# The Book of SCSI, 2nd Edition

# THE BOOK
## of
# SCSI
## 2nd Edition
### I/O FOR THE NEW MILLENNIUM

**Gary Field, Peter M. Ridge et al**

No Starch Press
San Francisco

Printed in the United States of America

1 2 3 4 5 6 7 8 9 10 — 02 01 00

Trademarked names are used throughout this book. Rather than use a trademark symbol with every occurrence of a trademarked name, we are using the names only in an editorial fashion and to the benefit of the trademark owner, with no intention of infringement of the trademark.

Publisher: William Pollock
Project Editor: Karol Jurado
Cover and Interior Design: Derek Yee Design
Composition: Derek Yee Design
Technical Review: John Lohmeyer, Ron Engelbrecht
Copy Editor: Carol Lombardi
Proofreader: Christine Sabooni
Indexer: Nancy Humphreys

*Distributed to the book trade in the United States and Canada by:*
Publishers Group West, 1700 Fourth Sreet, Berkeley, CA 94710
phone: 800-788-3123; fax: 510-528-5511
For information on translations or book distributors outside the United States, please contact No Starch Press directly:
No Starch Press
555 De Haro Street, Suite 250, San Francisco, CA 94107
phone: 415-863-9900; fax: 415-863-9950; info@nostarch.com; http://www.nostarch.com

The information in this book is distributed on an "As Is" basis, without warranty. While every precaution has been taken in the preparation of this work, neither the author nor No Starch Press shall have any liability to any person or entity with respect to any loss or damage caused or alleged to be caused directly or indirectly by the information contained in it.

*Library of Congress Cataloging-in-Publication Data*
Field, Gary.
     The book of SCSI : I/O for the new millennium / Gary Field, Peter
       M. Ridge et al. -- 2nd ed.
          p. cm.
     ISBN 1-886411-10-7
     1.  SCSI (Computer bus)   I.  Ridge, Peter M.   II.  Title.
   TK7895.B87F44   1999
   004.6'2.--dc21                     98-52364

# YOUR TOUR GUIDES

This book is the work of many hands and has been guided by many minds. Whether you're a computer novice or a seasoned expert, these contributors will help you make the most of your SCSI hardware and supply you with a wealth of practical know-how and reference material.

### Gary Field

Gary Field has a Computer Engineering degree from Northeastern University and has worked with device level software since 1978. In 1985, while at Wang Laboratories, he became involved with SCSI on MSDOS platforms, and later led the development of an ANSI CAM SCSI subsystem for the support of optical disks on several UNIX platforms. He has also maintained the Usenet comp.periphs.scsi FAQ list since 1994. In 1996 Gary joined Digital Equipment Corp. (now Compaq Computer Corp.) as a principal software engineer in their Tru64 UNIX device driver development group. His "SCSI Info Central" (http://www.scsifaq.org/) web site is a popular oasis for weary SCSI explorers. In his home life, he is involved in scouting, and in spare moments he enjoys photography, electronic and computer tinkering, home automation and astronomy, as well as camping, boating, and fishing with his wife and son.

### John Lohmeyer

John is a principal engineer with LSI Logic in Colorado Springs, Colorado. He began his involvement with SCSI when it was still called SASI in the summer of 1981. Since then, John has contributed to the SCSI effort as a member of the design team on the first SCSI chip (NCR 5385), technical editor of SCSI-1, and chair of the T10 Technical Committee, which is responsible for the ANSI SCSI standards. He also maintains the T10 web site (www.t10.org) to disseminate information about SCSI and other I/O interface standards.

### Gerhard Islinger

Gerhard works for Siemens in Munich, Germany as a security consultant. While his first experiences with computers were far before SCSI, since 1982 he has done technical and user support in many fields, most of them associated with high-speed interfaces. Recently he got sidetracked into firewalls and network security issues, but SCSI and related interfaces still are a main part of his work and hobby time.

**Stefan Groll**

Stefan was born in Munich, Germany. After finishing school and a long stint in sports, he began work in freelance software development with a security services company. In 1986 he began his study of electronics. While developing diagnostic systems and self-test software, he acquired PC and UNIX know-how, which resulted in his troubleshooting security products for these environments. After some time in the publishing business developing electronic books and retrieval systems, he returned to security management, where he currently works in a mixed mainframe and workstation environment.

**Peter Ridge**

Peter, who has a degree in Electrical Engineering, has worked in a variety of areas of computer technology, including multimedia, speech recognition, speech synthesis, artificial intelligence, intelligent agents, SCSI, telephony, and interactive entertainment during his fourteen years in the PC industry. He is currently the General Manager and Vice President of Product Development at Game Commander Interactive (www.gamecommander.com), where he designed the award-winning Game Commander voice control software for games. He has contributed to several books about computer and multimedia hardware and software including *The Book of SCSI: A Guide for Adventurers* (No Starch Press), *Sound Blaster: The Official Book* (Osborne/McGraw-Hill), and *The Business Week Guide to Multimedia Presentations* (Osborne/McGraw-Hill).

# DEDICATION

I would like to dedicate this book to my wife Mary and my son Danny who took up the slack and gave me the time out from my household duties to enable me to work on this book. I couldn't have done it without their support. —G.F.

# BRIEF CONTENTS

**Chapter 1**
Welcome to SCSI
1

**Chapter 1.5**
A Cornucopia of SCSI Devices
15

**Chapter 2**
A Look at SCSI-3
23

**Chapter 3**
SCSI Anatomy
33

**Chapter 4**
Adding SCSI to Your PC
55

**Chapter 5**
How to Connect Your SCSI
Hardware
83

**Chapter 6**
Troubleshooting Your SCSI
Installation
103

**Chapter 7**
How the Bus Works
125

**Chapter 8**
Understanding Device
Drivers
171

**Chapter 9**
Performance Tuning Your
SCSI Subsystem
179

**Chapter 10**
RAID: Redundant Array
of Independent Disks
191

**Chapter 11**
A Profile of ASPI
Programming
205

**Chapter 12**
The Future of SCSI and
Storage in General
309

### Appendix A
All-Platform Technical
Reference
313

### Appendix B
PC Technical Reference
359

### Appendix C
A Look at SCSI Test
Equipment
363

### Appendix D
ATA/IDE versus SCSI
367

### Appendix E
A Small ASPI Demo
Application
375

### Glossary
389

### Index
399

# CONTENTS IN DETAIL

# 1

## WELCOME TO SCSI

| | |
|---|---|
| A Few Well-Chosen Words | 1 |
| The Birth of SCSI | 3 |
| *The Prequel* | 3 |
| *Intelligent Life* | 3 |
| SCSI-2: The First Major Improvement | 4 |
| New and Improved SCSI | 5 |
| *Fast SCSI: Just Exactly That!* | 6 |
| *Wide SCSI: Two Lanes Are Better Than One* | 6 |
| *The Best of Both Worlds* | 7 |
| SCSI-3 Is on Its Way | 7 |
| *Serial versus Parallel* | 8 |
| *Why Choose SCSI?* | 9 |
| *Multi-Platform Capability* | 9 |
| *Devices Supported* | 11 |
| *Expandability* | 11 |
| *External Device Support* | 11 |
| *The Speed Thing* | 12 |
| *Multitasking* | 12 |
| *Built-In Error Checking* | 12 |
| *Cost* | 12 |
| SCSI Is Easy to Use | 13 |
| *. . . but Not a Panacea* | 13 |

# 1.5

## A CORNUCOPIA OF SCSI DEVICES

| | |
|---|---|
| Storage Devices | 15 |
| Hard Disks | 15 |
| *Sidebar: Terminology Wars* | 16 |
| Removable Media Disk Drives | 17 |
| Tape Drives | 17 |
| *Quarter-Inch Cartridge (QIC)* | 17 |
| *Digital Audio Tape (DDS DAT)* | 17 |
| *8mm Tape* | 18 |

DLT                                                                                    18

Optical Disk Drives                                                                    18

*Magneto-Optical (MO) Drives*                                                          *18*

*Write Once Read Many (WORM) Drives*                                                   *19*

*CD-ROM Drives*                                                                        *19*

*CD-ROM Recorders (CD-R and CD-RW)*                                                    *19*

*DVD-ROM Drives*                                                                       *20*

Printers and Scanners                                                                  20

*Printers*                                                                             *21*

*Image Scanners*                                                                       *21*

Variety Is the Spice of Life                                                           21

# 2

## A LOOK AT SCSI-3

*Sidebar: What's in a Name?*                                                           *25*

Physical SCSI-3 Interfaces                                                             27

*Parallel SCSI*                                                                        *27*

*Serial SCSI*                                                                          *29*

SCSI's Greatest Value: The Command Sets                                               31

Is SCSI-3 Done Yet?                                                                    32

# 3

## SCSI ANATOMY

SCSI Devices Can Be Initiators or Targets                                             33

SCSI IDs and LUNs Identify Individual SCSI Devices                                    34

*Ah, the Mysteries of LUNs*                                                            *35*

The SCSI Bus Allows Communication Between Your Computer and Your SCSI Devices         35

*Types of SCSI Buses*                                                                  *36*

*Sidebar: The Differences Between Single-Ended and Differential SCSI*                  *37*

SCSI Cables and Connectors                                                            39

*Sidebar: Cable Specifications*                                                        *40*

Adapters                                                                              40

*SCA Adapters*                                                                         *42*

Terminating the SCSI Bus                                                              42

The SCSI Bus Is a Transmission Line ........................................... 43
What's That He Said? ........................................... 44
*Passive Termination* ........................................... 45
*Active Termination* ........................................... 45
*Sidebar: Passive Termination in Detail* ........................................... 46
*Forced Perfect Termination (FPT)* ........................................... 46
*Don't Forget Differential* ........................................... 46
*Sidebar: Active Termination in Detail* ........................................... 47
*Sidebar: How Parity Checking Works* ........................................... 48
Using Parity Checking ........................................... 49
*Is Parity Really Enough?* ........................................... 50
Your SCSI Devices Can Communicate Either Synchronously or Asynchronously ... 50
*Asynchronous Communication* ........................................... 50
*Synchronous Communication* ........................................... 51
Disconnect/Reconnect ........................................... 51
*Once More for Luck* ........................................... 53

# 4

## ADDING SCSI TO YOUR PC

Types of SCSI Host Adapters for the PC ........................................... 56
*A Bus by Any Other Name . . . ISA, EISA, MCA, VESA Local Bus, PCI, AGP* ... 56
*The Decisions* ........................................... 57
Caching Host Adapter Cards Can Increase Performance ........................................... 57
*Software Caching Is Flexible* ........................................... 58
*Hardware Caching Can Duplicate Software Caching* ........................................... 58
*Which Form of Caching Is Right for You?* ........................................... 59
One Bus or Two? ........................................... 60
BIOS on the Host Adapter Lets You Boot from SCSI Devices ........................................... 60
How About Mixing SCSI and Non-SCSI Host Disks in One System? ........................................... 61
What Performance Level Do I Really Need? ........................................... 61
Installing the SCSI Interface Card ........................................... 62
PCI Cards Solve Most of the Problems ........................................... 62
*Setting the Port Address—the Front Door to the Interface* ........................................... 62
*Setting Interrupts* ........................................... 63
*Sidebar: A Note About Interrupts* ........................................... 64
*Using DMA for High-Speed Data Transfer* ........................................... 65

*Sidebar: Data Transfer Methods: DMA, Bus Mastering, Programmed I/O*      66
*Set the SCSI ID on Your Interface Card*      68
Install the Right Drivers      68
*Layered Drivers*      69
*Get the Latest SCSI Drivers*      70
*Software That Will Simplify Your Driver Installation*      70
DOS Drivers      70
*Windows 3.1 Drivers*      73
*Windows 95/98 Drivers*      74
*Windows NT Drivers*      75
*OS/2 Drivers*      76
Linux Drivers      77
More About Drivers Later      77
Tips for a Successful Installation      77
*SCSI CD-ROM Drives*      78
*SCSI Hard Drives*      78

# 5

## HOW TO CONNECT YOUR SCSI HARDWARE

Use Quality Cables and Connectors      84
*The Shorter, the Better*      84
*Sidebar: Finding the Right Cable*      85
*Internal versus External Cables*      87
*Know Your Connectors*      89
Connecting Devices to the Bus      91
*Find Pin 1*      92
*A Daisy-Chained SCSI System*      94
Terminating the SCSI Bus      94
*The Host Adapter Is a Device, Too*      95
*Terminating Your Particular Device*      96
*Sidebar: Mix and Match: Combining Regular and Wide SCSI*      96
Terminator Power      98
SCSI IDs      98
*Setting SCSI IDs*      99
Why Set One Device's ID Higher than Another?      99
Parity Checking      100
Another Way to Do All This      101
That's That, I Guess!      101

# 6

## TROUBLESHOOTING YOUR SCSI INSTALLATION

Common Problems 105
Problem: Host Adapter Not Recognized by the System 105
Problem: One Device Not Found 107
Problem: No Device Found 109
Problem: System Can't Boot from SCSI Hard Disk 110
Problem: Intermittent Lockups and Communication Errors 112
How to Check Typical Issues 113
Two Devices with the Same ID 113
Dead Devices 115
Termination 115
Termination Power: Active versus Passive 117
Cables 118
Connectors 119
Tricky Devices 119
Driver Problems 119
General Rules for Troubleshooting Drivers 122
Driver Combinations 122
Useful Tools 122

# 7

## HOW THE BUS WORKS

An Intelligent Interface 125
SCSI Supports Generic Software 126
A True Peripheral Interface 126
Initiators, Targets, and Logical Units 126
What Is an I/O Process? 127
SCSI Configurations 127
Bus and Device Characteristics 127
Initiators 129
Targets 130
SCSI IDs 130
SCSI Cables 132

Cable Evolution                                              132
SCSI-1, SCSI-2, and SCSI-3 Cabling Diagram                  134
SCSI Bus Signals                                            134
Data Bus Signals                                            134
Control Signals                                             135
The SCSI Protocol                                           137
Phase Sequence Diagram                                      140
Bus Phases                                                  143
Connect, Disconnect, and Reconnect Concepts                144
Connect                                                     145
Disconnect                                                  147
Reconnect                                                   149
Tagged Command Queuing                                      150
How Disconnects and Reconnects Work                        151
Information Transfer Phases                                 151
Characteristics of the Information Transfer Phases         154
MESSAGE Phase and Code Descriptions                        155
Protocol Example of a Synchronous Negotiation             158
COMMAND Phase and Code Descriptions                        160
Status                                                      164
Check Condition                                             165
Contingent Allegiance Condition                            166
Handshaking of Information                                  166
Asynchronous Handshake Method                              167
Synchronous Handshake Method                               168
Ever Onward and Upward!                                    170

# 8

## UNDERSTANDING DEVICE DRIVERS

In the Beginning . . .                                      171
The PC BIOS                                                 172
MS-DOS Drivers                                              173
Windows 3.x Drivers                                         174
Windows 95/98 Drivers                                       174
Windows NT Drivers                                          175
UNIX Drivers                                                176
Enough Already!                                             178

# 9

## PERFORMANCE TUNING YOUR SCSI SUBSYSTEM

SCSI Cable Types 183
Passive Termination 184
Active Termination 184
Where to Terminate 185
*TERMPWR Bypassing* 186
High Voltage Differential SCSI 187
Low Voltage Differential 187
Tricks 188
How Daring Are You? 188
Let's See How We Did 188
Keep Your Expectations Realistic 189

# 10

## RAID: REDUNDANT ARRAY OF INDEPENDENT DISKS

*Name Games* 192
*RAID Levels* 192
*Analyze Your Needs* 199
*RAID and the RAB* 199
How Does All This Stuff Connect to My System? 202

# 11

## A PROFILE OF ASPI PROGRAMMING

ASPI Developer Information 206
ASPI for DOS Specification 207
Accessing ASPI 207
Getting the ASPI Entry Point 208
Closing ASPI 208
Calling ASPI 209
SCSI Request Block (SRB) 210
*Command Codes* 210

| | |
|---|---|
| *Status* | *211* |
| *Host Adapter Number* | *211* |
| *SCSI Request Flags* | *211* |
| *Reserved for Expansion* | *211* |
| ASPI Command Codes | 211 |
| ASPI for DOS under Windows 3.*x* | 221 |
| ASPI for Windows Specification | 221 |
| ASPI Managers for Windows | 222 |
| GetASPISupportInfo | 222 |
| SendASPICommand — SC_HA_INQUIRY | 224 |
| SendASPICommand — SC_GET_DEV_TYPE | 226 |
| SendASPICommand — SC_EXEC_SCSI_CMD | 228 |
| SendASPICommand — SC_ABORT_SRB | 233 |
| SendASPICommand — SC_RESET_DEV | 235 |
| ASPI Polling | 238 |
| ASPI Posting | 239 |
| Miscellaneous | 241 |
| Error Codes and Messages | 242 |
| ASPI for Win32 Specification | 243 |
| Programming Conventions | 244 |
| Calling ASPI Functions | 245 |
| *Explicit Dynamic Linking* | *245* |
| *Implicit Dynamic Linking* | *247* |
| GetASPI32SupportInfo | 247 |
| SendASPI32Command | 248 |
| SC_HA_INQUIRY | 250 |
| SC_GET_DEV_TYPE | 253 |
| SC_EXEC_SCSI_CMD | 255 |
| SC_ABORT_SRB | 259 |
| SC_RESET_DEV | 261 |
| SC_GET_DISK_INFO | 263 |
| SC_RESCAN_SCSI_BUS | 265 |
| SC_GETSET_TIMEOUTS | 266 |
| GetASPI32Buffer | 269 |
| FreeASPI32Buffer | 270 |
| TranslateASPI32Address | 271 |
| Waiting for Completion | 273 |
| *Event Notification* | *273* |
| *Posting* | *274* |
| *Polling* | *275* |

ASPI for Win 32 Errors                                      276
ASPI for OS/2 Specification                                 279
Calling ASPI                                                280
Accessing ASPI at Initialization Time                       280
ASPI and OS/2 2.x                                           281
Target Allocation with OS/2 2.x                             281
Sample Code for OS/2 2.x                                    282
SCSI Request Block (SRB)                                    282
*Command Code*                                              283
*Status*                                                    283
*Host Adapter Number*                                       283
*SCSI Request Flags*                                        283
*Reserved for Expansion*                                    283
ASPI Command Codes                                          283
*Valid ASPI Command Codes*                                  283
*ASPI Status Bytes*                                         284
*ASPI Command Code = 0: Host Adapter Inquiry*               284
*ASPI Command Code = 1: Get Device Type*                    285
*ASPI Command Code = 2: Execute SCSI I/O Command*           286
*The SCSI Request Flags Byte Is Defined As Follows*         287
*ASPI Command Code = 3: Abort SCSI I/O Request*             290
*ASPI Command Code = 4: Reset SCSI Device*                  291
*The SCSI Requests Flags Byte Is Defined as Follows*        292
*ASPI Command Code = 5: Set Host Adapter Parameters*        292
ASPI for NetWare Specification                              292
ASPI Routine: ASPI_Entry                                    293
*Syntax*                                                    293
*Return Values*                                             293
*Parameters*                                                293
*Assembly Example*                                          293
*Remarks*                                                   294
SCSI Request Block (SRB)                                    294
*Command Code*                                              294
*Status*                                                    294
*Host Adapter Number*                                       294
*SCSI Request Flags*                                        294
*Reserved for Expansion*                                    295
ASPI Command Codes                                          295
*Valid ASPI Command Codes*                                  295
*ASPI Status Bytes*                                         295

Handling Greater Than 16 Megabytes                                                    303
*Host Adapters Handling > 16 MB*                                                       *304*
*Host Adapters Handling PIO or Second-Party DMA Host Transfers*                        *304*
*Host Adapters Handling Bus Mastering ISA Mode Host Transfers*                         *304*
*Host Adapters Handling EISA or PCI Mode Host Transfers*                               *304*
Scanning for New Devices                                                              305
ASPI Specification Addendum                                                           305
What Is Residual Byte Length?                                                         305
How Do I Find Out If the ASPI Manager Loaded Supports This New Feature?               305
Now That I Know My ASPI Manager Supports Residual Byte Length,
How Do I Make Use of It?                                                              308
*The SCSI Request Flags Byte Is Currently Defined in the Various ASPI*
*Specifications as Follows*                                                            *308*
*The New Definition for this Byte is as Follows*                                       *308*

# 12

## THE FUTURE OF SCSI AND STORAGE IN GENERAL

If You Can't Beat 'em, Buy 'em!                                                       309
Coming Down the Pike                                                                  310
*Ultra3 (Fast-80) LVD*                                                                 *310*
*IEEE-1394*                                                                            *310*
*Fibre Channel*                                                                        *311*
*Device Bay*                                                                           *311*
*SCSI Harbor*                                                                          *311*
*Storage Area Networks*                                                                *311*

# A

## ALL-PLATFORM TECHNICAL REFERENCE

Electrical Specs                                                                      314
*Single-Ended SCSI Interface*                                                          *314*
*Differential SCSI Interfaces*                                                         *315*
Cable Specs                                                                           317
*Internal Cables*                                                                      *317*
*External Cables*                                                                      *318*

Connector Specs 319
*Unshielded Connectors* 321
*Shielded Connectors* 327
*Vendor-Specific SCSI Connectors* 333
*Obsolete Connectors* 337
SCSI Bus Signals 342
Bus Phases and Timing Diagrams 343
*Bus Phases and Conditions* 343
*Phase Sequence* 345
*Bus Timing* 347
Termination 352
*Termination Circuits* 354

# B

## PC TECHNICAL REFERENCE

# C

## A LOOK AT SCSI TEST EQUIPMENT

Your Mission . . . 364
*Rent or Buy?* 364
Types of SCSI Analyzers 365
*Analyzer Output* 365
*Manufacturers* 366

# D

## ATA/IDE VERSUS SCSI

History 367
*SCSI* 367
*ATA* 368
Speed—and Why It Isn't Everything 368
Features That Make a Difference 369
*I/O Device Independence and Multitasking* 369
*Cable Length—and What It Means in Real Life* 370

Devices per Channel: Why Should You Care?                    371
What to Choose?                                              371
Consider Your Requirements                                  372
The Bottom Line                                             373

# E

## A SMALL ASPI DEMO APPLICATION

Program Structure                                           375
Why Use Three Layers?                                      376
Implementation of the Load/Eject Functionality in ASPI_Interface     382
Implementation of the Load/Eject Functionality in ASPIApplication    386
Implementation of the Load/Eject Functionality in the GUI            386

## GLOSSARY

### 389

## INDEX

### 399

# ACKNOWLEDGMENTS

The details involved in producing a book as technical as this can be mind-boggling! I would like to hereby thank John Lohmeyer, our technical editor and contributing author for his invaluable input. And also, Gerhard Islinger and Stefan Groll for their hard work on several chapters and appendices. All the previous authors who contributed to the first edition deserve recognition as well. Much of their work is still contained herein.

My colleagues at Compaq unknowingly also contributed to this book through their everyday thoughts and comments. I recognize the value they offer.

Thanks also go to No Starch Press for giving me the opportunity to share my SCSI experience with the world.

And last but certainly not least Karol Jurado, my project editor, who kept the many loose ends from unraveling, and Mike Flynn, who saw to it that the world would see this book, and the rest of the team that handled all the required processes that put the book in the form as you now see it.

Many thanks to one and all!

**Gary Field**

# FOREWORD

SCSI amazes me. Each time I begin to think SCSI cannot evolve further, it does. The standards committees are now working on SPI-4, the fourth generation of the physical layer of SCSI-3. This is the eighth generation of parallel SCSI. And still there is no end in sight!

No wonder there is now a second edition of *The Book of SCSI*. All the great stuff from the first edition is still here, along with numerous enhancements. I know because I naively agreed to be the technical reviewer of this second edition. I thought it would be a piece of cake; how much could they change? A great deal. I enjoyed every minute spent reviewing this book. Even when those minutes turned into hours and days, I got to read it first!

This book continues to be a practical book aimed at helping SCSI's real users. It is chock-full of helpful hints on making SCSI work for you. You'll find arcane SCSI concepts explained simply and clearly. Whether you already have SCSI on your PC or are contemplating adding it, this book is definitely worth reading.

You will find discussions on terminating your SCSI bus (not with a gun); setting SCSI IDs; choosing cables; choosing controller card features; setting up I/O addresses, IRQs, and DMA channels; installing device drivers; and more. Modern operating systems support SCSI better than ever before, but they do not do everything. You still need to understand these concepts to get the most out of your SCSI investment.

As the chair of the T10 Technical Committee on SCSI, I am occasionally told that standards committees are slow and plodding organizations. We often are—for good reason. We are required to achieve consensus on highly technical concepts and our only resources are volunteers who work for competing companies. Some might think it is amazing that we accomplish anything at all! In spite of the obstacles, much is achieved (often on evenings and weekends) by some dedicated individuals who want to have an impact on the industry.

The fact is that most users cannot afford to attend standards committee meetings and are thus underrepresented in the SCSI standards development process. If you think your needs are not being met, there are ways you can have input without appearing at meetings or spending a lot of money. All standards go through a public review process, which is your formal chance to comment on pending standards. You can find out about these public review periods by checking the NCITS web site (www.ncits.org). The public review comment periods are only two months long, so you'll need to check monthly.

You'll probably get even better results if you lurk on the T10 web site (www.t10.org) and join the T10 Reflector (it's free!). To join, send an email to majordomo@t10.org and include the following line in the message body:

```
subscribe t10
```

If you are crazy enough to want to join the T10 Technical Committee, I urge you to visit the T10 Web site or contact NCITS (our parent organization) in Washington, DC by email at ncits@itic.org or by voice at 202-737-8888.

**John Lohmeyer**
***Chair T10 Technical Committee***
***LSI Logic Corp.***
***<lohmeyer@t10.org>***

# INTRODUCTION

This is the second edition of this book. Time marches to a rapid beat in the computer industry and to keep up you need to constantly adapt to the rapidly improving computing environment. This book is an effort to provide an up to date guide for those who desire to keep their computer performance in line with the state of the art. The subtitle: "I/O for the New Millennium" is intended to be more than a catch phrase. I truly believe that SCSI has the necessary ingredients to be the leading storage architecture well into the coming century.

Most of the information presented is generic enough that it should apply to any type of computer (Macintosh, PC, or UNIX workstation), however, where system specific information is required, the details are aimed at the IBM PC clone platform running Microsoft Windows 95/98 or NT 4.0. This detailed information is mostly in the area of installing SCSI host adapter cards and loading device drivers. Most aspects of SCSI relating to the connection of peripheral devices are the same regardless of platform type and so would be helpful to Macintosh and UNIX users as well.

The central theme is to provide readers with the practical information necessary to purchase appropriate SCSI hardware, and then implement SCSI I/O in their computers. However, it's not just a cookbook. There's enough theory and variety of information to give readers a depth of understanding, not just get them into trouble.

The chapters are presented in an order that is appropriate for a reader who is new to SCSI, but if you're already familiar with SCSI you'll be able to easily find the updated information you're looking for. Here's what we've got in store for you:

**Chapter 1:** Welcome to SCSI: Introduces the readers to what SCSI is all about and why they might want to use it.

**Chapter 1.5:** A Cornucopia of SCSI Devices: A glimpse at the variety of device types that SCSI has to offer and a little background on each.

**Chapter 2:** A Look at SCSI-3: An update on the latest SCSI standards as told by John Lohmeyer, who has been there since the beginning.

**Chapter 3**: SCSI Anatomy: Describes the basic concepts and terminology of SCSI to help ready you for what follows.

**Chapter 4:** Adding SCSI to Your PC: Explains what you need to get your system ready for SCSI devices and how to install it.

**Chapter 5:** How to Connect Your SCSI Hardware: Describes in detail how to connect a collection of SCSI devices to your system.

**Chapter 6:** Troubleshooting Your SCSI Installation: OK, so you didn't get it all right from the beginning. Now you'll learn a few things.

**Chapter 7:** How the Bus Works: For the curious, we explain how all the little bits do their thing to get the job done.

**Chapter 8:** Understanding Device Drivers: What a device driver really is and how it can affect your system.

**Chapter 9:** Performance Tuning Your SCSI Subsystem: How to squeak all the performance you can out of your SCSI hardware.

**Chapter 10:** RAID: Redundant Array of Independent Disks: What RAID is, and why you might care.

**Chapter 11:** A Profile of ASPI Programming: This chapter provides the complete ASPI specification, which gives all the details you would need to write a SCSI application program for MSDOS, Windows 95/98/NT, OS/2, or Netware. Such a program is the subject of Appendix E.

**Chapter 12:** The Future of SCSI and Storage In General: My view of storage industry trends and what's on the horizon.

**Appendix A:** All-Platform Technical Reference: This is a comprehensive collection of diagrams and pinouts for all the SCSI connectors as well as a guide to solving SCSI problems that can crop up in almost any SCSI based system.

**Appendix B:** PC Technical Reference: Tables of PC specific information that are useful when solving SCSI problems that are specific to the PC architecture.

**Appendix C:** A Look at SCSI Test Equipment: While aimed at professionals who need to solve tough system integration problems, this chapter might interest any technically minded reader as well.

**Appendix D:** ATA/IDE versus SCSI: The battle rages on between price and performance.

**Appendix E:** A Small ASPI Demo Application written using Delphi/Pascal. The source code referred to here is contained on the CD-ROM.

But wait … there's more!

The CD-ROM includes an easy to use HTML index which provides hot links to the CD contents and links to other SCSI related stuff out on the Internet.

(Just point your browser (either Netscape or IE) to: drive:\BOS_CDtour.html)

- ASPI source code examples

- ASPI tar utility (example tape backup utility)

- SCSIDRVR.C

- SCSI test programs and benchmarks

- SCSIReset

- Some useful SCSI utilities courtesy of Western Digital

- ASPIMenu, SCSIBench, SCSIScan etc.

- The comp.periphs.scsi FAQ and SCSI Quick Start Guide

- SCSI: A Game With Many Rules and No Rule Book: A Light hearted look at hooking up SCSI devices and getting them to work in your system

- Linux SCSI HowTo

- Linux SCSI Programming HowTo

- A collection of some of the most useful links to SCSI information on the Web

And now to properly set the tone for the reader:

## ODE to SCSI

You know that SCSI is the greatest.
Its performance can't be beat.
For any storage situation,
Its bus bandwidth's really neat.
Though the cables can get gnarly,
And termination's such a treat,
The flexibility is worth it,
And the multitasking's sweet.
When you need to add a scanner
To your disk and CD-ROM,
You just plug it on the bus,
(Which can only be so long).
Then you load a device driver,
And scan and print with glee,
Without using another resource,
Try *that* with IDE!

Well, that's as close as an engineer gets to poetry. And now, let's get to the subject at hand!

**Gary Field**

# 1

## WELCOME TO SCSI

We begin this adventure by getting the
lay of the land, so to speak: some basic
vocabulary followed by a short background
on the birth of SCSI (pronounced "scuzzy"),
then a quick look at what it is and where it's going.

### A Few Well-Chosen Words

Since this may be the first time you've ventured into SCSI territory, here are a
few terms you'll need to be familiar with before we embark.

> **bus** The bus is the path or channel that carries data between the
> computer and other devices (like a printer or scanner) or between a
> series of devices. Although cables, wires, and optical fiber are components
> commonly used to form a bus, the bus itself is not a single physical object
> that you can hold in your hand. Rather, it is the entire *collection* of cables
> and wires used to make up the communications pathway. The size of the
> bus changes in direct proportion to the number of connections.

**bus slots** Bus slots are connectors inside the computer that attach add-on cards (like sound or video cards) and devices to a bus. Examples would be an ISA slot or PCI slot.

**controller card** (or **host adapter card**) Host adapters are circuit boards that plug into the motherboard on the computer. They allow the computer to communicate with and control devices. SCSI, IDE, and ESDI cards are examples of hard disk controller cards. Some printers and scanners require their own special controller cards. SCSI host adapter cards are often referred to as controllers.

For instance, the Windows 95/98 Device Manager menu refers to "SCSI controllers," although technically a SCSI controller is a chip on a target device that controls the operation of the device. They really are referring to host adapters.

Throughout this book I'll try to consistently call a card that plugs into a PC a "host adapter," but if someone calls it a controller, don't jump down his throat.

**data transfer rate** Data transfer rate is a measure of how quickly information can be passed between the computer and another device or between devices. The higher the data transfer rate, the less you'll have to wait for data to get to its destination. It is commonly expressed in megabytes per second (MB/sec).

**device** Device generally refers to hardware that can be connected to the computer (such as printers, hard disks, scanners, and modems), although sometimes the computer itself is referred to as a device as well. Devices can also be interface cards, such as video cards, SCSI cards, and sound cards.

**hardware interface** A hardware interface consists of the electronics necessary to communicate with and control devices. When you put these electronics on a card you have an interface card, also known as a host adapter. In this book, we'll often refer to the hardware interface as simply "the interface."

**multitasking** Multitasking simply means performing more than one function simultaneously. Multitasking operating systems, such as Windows 95/98, Windows NT, OS/2, and UNIX, can run many programs simultaneously. When your software or devices are multitasking, they don't have to wait for one program to finish before they can do their work. They all work simultaneously. And, as a user of a multitasking system, you don't have to wait, either.

**IDE**  Integrated Drive Electronics, or IDE, is a common, parallel bus standard for hard disk drives. All the control electronics for IDE reside on the hard disk drive, not on the interface card. Because IDE is not an intelligent bus, simpler, low-cost electronics can be used. The low cost of IDE makes it an ideal interface for the mass market. The more appropriate industry term for this type of interface is ATA, which stands for advanced technology attachment.

**EIDE**  Enhanced IDE is an updated version of IDE that improves on IDE's speed and adds support for drives larger than 528 MB.

**ATAPI**  ATA Packet Interface is a software protocol that allows support for CD-ROM drives on IDE/EIDE interfaces.

## The Birth of SCSI

### The Prequel

Minicomputer interfaces prior to SCSI were not intelligent; they were each designed specifically for one device, so a special interface was required for each different device, such as a hard disk interface for a hard disk. Prior to SCSI, minicomputer users had to change both software and hardware to support new devices.

### Intelligent Life

SCSI began life in 1979 as the *Shugart Associates Systems Interface* (abbreviated *SASI* and pronounced "sassy"). SASI was the first small-scale intelligent hard disk interface designed to work with smaller minicomputers. SCSI was developed based on SASI. SCSI's birth was a major leap forward in hardware interfaces.

Intelligent interfaces, like SCSI, know what types of devices are connected to the computer and how to deal with each. Intelligent interfaces are designed to support multiple data rates and use logical command sets that hide the implementation details of the devices. This allows system software to accommodate the addition of newer devices as they become available.

As an intelligent interface, SCSI allows users to mix and match devices on one controller rather than needing to install a separate controller for each device.

But in order to get everyone to use SCSI and to make sure that every company's SCSI devices would be compatible, a SCSI standard had to be defined. And so, in 1981, Shugart Associates and NCR (National Cash Register) presented their SASI proposal to the X3T9.2 committee for a standard to be published by the *American National Standards Institute* (ANSI, pronounced "ANN-see"), the standard-setting organization in the U.S. After many long years of debate on the exact specifications for this new bus, ANSI finally gave its approval in June, 1986. The new standard, document X3.131-1986, was named the *Small Computer System Interface* (SCSI), and thus SCSI was born. That first version of SCSI is now referred to as SCSI-1, because newer standards have been released since 1986.

SCSI-1 defined a universal, parallel, system-level interface, called the *SCSI bus,* for connecting up to eight devices along a single cable. Parallel devices (such as the majority of printers) send a group of bits (binary digits) at a time, as opposed to serial devices (such as modems and mice), which send data one bit at a time.

As a system-level interface, SCSI is very different from a device-level interface such as the older *ESDI* (enhanced small device interface).

SCSI is an independent and intelligent local I/O bus through which a variety of different devices and one or more controllers can communicate and exchange information independent of what the rest of the system is doing. ESDI, on the other hand, was limited to two devices, both of which could only be ESDI drives.

SCSI's benefits were clear; however, because it was a groundbreaking standard, the system software took a while to become flexible enough to take advantage of them.

SCSI-1 devices were also limited to a peak throughput of five megabytes per second (5 MB/sec), which was comparable to the transfer rate of ESDI. ESDI didn't have all the compatibility headaches that SCSI-1 did, either. But ESDI had a significant problem: a lack of flexibility. Although ESDI was fast, ESDI drives worked only with ESDI controllers, which brings us back to the one controller–one device problem. So whereas SCSI had the advantage of flexibility over ESDI and had comparable speed, something had to be done to solve the integration problem in order to make SCSI a more attractive solution.

## SCSI-2: The First Major Improvement

Even before SCSI-1 was made an official standard in 1986, improvements to it were in the works. SCSI-1 had significant shortcomings: It wasn't as general purpose as it needed to be, and, although it was fast, some felt that its speed could be improved. One of the essential shortcomings was a lack of standardization of command sets. Almost immediately after SCSI-1 was adopted, an industry group developed an addendum to it called the SCSI Common

Command Set, or CCS, which solved this problem. This standard was a major milestone, but the technical committee was already working on improvements.

In January, 1994 (after almost four years of deliberation), ANSI approved the X3T9.2 committee's updated draft standard, SCSI-2. The standard was designated X3.131-1994 to indicate that it replaced SCSI-1.

Everyone had been calling this new standard SCSI-2 as early as 1986, when it was first proposed. In fact, just as there are a variety of unofficial SCSI-3 devices on the market today (with the SCSI-3 family of standards still not all finalized), there had been a number of SCSI-2 devices on the market prior to the 1994 adoption of the SCSI-2 standard.

**NOTE** *Because SCSI-2 devices were on the market before the adoption of a SCSI-2 standard, compatibility problems occurred between SCSI-2 devices. You may encounter these problems if you still have any SCSI-2 hardware developed prior to 1994. Newer SCSI-2 devices were developed to adhere to the official ANSI SCSI-2 standard and have proven to be very compatible, even between different vendors' products.*

## New and Improved SCSI

The following is a list of the improvements provided in the SCSI-2 standard, together with a brief description of what makes these advances important. We'll explore them in more detail in Chapter 2.

1.  New 50-pin and 68-pin high-density connectors were standardized, which shrank the size of the connector and made for more efficient and trouble-free connections. This was especially important for IBM PC SCSI host adapters, because the older connectors were extremely difficult to fit onto an option card rail.

2.  The speed of data transfer along the SCSI bus was increased by allowing for synchronous transfers. This is now standard with optional fast synchronous data transfer mode (Fast SCSI-2).

3.  The speed of data transfer was further increased by widening the size of the bus. Both 16-bit and 32-bit buses were defined (Wide SCSI-2).

4.  The reliability of device-to-device communication was increased by allowing synchronous negotiation to be invoked whenever the initiator or target device detects a change. Previously, many target devices refrained from starting such negotiations because some early host adapters locked up.

5.  Signal integrity was improved with the addition of mandatory SCSI bus parity checking.

6. Command queuing was added to improve performance.

7. Command sets were added for CD-ROMs, scanners, medium changers, and communications devices.

8. Extensive enhancements were made to the existing command sets.

### Fast SCSI: Just Exactly That!

The SCSI bus allows for both asynchronous and synchronous data transfer modes (see Chapter 3 for a detailed discussion of these transfer modes). Synchronous transfer is considerably faster than asynchronous. SCSI-1 allowed asynchronous transfer rates of 1.5 MB/sec and synchronous transfer rates at a maximum of 5 MB/sec. In order to improve on this, Fast SCSI was introduced as an optional SCSI-2 operating mode.

Fast SCSI squeezed some of the timing margins so that faster handshaking (connections) could occur, doubling the synchronous transfer rates of SCSI. The maximum SCSI-1 synchronous transfer rate doubled, from 5 MB/sec to 10 MB/sec.

The term "fast" is generally used to describe SCSI devices that can support synchronous transfers at this improved rate of 10 MB/sec. "Fast SCSI" may be used only when describing SCSI-2, because SCSI-1 did not support this faster synchronous transfer mode.

But this increase in speed did not come without added costs and demands. Sending data twice as fast meant that devices needed better electronics to ensure error-free data transfers. Similarly, faster data transfer also required that the cables used for the SCSI bus be of higher quality than those used for SCSI-1 or regular SCSI-2. (We'll talk more about cables in Chapters 3 and 4.) This is the typical progression of SCSI — indeed, of any advancing technology: Faster and better always means that all supporting technology needs to advance, too.

**NOTE** *In order to use Fast SCSI, both your SCSI interface and SCSI devices must have Fast SCSI capability. Be sure to check the device's specifications if you're interested in using Fast SCSI, because not all SCSI-2 devices support it. Remember, Fast SCSI is an option with SCSI-2; you don't need to use Fast SCSI in order to use SCSI-2-compatible devices.*

### Wide SCSI: Two Lanes Are Better Than One

Besides doubling the rate at which data can be transferred over the SCSI bus or pathway, SCSI-2 also provided the option to double or quadruple the width of the SCSI bus with Wide SCSI.

**NOTE** *Although SCSI-2 defined Wide SCSI using a two-cable approach, Wide SCSI didn't catch on until SCSI-3 introduced the single "P" cable method of implementing Wide.*

The width of the bus is the number of its data lines. By increasing the width of the bus from 8 bits to either 16 or 32 bits (although 32-bit Wide has yet to catch on), the Wide SCSI bus can transfer two to four times more data in the same amount of time than regular 8-bit SCSI-2 did. Of course, this also means that the size of the cables must be increased, because more bits require more wires.

**NOTE** *As with Fast SCSI, both the SCSI interface and SCSI devices have to support Wide SCSI in order to take advantage of the Wide capability. If your SCSI controller supports Wide SCSI but your device does not, or vice versa, communication between the controller and device will take place at regular 8-bit SCSI-2 speed, and you won't be able to take advantage of Wide SCSI. But even if your system won't use Wide SCSI, communication will still take place without a hitch; it will simply be slower.*

### The Best of Both Worlds

Although Fast and Wide SCSI can certainly operate independently, a combination of the two features provides even greater improvement in the rate of data transfer. The faster transfer rate of Fast SCSI and the extra bus width of Wide SCSI can be combined to create Fast Wide SCSI, which can send data at 20 MB/sec (on a 16-bit Wide bus).

Data on a SCSI-2 bus won't travel any faster than the 20 MB/sec achieved with Fast Wide SCSI, and this speed is probably more than most people need on their desktop. However, if Fast SCSI still leaves you hungry for more when you get into tasks such as full-motion digital video (for editing movies) and large-scale computer networks, read on. In fact, in such demanding SCSI applications, you're likely to find that even Fast Wide SCSI isn't enough and you'll need even more speed. Don't worry, help is on the way with SCSI-3.

## SCSI-3 Is on Its Way

Throughout the history of SCSI, ever-newer SCSI standards have always been waiting in the wings, and today is no different. Proposals are currently before the T10 Technical Committee for the next generation of SCSI, called SCSI-3. For several reasons, including size and flexibility, SCSI-3 is being partitioned into a family of about fourteen standards. These standards will be used as building blocks, much like communications standards, to create various combinations of SCSI-3 features, including serial versions. And, although the entire family of SCSI-3 standards is not all officially approved, you will notice a bunch of devices claiming to include SCSI-3 features cropping up on store shelves.

Fast-20 SCSI and Fast-40 SCSI, also marketed as Ultra SCSI and Ultra2 SCSI, may be the SCSI-3 feature most commonly found in new devices. These Ultra SCSI rates are basically an extension of the Fast SCSI, found in the SCSI-2 specification, except that Ultra SCSI offers double or quadruple the old "Fast" rate. Fast-20 SCSI (or Ultra SCSI) will provide 20 MB/sec over the 8-bit bus or 40 MB/sec over the 16-bit Wide SCSI bus. Fast-40 (Ultra2 SCSI) is twice as fast as Fast-20. The future even promises an Ultra3, Fast80 option (up to 160 MB/sec). These aspects of the SCSI-3 protocol are covered in the SPI (SCSI Parallel Interface) standard and its successors.

NOTE *Unfortunately, as with everything in real life, speed has its price. The high data transfer rates promised by Fast-20 SCSI will limit the SCSI bus length to 1.5 meters (about 5 feet) for 8 devices, 3 meters (about 10 feet) for 4 devices, and will require even higher-quality cables.*

*Furthermore, single-ended buses are not acceptable for Fast-40! You will need a host adapter with "low voltage differential" bus drivers to use this option.*

Another hot — but perhaps deferred — feature of the SCSI-3 protocol is *SCAM* (SCSI Configured "AutoMagically").

SCAM, along with Intel PCI and Microsoft's Plug-and-Play, will allow users to plug in SCSI interface cards and attach SCSI devices without worrying about jumpers, switches, wheels, or any other kind of configuration option. All configuration options will be handled by the computer — no more headaches. At least, that's what ANSI had in mind when they created SCAM. After all was said and done, however, Microsoft didn't implement SCAM in their operating systems and ANSI is considering removing it from SPI-3.

### Serial versus Parallel

Perhaps SCSI-3's most notable addition to SCSI will be its introduction of support for a new breed of very high speed serial devices. The existing standards for serial communication, such as RS-232, are much too slow for hard disks and other SCSI devices. In general, parallel data transfer is faster than serial, but this doesn't always apply in SCSI. SCSI-3 defines both serial and parallel communication, and its serial buses are very fast. However, parallel bus development is not standing still and is currently on par with Fibre Channel. Today's silicon electronics can operate at speeds approaching 1 GHz (GigaHertz, or billions of cycles per second), and SCSI-3 will make use of every bit of it. In fact, expensive gallium arsenide chips offer speeds in excess of several GHz. That's blazing speed, compared with the 5 MHz bus rate of SCSI-1. There is a real horse race going on between parallel and serial SCSI with no clear winner.

#### The Serial Future

Two interfaces are competing to provide the link between the new high-speed SCSI-3 serial devices: Fibre Channel and IEEE-1394 (Apple's FireWire). These interfaces offer transfer rates of 400 to 1000 Mb/sec (Megabits per second) as opposed to the 20 MB/sec parallel transfer rate of SCSI-2, which is equivalent to 160 Mb/sec. (There actually is a third serial interface option called SSA, but it seems to have run out of steam and probably won't see widespread acceptance.)

Each interface promises quick and easy cabling between devices and the SCSI interface card via small, keyed connectors. (For those of you who struggle with SCSI device connections, this is sure to be a welcome improvement.)

Going serial also means that cables will have fewer wires (or fibers, as the case may be). Rather than the monstrous 50 and 68 wire cables required by parallel SCSI implementations, serial SCSI will only need 6 (or fewer) wires.

However, the change to serial will require a different way of thinking for device driver writers. For example, parallel buses supported no more than 15 devices. Scanning the bus for devices took no more than four seconds (that is, 1/4 second to timeout on each device). With Fibre Channel supporting 16 million devices, clearly a different approach is needed! Also, drivers frequently used bus reset to recover from certain types of error conditions — and there is no such thing on Fibre Channel!

For the latest information about SCSI developments, for SCSI standards, and for the latest on SCSI-3, you can access the T10 Technical Committee's web site at http://www.t10.org/.

You can also write to:

Global Engineering Documents
15 Inverness Way
Englewood, CO 80112
(800) 854-7179

We'll hear more about the latest developments in SCSI-3 from the chair of the T10 Technical Committee himself in Chapter 2!

## Why Choose SCSI?

If you're reading this book, you've probably either already purchased SCSI hardware, you're thinking about it, or you're just wondering what SCSI is. But have you thought about why you should use SCSI and not some other standard, such as the mass-market IDE or EIDE? Well, take a look at the benefits SCSI brings, as well as the pitfalls, as shown in Table 1.1.

### Multi-Platform Capability

As you can see in the first row of Table 1.1, SCSI is a cross-platform interface. As such, it is highly flexible. In most cases, a SCSI device taken from one type of computer system (like a Mac or a PC) will work on a completely different system without your having to modify it in any way. As long as your computer has a SCSI host adapter card, you simply buy a SCSI drive.

## Table 1.1: Comparison of Features

| Feature | SCSI | IDE/ATA/EIDE/UDMA |
|---------|------|-------------------|
| Computers supported | PC, Macintosh, UNIX servers, and workstations | PC, some newer low-end workstations, newer Macintosh |
| Device types supported | Hard disk, CD-ROM, DVD,scanner, tape drive, printer, optical WORM and MO | Hard disk, CD-ROM, DVD, low-end tape drive |
| Maximum number of devices supported (per bus or channel) | Narrow SCSI = 7<br>Wide (16) = 15<br>Fibre Channel AL = 126<br>Fibre Channel fabric = 16 M<br>Unlimited number of buses per host | 2<br>n/a<br>n/a<br>n/a<br>Maximum of 2<br>buses per host |
| External device support? | Yes | No |
| Data transfer rate<br><br>Note: This is the maximum burst rate for the interface bus. No individual drive will achieve these rates. | SCSI-1 = 5 MB/sec<br>FAST-10 = 10 MB/sec<br>FAST-10 Wide = 20 MB/sec<br>…<br>FAST-20 Wide = 40 MB/sec<br>…<br>FAST-40 Wide = 80 MB/sec<br>FAST-80 Wide = 160 MB/sec<br>Fibre Channel = 100 MB/sec | EIDE (PIO) = 3 to 16 MB/sec<br>EIDE (DMA) = 2 to 8 MB/sec<br>UDMA = up to 33 MB/sec<br><br>Note: Although PIO might seem fast according to these figures, it consumes the CPU, causing multi-tasking to suffer severely. |
| Multitasking ability | Excellent<br>• Bus master DMA<br>• Disconnect/reconnect<br>• Tagged queuing | IDE = Poor owing to polled I/O<br>EIDE = Fair owing to DMA<br>UDMA = good<br>• Only one device active per bus |
| Error detection | Yes = Bus parity, CRC will be introduced with FAST-80. | None currently.<br>(Rumor has it that, when UDMA66 is introduced, it will use CRC.) |
| Cost | Relatively expensive because of the need for terminators, more involved device firmware testing, and also because a premium is charged for the extra performance. | Inexpensive because of high-volume production, no need for terminators (because of short bus length) and simplified testing owing to single-threaded structure. |

In contrast, this is definitely not the case with IDE and many other kinds of drives. PC IDE drives will not work with your Mac. When buying a drive for an IDE system, you must buy the specific IDE drive made for your system.

**NOTE**
*SCSI's ability to allow swapping peripherals between platforms comes in particularly handy if you've got both a Mac and a PC at home or in the office. As long as the PC is SCSI-based, you'll be able to swap SCSI devices — whether hard drive, CD-ROM, or the like — between both systems. Of course, whereas you can interchange the drives, you won't necessarily be able to read the data on the drive, because Macs and PCs format their drives differently and the file structures are different.*

SCSI is widely supported by many operating systems and platforms, including Macintosh, UNIX, DOS, Windows, Windows NT, OS/2, and a variety of other operating systems. Most of these operating systems have built-in support for SCSI, which makes it even easier to use, install, and swap SCSI devices among all operating systems.

### Devices Supported

The second row of Table 1.1 compares the number of devices supported by SCSI with that supported by IDE. You'll notice that the list for SCSI is considerably longer. In fact, IDE and EIDE support only hard drives, CD-ROM drives, and some inexpensive tape drives. SCSI can support just about any device you throw at it. When new device types are developed, the earliest models are typically equipped with SCSI interfaces.

### Expandability

SCSI offers efficient expandability. As you can see in the third row of Table 1.1, if you have a SCSI-1 based system, you'll be able to connect up to seven devices to one interface card, as opposed to a maximum of four if you have EIDE. These seven devices could be any combination of hardware, such as hard disks, CD-ROMs, tape drives, image scanners, or even printers. If seven devices aren't enough, just add a second SCSI adapter, and you're ready for the next seven devices. With Wide SCSI, you can connect fifteen devices (with 16-bit Wide SCSI); with Fibre Channel Arbitrated Loop you can connect 126. We're talking about a real system of devices here.

### External Device Support

Unlike IDE or EIDE, SCSI supports devices connected to your computer externally. With IDE or EIDE, all drives that you connect must fit inside your computer (in fact, the cables are restricted to about 0.5 meter (18 inches) in length. This presents some limitations. If you're using IDE or EIDE and you've maxed out your computer case's expandability with something like two floppy drives, a CD-ROM, tape backup, and a hard disk, you won't have room to add anything else. On the other hand, with SCSI you can buy devices that are housed in their own cases and simply connect them to the back of your computer with a SCSI cable. You therefore won't need a refrigerator-sized computer case, and your system's expandability will be much greater. With Fibre Channel, your devices can be spaced up to 10 kilometers (about 6.2 miles) apart with an unlimited number of hops of 10 km each using fibre optic cable! This makes a terrific backup strategy, which allows for off-site backups in case of fire.

### The Speed Thing

Although SCSI isn't always as fast as simpler interfaces (like IDE or EIDE), if you're using just one hard disk, it leaves them behind when you attach several drives. (That's the reason network servers use SCSI drives: They provide the flaming speeds required by heavy network use.) Also, because SCSI supports multitasking environments, multitasking operating systems such as UNIX, Windows NT, and OS/2 can realize better performance with SCSI than with IDE or EIDE.

### Multitasking

Only SCSI devices will really multitask in multitasking operating systems. IDE and EIDE devices are single-tasking, so although they'll work in a multitasking environment, only one drive per bus can be active. (See Appendix A, "The All-Platform Technical Reference," for more detailed comparisons of IDE, EIDE, and SCSI.)

### Built-In Error Checking

Unlike IDE or EIDE, SCSI offers built-in error checking. This capability ensures that data transferred through your system from card to device and back will be error-free. (We'll talk more about SCSI's error-checking ability in Chapter 2.) IDE depends on short cables to reduce the likelihood of errors. But if errors do occur, they may well go undetected.

### Cost

Price seems to be the only thing that matters in PCs these days; even at the expense of performance. There's no doubt that ATA/IDE drives cost less, but in my opinion many people who buy them probably regret it later when they want to add spiffy new stuff onto their system. But, c'est la vie.

## SCSI Is Easy to Use

And finally, believe it or not, SCSI is easy to use. For example, when you connect a new SCSI hard disk, you don't have to worry about all the things that plague many IDE hard disk installations, such as the number of heads, cylinders, and sectors per track in your hard drive. Even the computer doesn't worry about such details. The SCSI interface takes care of all that. In essence, all you have to do is plug it in. And Windows 95/98 and OS/2 Warp make this installation even easier with their built-in detection of SCSI cards and devices.

### ... but Not a Panacea

Although SCSI has a tremendous amount to offer its users, it's not without its drawbacks. You should be aware of these drawbacks before going out to buy a SCSI system.

### Installation

For one, interface cards aren't all that easy to install. If you've had problems installing interface cards before, SCSI is no less a challenge. This book is intended to help you through as much of the installation as possible, but the best way to minimize problems is to look for PCI Plug-and-Play SCSI interface cards that configure themselves. (Or, have your dealer do the installation.) A system with PCI slots (almost all Pentium- or Pentium II–based systems) simplifies the process and increases performance greatly. If you have Microsoft's Windows 95 or 98 you should look to its built-in tools for step-by-step help with the installation of your SCSI card. Similarly, IBM's OS/2 Warp's installation program scans for the most popular SCSI host adapters and installs them automatically.

### That Cost Issue

Another drawback to SCSI is the cost of the interface card. Although you can pick up interface cards for less than $50, the performance you'll get out of them often isn't worth the trouble. To take full advantage of SCSI you need a "real" SCSI host adapter, and it's going to cost upward of $100, depending on its capabilities. At a minimum, we consider a real SCSI card to be one with built-in BIOS, which has the ability to boot the system from a SCSI hard disk — and preferably from a CD-ROM as well. Cheap cards do not have built-in BIOS, which means you'll have to boot your system from a floppy disk or non-SCSI hard disk.

The first thing people notice is that SCSI devices cost more than EIDE or UDMA devices. In order to be flexible, fast, and easy to use, SCSI devices need more built-in intelligence than simple IDE devices tend to have — this costs money. Beyond this, the difference in price is due primarily to three things.

First, because IDE was less expensive when it was introduced, more of them were sold. Volumes went up, which drove their prices down even farther. Second, because SCSI performance is better, vendors feel justified in charging a premium for it. Third, testing SCSI devices is far more difficult than testing IDE devices, because the multi-threaded nature of SCSI makes the device firmware more complicated. When you consider the benefits of SCSI (speed, flexibility, and expandability), the slightly higher cost of SCSI is easily justifiable.

**NOTE** *SCSI is for you if, like us, you struggle to have a useful computer without upgrading annually. SCSI devices tend to be used longer than any others. Because the interface isn't changing so often, a lot of SCSI disks from as far back as 1988 are still in use, whereas other early drives (like ST-506 and ESDI) from the same period in time were generally replaced with SCSI or IDE disks. And, unlike with IDE- or EIDE-based systems, you're not likely to run out of bus slots or IRQs (interrupt requests) with a SCSI system. This means that you can easily add a second or even a third hard disk to your system and still have room to add more devices to the SCSI bus.*

### Upgrading the User

Finally, in order to use SCSI effectively, you'll need some basic knowledge of SCSI technology. You need to know how to install and configure the interface card (if it isn't Plug-and-Play), how to set device IDs, how to terminate the SCSI bus, how to choose and load device drivers, and how to optimize your system and keep it healthy.

Not to worry—we'll show you how to handle all of these tasks.

# 1.5

## A CORNUCOPIA OF SCSI DEVICES

One of the great advantages of using SCSI is that it gives you the flexibility to connect to your system a variety of devices, not just hard disks. Following are descriptions of just a few of the many devices you can connect to a SCSI system.

### Storage Devices

When you're shopping for a storage device, the first thing you look at is its *capacity* (how much data you can store on it). The capacity of these devices is specified in *megabytes* (MB) or *gigabytes* (GB).

### Hard Disks

Of all the types of hardware you can connect via SCSI, hard disks are by far the most commonly used. Hard disks are generally mounted inside the computer,

**TERMINOLOGY WARS**

Computer engineers have always used the convention that "kilo" means 1024, "mega" means 1024×1024 and "giga" means 1024×1024×1024. This is because everything in a computer works in binary (base 2), and 1024 is $2^{10}$ (two raised to the tenth power). A megabyte (MB) is therefore $2^{20}$ and a gigabyte (GB) is $2^{30}$. Using this convention makes calculations easy for engineers. The exponents come out to nice round numbers.

Then along came the marketing people, who are not used to binary and use decimal like most other people. When a marketing person writes an ad for a disk drive, they use decimal numbers (thousands, millions, and so on) to describe the capacity of the device. This practice, likely originated by the fact that most folks dislike using unfamiliar systems, coincidentally makes the capacity of the device *sound* bigger. As a result, almost any ad you see for a 9.1 GB disk will be referring to a capacity of 9,100,000,000 bytes. An engineer would refer to that same drive as an 8.475 GB disk.

The main reason I bring all this up is that, when your new 9.1 GB drive (which was thus described in an ad) arrives and you install it in your computer (which was designed by engineers), the BIOS and operating system will tell you it has a capacity of 8.475 GB! Don't get upset—you didn't get cheated! It's simply a lack of agreement about the definition of a gigabyte.

enclosed in a sealed case. The PC industry coined the phrase *hard disk* to differentiate them from *floppy disks,* which were the main storage medium on early PCs. Because the media platters inside the drive are permanently fixed inside of it, they are also called *fixed disks.* Removable media hard disk drives, such as those from SyQuest, allow you to take them with you, ship them, or lock them up for safekeeping. Another method that helps keep data secure is to enclose the entire fixed disk drive in a docking case that is constructed to allow the entire drive mechanism to be pulled out and stored separately.

One benefit of using SCSI hard disks is that they are available in higher-performance models with larger capacities than the IDE hard disks generally offer. Although recent developments have made 36 GB hard disks available for IDE, SCSI hard disks are now available with capacities of 73 GB, and even bigger disks are on the way. Also, IDE drives have just become available with rotation speeds of up to 10,000 RPM, but SCSI drives have sported 10,000 RPM for a while—and word has it that 14,400 RPM is just around the corner. The higher the rotational speed of the media, the less time the user has to wait for his data to come around to the heads that will read or write it. This waiting time is called *rotational latency* and is one of the most important performance parameters.

# Removable Media Disk Drives

This class of drives has gotten quite popular. Some examples are the 100 MB and 250 MB ZIP drives, the 120 MB LS-120 SuperDisks and the 2.2 GB ORB drives. These make handy back-up drives and are good for storing sensitive data that can't be left on the system, but are generally too slow to act as the main storage in a system. Also, they are not really designed to be operated continuously, or in severe environments where hard disks are a much better choice.

# Tape Drives

Tape drives can easily be attached to the SCSI bus. Tapes come in various types and are used to store large amounts of data (usually as backup, in case something happens to the computer's hard disks). They are not generally used for primary storage because the data can only be accessed sequentially, not randomly, as a disk drive allows. The low cost and large storage capability of tape cartridges make them ideal for archiving purposes. Because tape drives are rather slow (rewinding a tape can take 30 minutes!), SCSI's ability to let them disconnect from the bus and allow other devices to go about their business is a big plus. Several types of tape drives are discussed below. Most of the tape drives mentioned here are only available with a SCSI interface. IDE just isn't suitable.

### Quarter-Inch Cartridge (QIC)

Quarter-inch cartridge tapes aren't as common on PCs as they once were. They are so named because the tape used in the first cartridges was one-quarter of an inch wide. QIC tapes can hold from 40 MB to as much as 2 GB. QIC-150, QIC-1350, and QIC-2100c are common tape formats. Because they have well-standardized formats, these tapes have also been used extensively as a medium of data exchange between UNIX systems. Tape drives that adhere to these standards are available with SCSI interfaces.

### Digital Audio Tape (DDS DAT)

Digital audio tape is well known in the music industry for recording digital audio. In the PC world, the DAT system provides huge data storage capacity in a small form factor cassette. 4mm DAT drives employ helical scan similar to a VCR to increase the bit density on the tape. *DDS* (digital data storage) standard DAT tapes hold from 1.3 GB to 2 GB and cost less than one-third the price of QIC tapes per megabyte. The DDS-2 tapes store up to 4 GB on one tape. DDS-2 and newer 4mm drives also employ data compression to increase the data capacity per tape cassette even more.

### 8mm Tape

An 8mm tape, similar to the tape used in camcorders, can also be used for recording data. As in a camcorder, a helical scan technique is used. It provides slightly more storage capability than DDS-1, weighing in at 2 GB to 5 GB per cartridge. This format was primarily supported by one manufacturer (Exabyte) and didn't become as popular as DDS.

## DLT

Digital Linear Tape provides very fast transfer rates and high storage capacity, but unfortunately, also at a high price. The cartridges consist of a 4" square cassette with 1/2" tape inside.

# Optical Disk Drives

Optical drives are so named because they use light (optics) in the form of a laser to read and write data, as opposed to magnetic field changes that are the basis for most other computer storage. Until 1993 or so, optical drives could store more data than magnetic drives such as hard disks, but in recent years magnetic storage has improved in leaps and bounds while most optical drives improved only slightly. Optical drives come in two types: *Magneto-Optical* (MO) (which can be written and re-written many times), and *Write Once Read Many* (WORM).

As magnetic storage has gotten larger, cheaper, and faster, reasons to use optical disks have dwindled. WORM media, however, has a loyal following that actually *appreciates* the fact that the media cannot be altered after writing: This provides confidence that the data has not been altered and is used where data authenticity is very important, such as in storing government records.

### Magneto-Optical (MO) Drives

Magneto-optical drives are a cross between an optical drive and a hard disk. MO drives read data using a laser, and some are almost as fast as hard drives. The fastest MO drive access time — around 30 ms (milliseconds) — is considerably slower than the average hard disk access times (around 15 ms or less), and the transfer rates of MOs are slower than hard disks as well.

Magneto-opticals also use a high-powered laser to write to the disk. The laser heats up the surface of the disk and, once the disk material is hot enough (a temperature known as the curie point), a magnetic field changes the heated material so it either absorbs or reflects light.

In spite of the speed difference, magneto-optical disks have several advantages over hard disks: Their storage space is large and expandable for relatively little money; the disks themselves last for a very long time (about 30 years, or nearly 100,000 rewrites); and data stored on magneto-opticals lasts for several decades.

### Write Once Read Many (WORM) Drives

WORM drives are similar to CD-ROM writers in that both burn data onto the disks and cannot be erased or overwritten. WORM drives are slightly cheaper than MO drives, but because the disks can't be reused, this system is more expensive in the end and is generally only used for specific archival purposes.

### CD-ROM Drives

CD-ROM (compact disk read-only memory) made its mark in the industry with the birth of multimedia because of the large storage requirements of audio and video data. CD-ROMs are manufactured in the same way as audio CDs and are designed to be read-only. As a result, they are used to distribute programs and data files, not to back up your hard disk. CD-ROMs can store up to 650 MB of data. This medium has become extremely popular for distributing software because each disk holds so much data and the disks can be mass produced for less than $1.00 each. CD-ROM disks come in many data formats, which are governed by a set of standards defined by Sony and Philips called the colored books, because each standard has a different color cover. Almost all CD-ROMs have their files stored in ISO-9660 file system format (which is sometimes also called "High Sierra format" after the name of the hotel where the standards meeting took place). CD-ROM has become the standard media for software distribution since every new system shipped can read them.

If copying audio data from music CDs is something you want to be able to use your drive for, you should check the drive's spec sheet for its ability to "rip" audio tracks as data. Some drives cannot do this at all and some can only do it at the 1x speed (the base speed of 1x being 150 kbytes/sec). A few drives have been optimized for this use and can rip audio tracks at 11x and even 20x.

### CD-ROM Recorders (CD-R and CD-RW)

CD-ROM recorders take the read-only aspect out of CD-ROM. By using a special kind of CD called a *CD-R* (compact disk recordable), the CD-ROM recorder makes a CD-ROM by altering the color of a special dye on the media using a laser. There are two types of dye that can be used to make blank CD-Rs: cyanine (a dark blue/green color) and pthalocyanine (a gold color). CD-ROM recorders are also referred to as CD-ROM burners. The data can only be burned in once. You can't erase or overwrite data on CD-R, but data can be written to it in multiple "sessions." The best-known example of this is Kodak's PhotoCD system.

CD-R drives present special problems to the host system and interface. They are burned sequentially and must receive a continuous flow of data or the disk being written will become useless. (This is known as "making a coaster.") To improve this situation, CD-R drives usually contain a large amount of buffer memory (usually about 1 MB), which helps even out the flow of data.

CD-RW, a variation on the CD-R, creates disks that can be erased and re-written. The drawback is that these disks aren't compatible with most older CD-ROM drives. CD-RW drives make great backup devices.

The rating for these drives is usually given as the speed multiple that it can perform each of its functions at. For example, a drive that can record CD-R media at 6x, CD-RW media at 4x, and read CD-ROM media at 24x might be referred to as a 6x4x24 CD recorder.

### DVD-ROM Drives

*DVD-ROM* (Digital Versatile Disk Read-Only Memory) is the latest arrival in the world of multimedia. DVD is fundamentally a CD with huge capacity (up to 17 GB per disk). DVD-ROMs are manufactured in the same way as CDs are and, like CDs, are read-only. These drives can also read all existing CD-ROM disks. The main purpose of this medium is to contain very high quality, full-length movies complete with multiple audio tracks, closed captions, and so on. The film master is converted into a high-quality video master and then digitized and compressed using MPEG-2 encoding. This highly compressed data is then stored on the DVD in large files using the newly developed UDF file system format. Three different storage densities are available: single-sided, single layer for 5 GB; single-sided, dual layer for 9 GB; and double-sided, dual layer for 17 GB. These disks can also be used to store ordinary computer data and should become popular for distributing software that currently takes multiple CD-ROM disks. The price of these drives is expected to come down to about the same as a current CD-ROM drive. Therefore, it is expected that ordinary CD-ROM drives will soon become extinct. For some reason, the IDE interface became much more popular for DVD-ROM drives, and I'm only aware of two manufacturers producing SCSI DVD-ROM drives, but I think that will change when DVD-R becomes standardized—forecast to occur late in 2000.

## Printers and Scanners

Storage devices aren't the only devices that work with SCSI. Even printers and scanners are available with SCSI interfaces.

### Printers

Printers with SCSI interfaces aren't commonly used now, but more will likely appear in the high-end market. Why? Because the amount of data transferred to the printer increases with color images, so a bi-directional high-speed interface, like SCSI's, is very desirable. Many high-end PostScript printers have an internal SCSI interface for attaching hard disks as font, macro, or cache memory that is used by the printer when printing large files with a variety of typefaces. Perhaps the longer allowed cable lengths of the IEEE-1394 flavor of SCSI will be more appropriate for SCSI printers and also increase their popularity.

### Image Scanners

Some of the most common SCSI devices are image scanners. The amount of image data increases dramatically with *color depth* (the number of colors in the image), in fact, it's not unusual for scanners to generate files of over 20 MB for a single image, so SCSI is the interface of choice for most scanner manufacturers. Non-SCSI full-page scanners are generally too slow for professional scanning. Recently released USB scanners are lower cost, and slightly easier to install, but they can't keep up with SCSI-equipped devices.

## Variety Is the Spice of Life

As you have seen, SCSI allows you to connect quite a spectrum of peripherals to your system. This is largely due to its high speed and flexible connection schemes. In my opinion this is one of the strongest reasons for choosing SCSI I/O for your system.

# 2

# A LOOK AT SCSI-3

*by John Lohmeyer, Senior Consulting Engineer, LSI Logic Corp.,*
*and Chair of the T10 Technical Committee on SCSI*

SCSI-3 departs from SCSI-1 and SCSI-2 in that it is not a single standard. SCSI-3 is a collection of over a dozen standards that are arranged in a building-block fashion. This provides greater flexibility: SCSI-3 supports the traditional parallel bus plus at least three serial interfaces. Also, the building-block approach permits publication of the various pieces of SCSI-3 when they are ready rather than requiring that developers wait for all of the pieces to be ready at the same time (which is nearly impossible).

Unfortunately, the building-block approach is not as easy to comprehend as is the structure of SCSI-2, where everything you needed to know was in one standard. Figure 2.1 shows the various building blocks planned for SCSI-3.

When developing a SCSI-3 product, designers must first conform to two of the standards, namely SCSI-3 Architecture Model and SCSI-3 Primary Commands. Then they must pick a *physical interface* (usually a pair of associated standards) and a *command set* (one of the standards—SBC, RBC, SSC, and so on—shown across the top of Figure 2.1). In sum, each SCSI-3 peripheral product must conform to at least four standards. Although this may be a bit confusing at first, don't forget that this is a powerful architecture. And a bit of confusion will be well worth it—there will be no need to rewrite SCSI-3 driver software when you move from one physical interface to another!

If you are already familiar with communications standards, then you probably recognize that SCSI-3 has essentially adopted the layered-standards architecture promoted in the ISO Reference Model, with one key difference: SCSI-3

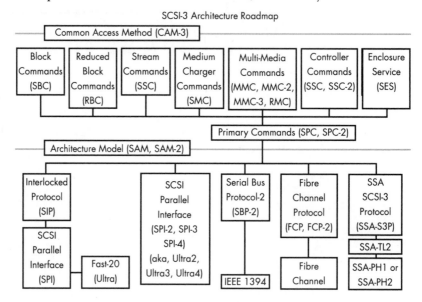

Figure 2.1: SCSI-3 Organization Chart

is optimized for storage and local I/O applications. It is not optimized to operate over the long distances typically associated with communications, although these distances can be supported using the Fibre Channel serial interface.

The SCSI-3 family has undergone several changes since the first edition of this book.[1] Many of the SCSI-3 standards have been completed, approved, and published. Some second-generation SCSI-3 standards have also been published, and one third-generation SCSI-3 standard (SPI-3) is well along in development. Rather than calling these standards SCSI-4 or SCSI-5, the T10 Technical Committee has instead added a "-2" or "-3" to the base acronym. For example, the second generation of SPI is SPI-2; the third is SPI-3. And a

1. *The Book of SCSI: A Guide for Adventurers,* No Starch Press, ISBN 1-886411-02-6

# WHAT'S IN A NAME?

SCSI terminology is confusing for a lot of good and some not-so-good reasons. Part of the problem stems from multiple naming sources, the *T10 Technical Committee* (T10), the *SCSI Trade Association* (STA), and various industry groups.

In spite of the confusing names, there is remarkable interoperability between the various SCSI products. This is because devices negotiate for advanced speeds and features. In almost all cases, a compatible speed and a compatible set of features can be found.

Here is a short guide to SCSI names you may encounter:

| Name | Defined by | Meaning |
|------|-----------|---------|
| **narrow SCSI** | STA | The original 8-bit Wide SCSI. |
| **Wide SCSI** | T10 | 16-bit Wide SCSI. Doubles the data transfer rates as compared to 8-bit SCSI. First documented as a single-cable feature in the SCSI-3 Parallel Interface (SPI) standard. |
| **Fast-xx** | T10 | The maximum data transfer rate xx in megatransfers per second. Multiply this number by 2 to get megabytes per second for a Wide (16-bit) SCSI bus. Fast-xx is mostly used in the various SCSI standards; marketing names usually include the word "Ultra." |
| **SCSI-2** | T10 | The second-generation all-in-one SCSI standard adopted in 1994. (ANSI X3.131:1994) |
| **SPI** | T10 | The first SCSI-3 standard for the parallel physical interface layer. This standard defined "Fast SCSI" later called Fast-10. (ANSI X3.253:1995) |
| **Fast-20** | T10 | A "delta" standard that, used in conjunction with SPI, defines the Fast-20 data rate. (ANSI X3.277:1996) |
| **Ultra SCSI** | Industry | Fast-20 SCSI — 20 MB/sec on a narrow SCSI bus and 40 MB/sec on a Wide SCSI bus as defined in SPI and Fast-20. |

| Name | Defined by | Meaning |
|------|-----------|---------|
| **SPI-2** | T10 | The second-generation SCSI-3 standard for the parallel physical interface layer. This standard introduced low-voltage differential (LVD) technology. (ANSI X3.302:1999) |
| **Ultra2** | STA | Fast-40 SCSI — 40 MB/sec on a narrow SCSI bus and 80 MB/sec on a Wide SCSI bus as defined in SPI-2. |
| **SPI-3** | T10 | The draft third-generation SCSI-3 standard for the parallel physical interface layer. This standard introduced double transition (DT) clocking, CRC protection, packetized protocol, and quick arbitrate and selection (QAS). |
| **Ultra3** | STA | Fast-80 SCSI — 80 MB/sec on a narrow SCSI bus and 160 MB/sec on a Wide SCSI bus as defined in SPI-3. |
| **Ultra160/m** | Industry | Ultra3 on a Wide bus with the Domain Validation feature (does not include packetized or QAS features). |
| **Ultra160** | Industry | Same as Ultra160/m. The "/m" was dropped to reduce complexity. |
| **Ultra3+** | IBM Corp. | Ultra3 plus the packetized and QAS features. |
| **SPI-4** | T10 | The draft fourth-generation SCSI-3 standard for the parallel physical interface layer. At the time of publication, this draft standard project was just getting started. |
| **Ultra4** | — | This term was dropped in late 1999 in favor of Ultra320. |
| **Ultra320** | STA | Fast-160 on a Wide bus plus packetized and QAS as defined in SPI-4. |

SPI-4 project is likely. In a somewhat futile attempt to avoid further confusing layers of dashes, developers of the second-generation SCSI-3 projects dropped the "-3" on SCSI-3, so that SPI-2 was called "SCSI Parallel Interface-2" instead of "SCSI-3 Parallel Interface-2."

If you aren't confused yet, another set of names may do the trick. The SCSI Trade Association has created the marketing names Ultra SCSI, Ultra2 SCSI, and Ultra3 SCSI to correspond to SPI + Fast-20, SPI-2, and SPI-3, respectively. You'll probably also see the name, Ultra 160, which is Ultra3 SCSI minus a few, less popular features.

## Physical SCSI-3 Interfaces

### Parallel SCSI

#### Ultra SCSI

The first generation of parallel SCSI-3 consisted of two standards, the *SCSI-3 Parallel Interface* (SPI, pronounced "spy") and the *SCSI-3 Interlocked Protocol* (SIP, pronounced "sip"). A close follow-on standard was *SCSI-3 Fast-20 Parallel Interface* (Fast-20). Together these three standards defined new features that the marketing people dubbed "Ultra SCSI." The features included a single-cable, 16-bit interface, 16-device support, and up to 20 MB/sec transfers on narrow cables or 40 MB/sec transfers on wide cables.

#### Ultra2 SCSI

As good as Ultra SCSI was, it had some serious shortcomings. Each time the speed was doubled, the maximum cable length was cut in half. This was due to the marginal signal characteristics of single-ended drivers and receivers used in over 80 percent of SCSI designs. If Ultra2 SCSI retained single-ended drivers and receivers, the maximum cable length would be 0.5 meters (about 20 inches)—too short to be useful. And if the high-powered differential drivers and receivers previously in use were also used for another generation, the system costs would be too high, because these parts required so much power that they had to be in separate chips from the protocol logic. Furthermore, doubling the speed meant cutting the skew budget in half—a nearly impossible feat if the drivers and receivers were on separate chips. It appeared that SCSI was at the end of its life unless a new driver and receiver technology could be adopted.

That is when *low-voltage differential* (LVD) came to the rescue. LVD had almost all of the benefits of the high-powered differential plus it could be integrated directly on the protocol chip. Besides that, it is 3-volt and 2.5-volt friendly, so it is compatible with the newest silicon processes. LDV SCSI could support 16 devices on a 12-meter cable (about 39 feet), and it was possible to design a multi-mode driver and receiver that could also operate in single-ended mode (although at Ultra SCSI speeds)—a real win-win situation.

The standard that documents LVD SCSI is called SPI-2. Besides defining this new technology, it also documents all the rest of the SCSI physical layer, including SPI, Fast-20, SIP, and the various SCSI-2 connectors. SPI-2 contains everything you need to know about the physical layer of parallel SCSI.

### Ultra3 SCSI

Of course, we are not done yet. The SPI-3 draft standard defines another doubling of SCSI speed and also adds several new features. The standard is still in development, so it might change yet. However, the following features appear locked in:

1. Fast-80 synchronous data rates. This is done by keeping the REQ and ACK signal timing the same as for Fast-40 (Ultra2 SCSI), but both the rising and falling edges are used. This means that data is transferred twice as fast without doubling the clocking signal frequencies. This signaling method is called *double transition* (DT) as compared to the older method of *single transition* (ST). Also, DT is defined only for 16-bit bus widths, because virtually all devices are now 16 bits; this simplifies product testing.

2. CRC has been added to protect data integrity on DT transfers.

3. Domain validation has been defined to verify that the system is capable of running at the higher rates. This works a bit like modems in that the system will verify that data can be transferred reliably at the negotiated rate; if verification fails, the system falls back to a lower speed.

4. Packetized protocol. A new protocol for transferring commands, status, and data sends this information in packets that are protected with a CRC. These packets are also sent synchronously (instead of asynchronously) to reduce the protocol overhead.

5. *Quick arbitrate and select* (QAS) reduces the time from one pair of devices using the bus to the next pair of devices using the bus.

The last two features have been somewhat controversial because of the amount of work needed to reduce SCSI overhead. Some companies think the work is not justified and have coined the term Ultra160 to refer to only the first three features—the "160" is the 16-bit data rate (MB/sec).

### Ultra4 SCSI

This concept is just a gleam in the eyes of the SCSI architects. However, it will almost certainly involve yet another doubling of SCSI data rates. Stay tuned. The standards committee will call this standard SPI-4, while the SCSI Trade

Association has already dubbed this effort Ultra320 (abandoning their previous UltraN naming scheme).

## Serial SCSI

Serial SCSI means different things to different people. It is used here as a generic term to describe the process of transporting SCSI commands over any serial interface. The T10 Technical Committee has defined SCSI mappings for three serial interfaces: Fibre Channel (FC), serial storage architecture (SSA), and high-performance serial bus (IEEE 1394).

### Fibre Channel

*Fibre Channel* is being positioned as the high-end "universal pipe." It is capable of connecting almost anything to anything else at speeds up to 100 MB/sec (1 Gbit/sec) using either coaxial cable or fiber optics. FC devices are connected through networks that are called *fabrics*, most of which are actually made up of circuit switches.

The only trouble with Fibre Channel is that its flexibility and speed are expensive, and the challenge for its proponents is to get the costs of its fabric down to a competitive level. One approach, called the *Fibre Channel Arbitrated Loop* (FC-AL), simplifies connections by including a piece of the fabric in each FC-AL device. A number of FC-AL devices can be connected in a loop or ring, referred to as an arbitrated loop, in theory reducing the system costs. (The loop is called "arbitrated" because, like parallel SCSI, FC-AL devices arbitrate for exclusive use of the loop. The winning device gets access to the loop and, once finished, the winning device gives up control of the loop so that another device may arbitrate.) I say "in theory" because FC-AL devices are almost always used in high-availability systems which then must include *Loop Resiliency Circuits* (LRC) to bypass failed devices. The LRCs add cost and complexity, so circuit switches may still be the best solution.

### Serial Storage Architecture

*Serial storage architecture* (SSA) is less of a general-purpose interface than FC, because IBM designed it principally as a storage interface. Although SSA could be used for many of the same applications as FC, it does not extend as far or connect as many devices as FC. Still, SSA is a powerful interface that can connect more devices than any PC system is ever likely to need.

Although SSA transfer rates (20 or 40 MB/sec) are somewhat lower than those of FC, SSA loops work differently from FC-AL loops. SSA loops are full-duplex, allowing for simultaneous two-way conversations. The whole loop is not dedicated to a conversation, so several separate conversations can occur at the same time. SSA proponents call these multiple conversations spatial reuse. In the best case, spatial reuse could give SSA an effective quadrupling of bandwidth. However, the reality is that, because many of today's operating systems (particularly DOS and Windows) are not multithreaded, they cannot exploit spatial reuse. Of course, multithreaded 32-bit operating systems, like Unix, Windows NT, and OS/2, could exploit it handily.

### IEEE 1394

The third contender for the title of serial SCSI is *IEEE 1394,* which you may have heard called Firewire or I.Link, Apple Computer's and Sony's names for their versions, respectively. 1394 was designed to be a serial replacement for parallel SCSI, and it solves almost every problem that Apple's engineers perceived was wrong with SCSI. It uses simple flexible cables that can be plugged into almost any empty socket, there are no terminators to worry about, no IDs to set, and it logically appears to be a bus, just like parallel SCSI. Furthermore, 1394 supports isochronous services. (Isochronous, "having equal duration," here means guaranteed timely delivery of certain data. It's a great way to deliver voice and video data.)

Early 1394 chips support only 100 Mbit/sec data rates — clearly not competitive with FC and SSA. To remedy this problem, chips are under development to support 200 Mbit/sec, and a 400 Mbit/sec version is planned. 1394 is not a true serial interface, but a 1-bit wide parallel interface. A data signal and a strobe signal are used to move data. This approach simplifies the interface logic, but it limits the upper data rates. A third "signal" power keeps the low-level interface logic alive in powered-down devices, thus keeping the bus intact even when a device is unplugged. Because 1394 has these three signals, its cables have three twisted pairs.

### Which Serial SCSI Will Win?

In the first edition of this book, these interfaces were described as being in a three-horse race to determine which, if any, would become an important PC interface. Although we still have not declared a winner, it is safe to say that SSA has dropped out of the race. Although SSA remains an important interface within IBM Corp., it has not attracted an outside following.

Fibre Channel is gaining ground as a high-end system-to-subsystem interface. Although a few disk drives are available with Fibre Channel Arbitrated Loop interfaces, they are currently shipping in low volumes.

IEEE 1394 is attractive for consumer applications such as VCRs and video cameras, but most storage vendors have panned this interface as too expensive and too slow for disk drives. Still, a few vendors have prototype 1394 disk drives available; these drives target audio/video applications rather than traditional storage.

Some new serial contenders have entered the race. The *Universal Serial Bus* (USB) is starting to gain acceptance. However, it is much too slow to seriously consider for disk drive applications. Also, the InfiniBand™ interface proposal (Intel's NGIO and Compaq's, IBM's, and HP's SIO, which were worst-kept secrets until they recently merged) is vying for consideration as an alternative to Fibre Channel. The serial race is far from over.

## SCSI's Greatest Value: The Command Sets

The part of SCSI that has the most value to systems integrators, software developers, and peripheral manufacturers is its command sets. Because the computer industry has made a huge investment in SCSI driver software, all of the serial interfaces need SCSI command set mappings to leverage the computer industry's command set investment and to get to market quicker. Even IDE proponents have leveraged the SCSI command sets: The ATAPI protocol maps the SCSI CD-ROM command set onto the IDE interface to permit internal IDE CD-ROMs.

The command sets that were in SCSI-2 are partitioned across several SCSI-3 command set documents near the top of the chart in Figure 2.1. Enhancements are being made, but most of the changes are evolutionary so old software continues to run with the new hardware.

Two SCSI-2 command sets are not included in the SCSI-3 standards: Scanner Devices and Communications Devices. If you were building one of these devices for SCSI-3, you would need to refer to SCSI-2 for the command set.

Also, SCSI-3 offers several new command sets:

- The *SCSI-3 Controller Commands* (SCC) and the *SCSI Controller Commands-2* (SCC-2) are new command sets for RAID controllers.

- The *Reduced Block Commands* (RBC) is a greatly simplified command set (as compared to SBC) for disk drives.

- The *Multimedia Commands-2* (MMC-2) adds DVD support to the CD-ROM command set.

- The *SCSI Enclosure Services* (SES) defines a command set for communicating with an enclosure that holds disk drives or other devices. In high- availability systems, SES allows the system to find out the status of power supplies, fans, and so on.

## Is SCSI-3 Done Yet?

People not familiar with the SCSI-3 architecture and the standards process often ask this question. Of course, each draft standard goes through the standards approval process individually, so one cannot name a single specific date. Most SCSI-3 standards, including SBC, SMC, MMC, SCC, SCC-2, SES, SPC, SAM, SPI, SIP, Fast-20, SPI-2, SBP-2, FCP, and the six SSA standards are approved ANSI standards. Most of the others are nearing completion of their development phases that will be followed by approval phase, which usually takes about nine months. The fact is that manufacturers rarely wait for final ANSI approval before starting product development. Although SCSI-2 is still often referenced, most SCSI products shipping today use at least some of the features documented in the SCSI-3 standards.

# 3

## SCSI ANATOMY

Before venturing deep into the heart of connecting and configuring SCSI devices, you should know some of the basics of SCSI technology. Once we've cut through the morass of techno-babble, we hope you'll find that the principles behind the way SCSI works are actually quite easy to understand.

### SCSI Devices Can Be Initiators or Targets

Although the different kinds of SCSI devices are numerous—such as interface cards, hard disks, CD-ROMs, and scanners—all of them fall into two fundamental categories: initiators and targets. The *initiator* device is also called the host, and it starts or initiates device-to-device communication. The *target* device receives the communication from the initiator and responds. For example, when reading a file from a SCSI hard disk, the SCSI interface card (the initiator) requests data from the SCSI hard disk, and the hard disk (the target) responds to the request by sending the data. This is the most common initiator–target interaction in a SCSI system.

In general, the SCSI host adapter card will be the initiator on the bus. Most of your other devices will probably be targets.

SCSI peripherals can act both as initiators and as targets. For example, if you were to use the SCSI Copy command to copy data from one SCSI hard disk to another, the disk that holds the data to be copied (the source disk) acts as the initiator, and the hard disk that receives the file is the target.

**NOTE** *To avoid confusion, I want to point out that operating systems do not use the Copy command to copy data from one disk to another. In general, the data is read from the source drive into memory and then written from memory to the destination drive. This may seem inefficient, but it is necessary to implement the file systems that we all know and love. Without this convenience, you would need to remember the block numbers on the disk that your data is stored in! I think you'll agree that this convenience is worth a little inefficiency.*

SCSI systems can have up to eight devices connected in a daisy chain (16-bit Wide SCSI can have up to sixteen devices). These devices can be any combination of initiators and targets, but at least one must be an initiator and one a target in order to have a useful system. Typically, a system will have one host adapter card and one or more peripheral devices, such as hard disks and CD-ROM drives.

## SCSI IDs and LUNs Identify Individual SCSI Devices

If you have a system with only one initiator and one target, you have a pretty simple system—no confusion here. But what happens if you have one initiator and more than one target? How do you tell one target from another? For example, if you've hooked three hard disks—E, F, and G—onto the bus and want to talk to F, how do you send the command to F, bypassing E and stopping before G?

SCSI's answer is to give each device on the SCSI bus, including the SCSI host adapter, a kind of unique identification called a *SCSI ID*. These IDs, or addresses, are a lot like house numbers in a street address, which identify each house uniquely so that the mail gets to the right place. Without this identification, there would be no way to know where to send commands and data along the bus and no way to direct signals to a specific device.

Every SCSI device is assigned its own unique SCSI ID number. In our example above, hard disk E might get ID 2, hard disk F might have ID 3, and hard disk G could get ID 4. Given that SCSI-1 and SCSI-2 allow you to attach up to eight SCSI devices on the bus, you can have eight possible SCSI IDs. These SCSI IDs range from 0 to 7, counting 0 as the first number. Note that

16-bit Wide SCSI allows a maximum of 16 devices, with IDs ranging from 0 to 15; and 32-bit Wide SCSI allows for 32 devices, ranging from 0 to 31.

### Ah, the Mysteries of LUNs

If you've been working with SCSI, then you may have encountered *LUNs* (logical unit numbers). LUNs can be really confusing, but don't fret. They're similar to SCSI IDs in that they identify SCSI devices. The difference between LUNs and SCSI IDs, though, is that LUNs represent devices within devices; they're divisions within IDs. The way this works in practice is that every device ID, from 0 to 7, can have up to 8 LUNs (64 LUNs in SCSI-3), also numbered 0 to 7 (0 to 63 in SCSI-3), for a total of eight subdevices within each ID. LUNs give SCSI a certain added flexibility.

If you were a device manufacturer and wanted to allow your customers to have more than eight devices on a SCSI bus, you consider using Wide SCSI, which allows up to 16 devices (because it uses a 16-bit bus instead of regular SCSI's 8-bit bus). But that's not the only alternative. You could also make your device respond to a single device ID but have each subdevice device respond to a different LUN for that ID. So, for example, three hard drives, labeled E, F, and G, could be put together into one drive case and assigned SCSI ID 2, but each drive would have a different LUN number: drive E might be LUN 0, drive F might be LUN 1, and drive G might be LUN 2. This is what is done in RAID systems. We'll talk more about RAIDs in Chapter 10.

**NOTE** *The sad fact is that a SCSI user cannot independently decide to use LUNs for some purpose. The hardware needs to be designed with this in mind. Also, LUNs are so seldom used that many host adapters don't check for them by default — a practice that speeds up the bus scanning process and saves a little memory. If you have a device that uses LUNs (like a CD-ROM changer), you may need to enable LUN support in the host adapter BIOS or device driver.*

## The SCSI Bus Allows Communication Between Your Computer and Your SCSI Devices

Once you have an initiator and a target identified, you have to provide a means for communicating between them so the devices may send and receive commands and data.

Cables are the answer here. When you connect a cable between the two devices, you provide a bus or pathway between them. This pathway is the SCSI bus, and it is the communication channel between all SCSI devices. The SCSI bus begins at one end of the cable, which is usually attached to a target device, and ends at the other end of the cable, which is usually attached to the SCSI

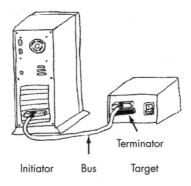

Terminator

Initiator     Bus     Target

*Figure 3.1: A Typical SCSI Bus*

host adapter card. We'll go into more detail about using connectors and cabling in Chapter 5.

A SCSI bus with one initiator and one target might look like that in Figure 3.1.

### Types of SCSI Buses

SCSI buses come in two electrical types: *single-ended* and *differential.* The essential difference between the two is that, on a single-ended bus, the devices signal each other over one wire (and a ground reference), whereas on a differential SCSI bus, the devices communicate over a pair of wires per signal.

Differential SCSI gets its name from the fact that it subtracts (takes the difference) between the two wires for each signal. When compared with differential SCSI, single-ended communication is relatively inexpensive, and it's fine for short distances. Differential SCSI is more expensive than single-ended SCSI, but it allows your system to communicate over longer distances.

### Single-Ended SCSI Is Cheap, and It's Fine for Short Distances

Most SCSI systems use a single-ended bus, which is a bus with only one wire (plus a ground reference) per signal. Single-ended buses are the most economical way to communicate between devices, because the electronics used to send and receive the signals are very simple and inexpensive. Single-ended buses provide high-speed communication for short distances (see Table 3.1 for maximum lengths allowed). The maximum length of the single-ended bus cable for Fast SCSI is shorter than that for regular SCSI, because Fast SCSI is more error-prone than regular SCSI. The longer the cable, the greater the chance of introducing errors into the signal, so the Fast SCSI bus cable is kept short. Put another way, the faster the signals on the bus are, the harder it is to distinguish them from noise.

### Differential SCSI Allows Communication over Longer Distances

When you want to go beyond the maximum distance allowed by single-ended SCSI, you risk encountering signal loss and noise problems due to the extended length of the cable. Differential SCSI offers an alternative to single-ended SCSI when you want a system to communicate over greater distances. The differential SCSI bus carries commands and data over pairs of wires, taking the difference in voltage between each of the two wires (see the sidebar entitled "The Differences Between Single-Ended and Differential SCSI" for more information on this process).

Because the subtraction process also subtracts off any noise that is the same on the two signals, differential SCSI extends the maximum bus cable length to 25 meters (about 82 feet).

## THE DIFFERENCES BETWEEN SINGLE-ENDED AND DIFFERENTIAL SCSI

Table 3.1 illustrates the differences between single-ended and differential SCSI by comparing a 50-pin cable for each. In the single-ended configuration, wires 26 through 50 carry signals between devices. Wires 1 through 25 are ground returns. Because signals are present on only one set of wires, information is interpreted by the Voltage (the strength of the signal) on the wire relative to ground. Unfortunately, electrical noise from the outside world can cause the voltage to fluctuate, resulting in corrupted data.

In the differential configuration, each signal is sent on two wires. The information is interpreted by the difference in voltage between the wires, not as the voltage of the signal on a single wire relative to ground. When noise interferes with the signal in this bus configuration, both wires are disturbed equally. However, because the noise on one wire is the same as the noise on the other wire and both are affected equally, the difference in Voltage is zero. The result is that the device receives the information free of noise.

Don't worry about the details in Table 3.1, but notice that the wires in a single-ended bus are used differently than the wires in a differential bus and consequently the two cannot coexist. You must have single-ended SCSI devices on a single-ended SCSI bus and differential SCSI devices on a differential SCSI bus. You cannot have single-ended SCSI devices connected to differential SCSI devices. In LVD, the signals were aligned with the single-ended signals so interoperation between the two signaling standards would not be a problem; avoiding the confusion that occurred with HVD and single-ended being connected.

**Table 3.1: Single-Ended versus Differential SCSI 50-pin Cables**

| Single-Ended | | | | Differential | | | |
|---|---|---|---|---|---|---|---|
| Pin | Signal | Pin | Signal | Pin | Signal | Pin | Signal |
| 1 | GROUND | 26 | D0– | 1 | GROUND | 26 | GROUND |
| 2 | GROUND | 27 | D1– | 2 | D0+ | 27 | D0– |
| 3 | GROUND | 28 | D2– | 3 | D1+ | 28 | D1– |
| 4 | GROUND | 29 | D3– | 4 | D2+ | 29 | D2– |
| 5 | GROUND | 30 | D4– | 5 | D3+ | 30 | D3– |
| 6 | GROUND | 31 | D5– | 6 | D4+ | 31 | D4– |
| 7 | GROUND | 32 | D6– | 7 | D5+ | 32 | D5– |
| 8 | GROUND | 33 | D7– | 8 | D6+ | 33 | D6– |
| 9 | GROUND | 34 | DPAR– | 9 | D7+ | 34 | D7– |
| 10 | GROUND | 35 | GROUND | 10 | DPAR+ | 35 | DPAR– |
| 11 | GROUND | 36 | GROUND | 11 | DIFFSENS | 36 | GROUND |
| 12 | RESERVED | 37 | RESERVED | 12 | RESERVED | 37 | RESERVED |
| 13 | OPEN | 38 | TERMPWR | 13 | TERMPWR | 38 | TERMPWR |
| 14 | RESERVED | 39 | RESERVED | 14 | RESERVED | 39 | RESERVED |
| 15 | GROUND | 40 | ATN– | 15 | ATN+ | 40 | ATN– |
| 16 | GROUND | 41 | ATN– | 16 | GROUND | 41 | GROUND |
| 17 | GROUND | 42 | GROUND | 17 | BSY+ | 42 | BSY– |
| 18 | GROUND | 43 | BSY– | 18 | ACK+ | 43 | ACK– |
| 19 | GROUND | 44 | ACK– | 19 | RST+ | 44 | RST– |
| 20 | GROUND | 45 | RST– | 20 | MSG+ | 45 | MSG– |
| 21 | GROUND | 46 | MSG– | 21 | SEL+ | 46 | SEL– |
| 22 | GROUND | 47 | SEL– | 22 | C/D+ | 47 | C/D– |
| 23 | GROUND | 48 | C/D– | 23 | REQ+ | 48 | REQ– |
| 24 | GROUND | 49 | REQ– | 24 | I/O+ | 49 | I/O– |
| 25 | GROUND | 50 | I/O– | 25 | GROUND | 50 | GROUND |

### Low Voltage Differential

So far when we mentioned differential, we have been referring to what is now known as *High Voltage Differential* (HVD). From here on, we will distinguish HVD from *low voltage differential* (LVD), which is a new signaling standard introduced by SCSI-3 (SPI-2).

As SCSI speeds got faster and faster, the allowable length of its cabling got shorter and shorter. Using differential bus driver chips allowed longer buses, but greatly increased the cost of both the host adapters and drives, especially for Wide SCSI, which requires 27 bus drivers. This is because the HVD bus drivers couldn't be integrated into the SCSI protocol chips because of the amount of power dissipated by them. Also the higher speeds made it increasingly important that the propagation delays in all the bus drivers be matched quite accurately. What to do, what to do?

The T10 Technical Committee decided on a compromise. They came up with an interface that had the advantage of differential signaling, but with low enough power dissipation that the bus drivers could be integrated into LSI chips. Also, putting all the bus drivers on the same piece of silicon helps to match their speeds! To make it even better, they decreed that the devices using this new LVD interface should be able to determine whether all the devices on the bus are able to use LVD or switch to single-ended mode to remain compatible.

As a result, LVD devices go by the Voltage they see on the DIFF SENSE signal to decide whether any single-ended devices are present. If the Voltage is less than .6 V, there are single-ended devices; if it's between .7 V and 1.9 V, it's all LVD; and if it's over 2.2 V, there are HVD devices present. If HVD devices are present, the LVD device shuts off its bus drivers to avoid damage. Wow! That's one less thing we need to worry about when connecting things up. Starting with Fast-40 devices, this LVD interface became standard. LVD has been designed to accommodate devices as fast as 320 MHz, so we can expect to see more of these devices appearing in the future.

**NOTE** *Single-ended SCSI is based on sending a single signal, whereas differential SCSI takes the difference between two signals. As a result, the two cannot coexist. You must have single-ended SCSI devices on a single-ended SCSI bus and HVD SCSI devices on a HVD SCSI bus. You cannot have single-ended SCSI devices (or even LVD devices) connected to HVD SCSI devices. LVD bus driver chips are able to identify a single-ended bus and switch modes to accommodate it, but are not compatible with HVD. You can expect HVD equipment to be phased out as LVD replaces it.*

## SCSI Cables and Connectors

Cables are the physical makeup of the SCSI bus. As a result, they become the lifeline of the entire system. To ensure that the correct cables are used to build the bus, SCSI-2 and SCSI-3 define minimum requirements for the number of wires needed as well as the electrical properties of the cable. SCSI systems can utilize cabling both inside and outside the device cabinet (or case). Internal cables are typically flat, unshielded ribbon cables; external cables are generally round and shielded. Because flat cables can cause excessive cross-talk on differential signals, newer LVD systems use round cables internally.

Tables 3.2 and 3.3 summarize the number of wires, maximum transfer rate, maximum length, and type of cables for the different SCSI standards. Note in Table 3.2 that, for SCSI-3 32-bit, you need to use two cables, P and Q, each with 68 wires. This is why you don't see any 32-bit devices for sale. Table 3.3 lists the maximum and minimum lengths for different parts of the bus for each SCSI standard.

## Adapters

As mentioned above, there are two kinds of SCSI cables, 50-pin and 68-pin. If you look at the two quickly you may confuse which one is considered "wide." The 68-pin ribbon cable is actually narrower than the 50-pin ribbon because the wires in the 68-pin cable are spaced only half as far apart. So the "width"

**Table 3.2: SCSI Cable Reference Table**

| Bus Standard | Width | Maximum Transfer Rate (MB/sec) | Cable Type | Number of Conductors |
|---|---|---|---|---|
| SCSI-1 | 8-bit | 4 | Not specified | Not specified |
| SCSI-2 | 8-bit | 5 | A | 50 |
| | 16-bit | 10 | B | 68 |
| SCSI-3 Parallel | 16-bit | 80 | P | 68 |
| Interface (SPI) | 32-bit | 60 | P and Q | 68 and 68 |

Note: In SPI-3, support for the Q-cable has been dropped.

**Table 3.3: SCSI Bus Length Specifications**

| Bus Type | Property | Single-Ended | Differential (HVD) | LVD |
|---|---|---|---|---|
| Sync (5 MHz) | Maximum bus length | 6 meters (20 feet) | 25 meters (82 feet) | 12 meters (39 feet) |
| Fast-10 | Maximum bus length | 3 meters (10 feet) | 25 meters (82 feet) | 12 meters (39 feet) |
| Fast-20 (Ultra) | Maximum bus length | 1.5 meters (5 feet) | 25 meters (82 feet) | 12 meters (39 feet) |
| Fast-40 (Ultra2) | Maximum bus length | Don't do it | 25 meters (82 feet) spec. but not available** | 12 meters (39 feet) |
| Fast-80 (Ultra3) | Maximum bus length | Don't do it | Don't do it | 12 meters (39 feet) |
| All | Maximum stub* length | 0.1 meter (4 inches) | 0.1 meter (4 inches) | 0.2 meter (8 inches) |
| All | Minimum stub* spacing | 0.3 meter (12 inches) | n/a | n/a |

* A section of cable that runs between the device and the bus. Considered a defect in the bus, stubs should be as short as possible.

** Although the SCSI spec. defines HVD transceivers for Fast-40, none are manufactured.

used in this context concerns the number of pins, not the measured width, of the cable.

The next thing that may occur to you is "If I get a 68-pin Wide host adapter and a Wide disk drive, how am I going to be able to connect my existing 50-pin narrow CD-ROM drive to the same bus?" The answer is adapters.

Additionally, there is another consideration: If you adapt the 16-bit Wide bus down to 8-bit narrow, you need to terminate the upper half of the bus where the adapting takes place. You will see adapters that say they contain "Hi-9 termination," which means that the high order bits and their parity bit will be terminated right in the adapter. This is what would typically be needed if your host adapter has an external connector on its back rail that is 68-pin and you want to connect several narrow devices, like CD-ROMs and scanners, that are external to the system case. This type of adapter would be called a 68-pin male to 50-pin female. The 50-pin side is usually either a Centronics type or High Density type.

If a narrow device, like a CD-ROM for instance, will be placed internal to the system, and connected to the 68-pin cable, you would use a 68-pin male to 50-pin female IDC adapter that doesn't have any terminators in it, and you would plug it directly onto the back of the narrow device. Then the adapter can plug directly onto an available connector on the internal 68-pin cable.

### SCA Adapters

Another type of connector you might encounter is the 80-pin *SCA* (single connector attachment). There are no host adapters with 80-pin connectors. Drives with this type of connector are designed to be plugged into bays in "hot-swap" cabinets. A common use for this type of mounting is in RAID arrays, where you can replace defective drives without even powering down the system. Sun Microsystems developed this connector arrangement, and it was standardized by the *Small Form Factor* (SFF) Committee. SCA just combines the normal Wide SCSI signals with the four ID bits and power supply connections. In addition, SCA drives usually lack built-in terminators, so other arrangements will need to be made for termination. SCA Adapters are available that bring out these connections separately, so you can connect an SCA drive to a regular SCSI bus.

## Terminating the SCSI Bus

If there's one aspect of SCSI that always raises the hair on even the wisest technician's head, that honor must go, unequivocally, to properly terminating the SCSI bus. This section covers the types of termination. How to terminate the bus will be discussed further in Chapter 5.

## The SCSI Bus Is a Transmission Line

(Drum roll, please. . . .)

I am now going to attempt to explain, in a few paragraphs, the technical reasons that a SCSI bus needs terminations. This discussion will require mention of radio frequency transmission line theory and similar heavy-duty stuff that most computer people (even computer engineers) have never studied. If this sounds too scary, just skip to the next section (on page 44), where I'll explain it in simpler terms.

A *transmission line* is a pair of wires, parallel to each other, used to send a signal from one place to another. *Impedance* is the ratio of voltage to current in a circuit. The characteristic impedance of a transmission line is the result of the distributed inductance of the wire it's made of and the distributed capacitance caused by the proximity of the two wires to each other.

The mathematical formula for the characteristic impedance of an ideal transmission line (one where the wires have zero resistance and the insulation between the wires has zero dissipation) is:

$$Z0 = 276 \log_{10} (2D \, / \, d) \text{ Ohms}$$

where

$D$ = the center-to-center distance between the two wires
$d$ = the diameter of each wire

A digital signal (a change in voltage from 0 volts to 3 volts, for example) can be thought of as an incident wave. A transmission line of infinite length does not need to be terminated, because the incident wave will never reflect back from anything. A finite transmission line needs a terminating resistance at the end to absorb the signal wave so it will not reflect.

The effect of a reflection returning from the end of a transmission line is that the reflected voltage adds to the forward voltage and distorts the wave form.

Digital circuits require that the signal transitions be sharp rises or falls in voltage. A signal distorted by reflection — in which the voltage comes part way down, stays the same for a while, and then falls the rest of the way — confuses the circuit that's trying to determine whether it sees a 1 or a 0. Many types of signal distortion can happen because of reflected signals combining with forward moving ones.

Because the SCSI bus has devices (any one of which can generate signals) all along it and not at just one end, both ends need to be terminated — even on a "single-ended" bus. :-)

## What's That He Said?

Let's try that again without the math and electronic theory.

Because the SCSI bus is a chain of devices with definite ends, the two ends of the bus must be capped off or terminated. Every wire, even though it conducts, presents a slight impediment to the passing of electrical signals. The SCSI bus, too, has a specific impedance; but when the signals reach the end of the cables that make up the bus, they encounter the air, which has very high impedance and acts as a wall. (That's why the electricity doesn't jump out of your wall outlet: The air keeps it in.) The only problem with the high impedance at the end of the bus for electrical signals is that any signal coming down the bus is reflected back in the other direction once it hits this barrier. (Although this is good in racquetball, it's bad in SCSI.) That's where termination comes in.

*Termination* is an electrical requirement that must be met in order to prevent the reflection of signals when they reach the ends of the bus. You terminate the bus by attaching a resistor (the terminator) to the physical ends of the SCSI bus. The terminator provides an impedance that matches the cable's, thereby preventing the signal from bouncing back.

The terminators on a single-ended SCSI bus serve a second purpose, too. The terminator resistors act as a supply of current to pull the voltage on idle signals up to about +3 volts. Yes, you heard me correctly. The SCSI bus is active low. A "one" (asserted signal) is represented by pulling the bus signal line toward ground. The terminators get this current from the SCSI bus by way of the termination power (TERMPWR) wire on the bus. (You'll see this wire in the Cabling and Connector Pin Out diagrams in Appendix B.)

**NOTE**
*This TERMPWR Voltage must be provided by at least one device on the SCSI bus. In SCSI-2 and beyond, it is specified that host adapters must supply TERMPWR. One exception to this that I have seen is PCMCIA host adapters that plug into laptop computers. The manufacturers of these apparently feel that portable computers, which typically run on battery power, cannot afford to supply TERMPWR. Also, the connector pins on a PCMCIA card are too thin to carry the current required by terminators. When attaching SCSI devices to laptop systems, set (usually with an internal switch or jumper) one of the external devices to supply TERMPWR and everyone will be happy.*

There are three methods for terminating the bus: passive, active, and forced perfect termination.

### Passive Termination

*Passive termination* is the oldest method of termination and was defined in the specifications for SCSI-1.

A passive SCSI terminator is a set of 18 voltage dividers, each containing two resistors. The resistor pairs have values such that the voltage at their center junction will be about 3.3 volts when TERMPWR is about 5 volts. That is, for each signal there is a 220-ohm resistor pulling the signal up to TERMPWR and a 330-ohm resistor pulling it down to ground.

Any two resistor values having the ratio of 2/3 and connected to a 5-volt source, would give 3.3 volts at their junction, but these values are chosen because, when placed in parallel (as they appear to be on the SCSI bus), their combined value — (R1 × R2) / (R1 + R2) — becomes 132 ohms. This is pretty close to the value specified for the cable that SCSI buses are made of (but not as close as we'd like, as we'll soon see)!

Three fundamental problems occur using passive terminators:

- Much of the power drawn from TERMPWR (.16 Amps idle, to a max. of .40 Amps per terminator) is being wasted in the voltage dividers.

- If the TERMPWR voltage isn't high enough or has noise on it, that problem will be passed on to the SCSI signals being terminated.

- The 132-ohm impedance they present turns out not to match typical cable as well as it should.

### Active Termination

*Active termination* takes a different approach to providing a resistance equal to the transmission line's impedance. Instead of a pair of resistors at the end of the bus, an active terminator has only one. On each of the 18 (or 27 for Wide) signals is a 110-ohm resistor connected to a 2.8-volt power supply. The 2.8 volts is provided by putting an active voltage regulator in series with the TERMPWR line. Because of this active regulation, the power that each signal gets from the TERMPWR source is more stable and noise-free than is possible with passive termination. Also, it has been found that 110 ohms is closer to the real impedance of most of the cables being manufactured.

**NOTE** *Active terminators are highly recommended when using any devices faster than 5 MHz.*

### Forced Perfect Termination (FPT)

*Forced perfect termination* is the most complex of the terminators. Beyond merely stabilizing the power applied to the terminator, it can minimize distortion caused by reflections. It is usually used in high-speed SCSI systems that have many different devices, cables, and terminator types. The complexity of such a system can introduce many impedance mismatches that will degrade the signals sent through the bus. FPT actively compensates for these impedance variations by means of diode switching and biasing to clamp the voltage levels of the signals so they go no higher than +3 volts nor any lower than ground. There is a lot of controversy surrounding FPT termination: Although it can permit a complex bus to work that would otherwise fail, it technically violates the SCSI standards by supplying more current than allowed under certain conditions. This could cause SCSI protocol chips to fail prematurely. Figure 3.2 shows a schematic of a typical FPT.

### Don't Forget Differential

Differential buses use passive and active terminators that have a different arrangement of resistors to accommodate the fact that the signaling is done on two wires instead of one. As with everything else pertaining to HVD, you cannot mix differential terminators with any other kind.

As if we didn't already have enough different terminators already, now we need a new type! Earlier in this chapter we mentioned a new differential interface called Low Voltage Differential (LVD). LVD drives don't have terminators built in as do most single-ended drives. You need to put an LVD terminator on an unused connector at the end of the cable. This technique can also be used with single-ended drives and eliminates the need to check all the devices

## ACTIVE TERMINATION IN DETAIL

In order to solve the above mentioned problems (which is especially important on SCSI buses running at 10 MHz and faster) use active termination. This type of termination is known as Alternative-2 in SCSI-2 and uses only a 110-ohm resistor on each signal line connected to a Voltage regulator. This regulator actively adjusts its output to maintain 2.85 V, thereby offering partial immunity to voltage drops on the TERMPWR line.

By using 110-ohm resistors, the terminator's impedance is a much closer match to the impedance of the cable (105 to 108 ohms) than passive termination (132 ohms). A closer impedance match between terminators and cables minimizes reflections at the ends of the bus to reduce data errors.

The lower resistor values in the terminator also result in higher pull-down currents. As a result, actively terminated buses don't suffer from rising ("staircase") waveforms commonly seen on weakly driven transmission lines.

Studies by Kurt Chan and Gordon Matheson, both of Hewlett-Packard, have shown that mixing termination types will yield better performance than using passive termination alone. Wherever possible, use SCSI devices that employ active termination. If necessary, add stand-alone active terminators and disable the internal terminators (usually by setting a switch or jumper in the device).

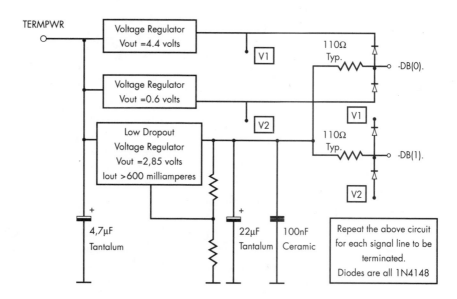

*Figure 3.2: Schematic of Forced Perfect Terminator (FPT)*

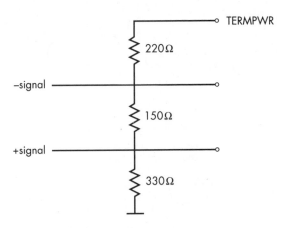

*Figure 3.3: Schematic of Differential (HVD) Terminator*

to see which ones have their terminator enabled. You just terminate the ends of the cable and can move devices around later without worry. Figure 3.3 shows a schematic for differential terminator.

## HOW PARITY CHECKING WORKS

When a device receives a byte of data, it can check the data for errors by counting the number of bits that are set to 1. Because SCSI uses odd parity, the number of bits set to 1, including the parity bit, must always be odd. For example, the decimal value 35 in binary format is 00100011. Looking at this byte, you see a total of three 1's (an odd number of 1's). Therefore, the parity bit for this byte is 0 so that the total number of 1's is still odd. The data actually sent is therefore 001000110. The trailing 0 is the parity bit. When the receiving device gets this data, it counts the number of 1's in the nine data bits, sees that the total is odd, and accepts it as correct.

If the number of 1's received isn't odd, the device knows that an error has occurred in the data transmission, and it asks to have the data sent again. However, parity checking is not foolproof. As you can see in the last rows of Table 3.4, as long as there is an odd number of 1's, it doesn't matter if one, three, five, seven, or nine 1's are received—an error is not generated. This is definitely a limitation of parity checking. But because it's fast and inexpensive to implement, it provides a satisfactory level of security. IDE and EIDE don't offer any error checking of the data that's transmitted over the cable.

## Using Parity Checking

When working with SCSI systems, you'll probably encounter the term *parity checking*. Parity checking is built into all SCSI-2 devices, and it will be part of all future SCSI devices. It's not always present in older, SCSI-1 devices, because parity checking was an option in the SCSI-1 specification. So, if you have a SCSI-1 device, be sure to check your manual to see whether your device supports parity checking.

**Table 3.4: Odd Parity Checking (Odd Number of 1's)**

| Data Value (8 bits) | Number of 1's Sent | Odd Parity Bit | Data Received (9 bits, includes parity bit as LSB) | Number of 1's Received | Error? |
|---|---|---|---|---|---|
| 00100011 | 3 (odd) | 0 | 001000110 | 3 (odd) | No |
| 00100011 | 3 (odd) | 0 | 001010110 | 4 (even) | Yes |
| 00100011 | 3 (odd) | 0 | 001011110 | 5 (odd) | No |
| 00100111 | 4 (even) | 1 | 001001111 | 5 (odd) | No |
| 01111011 | 6 (even) | 1 | 011110111 | 7 (odd) | Yes |

There are two types of parity, even and odd. In even parity, there is always an even number of bits set to 1, including a reference bit called the *parity bit*. In odd parity, there is always an odd number of bits set to 1, including the parity bit.

Briefly, parity checking is a simple and fast way to detect errors in the data sent through the SCSI bus by (1) checking the number of 1's carried in a byte (eight bits) of data and (2) checking the parity bit.

When you send eight bits of data, you count how many ones there are, and you set the parity bit to either 0 or 1, depending on the type of parity being used. (See the sidebar "How Parity Checking Works" and Table 3.4 for a detailed explanation of setting the parity bit.) When the target receives the data, it counts the number of bits that are set to 1. If the number of 1's is odd when it should be even or vice versa, the target knows that a data error has occurred, and it can request that the device send the signal again.

SCSI uses odd parity, which means that the byte of data always contains an odd number of bits set to 1. If there is an even number of 1's, then something went wrong with the data transfer. The parity bit is included with each byte of data that is transferred. Thus, rather than sending eight bits of data with each byte, nine bits are sent. The ninth bit is the parity bit.

Although parity checking is simple and effective, whether you'll be able to use it depends on the capabilities of all of your SCSI devices. All devices on the bus must be able to perform parity checking in order for you to enable it. In fact, if even one device lacks support for parity checking, you must turn parity checking off on your host adapter. Otherwise, the one device that doesn't set the parity bit properly will cause errors, and your system won't work properly.

### Is Parity Really Enough?

As bus speeds continue to increase, the T10 Technical Committee is concerned that simple parity checking may not catch all the errors that may occur. Therefore, in SPI-3, they are adding *CRC* (Cyclic Redundancy Check) to be used with Fast-80.

## Your SCSI Devices Can Communicate Either Synchronously or Asynchronously

SCSI devices have two methods of sending and receiving data between devices: asynchronous and synchronous. Their names are clues to their methods of operation. In *asynchronous communication*, every byte of data sent from initiator to target must be acknowledged by the target, with a kind of return receipt. Whereas this is a safer way to communicate, it's also slower because the target needs to send a receipt and the initiator needs to receive it before another byte of data is sent, resulting in a delay in communication.

*Synchronous communication* also requires acknowledgment, but allows the initiator to send many bytes without having to wait first for an "acknowledge" for each byte from the target. So the initiator can send a whole stream of data, and it doesn't matter when the stream of receipts comes back. Thus, synchronous communication is much faster than asynchronous, because instead of a delay between each byte sent, a flood of data is sent, followed by a delay until a flood of receipts comes back. In effect, you have one delay rather than a whole bunch of delays.

### Asynchronous Communication

SCSI devices communicate with the host adapter asynchronously by default. Asynchronous "handshaking" ensures that the data reaches the target. Because devices wait for a return receipt before sending another byte of data, communication between devices sending and receiving at different speeds is possible.

For example, let's say that your SCSI hard disk and host adapter need to communicate with each other, but they send and receive data at very different speeds: Your hard disk receives data much more slowly than your host adapter can send it. If your hard disk were to keep sending data to your host adapter, you shouldn't have a problem because the host adapter can keep up. But reverse the flow of information—assume it's moving from the fast host adapter to the slow hard disk—and you have a bottleneck. The host adapter dumps out data faster than the hard disk can receive it, and the transfer falls apart.

Asynchronous transfer mode provides the solution for the latter case. With asynchronous transfers, the host adapter will wait for the hard disk to send acknowledgment that it has received the data. Once the host adapter receives this acknowledgment, it will send its next byte of data, and so on. Thus, asynchronous negotiation allows for compatibility between devices despite variations in communication speed.

Because asynchronous transfer mode has this built-in "receipt requested" feature, it's also a great method for protecting the integrity of data, because data is sent only after the previous data has been received successfully. But because of the overhead of the return receipt process, the maximum speed over the SCSI bus is reduced when using asynchronous transfer.

### Synchronous Communication

To speed up the communication process over the bus, synchronous transfer mode was included in the SCSI specification. "Synchronous" means that the initiator can issue multiple requests without waiting for the target to acknowledge each one. As a result, the overhead of transferring data is greatly reduced. However, we have a new problem in the example of our host adapter sending data faster than the hard disk can receive it. Because the acknowledgments don't have to be returned after every byte, how would the host adapter know not to send data too quickly for the hard disk? Simple. Before a transfer is going to take place, both devices must agree on the maximum data transfer speed between them and on the number of bytes that can be sent before receiving an acknowledge — a process called *synchronous transfer negotiation*. For example, a synchronous transfer from host adapter to a hard disk would be negotiated at the maximum speed of the hard disk, given that it's the slower device. Problem solved.

How do you know if your devices can communicate synchronously or only asynchronously? Choosing the wrong method could lead to trouble with devices that don't support synchronous transfers. Synchronous transfer negotiation takes care of this problem as well. Before a synchronous transfer is attempted, the devices negotiate whether to use synchronous or asynchronous transfer modes. If the target device can handle synchronous transfers, then synchronous transfer mode is used. Otherwise, asynchronous mode is used for maximum compatibility between the devices.

## Disconnect/Reconnect

Even though SCSI provides features such as synchronous transfer mode, Fast SCSI, and Wide SCSI to increase the performance of data transfers, all of its attempts to speed up communication are for naught if you have to wait for the bus to be available while other devices are seeking their heads or positioning their tape to prepare to send or receive data. To overcome this problem of having to wait for devices to respond, SCSI offers *disconnect/reconnect*.

SCSI transfers data so quickly that, given the speed with which parts in a device can move, almost any device can become a time-waster. The simple fact is that operations such as positioning hard disk heads, fast-forwarding or rewinding tape cartridges, or changing CDs in a CD-ROM jukebox take a long time (in terms of computer speed). In cases such as these, where the hardware itself becomes the time-waster, the device can get off the bus to go about its own work and stop holding up the works.

In the meantime, with the "otherwise occupied" device out of the way, other SCSI devices can go about their business performing various operations, like sending and receiving data, and so on. When the device finally has its act together and is ready, it reconnects to the host that gave it the command in the first place and performs its data transfer. This feature is what gives SCSI its excellent multitasking capability.

**NOTE** *On an active SCSI bus, it's not unusual to have several devices with operations pending in a disconnected state, waiting to get their shot at the bus. By planning your system carefully, you can improve performance by placing heavily used filesystems on different drives so that operations to them can be overlapped as much as possible.*

Consider the case in which you request a file from your tape backup. Because the tape in the cartridge is very long, a considerable amount of time can be spent fast-forwarding or rewinding the tape to a specific position in order to read a file. Rather than tie up the SCSI bus while the tape drive whirrs away, the device can disconnect from the bus so that you can still access hard drives and any other SCSI devices attached to the bus, thus preventing devices from hogging the communication channel. When the tape drive has found the file and is ready to send, it reconnects to the bus and sends the file. Whew — what a relief!

Disconnect/reconnect is particularly important in multitasking environments, where more than one program might need to send and request data at the same time. Because devices can disconnect during slow operations, programs that are running concurrently within the multitasking environment don't have to wait to access other devices on the bus while one device is busy. By using disconnect/reconnect in a multitasking environment, the bus can be shared by many devices for greater efficiency and ensure that the bus is not tied up waiting for a device to be ready.

*Although SCSI's disconnect/reconnect feature allows you to overlap the use of devices in multitasking environments (like Windows NT, OS/2, and UNIX), IDE and EIDE are poor at multitasking because they lack any similar feature.*

### Once More for Luck

Although the name may imply the contrary, a "single-ended" SCSI bus needs terminators on *both* ends, as do HVD and LVD buses.

# 4

## ADDING SCSI TO YOUR PC

In the first few chapters we've tried to give you an idea of what SCSI is, explain why you might want to use it in your computer, and introduce some of the terminology and technical issues. If you've read this far, we hope you've decided to add SCSI to your PC. Your reason may be one of several: you want the flexibility of SCSI; you've got to have the ultimate in performance; or maybe you need to install a type of device that's only available with a SCSI interface.

Whatever the reason, the first thing you'll need to do is select and install a SCSI host adapter card. So what are you going to get? Single-Ended, Differential, or Low Voltage Differential? Bus mastering or not? ISA? PCI? VLB bus? Fast-10, Fast-20, Fast-40, or maybe Fibre Channel (for the high rollers)? And then, of course, once you've bought the host adapter, you still have to install it and get it working. Do you know what interrupt to use? DMA channel? Port address? Because none of these questions have a single answer that's right for all installations, it's important to understand the concepts behind the hardware so that you can figure out what's right for your system.

## Types of SCSI Host Adapters for the PC

Before you go out and buy a host adapter, you need to know a few things about your PC. Nowadays, PCs have different types of slots, and option cards will work only in their own specific type of slots.

### A Bus by Any Other Name . . . ISA, EISA, MCA, VESA Local Bus, PCI, AGP

A bus is just a set of electronic signals that conform to a known specification to allow the transfer of information across an electronic boundary in a computer. You undoubtedly have heard of one or more of the following bus architectures: ISA, EISA, MCA, VESA Local Bus, PCI, and AGP. Whereas SCSI is a bus for transferring data between the computer and a device such as a hard disk, the above-mentioned buses provide the means for sending data between the computer's CPU and its interface cards.

*ISA,* or industry-standard architecture, is the bus used on the original IBM PC or PC/XT. It is an 8-bit bus running at a maximum data rate of 8 MHz, or 8 MB/sec—very slow by today's standards. Upon introduction of the IBM PC/AT and the 16-bit Intel 80286, the ISA bus was extended to support 16-bit data transfers and 16-bit cards. However, the data rate stayed the same. This proved to be a performance bottleneck once 32-bit (386, 486, and Pentium) computers came on the scene, because their higher performance demanded more data faster than the bus could send it.

IBM decided that the only way to increase the data rate performance between the computer and plug-in cards was to totally redesign the bus. (IBM also wanted to eliminate the plethora of PC clones.) The *micro-channel architecture* (MCA) was developed to provide 32-bit data transfers at up to 33 MHz. But, because it wasn't compatible with existing ISA cards, the MCA standard fell by the wayside.

In another attempt to improve performance, an extension to the ISA standard was developed. The *enhanced industry-standard architecture* (EISA, pronounced EE-sa) provides 32-bit data transfers at up to 33 MHz, but it can also accept older ISA cards. The cost of EISA was high, thus restricting its use to expensive network servers and users with large pocketbooks.

Later the *Video Electronics Standards Association* (VESA, pronounced VEE-sa) stepped in and proposed an inexpensive 32-bit bus that could be used in conjunction with ISA. The *VESA local bus* (VL-Bus, or VLB) allows data to be transferred at up to 40 MHz between the computer and VL-Bus–compatible cards. (A 50 MHz version was also defined but was problematic.) Although VL-Bus is limited to two or three slots for interface cards, it was quite popular on 386 and 486 computers because of its speed, low cost, and compatibility with existing ISA cards. With the coming of Pentium class CPUs, VLB options slots faded from inclusion in new systems.

Most recently, Intel introduced PCI to remove the bottleneck between the CPU and the peripheral cards. This new bus offers 32-bit or 64-bit data transfers at 33 MHz, and it supports more slots than VL-Bus. The maximum number of card slots depends on the manufacturer's design. But beware: PCI is not compatible with existing ISA, EISA, or VLB cards, so you'll need to buy new cards for a PCI machine.

During the transition period from ISA and VL-Bus to PCI, many machines had both ISA/VL-Bus and PCI slots so users wouldn't have to throw away their old cards. PCI is the bus of choice if you're running a Pentium or faster machine, because the speed of the computer won't be bogged down waiting for data to come over a sluggish bus.

AGP is a new bus standard that is intended specifically for video cards. There is typically only one AGP slot per motherboard. SCSI host adapters are not available for AGP bus slots.

**NOTE** *Many motherboard manufacturers are beginning to include SCSI host adapter logic on the motherboard. If you buy a motherboard with built-in SCSI, you won't need to buy a separate SCSI host adapter card. If you're considering one of these motherboards, be sure to ask around (check out the hardware forums online if you can) to see which combinations from which manufacturers are working well for people.*

### The Decisions

As with most things in the world of PCs, a trade-off exists between price and performance when it comes to SCSI host adapters. You can expect to pay more for a high-speed PCI host adapter than you would for a slower ISA one. However, it doesn't do any good to install an adapter card that supports DMA rates faster than the bus allows.

For example, the Adaptec 1542CF supports DMA bus mastering speeds of up to 10 MB/sec, which is fast enough for Fast10 SCSI; but because the ISA architecture supports only 5 MB/sec DMA throughput, there would be a bottleneck at the bus, and your system wouldn't be able to take advantage of the higher transfer rate.

## Caching Host Adapter Cards Can Increase Performance

Caching SCSI host adapter cards can improve your system performance by increasing the disk I/O performance. Caching works by keeping a copy of certain data segments in memory so that they are immediately handy if the CPU asks for them. Because it's faster for the system to retrieve a block of data from memory than to read it off the disk, caching results in faster data transfer. Caching data that was read from a device is called *read caching*.

A cache can also be used to improve performance by postponing the writing of changed blocks of data to disk. This process is known as *write caching*. Although write caching doesn't usually significantly decrease the number of disk accesses, it can compel the accesses to take place when the system isn't busy doing something else. When the system is idle (waiting for you to figure out where your mouse cursor just went, for example) the blocks in the cache that are marked as changed (or "dirty") are written (or "flushed") out to disk.

Because these changed blocks of data are written to disk only when the CPU is idle, the CPU is free to finish other processing tasks, and idle time is minimized. However, because the writing of data to the disk is delayed, if power fails before the data is written out, that changed data will be lost. This could potentially result in filesystem corruption. This is one of the reasons you need to shut down your system properly rather than simply turning off the power. This situation might prompt you to invest in a *UPS* (Uninterruptable Power Supply) backup for your computer so it has time to flush its cache when the power goes out.

### Software Caching Is Flexible

Caching can be maintained either through software or hardware. The advantage of software caching is that, unlike a hardware cache, it doesn't require dedicated memory on the host adapter card. A software cache uses a portion of the system memory to cache data, and you can adjust the size of the cache to suit your needs.

Most operating systems use software caching to increase disk performance, and many caching host adapters simply duplicate the caching algorithms of the operating system software. For example, UNIX and Novell are already heavily software cached, and MSDOS comes with a software caching program called SmartDrive (smartdrv.exe), which provides both read and write caching capabilities. Windows 95 and 98 also cache certain filesystem data. A software disk cache can dramatically increase its performance and minimize "thrashing" your hard disk with repetitive reads and writes of the same data.

### Hardware Caching Can Duplicate Software Caching

*Hardware caching* is another form of caching that uses the host adapter as the location of the cache. However, because the memory exists on the host adapter card itself, you cannot use that memory for any purpose other than the cache. Also, if you need more cache memory, you have to buy more memory specifically for that purpose. The benefit of a hardware cache, though, is that the cache management and maintenance is performed by the host adapter card's own CPU, not the main system CPU. As a result, there's no overhead when using a hardware cache.

So, if a software cache is good and a hardware cache is good, why not use both? Well, because using software-caching environments like UNIX, Novell, Windows 95/98, or DOS with smartdrv.exe, along with a hardware cache in the SCSI host adapter duplicates the caching algorithms. This double-caching of the same data adds extra overhead, and it usually slows down the system.

### Which Form of Caching Is Right for You?

Should you switch to a caching host adapter card if you're already using software caching? Not if yours is a single-user system. Single-user systems running MSDOS and Windows and already using software caching won't see much improvement in disk performance with the extra cost of a hardware cache. The zero cost (it's included!) and flexibility of a software cache is the best solution. Also, single-user systems generally have plenty of available idle time to write data to disk, so you'd probably want to avoid write caching on your PC.

On the other hand, a caching SCSI host adapter can give a big performance boost if you're building a multi-user system like a Novell fileserver. The reason is that such a heavily loaded system may not have enough idle time for the software cache to keep up with all the requests for disk access. This causes two bad things to happen: First, as the system becomes more heavily loaded, the software cache begins to fill up with dirty sectors waiting to be written to disk. These sectors take up space in the software cache that could otherwise be used for read caching—an operation at which the software cache is much more effective. Second, the software cache flushing operations can begin to interfere with other system activity as more users are added to the system and less idle time results. In fact, when the system is under heavy loads with no idle time, the benefit of soft- ware write caching completely disappears, and hardware caching is an excellent alternative.

Some caching host adapters are specifically designed to work cooperatively in software-caching environments like UNIX or Novell. These host adapters are engineered to make the process of writing changed data blocks more efficient. Installing one of these specially designed hardware caching host adapters in a software caching system doesn't eliminate the need for the operating system's cache buffers to flush the dirty blocks from cache to disk, but it improves the efficiency and speed of this operation. The hardware cache receives the flushed data in a fraction of the time it would take without hardware caching, and it then proceeds to copy the data back to disk concurrently without interfering with other system activity.

## One Bus or Two?

If you expect to have many devices on your system, you might want to consider getting a dual host adapter card. Even though SCSI protocol allows each device to operate at its own speed on the bus, really slow devices like scanners and CD-ROM drives can take away performance from your hard disks. If you expect that these devices will be operated heavily simultaneously (as they might be in a server), you might want to consider getting either two host adapters, or a dual channel one. The main advantage to a dual channel adapter versus two separate ones is the dual will only require one *IRQ* (interrupt request), whereas the two separate ones will probably need two.

If your system contains LVD devices, you should know that, if you mix single-ended devices with LVD devices, the LVD devices won't be able to operate in LVD mode, which will limit their performance. The solution to this is to get a host adapter that has two bus segments. Your system still has only one SCSI bus, but dividing the bus into segments allows LVD devices to use LVD mode on their segment and leave the second segment running in single-ended mode.

In a two-segment bus, each segment is separated by a signal conditioner chip that isolates and re-clocks (cleans up) the signals. This also prevents reflections from one segment from messing up the signals on the other segment(s). Because of this, somewhat longer cables are permitted also.

This technique also allows the host adapter to provide three connectors (50-pin and 68-pin internal and a 68-pin external, for example) that can all be used simultaneously. Without a separate segment for the internal devices, you would be limited to using only two of the three connectors, because using all three would form a Y-shaped bus, which is not allowed. An example that illustrates this is the Adaptec 2940UW. It has three connectors but all are on one segment. The newer version of the host adapter, the 2940UW Pro, has a second segment, which allows the use of all three connectors simultaneously.

## BIOS on the Host Adapter Lets You Boot from SCSI Devices

Unfortunately, the main BIOS in most PCs doesn't know how to control a SCSI drive. On the other hand, the PC BIOS does know how to load extensions to itself in the form of PROM-based code on option cards. Therefore, if you want to boot up your system from a SCSI hard drive, you must have a SCSI host adapter with a built-in BIOS extension. During the boot process, the BIOS on the computer's motherboard first checks the setup for a bootable disk. If it doesn't find one, it scans for another BIOS on a peripheral card. When it finds the BIOS on a SCSI host adapter, it allows the SCSI BIOS to handle the boot process. If you don't have a BIOS on your SCSI card, you'll have no choice but to boot from another type of hard disk (such as IDE or EIDE) or via floppy disk, because the system's BIOS will recognize all of these.

### How About Mixing SCSI and Non-SCSI
### Host Disks in One System?

Even if you already have non-SCSI types of hard drives (like IDE, EIDE, or ATA) in your system, you can still add a SCSI hard drive. The only catch is that, unless your motherboard is equipped with a modern BIOS, which allows boot device specification, the system will boot from the non-SCSI drive rather than the SCSI drive. The reason is that, during the boot process, the motherboard BIOS first looks for bootable drives that have been set up in its BIOS configuration. Because most SCSI host adapters (except ones built onto the motherboard) are supported by option BIOSes on the host adapter, SCSI drives are seen after the drives supported by the motherboard BIOS.

SCSI host adapters will, in general, coexist with other disk controllers as long as you make sure there are no IRQ or port conflicts between the controllers.

**NOTE** *When choosing a SCSI host adapter, it's important to consider what other features the BIOS offers. Many SCSI cards offer additional features, such as the ability to format a drive, extra diagnostics, and the ability to configure IRQ, DMA settings, SCSI ID, and selection of SCSI options through software instead of with jumpers.*

## What Performance Level Do I Really Need?

If you've begun looking through all the Web sites, catalogs, and magazines, you already know that the best-performing host adapters generally command premium prices. If you just want to hook up a CD-ROM or scanner, you can safely opt for the lower-cost cards. If you will be using SCSI for your main hard disk storage, however, you should consider getting the best-performing card you can afford. Read the magazine reviews and the Usenet comp.periphs.scsi newsgroup for a while to get a feel for what most people have found to be the best compromise among performance, price, and compatibility. One of the very important considerations is whether you can expect the manufacturer to remain in business long term so that you will continue to get driver updates and so on.

In choosing the performance level of the card, be aware that, unless you also plan to spend top dollar on the hard disks, going for the maximum bus speed (currently Fast-40) may not actually give you any more overall performance. For example, currently the fastest disk drives can read data off the media at about 20 MB/sec. Putting only one of these drives on a Fast-40 host adapter (which can hustle 80 MB/sec in Wide mode across the bus) is not very cost effective. If, however, you expect to have several of these drives on the bus (as you probably would in a departmental server), go for the speed! You can use all the bus bandwidth you can get.

There is more than bus speed to be gained with Fast-40, though. When the T10 Technical Committee defined Fast-40, they specified that, when it is used on single-ended buses, the maximum length of the bus would have been about 0.5 meter (about 20 inches)! To remedy this situation, they defined the low voltage differential (LVD) protocol. The increased noise immunity allowed the maximum length to be extended out to 12 meters (about 39 feet). So if you want to be able to space your devices out more, you might want to get a Fast-40 (Ultra2) LVD host adapter.

## Installing the SCSI Interface Card

The *SCSI interface card* is the link between your computer and all the SCSI devices you connect to it. Once you purchase the SCSI interface card, you have to configure and install it before you can start adding SCSI devices. If your card uses Intel/Microsoft's Plug-and-Play SCSI interface, the configuration is handled for you after you plug the card in and power up the computer.

For those of you who don't have a Plug-and-Play card, you will need to set the SCSI ID, I/O port, interrupt, and (on some cards) the DMA channel. We'll go over each of these settings, what they do, and what happens if you set them incorrectly.

## PCI Cards Solve Most of the Problems

PCI-type host adapters have registers that the CPU can read and write to find out who manufactured the card to set up the appropriate I/O ports, interrupts, and DMA channels automatically. About the only thing you might need to do is go into your BIOS setup menu and select which interrupts will be used by the PCI slots. PCI cards can share interrupts, so you don't need one for each card—as you do with many other types of option cards. If you have a PCI-based card, you can skip the next few sections, which explain how to set these things manually.

### Setting the Port Address—the Front Door to the Interface

Every interface card has a port address, also known as the *input/output* (I/O) *port*. The I/O port is the communication channel through which all commands are passed. Incorrectly setting the port address will render the interface card useless, because the computer won't know where the card is. Setting the port address incorrectly is like writing the wrong mailing address on a letter. The message won't go where you want it to.

The reason it's so important to know what I/O ports are in use is that, when two ports are set to the same address, your system ends up with a hardware conflict or, more specifically, an I/O port conflict. You'll know when you have a hardware conflict, because either your SCSI card, or the other interface card, or both will not function properly, if at all. This doesn't mean that the cards are broken. The solution is to simply change the port address on either the

SCSI card or the other conflicting card and try again. As long as there isn't a conflict, and assuming no other problems exist with your card or your system, your SCSI card should begin to work properly.

There's more than one way to select the port address, but the general procedure is that you change a set of switches or jumpers. More and more SCSI cards allow you to configure the port address through their configuration software, so you don't have to actually change any physical settings on the card. The only way to find out how to change the port address on your card is to read the manual that came with the card.

Regardless of how you set the port address on your card, you will have several three-digit addresses to choose from. Common addresses include numbers like 130, 134, 230, 234, 330, and 340, but your particular SCSI card may have other addresses. The particular address you select depends on one thing: It cannot be the same as an address already being used by another interface in your PC, like your printer or mouse, for example.

### Find Conflicting Addresses

To avoid choosing a conflicting port address, you need to know what ports are already being used by other devices. To help you to determine which ports are already being used in the PC, see Appendix B, which lists all the common I/O port addresses. In addition, check the manuals for the other interface cards in your computer to see what ports they're set to.

A variety of diagnostic programs, such as Microsoft Diagnostic (msd.exe), comes with DOS 6.$x$ and Windows 3.$x$, but they cannot always identify all the devices in your computer. A much better utility, provided in Windows 95/98, is called the Device Manager. To get to it, select **Control Panel • System**, then the **Device Manager** tab. Then you can select the device of interest (in our case the SCSI host adapter), and choose **Properties** to look at what driver has been loaded for it and what resources (in this case port addresses) are being used by it.

The only way to know for sure what you have in there and what I/O ports your devices use is to open the computer and take a look. Pull out those old manuals and compare the jumpers or switches on the interface cards in your system with the information in the manual. Once you determine the settings for the card, write them down so you won't have to go through this process next time you add a card.

### *Setting Interrupts*

Without the ability to be interrupted while running a program, your CPU would be oblivious to any hardware or software around it, including interface cards (unless the program were specifically programmed to check up on devices periodically to see if they were in need of attention). Your computer is a complex system, with different devices placing demands on the CPU at different times, regardless of whether the CPU is doing something else at the moment. What happens when your interface card wants to send data to the CPU but it doesn't want to wait around until a program asks for the data? The device uses a hardware interrupt to request the CPU's immediate attention.

*Hardware interrupts* are the vehicle with which your computer manages different devices requesting attention from the CPU. Your computer has a number of interrupt lines that carry these requests to interrupt the task the CPU is working on. When you set hardware interrupts, also called IRQs or interrupt requests, you're selecting the interrupt line (your CPU has several interrupt lines built in as pieces of hardware) in your system that will be used by a particular device when it wants to request attention from the CPU. Once IRQs have been set, your devices will use their assigned interrupt line to request the CPU's attention. The device, like your interface card or your modem, will put a signal on the bus via this interrupt line to signal to the CPU that the device needs attention. Setting the hardware interrupt simply means selecting which interrupt line the device will use to tell the CPU that the device needs something.

**NOTE**    *On host adapters, where interrupts are not used, polling is required. Polling is a process whereby the CPU goes out at regular intervals to see if a device needs attention. The biggest problem with polling is that it wastes a lot of time in your system. Each time a device needs attention from the CPU, it has to wait for the CPU to poll it. It can't interrupt the CPU with a request for attention, as it can when using IRQs.*

Just as you did with the port address, you set the interrupt on your card by changing a switch or jumper on the card. Interrupts can also be set on some cards by using the manufacturer's configuration software. See your card's manual for specifics on how to change or select your card's IRQ setting if the factory default setting won't work.

Your PC has 16 possible interrupts, ranging from 0 to 15. The interrupt you select should be free, meaning that it's not being used by anything else.

Use Appendix B, which lists the interrupts commonly used in most computers, as an aid to setting your interrupts, but be sure to check the other interface cards in your system to see exactly which interrupts are used and which ones are free. Take a look at IRQ 10, 11, and 15 first because these are most commonly available for use by a SCSI card.

One way to see which interrupts are in use in your system is to run Microsoft Diagnostics, msd.exe, from the DOS command prompt. This program comes bundled in DOS 6.x. A selection in the program will give you a list of all of the interrupts and their status (free or in use) in your system. Be sure to run the program from the DOS prompt, not from within Windows, for the most accurate picture of your system. Although this is all that was available under Windows 3.x, it wasn't a completely reliable tool. As we discussed under "Setting The Port Address," the Win 95/98 Device Manager can help with interrupts as well. The only way to know for sure is to open your system and log the settings for all the cards in your computer. Appendix C also lists IRQs used by the motherboard. This is important so that you don't run into an IRQ conflict with a built-in device such as the real-time clock.

When you assign the same interrupt to two or more cards, you create the potential for a hardware conflict commonly called an *IRQ conflict*. An IRQ conflict is like having two houses with the same doorbell. When you push the button, the people in both houses hear the ring and come running to the door. Funny thing is, you're probably at only one of the doors.

This is not to say that two devices cannot share one IRQ. In fact, interrupts can be shared between devices, but only if (1) the devices sharing the IRQs have some other way of identifying themselves to the host, or (2) the devices will never need to request CPU attention at the same time. The printer port is an example of such a device. For example, if you have a sound card at IRQ 7, it will share its interrupt with the printer port at IRQ 7. As long as you don't use both devices simultaneously, a conflict doesn't occur. Not all devices are good about sharing IRQs, and the risk you run when your devices share IRQs is that your computer will lock up when it encounters a conflict between the devices at the IRQ. The best rule of thumb is to give each device its very own IRQ.

### Using DMA for High-Speed Data Transfer

When your system accesses a peripheral device, like a disk or tape drive, large amounts of data are moved back and forth between the device and the computer's *RAM* (random access memory). One of the most efficient methods of moving this data is called direct memory access, or DMA. DMA is a method by which a plug-in card that controls a peripheral (also called a peripheral controller, or simply a controller) can read or write directly to RAM. In contrast, when DMA is not being used, the CPU, rather than the controller, reads or writes to RAM, thus taking time away from the CPU that could be used for other sorts of data crunching. Controllers that support DMA free up the CPU and, as a consequence, speed up the rest of your system.

# DATA TRANSFER METHODS: DMA, BUS MASTERING, PROGRAMMED I/O

## DMA

Two primary types of DMA are used in PCs: *third-party DMA* and *first-party* (or bus-mastering) *DMA*. Third-party DMA, used on floppy disk controllers in PC/AT ISA and EISA computers, is the slower and less expensive of the two types of DMA. It relies on an independent DMA controller, typically built into the PC motherboard, to move data between a peripheral card (the first party) and system RAM (the second party). Because it can be shared by multiple peripheral cards, the DMA controller is considered the third party.

## BUS MASTERING

*Bus-mastering* SCSI controllers can take advantage of the faster DMA, called first-party or bus-mastering DMA. These controllers can move data to and from system RAM much faster than either PIO or third-party DMA, because they control the DMA transfer themselves: They don't need the help of the CPU or a third-party DMA controller to transfer data. While transferring the data using first-party DMA, the DMA hardware on the peripheral controller suspends CPU operation and takes control of the system bus. The hardware then automatically moves the data between system RAM and a buffer on the controller, resulting in much faster data transfer, because the CPU is not being used—the data transfer is implemented by the controller.

Although DMA improves the multi-tasking performance of the SCSI adapter, controller cards that use bus mastering, rather than third-party DMA, will generally have the highest performance.

## PROGRAMMED I/O

If you don't have a bus-mastering controller card or a controller card that supports regular DMA transfers, your system uses a data transfer method called *programmed input/output,* or PIO. PIO was used by the hard disk controller on the first PC/AT. PIO uses the CPU to move data between a controller card and the computer's memory, with data transfer speeds reaching about 2.5 MB/sec. In comparison, data transfer rates on even a slow ISA machine with a bus mastering SCSI card can achieve more than 5 MB/sec, quite a significant increase in performance.

PIO's relatively slow data transfer is its primary drawback. Its performance is hampered by the fact that it needs the CPU to read or write each block of data. As a result, transfer speed is slow and the CPU is unavailable for other tasks, thus slowing down the entire system. PIO's drawbacks make it unsuitable for multi-user environments like Windows, UNIX, or Novell fileservers. DMA, by contrast, is a much more sophisticated and effective method of data transfer.

### Setting Your DMA Channel

If your SCSI card supports DMA, you will have to set its DMA channel. As you did with I/O ports and IRQs, make sure that you select a DMA channel that is unused by any other card in your system. Not to belabor the point, but the only way to really know what DMA channels are in use is to log the settings of all the cards currently in your system. Also check Appendix C for common DMA usage in the PC. That's the last time we'll say that. Promise.

In addition to setting its DMA channel, you may also have the option to set the DMA transfer speed on your SCSI card. Your choice of DMA transfer speed will depend on the type of bus slots in your PC. Following are the major types in order by speed:

**ISA**  Relatively speaking, ISA is slow, supporting DMA transfer rates of up to 5 MB/sec. In most machines, it has been replaced by newer and much faster bus alternatives, namely EISA, VLB, and PCI.

**EISA**  In contrast to ISA's top speed of 5 MB/sec, the EISA bus supports DMA transfer speeds of up to 33 MB/sec.

**VESA local bus**, also called *VL-Bus* or simply *VLB*, supports DMA burst speeds (transfers of small blocks of data) of up to 130 MB/sec, though the sustained rate (continuous data transfer) is closer to 32 MB/sec.

**PCI bus** can sustain a rate of 132 MB/sec, which beats even the highest measured burst speeds of VLB.

**Future PCI**  In a continuing attempt to improve on bus transfer rates, a forthcoming PCI standard will support DMA rates of 264 MB/sec, twice the current sustained rate for PCI.

It's important that, when you set the DMA transfer speed, you set it *no higher* than the highest transfer speed that the bus slot holding your card can handle. For example, because most ISA slots can handle data transfer rates no higher than 5 MB/sec, setting an ISA SCSI card higher than 5 MB/sec could introduce intermittent data corruption into your system resulting from the incompatible transfer rates. (This data corruption can be very hard to track down, too.)

When setting the DMA transfer speed, your best option is to use the card's factory-set default transfer rate. Don't experiment with faster DMA transfer speeds unless you know that your computer can support them.

Setting the DMA is similar to setting the I/O port and IRQ. A set of jumpers, a switch, or a configuration program will be available to make the changes. The installation section of your SCSI card's manual will show you which method to use.

### Set the SCSI ID on Your Interface Card

As with any SCSI device, when you install a SCSI interface card you have to assign it a SCSI ID. You set the host adapter's ID by changing a set of switches or jumpers on the card or by using the manufacturer's configuration software. See the manual that came with your SCSI card for specifics on how to set its host ID.

The host adapter's ID is normally set to 7, the highest priority ID on the SCSI bus—and you're probably safest setting it to 7, because many manufacturers of SCSI hardware or software default to a setting of 7. However, you can select any ID from 0 to 7 as the host ID, as long as the ID is not in use by another SCSI device. If your interface card is a Wide SCSI interface, you'll have more than the 0 to 7 IDs to choose from: 16-bit Wide SCSI offers IDs from 0 to 15; 32-bit offers IDs from 0 to 31. ID 7 is still the highest priority though, even when higher IDs are available.

#### Things to Keep in Mind When Setting SCSI Host Adapter IDs

If you're combining regular and Wide SCSI devices on the same bus, set the host adapter's ID to an ID between 0 and 7; otherwise, the 8-bit SCSI devices won't be able to talk to the host adapter. About the only reason to set the host adapters ID to anything other than 7 is if you plan to share SCSI devices between two host systems. In this case, one of the host adapters should be ID 7 and the other should be ID 6. This is an unusual situation, however.

## Install the Right Drivers

*Drivers* are programs that allow the operating system and your applications to communicate with peripheral devices. When you load a driver, you're actually loading a program in memory that the computer can use when it needs to access a device. Some devices, like floppy disk drives for example, have their driver built into the computer's BIOS, so you probably won't have to load a driver for them. Also, depending on what operating system you install, you may not need to load any driver for your interface card. If it has a built-in BIOS and you're only using it to access hard disk drives under a single-tasking operating system like MSDOS, its BIOS probably has all of the software that you'll need to access your hard disk.

Still, there are many types of SCSI devices on the market besides hard disk drives, and each requires its own special driver. But it's not the case that each type of SCSI adapter needs a different driver for each type of SCSI device. If this were the case, SCSI systems would end up with a multiplicity of drivers and a lot of confused users: People asking questions like "Where can I get a driver so my Adaptec AHA-1540CF can talk to my Toshiba XM-3301T CD-ROM?" would probably drive manufacturers crazy.

### Layered Drivers

To avoid this potentially unpleasant situation, SCSI card manufacturers have developed standards for drivers that allow most SCSI devices to talk to their particular interface card. These special drivers are called *layered drivers,* because they're built up of layers of different drivers. The bottom, or adapter-specific, layer is a driver that communicates with the hardware on the SCSI adapter. This is also called the *low-level driver.* You load drivers for your specific SCSI devices on top of this adapter-specific, low-level layer. Instead of communicating directly with the SCSI adapter card itself, these layered device drivers communicate only with the bottom-layer adapter driver, so that only this bottom-layer driver needs to be able to communicate with the SCSI device. The use of layered drivers really simplifies the problems of driver writing and compatibility, because host adapter manufacturers need only focus on the bottom layer of the driver, rather than what may be several layers of drivers on top.

Of course, the world of drivers isn't quite that simple. On PCs there are two competing standards for SCSI device drivers. The most widely used device-driver standard right now is *ASPI* (Advanced SCSI Programming Interface), which was developed by Adaptec and has since been adopted by most other card manufacturers. ASPI exists for MSDOS, all flavors of Microsoft Windows, OS/2, and NetWare. Another advantage to this layered driver approach is the potential to program the SCSI interface yourself, without needing to know much about the host adapter itself.

Another driver interface standard is *CAM* (Common Access Method), an ANSI standard (X3.232-1996) software interface for SCSI device drivers. CAM-3 is a draft standard that enhances CA as part of the SCSI-3 architecture model. Currently, CAM isn't as widely implemented on PCs as ASPI, though CAM drivers are available for most popular devices.

Windows 95/98 and Windows NT also use a layered driver architecture. The Windows 95/98 and NT device drivers are called Miniport drivers. Many ASPI and CAM device drivers written for DOS and Windows 3.*x* will work under Windows 95/98.

For non-PC systems like UNIX workstations, the driver interface is less standardized. Many manufacturers use their own proprietary driver interface. Digital Equipment Corporation (now owned by Compaq) uses CAM for their Digital

UNIX (now called Tru-64 UNIX) drivers. A few other workstation manufacturers do as well. ASPI's architecture is not flexible enough to accommodate the needs of UNIX systems.

### Get the Latest SCSI Drivers

Probably the most important thing to keep in mind when dealing with SCSI device drivers is that hardware manufacturers are constantly updating them. If you experience any problems, always make sure you have the latest drivers for your hardware. You can usually download the drivers from the manufacturer's web site or from the support conferences on online services like CompuServe or America Online. A list giving many of these URLs is contained in the SCSI FAQ which is on the CD-ROM accompanying this book. At the same time that you're making sure you've got the latest device drivers, you should also make sure that the latest drivers aren't buggy. Keep up with the latest information about device drivers by checking out the appropriate conference online or read the SCSI newsgroup on Usenet. A little knowledge about what's happening in the world of drivers can save you a lot of headache and frustration.

### Software That Will Simplify Your Driver Installation

The major SCSI host adapter manufacturers all have SCSI driver installation tools. For example, Adaptec's program is called EZSCSI, and Symbios (now LSI Logic) has SDMS. When you run these programs on your system, they analyze your hardware and software, load the appropriate drivers, and then add the necessary driver installation commands to your config.sys and autoexec.bat files (in MSDOS-based systems). In addition to the installation tools, the packages often include some extra utilities, like a disk formatter or a tape backup program as well as performance measuring tools. Also, the Plug-and-Play tools in Windows 95/98 greatly simplify driver installation.

### DOS Drivers

Although the major SCSI host adapter manufacturers supply an easy-to-use program to install and configure your drivers, you may have to change the configuration manually someday. To become familiar with the drivers that are commonly installed into a DOS SCSI system, let's take a look at the two standard types of SCSI drivers, ASPI and CAM, and what each driver does.

**NOTE** *The following examples give you a general idea of which DOS drivers might have been loaded by your adapter's installation program. You should check the manual for your SCSI interface to see exactly what drivers it uses and what drivers it comes with for the devices you want to attach. If you have a SCSI device that doesn't have drivers supplied by the host adapter manufacturer, the driver may have been included with the device. Check the documentation to see if it has its own SCSI drivers.*

## ASPI

The main ASPI driver is the low-level or adapter-specific driver. It's the driver that talks directly to your SCSI adapter. Each SCSI card has its own special low-level driver that presents a standard interface to upper-level drivers, so that drivers for specific devices don't have to worry about the brand of host adapter you're using. Although the exact name of the low-level driver changes from company to company and host adapter model to host adapter model, they often have "ASPI" as a part of the filename, like aspixx.sys. Some drivers also have "DOS" in the filename, so that you know it's a DOS driver. For example, Adaptec's 1542 SCSI host adapter's low-level driver is called aspi4dos.sys. The "aspi" at the beginning indicates that it's an ASPI-compliant driver; the "4" stands for the 4x model of the 15xx series of cards; and "dos" indicates that it's a DOS driver. If you have a different brand of SCSI card, your driver's name won't be exactly the same, but it will likely be similar.

All the drivers following the ASPI manager in the config.sys file (aspicd.sys in the example) are device-specific drivers. These drivers provide support for a certain type of device—a hard disk, for example. Once again, ASPI device-specific driver filenames will usually include "ASPI" as well as some indication of the type of device it supports. For example, Adaptec's aspidisk.sys provides support for hard disks, and aspicd.sys supports CD-ROM drives. Some drivers may use only the device name to identify the driver, such as cdrom.sys.

The DOS ASPI drivers are loaded by the config.sys file. Following is a sample config.sys file:

```
device=c:\aspi\aspi4dos.sys /d
dos=high
files=30
buffers=20
device=c:\dos\himem.sys
device=c:\aspi\aspicd.sys /d:mscd001
```

This file contains entries that load a low-level ASPI driver (device=c:\aspi\aspi4dos.sys /d) as well as device-specific drivers for hard disks (device=c:\aspi\aspidisk.sys) and CD-ROMs (device=c:\aspi\aspicd.sys/d:mscd001, where /d:mscd001 is an identifying label for the driver). Your installation may have additional options after the name of each driver, depending on the particular driver you're using. Refer to your host adapter's device driver manual for the use of any additional options. One useful option is to tell the low-level driver to display a list of what devices are seen at each SCSI ID. This provides useful troubleshooting info if you run into difficulty later.

If you're using DOS 5.0 or higher and EMM386 or a third-party memory manager such as QEMM or 386Max, you can load the ASPI driver into upper memory by using the **Devicehigh** command instead of the **Device** command, as shown by the series of devicehigh statements in the following config.sys (check your DOS manual for more information about upper memory and loading drivers into upper memory):

```
device=c:\dos\himem.sys
device=c:\dos\emm386.exe ram
dos=high,umb
file=30
buffers=20
devicehigh=c:\aspi\aspi4dos.sys /d
devicehigh=c:\aspi\aspidisk.sys
devicehigh=c:\aspi\aspicd.sys /d:mscd001
```

### CAM

Like ASPI, CAM also has a low-level or adapter-specific driver that talks directly to the SCSI adapter. As in the case of ASPI drivers, each manufacturer has its own version of the low-level driver. CAM drivers usually have "CAM" as a part of the filename, and some also have "DOS" in the filename so that you know it's a DOS driver. For example, Symbios's low-level CAM driver is called doscam.sys. The "dos" indicates that it's a DOS driver and "cam" indicates that it supports CAM functions. If you have a different brand of SCSI card, your driver will have a similar name.

Device-specific CAM drivers follow a naming convention similar to that used with ASPI device-specific drivers. They may have CAM in the filename and also the type of device supported. For example, Symbios's scsidisk.sys provides support for hard disks and cdrom.sys supports CD-ROM drives.

CAM drivers are loaded by entries in the config.sys file like the following:

```
device=c:\cam\doscam.sys
dos=high
files=30
buffers=20
device=c:\dos\himem.sys
device=c:\cam\scsidisk.sys
device=c:\aspi\cdrom.sys /d:mscd001
```

This sample config.sys file contains entries that load CAM drivers for a Symbios SCSI adapter (device=c:\cam\doscam.sys), as well as device-specific drivers for hard disks (device=c:\cam\scsidisk.sys) and CD-ROMs (device=c:\aspi\cdrom.sys /d:mscd001). Again, /d:mscd001 in this example is simply an identifier for the CD-ROM driver. Your installation may look different depending on your system configuration. (Refer to your host adapter's device driver manual for more information on the use of your host adapter's drivers.)

If you're using DOS 5.0 or higher and EMM386 or other memory manager, you can load the CAM drivers into upper memory with the **Devicehigh** command, as shown by the series of devicehigh statements in the following config.sys file (check your DOS manual for more information about upper memory and loading drivers into upper memory):

```
device=c:\dos\himem.sys
device=c:\dos\emm386.exe ram
dos=high,umb
file=30
buffers=20
devicehigh=c:\cam\doscam.sys
devicehigh=c:\cam\scsidisk.sys
devicehigh=c:\cam\cdrom.sys /d:mscd001
```

If you have a SCSI card that uses CAM drivers, you may also have an ASPI-to-CAM translation driver. This driver is used to translate commands from programs that only support ASPI to ones that your CAM driver can understand. It's only needed if you're using ASPI-specific programs and drivers that don't talk CAM, such as Central Point Tape Backup. This translation driver is called aspicam.sys, aspi2cam.sys, or something close to that.

**NOTE** *The ASPI-to-CAM driver should be loaded after the CAM low-level driver and before any ASPI-specific drivers.*

### Windows 3.1 Drivers

DOS SCSI drivers are compatible with Windows 3.1, so once you finish installing them, Windows will be able to access all your wonderful SCSI devices. Some manufacturers also include Windows-specific drivers to squeeze out an extra bit of performance or to support additional features used by their own utility programs, such as tape backup software, music CD players, or diagnostic tools. For example, Adaptec's software installs two files for Windows ASPI support: winaspi.dll and vaspid.386. Your particular SCSI card may not use Windows-specific drivers. If it doesn't, don't worry unless you can't access your SCSI devices from Windows, in which case you'll need to get a driver from the manufacturer of your host adapter or replace it with a different one.

If your card does use a Windows driver, make sure that it's been copied into the Windows System directory (usually c:\windows\system) and that the correct entry exists in the 386Enh section of your system.ini file. The example below shows this entry in a typical system.ini file, including the Adaptec Windows ASPI driver vaspid.386:

```
[386Enh]
device=vaspid.386
device=dva.386
keyboard=*vkd
device=*int13
```

And so on.

### Windows 95/98 Drivers

Windows 95/98 includes drivers for SCSI cards from the leading manufacturers. In most cases, Windows 95/98 will know when you install a SCSI card into your system, and you will be sent straight to the Add Hardware Wizard (in which case you should skip to step 5 below). If your card wasn't detected, you'll need to run the Add Hardware Wizard yourself as follows:

1. Click the **Start** button.

2. Click on the **Settings** menu option.

3. Click on **Control Panel**.

4. In the Control Panel window, double-click the **Add/Remove Hardware** icon.

5. At the Add Hardware Wizard opening screen, click the **Next** button.

6. You can now install hardware by auto-detection or you can install it yourself. Auto-detection isn't foolproof and can lock up your system in some cases. However, it is the simplest way to add new drivers, so try it first. To auto-detect, click on the button next to **Auto-detect**. To choose the type of hardware driver yourself, click on the button next to **Install Specific** and skip to step 1 under the "Install Specific" section below.

7. Now click the **Next** button to run Auto-detect.

#### Auto-Detect Installation

1. Windows will begin auto-detection. This may take a while. If the progress meter at the bottom of the window stops for a long period of time (say, 15 minutes), the computer has probably locked up, and you'll have to restart your system.

2. After all devices have been properly detected, a new window will come up. If you want to see what devices were detected, click the **Details** button. Otherwise, click the **Finish** button to install the new drivers.

3. If the required drivers aren't already on your system, Windows will ask you for the appropriate disk. Follow the instructions from Windows for any drivers it needs.

4. After all the drivers are installed, you will need to restart the system for the changes to take effect. Click the **Restart** button to restart Windows.

## Install Specific

1. To use Install Specific, first scroll down the list of hardware devices until you get to SCSI Controllers and then double-click on **SCSI Controllers**.

2. Select the manufacturer of your SCSI controller from the list on the left by clicking on it. If the manufacturer is not listed, click on the **Have Disk** button.

3. Select the model of SCSI card that you installed from the list on the right by clicking on it.

4. If you have updated drivers on a disk that came with your SCSI card, you can install the newer version by clicking on the **Have Disk** button.

5. Click the **Next** button to install the driver(s).

6. A window will come up showing you the current settings for your SCSI card. Write this down for future reference so that you can avoid an I/O, IRQ, or DMA conflict with the SCSI card when installing an interface card into your system. Click the **Next** button after you write down the settings.

7. Click the **Finish** button to finish installing the driver(s).

8. After all the drivers are installed, you will need to restart the system for the changes to take effect. Click the **Restart** button to restart Windows.

## Windows NT Drivers

Windows NT includes drivers for many SCSI interfaces. After installing your SCSI card, start Windows NT and see if you can access your SCSI devices. If not, you have to install the NT drivers for your SCSI interface as follows:

1. Open Program Manager if it isn't already opened.

2. Open the **Main** group window and start the **Windows NT Setup** program.

3. Select **Add/Remove SCSI Adapters** from the **Options** menu.

4. Click the **Add** button and select the type of SCSI adapter you've installed.

5. If Windows tells you that the driver already exists on the system, you can click **Current** to use the existing driver or **New** to install a new copy.

6. If you choose to use the current driver, it will be installed and you will return to the main window where the new SCSI card will be listed.

7. If you choose to install a new driver, Windows will ask you for the full path to the location of the driver. Type in **A:\** or **B:\** (or perhaps the drive letter of a non-SCSI CD-ROM), depending on which drive you inserted the driver disk in, and click **OK.**

8. After the driver is installed, you will see it listed in the **Main Setup** window. Click the **OK** button to close the setup program.

9. Restart Windows NT by clicking on the **Restart** button for the changes to take effect.

### OS/2 Drivers

OS/2 has its own set of standards and conventions for SCSI device drivers. Beginning with version 2.0, OS/2 includes drivers that allow for direct SCSI access. OS/2 includes drivers for SCSI disks, CD-ROM drives, and optical disks, as well as an ASPI driver for communicating with other devices.

The concept behind OS/2's drivers isn't that different from that of ASPI in DOS. If you're running OS/2 and adding a new SCSI device, you have to load a hardware-specific driver for your host adapter card. Either you'll find this driver on a disk that came with your card or you'll need to get it directly from the card's manufacturer or its BBS (see Appendix A for a listing of manufacturers, including their BBS numbers). This hardware-specific device driver will probably have a filename with a .add extension.

To load these device drivers, choose **Device Driver Install** from **System Setup**. Follow the directions on your screen, and you should be on your way. Once you've loaded your hardware-specific .add driver, you may be asked to load OS/2's device type–specific drivers, which usually have a .dmd extension. Again, either you'll find this driver on a disk that came with your card or you'll need to get it from the manufacturer.

Finally, some devices running under OS/2 may require that you load drivers to change or enhance their operation. These drivers will have an .flt extension.

**NOTE** *Before direct SCSI support was implemented in version 2.0 of OS/2, Microsoft and IBM developed a standard driver interface called LADDR (Layered Device Driver), which was used in OS/2 versions 1.2 and 1.3. It is not needed in later versions of OS/2.*

## Linux Drivers

Let's not forget about Linux. This freely distributable UNIX clone is really taking off in some segments of the market. One of the fastest growing uses for Linux is in Web servers.

Because the support for new hardware is provided by volunteer developers who are highly motivated, Linux supports nearly every host adapter and SCSI device out there. For the most part, if you buy a bootable CD-ROM distribution of Linux, like Red Hat, the drivers that your host adapter needs will be automatically detected and loaded during installation. If you buy a card that is so new that Linux doesn't support it yet, you can always volunteer to write the driver for it.

**HINT** *Unless you're a UNIX kernel/driver guru, stick with a card that is supported.*

For more information on SCSI under Linux, take a look at the Usenet comp.os.linux.hardware newsgroup.

## More About Drivers Later

This chapter's coverage of device drivers concentrated primarily on how to install them. If you're interested in knowing more about the inner workings of device drivers, take a look at Chapter 8, "Understanding Device Drivers." It contains more detail that can aid in understanding and isolating problems you may encounter in your system.

## Tips for a Successful Installation

- Before you remove the SCSI interface card from the package, be sure to ground yourself. Touch a static discharge plate or your computer's case to make sure you aren't carrying a static charge. If you do zap your card with a static discharge, you're liable to fry it with as much as 10,000+ volts! They're never quite the same after that!

- Before getting started, print out the BIOS setup for your system. You can usually do this by going into the setup program (usually by pressing the **DELETE** key at bootup) and then pressing the **Print Screen** key. If that doesn't work, jot down the values that you see on your screen. You should also print out your autoexec.bat and config.sys files before you start changing them, so that you can recreate them if something goes wrong. (Actually, this is good advice anytime you install anything.) You can also copy the files to another directory to save a lot of typing in case you have to return your system to its original state.

- Be sure you have a bootable floppy disk handy before fiddling with the BIOS setups so that you can boot your machine if you really screw it up.

- Remember, when you load the drivers for your SCSI devices, you have to specify some of the same parameters, like the I/O port, which you determined when you set up your hardware. If you select an I/O port for the driver that's different from the one you set on your host adapter card, for example, you'll have to change the port on your host adapter card too.

### SCSI CD-ROM Drives

If you're installing a SCSI CD-ROM drive for use with DOS and Windows 3.*x*, be sure that you install the DOS CD extensions driver, mscdex.exe, in autoexec.bat. And, if you use smartdrv.exe for disk caching, be sure to load mscdex.exe before smartdrv.exe in your autoexec.bat file so that the caching program will recognize the CD drive.

An example of this setup might be the following:

```
MSCDEX /D:MSCD001 /M:12 /L:J
LOADHIGH SMARTDRV.EXE
```

This will cause the Microsoft CD-ROM extensions to be loaded (an ISO-9660 filesystem for MSDOS), allocate 12 sector buffers for caching CD sectors, and set the drive letter for the CD-ROM drive to J. This excerpt assumes that you have loaded a CD-ROM device driver and set its name to MSCD001 in config.sys as shown in one of the CAM examples above.

An MSDOS boot floppy with the above drivers loaded can also be useful as a rescue disk or for installing Windows 95/98.

### SCSI Hard Drives

Now that SCSI disks have grown so large (up to 73 GB as of this writing), operating systems and BIOSes have needed to increase their address range to be able to use all that space. If you have a hard disk larger than 8 GB, you need to enable a feature in your host adapter BIOS called "INT 13 extensions," which circumvents a longstanding limit in the INT 13 BIOS interface that hit a wall at 1024 cylinders. (Even though SCSI disks are addressed by logical block number instead of by cylinder head and sector, the PC BIOS still thinks in those terms). Without this extension feature, your disk will appear to be only 8 GB when it may actually be much larger!

**NOTE** *If you're wondering why the PC BIOS needed to be extended to handle larger disks, bear in mind that the largest hard disks available in 1985 (when the PC/AT BIOS was written) were about 33 MB! These new disks are about 1000 times that size. Hindsight is 20/20, but seeing the future is not so easy! (But that doesn't stop us from trying in Chapter 12!)*

## Extending the PC BIOS

Once you've installed a SCSI hard drive, it's usually a good idea to perform a low-level format on it. Generally a utility for doing this is provided with the host adapter, either in the host adapter BIOS or as a disk-based utility. This utility will send the **SCSI FORMAT UNIT** command to the disk. You need to be sure which SCSI ID you want to format, because this process will erase any data on the disk. The format operation can take as little as a few minutes or as long as several hours depending on what drive is being formatted. Once the disk is low-level formatted, you should verify the entire disk to make sure there are no bad sectors. A utility should be provided for this purpose as well. A good verify utility will also tell the disk drive to replace any bad sectors with good ones from its spare sector pool.

## Partitioning

Once the system is booted from an install floppy (or CD-ROM), the host adapter's BIOS will assign the new, blank disk a drive number (hex 80 for drive C or 81 for drive D). This number is used by FDISK or other operating system partitioning utility to make INT 13 hex BIOS calls to partition the disk. Partitioning is dividing up the available disk space into one or more pieces. In each of these pieces we need to create a filesystem so that the operating system can use it. When you boot the operating system, if it sees a properly partitioned and formatted filesystem, that filesystem will be assigned a drive letter.

If you're using DOS or Windows version 3.*x*, you will have to run FDISK, or a similar disk partitioning utility that came with your SCSI interface, to create a DOS partition. A FAT16 filesystem cannot be any larger than 2 GB. Starting with Windows 98 FDISK, if you have a disk larger than 2 GB, FDISK asks if you want support for large disks (larger than 2 GB). What it's really asking is whether you want to format your partitions with the FAT32 filesystem instead of the FAT16 filesystem (which has been used on all MSDOS and Windows 3.*x* systems since about 1987). FAT32, like many things, has advantages and disadvantages. The main advantage is that it will allow you to create partitions larger than 2 GB and use them more efficiently because the cluster size is smaller for the same size partition using FAT16. The main disadvantage of using FAT32 is that this filesystem is only supported by Windows 95 OSR2 and 98. Windows NT can't access them and neither can MSDOS. This means that if you boot different operating systems, or you need to rescue your disk by changing or adding a file that's been corrupted, you won't be able to access it using a DOS boot floppy.

After you finish partitioning, run the **FORMAT** command on the disk. If the O/S will be MSDOS or Windows 3.*x*, be sure to use the /s option of **FORMAT** to transfer system files if this will be a boot disk. Windows 95/98 takes care of installing the system files itself.

When creating a FAT16 partition with FDISK or the partitioning utility supplied by the SCSI interface manufacturer, don't create a partition that is larger than what you need even if you have a large hard disk. Larger partitions

**Table 4.1: The Relationship Between Partition and Cluster Size for FAT Filesystems**

| Partition Size (MB) | Cluster Size (Bytes) |
|---|---|
| **For FAT16** | |
| < 32 | 512 |
| 33–64 | 1024 |
| 65–128 | 2048 |
| 129–256 | 4096 |
| 257–512 | 8192 |
| 513–1024 | 16384 |
| **For FAT32** | |
| 513–8192 | 4096 |

**Table 4.2: DOS-Assigned Device Drive Letters**

| Device | Drive Letter |
|---|---|
| 5-1/4-inch floppy drive | A: |
| 3-1/2-inch floppy drive | B: |
| IDE primary partition (partition 1) | C: |
| SCSI primary partition (partition 1) | D: |
| IDE first logical partition (partition 2) | E: |
| SCSI first logical partition (partition 2) | F: |
| SCSI second logical partition (partition 3) | G: |

use larger clusters to store data. Because the sizes of most files aren't an even multiple of the cluster size, more space is wasted with larger clusters. Table 4.1 illustrates how the cluster size increases with larger partitions. On average half the cluster size is wasted for each file created on the disk. Because it's not unusual for a system to contain 10,000 files, this can really add up!

In order to choose the proper size, you need to have an idea of what the average size of files you will be storing is (not easy, we know). If the average file will be about 16 kB, you don't want to choose a cluster size nearly that big since that will waste on average half the space on the disk!

DOS and Windows assign drive letters to the primary partitions on drives before assigning any (extended dos) logical partitions. As a result, partitioning SCSI drives can result in some pretty interesting arrangements of drive letters. For example, let's say you have a setup that consists of a PC with two floppy drives, one IDE drive (the boot drive) with a primary and extended partition, one SCSI drive with a primary partition, and two logical partitions. Table 4.2 lists the devices, along with the drive letters, as they are assigned by DOS.

Windows NT needs a FAT16 filesystem to install into. It can convert it to NTFS during install, but the 2 GB FAT16 limit will still apply to that boot partition.

For more tips and hints on troubleshooting and perfecting your SCSI installation, see Chapter 6, "Troubleshooting Your SCSI Installation."

Now that you've gotten the host adapter installed and drivers loaded for it, I guess we're ready to hook all those SCSI goodies up and make them do something besides sit there! Interestingly enough, that's the purpose of the next chapter.

# 5

## HOW TO CONNECT YOUR SCSI HARDWARE

Once you've amassed a bunch of SCSI hardware, you'll probably want to connect it to your computer (unless you're simply an enthusiastic collector). This chapter focuses on attaching SCSI devices to the computer. The discussion applies to all SCSI devices and all systems. Regardless of whether you have a PC, a Macintosh, or a UNIX workstation, this chapter should help you get those SCSI devices hooked up properly.

(If you own a PC and you have a SCSI host adapter you need to install, then go to Chapter 4, which addresses PC-specific issues about plugging in and configuring a SCSI interface.)

# Use Quality Cables and Connectors

Before you even begin to connect anything together, you should know a bit about the cables that carry the commands and data between SCSI devices and the host adapter. If you don't have good-quality cables specifically meant for SCSI, you're liable to create headaches for yourself.

There is a direct relationship between the quality of your SCSI cables and the performance of your whole SCSI system. Cheap cables can cause data errors as well as performance loss. There is also usually a direct relationship between cable quality and price—high-quality cables often command a high price. Here is the best rule of thumb for buying cables: *If it seems like too good a deal, it probably is.*

When setting out to buy SCSI cables, do a little shopping and compare prices. For example, companies such as Amphenol and Adaptec sell their own brand of high-quality SCSI cables. The "hole in the wall" clone shops and warehouse superstores carry low- to mid-grade cables. These mid-grade cables will probably be just fine if you're using SCSI-1. On the other hand, Fast SCSI-2 is extremely sensitive to cable quality and will not be reliable at all if you're using low- to mid-grade cables. If you're using Fast SCSI, Wide SCSI, or SCSI-3, be sure that you buy only cables certified for SCSI-2 or SCSI-3. You should find some note of that certification on the cable's packaging. Then again, there is no agency overseeing the certification of SCSI cables. Just because it says "SCSI-2" doesn't always mean much. You really need to trust the vendor on this issue. Sometimes the only way to find out you have a bad cable is to eliminate all the other variables and that's not easy.

## The Shorter, the Better

Like a bridge, a SCSI cable should be no longer than it needs to be. Cable quality is not the only factor that will affect data integrity. Because cables carry signals, cable length is also important. Even though longer cables might make your connections neater, fight the temptation. In the case of SCSI cables, shorter is better. The reason is that signals weaken as they travel longer distances. Signals have energy and, as the signals pass through the wires in your system, they progressively lose some of that energy to the wires themselves.

The farther the signals have to travel, the weaker they get. As signals weaken, your devices and your host adapter start to have problems interpreting them. This is because, in addition to losing some of the desired signal, the cable is also picking up electrical noise along its whole length. Keeping the cables short minimizes both problems.

If you're having trouble imagining how signals lose their strength over greater distances, think of water rushing through a water pipe. As the water rushes through, it loses energy to the walls of the pipe and slows down. Eventually, if nothing pushes (that is, adds energy to) the water, the water will slow down until it stops.

# FINDING THE RIGHT CABLE

To ensure the best possible performance and data integrity of the SCSI bus, AMP Incorporated recommends the following specification in selecting cables.

External SCSI cables should be made up of twisted pairs of 28 AWG wire encased in a shielded jacket. A-type cables consist of 25 twisted pairs; P-cables consist of 34 twisted pairs. The single-ended impedance of the cable should be 80 ohms. A-cables are used for narrow SCSI devices and P-cables are used for Wide SCSI devices.

Four requirements, listed below, govern the arrangement of conductors in the external cable. These requirements are compatible with all single-ended and differential SCSI implementations.

1.  The conductors assigned to the single-ended REQ signal and its associated ground shoulde be a twisted pair located in the cable core. The conductors assigned to the single-ended ACK signal and its associated ground should also be a twisted pair located in the cable core. If there are more than three twisted pairs in the cable core, the REQ and ACK pairs should not be adjacent to each other.

2.  All conductors assigned to single-ended data and parity signals and their associated grounds should be twisted pairs located in the outer layer of the cable closest to the external shield.

3.  The conductors assigned to +SIGNAL and –SIGNAL in a differential configuration are associated as twisted pairs.

4.  Conductors are not to be connected together anywhere along the cable or within any connectors except in the case of P-to-A transition cables.

Internal SCSI cables can be either unshielded flat-ribbon or unshielded twisted-pair flat. Single-ended systems generally use flat-ribbon cable; this cable is available in 28 AWG with 0.050 inch (1.3mm) between the centers of each wire or 30 AWG with 0.025 inch (0.6mm) between centers. Normally, stranded wire is used for flexibility, but solid conductors can also be used for slightly higher impedance.

The SCSI standard recommends unshielded twisted-pair flat cables for use as internal cables in differential systems. The twisted-pair configuration helps to reduce cross talk between wires. Twisted-pair flat cables come in the same size/spacing as flat-ribbon cables and have flat sections spaced at intervals, such as every 12 inches (0.3 meter), for attaching connectors.

Similarly, the strength of the signals that travel through your SCSI system is finite: The signals are created (pushed) once and then they are moved along the bus. No wire has zero resistance and no insulation has infinite resistance, so the signal inevitably weakens as it meets these counter influences. Also, wires that are close together have capacitance unless they form an ideal, impedance-matched, transmission line. Added capacitance will cause the nice square edges of our SCSI signals to get rounded off (not good). Terminators keep our trans- mission line properly matched and minimize capacitance. Those darned terminators sure are important!

### How Long Can Your Cables Be?

According to the SCSI standards for SCSI-1 and SCSI-2 hardware, SCSI signals are good for a total bus length of only 6 meters (about 20 feet) when traveling through SCSI-compliant cables. If you're using Fast SCSI, the maximum cable length is cut in half to only 3 meters (about 10 feet). Of course, if you're using poorer-quality cables, your signals will be even weaker and will break up much sooner. The bottom line is this: Whenever connecting a SCSI device, use the shortest possible cable for the situation; don't exceed a total of 6 meters (about 20 feet) for regular SCSI hardware and 3 meters (about 10 feet) for Fast SCSI. Remember, this is the *total* length of the bus, including all internal and external cables.

**TIP** *As cables get longer, the signals weaken and are more susceptible to noise. Buying a longer cable than you need because it seemed like a good value is false economy. Use the shortest and best-quality cable you can afford.*

Given all the different speed and bus driver options available in SCSI-2 and SCSI-3, it takes a table to clearly show what lengths are permissible for the devices you have. When looking at Table 5.1, find the speed of the fastest device you have in Column 1 — unless your host adapter is slower, in which case you find the host adapter's speed.

### Going Farther Requires Repeaters

If you must extend the length of your SCSI bus, you will need to use *repeaters* (also called expanders). A repeater is placed at the end of the cable once the maximum bus length is reached. Then, another cable is attached to the repeater to extend the bus. The repeater picks up the signal from the host adapter and reproduces it on the next section of cable, thereby producing a clean, strong signal to the devices farther down the bus. Repeaters are pretty expensive, so lengthening your bus beyond the normal limits is not to be taken lightly. Also, make sure that the repeater is designed to operate at the speed of the fastest device beyond the repeater.

**Table 5.1: Maximum Allowable SCSI Bus Lengths for Various Transfer Rates and Bus Driver Types**

| Speed of Fastest Device | Maximum Single-Ended Bus Length | Maximum HVD Bus Length | Maximum LVD Bus Length |
|---|---|---|---|
| 5 MHz (SCSI1 synch.) | 6 meters (20 feet) | 25 meters (82 feet) | 12 meters (39 feet) |
| 10 MHz (SCSI2 FAST) | 3 meters (10 feet) (not recommended in SCSI-2) | 25 meters (82 feet) | 12 meters (39 feet) |
| 20 MHz (Ultra or Fast-20) | 1.5 meters (5 feet) (not recommended until SCSI3 SPI) | 25 meters (82 feet) | 12 meters (39 feet) |
| 40 MHz (Ultra2 or Fast-40) | Not recommended | 12 meters (40 feet) | 12 meters (40 feet) |

### Internal versus External Cables

When you shop for SCSI cables, you'll find two main types: *internal* and *external*. They're used just as you'd expect: the internal for internal connections; external for external hookups.

### Internal Cables Look Like Ribbons

Internal SCSI cables look a lot like the cables used for any other internal computer storage device. They're also called ribbon cables because they look like ribbons. If you haven't seen an internal ribbon cable (because you haven't dared to open your computer), an example is shown in Figure 5.1.

As you can see in Figure 5.1, flat-ribbon cables consist of a flat bunch of single wires all stuck together side by side and packaged in plastic, like a ribbon. One edge of the cable has a colored (often red) stripe, which indicates the first wire of the group. This becomes very important when you need to know how to orient the cable.

Differential SCSI systems usually use twisted-pair ribbon cables instead of the more common flat-ribbon cables to reduce interference between the wires. A twisted-pair flat cable looks similar to a flat-ribbon cable, except that each pair of wires is twisted together along the length of the cable. As a result, twisted-pair flat cable looks more like a bunch of twisted wires than a bunch of straight wires. At certain intervals along the cable, the wires are un-twisted so that the connectors can be attached to them, as you can see in Figure 5.2.

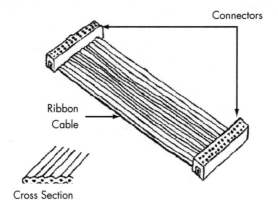

Figure 5.1: Typical Internal or Flat Ribbon Cable with Cross Section

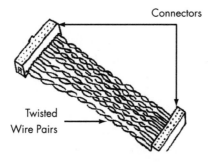

Figure 5.2: Twisted-Pair Ribbon Cable

### External Cables Are Round and Thick

External SCSI cables look similar to computer power cords: They are long, round, and rather thick. You'll often find similar cables attached to your printer, looking something like that shown in Figure 5.3.

**TIP** *Because external SCSI cables are thick and heavy, they have screws or clips on their connectors to keep them firmly attached to your computer. Always make sure that the screws or clips are properly fastened. If they fall off while you're saving an important file, you won't be a happy camper.*

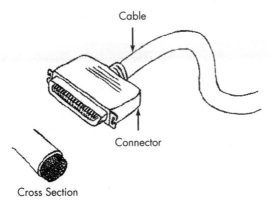

Cable

Connector

Cross Section

*Figure 5.3: Typical External Cable with Cross Section*

The two common types of external cables are:

- A cables with 50 wires (for regular [narrow] and Fast SCSI)

- P- and Q- cables with 68 wires (for 16-bit Wide and Fast Wide SCSI-3; P used alone for 16-bit; P and Q used together for 32-bit)

You don't need to worry about the number of wires in the cables, though. When buying SCSI cables, you'll need to know only the type of SCSI bus you're using (e.g., regular 8-bit or 16-bit Wide) and the type of connector.

### Know Your Connectors

Connectors attach the cables to SCSI devices and to the computer. They consist of a plastic or metal housing with either metal pins visible inside or with cavities into which those pins will fit. It may have screws or clips to hold it tightly in place. External and internal SCSI cables have different types of connectors, and it's important to recognize the differences so that you'll fit the right cable to the task.

Connectors are often referred to as being male or female. A connector is female if its contacts are female (they are hollow providing a place for a male pin to insert); male if its contacts are visible pins or other protrusions. The shape and size of a set of male and female connectors should match exactly. Remember, too, that it's the contacts that are being referred to, and not the connector housing or shell. Here's how to identify the different types of connectors.

### Internal Cables Usually Have Rectangular Connectors with Holes

Internal SCSI-1 and SCSI-2 cables usually have a rectangular plastic connector with 50 holes in it (so it's female). These connectors typically look like that in Figure 5.4. A male connector for this cable will have 50 pins whose arrangement matches exactly.

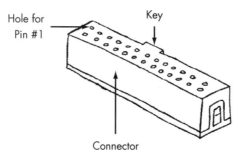

Figure 5.4: Typical Internal SCSI Cable Connector

Wide SCSI cable connectors have 68 pins (so they're male) spaced very close together. The female connector for such a cable will have 68 hollow contacts whose arrangement matches exactly.

### Four Common (and Some Not-So-Common) External SCSI Connectors

There are four main types of external SCSI connectors: the 25-pin D-sub, the Centronics 50-pin, the high-density 50-pin, and the high-density 68-pin.

**The 25-pin connectors** are used on Apple computers and some low-end SCSI adapters (such as those included with scanners); they can support only 8-bit SCSI and aren't actually official SCSI connectors at all, because they don't appear in any SCSI standard.

**NOTE** *If you must include any devices that have 25-pin connectors in your system, keep them to an absolute minimum. Also, keep as much of the bus as possible 50- or 68-pin — that is, locate a 50-to-25 pin adapter as close to the 25 pin device as possible and keep all the cables 50-pin to the extent you can. The popularity of drives which are 25-pin has caused many people to experience SCSI problems that are due to the 25-bus discontinuity. Because the 25-pin connectors share grounds between data signals they cannot be for differential and should not be used for anything running faster than asynchronous.*

**The 50-pin connectors** are used with 8-bit (narrow) SCSI. Most external SCSI-1 devices have the Centronics version; SCSI-2 devices have the high-density connectors.

**The 68-pin connectors** are used with Wide SCSI in order to handle the additional data bits and extra parity signals. You can use the connector outlines in Appendix A to see which kind you have or which kind you need.

Following are a few special connectors that were made specifically for a particular manufacturer's computer:

- IBM created its own version for the PS/2 models by adding 10 pins, which they marked as "reserved" but never actually used. If you have an IBM PS/2 with an IBM SCSI host adapter, you'll need a special IBM-to-SCSI adapter cable between your computer and the cable to the first device.

- Apple created a new, smaller connector for their PowerBook notebooks to save space. There isn't anything particularly special about it; it's just optimized for space reduction. You can find these cables in better-equipped shops, but they're more expensive than standard cables, of course.

Yet another new SCSI connector has appeared in recent years (whatever you may think about the fact that there are so many SCSI connectors to choose from, the connector manufacturers have got to love it!).

**The 80-pin SCA** (Single Connector Attachment) was designed to make it simpler to "hot-swap" SCSI drives in and out of systems, especially RAID arrays. Drives with SCA connectors typically don't provide their own termination or ID jumpers. They are intended to be plugged into special backplanes that provide these facilities. You can connect them to a regular SCSI bus though using SCA to 50/68 pin adapters.

## Connecting Devices to the Bus

SCSI devices are connected with cables to form a sequence known as a *daisy chain*. It begins at one end of the cable and continues from device to device until it reaches the last device, usually the SCSI interface inside the computer. The entire chain of connections is called the *SCSI bus,* and it carries commands and data between the host computer and the devices. External devices have two connectors on their housing so you can chain from one to the next. You can make an internal device into an external device by simply mounting it in a special case that has a power supply, an ID switch, and a Y-shaped cable with an internal connector in the middle and an external connector on each branch of the Y.

A typical SCSI daisy chain might look like that shown in Figure 5.5.

## Find Pin 1

To connect a cable to a device, you must orient it correctly. An external cable's connectors are shaped so that you can only connect them one way, so you don't need to worry that you'll connect them upside down. Internal cables, however, don't always have such a safeguard. As a result you should always be aware of the colored stripe on internal cables. The stripe on one edge of the cable indicates Wire 1, and hence Pin 1, on the connector. The connectors that are crimped onto the flat-ribbon cable often have their Pin 1 position indicated by a small triangle or arrow.

SCSI devices also have a mark of some kind to designate where Pin 1 is located. Sometimes a "1" is silk-screened on the circuit board, or it may be indicated by a small triangle embossed on the connector. If you can't find it, check the manual that came with the device to see which is Pin 1. Once you've established the orientation of the device's connector, match the orientation of the internal cable's connector to it, Pin 1 to Pin 1, and plug it in, as shown in Figure 5.6.

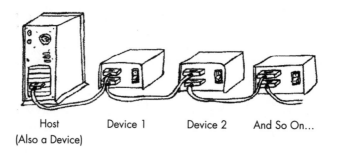

Host        Device 1        Device 2        And So On...
(Also a Device)

*Figure 5.5: Daisy Chain of SCSI Devices*

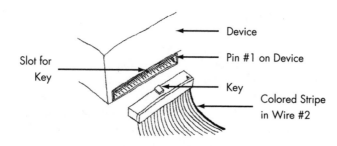

*Figure 5.6: Properly Oriented Internal Cables*

In general if you manage to plug in a SCSI cable reversed, no harm will be done. The designers of the SCSI standard were wise enough to define that the pin opposite TERMPWR be left open so that it won't be shorted to anything (which might cause damage).

If you want to add another device, say another hard disk, to your SCSI installation, you need to extend the bus to that device to make it part of the system too. To add a second hard disk to your system, you simply add a second cable between the first hard disk and the second one — *not* between the second hard disk and your computer. The resulting system is shown in Figure 5.7.

You now have three SCSI devices connected on your SCSI bus: the computer, the first hard disk, and the second hard disk. You've started the daisy chain — connecting the first device to another device, to another device, and so on. A more elaborate daisy chain, with a couple of hard disks, a CD-ROM, and an optical drive, might look like that in Figure 5.8.

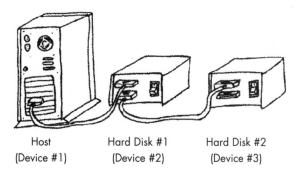

Host
(Device #1)

Hard Disk #1
(Device #2)

Hard Disk #2
(Device #3)

*Figure 5.7: Three Devices on the Bus*

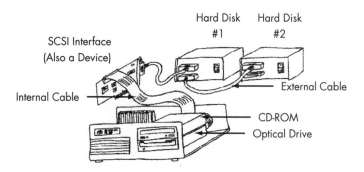

*Figure 5.8: Example of a Daisy-Chained SCSI System*

### A Daisy-Chained SCSI System

This is one of SCSI's greatest features — the ability to connect many devices to one slot on your motherboard, all coming off the same SCSI bus.

If you wanted to max out this daisy-chained system with other SCSI devices, you'd simply repeat the process of connecting device to device until the number of devices totaled the maximum for the type of SCSI you're using (8 devices for 8-bit SCSI, 16 for 16-bit SCSI). A maxed-out system would look like that in Figure 5.9.

Note that the device numbers do not refer to their SCSI IDs. The SCSI ID is independent of the device's position on the bus.

## Terminating the SCSI Bus

That's all there is to making the basic connections for the SCSI bus. But to have a fully operational SCSI bus, you must follow one more rule: Use only two terminators, one on each end of the chain. You want your signal to flow freely up and down the chain but not reflect from the ends. (For a more detailed discussion on the types of terminators, refer to Chapter 3.)

Figure 5.10 shows an example of what *not* to do.

**NOTE** *Correct placement of terminators is critical for proper system operation. Always terminate only the first and last devices on the SCSI bus.*

The most common mistake made when connecting devices to the bus is incorrect termination. Most SCSI devices can be terminated (not killed :-). Some devices have built-in terminators, and if you attach such a device to the middle

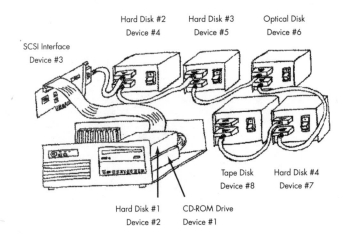

*Figure 5.9: Example of a Full 8-bit SCSI System (a Total of Eight Devices)*

of the bus but forget to remove the terminator, you'll have the configuration shown in Figure 5.10—and a headache. Make sure you check each device so that no devices in the middle of the bus are terminated. The only devices that must be terminated are the ones on the ends. (Technically, it's not the devices themselves that need to be terminated but the ends of the bus. However, it's sometimes less expensive to use the terminators provided in most devices rather than buying separate ones to plug onto the ends of the cable.)

Figure 5.11 shows a properly terminated SCSI system.

### The Host Adapter Is a Device, Too

Remember that the computer's host adapter card is also a device on the bus. As a result, if the host adapter is on one end of the bus, it must be terminated.

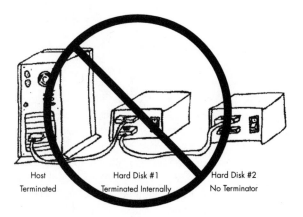

Figure 5.10: SCSI Bus Terminated in the Middle

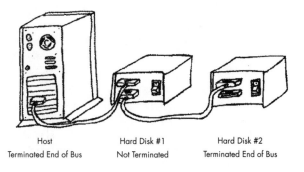

Figure 5.11: Example of a Properly Terminated SCSI System

However, if you have both internal and external SCSI devices, the host adapter is in the middle of the bus and must *not* be terminated. Figure 5.12 shows such a system.

### Terminating Your Particular Device

There is more than one way to terminate a SCSI device. Most SCSI devices have an internal terminator that can be turned on or off with a switch. The switch is either a jumper or toggle, or it may be software controlled on some interface cards. Some older devices have physical terminators that must be pulled off or plugged in to turn termination off or on, respectively. The manual for (or the manufacturer of) your particular device will tell you what system

## MIX AND MATCH:

## COMBINING REGULAR AND WIDE SCSI

Until now, we've only discussed methods of connecting devices of the same bus width: 8-bit devices on an 8-bit bus, 16-bit devices on a 16-bit bus, and so on. However, these devices can coexist to a certain extent.

When mixing devices, you must be aware of three important requirements:

1. The bus you use must be as wide as the widest device used on the bus. For example, you can connect an 8-bit device to a 16-bit bus, but not vice versa (unless you can disable Wide negotiation for that device, or the host adapter doesn't even attempt Wide).

2. You must terminate the entire width of the bus, regardless of the width of the last device. Just because the last device on your 16-bit bus is 8-bit doesn't mean you can simply use an 8-bit terminator. The full 16-bit bus must be terminated; otherwise, only the 8-bit devices will communicate properly.

3. You must not assign any two devices the same ID, regardless of their width. All 8-bit devices will have IDs from 0 to 7; 16-bit devices will have IDs from 0 to 15. As a result, the ID range for 8- and 16-bit devices overlaps from 0 to 7.

In a 16-bit Wide SCSI-3 system, a P- cable is used. In an 8-bit system, A cables are used. In order to attach 8-bit devices to a 16-bit bus, you will need a P-to-A (68-to-50 pin) transition adapter. Generally this adapter should have a terminator in it for the high byte. Also, care needs to be exercised in how pins 17, 18, and 51 on the 68-pin side are connected, because passing them through in the simplest manner will result in a short from TERMPWR to GROUND when using typical terminators.

your device uses. Figure 5.13 shows a typical physical terminator, just in case neither your device's manual nor your manufacturer is available.

External SCSI devices also might have a large physical terminator on the outside of the device, instead of a cable leading to another device, which might look like that in Figure 5.14. This particular type of external terminator looks like a cable connector without the cable.

If you've determined that you need to terminate a device (because it's either at the beginning or end of the chain), you'll do so by either turning on its terminator switch or inserting the physical terminator (as instructed by your manual). To turn off termination, turn off the switch or remove the physical terminator. Remember to check that none of the devices in the middle of the SCSI bus have their terminators switched on.

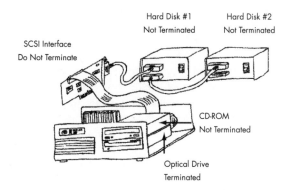

*Figure 5.12: A Correctly Terminated SCSI Bus with the Host in the Middle*

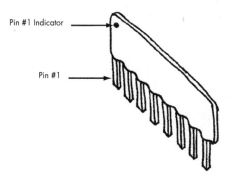

*Figure 5.13: A Typical Physical Terminator for Internal SCSI Devices*

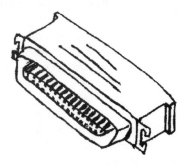

*Figure 5.14: A Typical Physical Terminator on an External SCSI Device*

## Terminator Power

SCSI terminators provide two functions: They prevent reflections (see Chapter 3 for details) from the ends of the bus and provide "pull-up" current to bring inactive signals up to about 3 volts. In order to provide this second function, they need a source of power or voltage. Because stand-alone terminators (ones not inside any device) may be out dangling at the ends of the SCSI bus, that power needs to be run along the whole bus. The TERMPWR line is provided for this purpose. The TERMPWR voltage can be supplied by several devices along the bus or only one device. The SCSI-2 specification requires that all host adapters (initiators) provide it, but any device can provide it too.

Your components may offer you the choice in this situation: Look for a jumper on your device marked TP or something similar. It may have two settings: (1) Provide power only to this device's terminator or (2) Let this device's terminator get power from the bus. It doesn't hurt to have more than one device supply TERMPWR — but no more than four should, or a short circuit on the bus could overheat the wires.

**NOTE**   *These settings are completely separate from whether the device's terminator is enabled or not.*

## SCSI IDs

Because all devices on a SCSI daisy chain are hooked together in one continuous string, each device on the bus (including the host adapter itself) must have a unique SCSI device ID. The number of available IDs is directly related to the width of the bus, like so:

- Regular SCSI-1 and SCSI-2 have eight possible SCSI IDs, one for each of the eight SCSI devices that can be attached to the bus. These SCSI IDs range from 0 to 7, counting 0 as the first number.

- 16-bit Wide SCSI has 16 IDs, ranging from 0 to 15, because it has a 16-bit bus.

- Likewise, 32-bit Wide SCSI has 32 SCSI IDs, ranging from 0 to 31. (You're not likely to see any devices like this, though.)

### Setting SCSI IDs

SCSI IDs are set by changing a numbered wheel, a group of switches, or a set of jumpers on each device. The method for each particular device will differ. Check your user manual for each device to see exactly how to set them. There will be a table of SCSI IDs showing the jumper or switch configuration that corresponds to each ID. If your device has a numbered wheel, just turn the wheel to the desired ID.

When choosing SCSI IDs, you can use any number you like, as long as it's not in use by another device on the bus and as long as it's within the range for the type of bus you're using.

**NOTE** *SCSI-3 will introduce new serial bus designs that will allow more devices on a single bus, but in general, they will be set automatically so you don't have to worry about them.*

Here's an example of how you might assign IDs to your SCSI devices. Let's say that you have one hard disk attached to your computer and you want to add a second SCSI hard disk and a SCSI CD-ROM drive. Assigning the IDs is simple. First of all, call the SCSI interface card on your computer ID 7, just so it's the last device. Now, give the first hard disk ID 0, the second hard disk ID 1, and your CD-ROM ID 2.

**NOTE** *Again, you'll set these IDs with some sort of wheel, switch, or jumpers. Check your manual.*

Figure 5.15 shows the results of assigning these three IDs.

## Why Set One Device's ID Higher than Another?

In order to avoid conflicts when more than one device tries to access the bus, the SCSI bus protocol provides a concept called *priority*. If two devices both put their IDs on the bus at exactly the same time, the one with the higher ID gets access and the lower one backs off and waits for the bus to be free again. This is one reason that the host adapter is usually assigned ID 7, because it is the most important and heaviest user of the bus. Using this line of thinking,

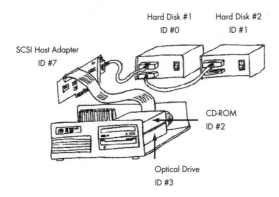

Figure 5.15: SCSI System with ID Numbers Assigned

you might be tempted to put your hard disk on ID 6, because you likely think of it as your next most important device. It turns out that this isn't always a good idea. Consider this scenario: Your CD-ROM is trying to return data that you asked for, but because you have so much hard disk activity at a higher priority, you'll never get anything from the CD-ROM. In general it is better to put slower, but less-used devices at the higher IDs and leave the hard disks at lower IDs. This is especially true of devices like CD recorders and streaming tape drives which fail to operate properly if their data stream is interrupted. If you have a CD-R drive and a tape drive, put them at ID 6 and ID 5 respectively.

## Parity Checking

When configuring your SCSI system, you'll probably encounter an option for parity checking. Parity checking is a simple and fast method of error checking (discussed in more detail in Chapter 3). You should turn parity checking on if your devices support it. Parity checking is turned on or off by either hardware or software, using a switch, jumper, or configuration program. (Check your manual to see which method your device uses.)

Whether you'll be able to use parity checking will depend on the capabilities of all of your SCSI devices. All devices on the bus must be able to perform parity checking in order for you to enable it. In fact, if only one device lacks support for parity checking, you must turn parity checking off for all of the others. Otherwise, the one device that doesn't know how to do the check won't understand the extra data, and your system won't work properly.

*Parity was optional under the old SCSI-1 standard but is required of all SCSI-2 and SCSI-3 devices. If you're unsure if all your devices support parity checking, check the manual that came with each device. Only old SCSI-1 devices may lack this feature.*

## Another Way to Do All This

Remember a while back we mentioned 80-pin SCA connectors and how they can be used to connect devices into RAID cabinets and the like? Well, let's just touch on that a little more. Now that you've seen all the details of connecting cables and setting IDs for your devices, you can better appreciate the value of avoiding that stuff altogether. An SCA backplane case allows the user to simply fasten drives to slide-in trays and install them without being concerned about individual data and power connections or ID jumpers. IDs are set either by the slot position the device occupies in the case or by thumbwheel switches on the outside of the case itself.

These cases aren't inexpensive, but make it very easy to replace individual drives (which may have become defective), in some cases without even turning the power off! SCA provides power pin sequencing which allows drives to be connected and disconnected from the SCSI bus without disturbing the other devices.

## That's That, I Guess!

So now you know how to select cables and connectors, hook up all of your hardware, and assign ID numbers to all devices. What's next? Well, what happens if it doesn't work?

# 6

## TROUBLESHOOTING YOUR SCSI INSTALLATION

Everyone hopes that troubleshooting will never be necessary—and then trouble strikes. Although some vendors still seem to make a company secret of it, troubleshooting a SCSI system is like all other troubleshooting jobs: Once you know a few basic rules, it's a logical process.

First off, if you do run into a problem and you've changed anything in your system, check for the typical faults during bootup. If you haven't changed anything, then some hardware must have developed a fault all by itself. If you encounter errors or other faulty behavior during normal bootup, the first rule is to "note all error messages." System error messages are your first clue. The best practice is to keep a log file containing the error messages or a hardcopy of the error message. If no log or hardcopy is available, write it down yourself.

However, sometimes error messages don't help; they may be cryptic, misleading, and unreadable for all but your resident system guru. In such cases, only a systematic search will help.

Before beginning the real troubleshooting process, run through the following list to check a few basics. In many cases, you'll be able to solve your problem by resolving one of these issues:

- Does the host adapter have any resource conflicts (namely I/O port, IRQ, or DMA)? (Remember sharing IRQs is OK with PCI cards.)

- Does each device have its own unique SCSI ID?

- Does termination appear only at the bus ends?

- Are cabling rules obeyed?

- Is the device connected properly? Most shrouded header connectors have a plastic guard around their perimeter with a notch on one side. To prevent you from incorrectly inserting connectors, these shrouded headers use a mechanical key (a slot or tab in the connector), which requires that the cable be inserted only one way into the shroud. Some cheaper devices (and a few high-end host adapters) use simple connectors, mostly for cost reasons. These simple connectors aren't keyed and won't prevent incorrect connections. If your host adapter has such connectors, look for a small white "1" or a similar label on the board marking pin 1.

Open the computer to be sure that internal devices are configured correctly—often they're not.

Test the system with whatever spare parts you have. You'll find the following parts especially useful for particularly pesky problems:

- At least one known good internal and external cable.

- Active and passive terminators.

- A cable with an unused connector (for the purpose of connecting test equipment, etc.).

- A multi-meter (for voltage and resistance measurements).

- One or more software tools for scanning your bus and formatting disks, etc. If your host adapter doesn't have a BIOS or the BIOS doesn't have a format utility or similar modules (all such tools need an installed ASPI or CAM driver), look on the CD accompanying this book for handy tools.

- For DOS users, a bootable floppy disk with DOS and your adapter's ASPI or CAM driver. If possible, have a newer DOS variant (DOS 6.0 or above) on this floppy with multiple boot configurations, which will allow you to decide which drivers should be loaded at startup.

- A spare host adapter and a small hard disk with a bootable partition on it — especially if you have to troubleshoot frequently.

- An oscilloscope or transient recorder is necessary for some very tricky things, like measuring RF distortion or noise on static signals like TERMPWR. There is no way around buying or borrowing these tools if you want to take measurements like these.

## Common Problems

Now that you know what tools you should have (and which, of course, you don't have handy when you need them most), here are some of the most basic system problems and their possible cures:

### Problem: Host Adapter Not Recognized by the System

#### Symptom

The host adapter isn't recognized on startup, or you get a message like "Couldn't initialize host adapter."

#### Possible Causes/Problems

1. The SCSI adapter isn't seated correctly in the computer's bus connector.

2. Your system's hardware is using conflicting system resources, like an I/O address, interrupt (IRQ), or DMA channel.

3. An illegal system resource is set on the host adapter.

4. The host adapter is plugged into the wrong type of bus slot.

5. A device on the SCSI bus is locking up the host adapter because of a conflict in SCSI settings, such as parity checking or duplicate IDs.

#### Explanations and Possible Remedies

**Problem 1:** Check to see that the host adapter is seated properly in the system's card slot. Make sure that it's not installed at an angle so that, although some functions seem to work, a few conductors are not making contact.

**Problem 2:** Check for a resource conflict with the host adapter. (If you encounter a resource conflict when installing a new SCSI host adapter, see the installation guidelines in Chapter 4, "Adding SCSI to Your PC.") Many systems work fine prior to the installation of a SCSI card, but then encounter resource conflicts immediately after you add a new adapter card. (Sound cards are especially notorious for causing resource conflicts, because many sound cards use the same I/O ports, interrupts, or DMA channels as SCSI host adapters.)

**Problem 3:** Verify your adapter's jumper and switch settings with its user manual. Some adapters have a set of jumpers or DIP switches, but allow you to set only a few specific combinations. If you set an undefined combination, you can create all sorts of problems in your system.

- If your system includes EISA or PCI, verify that each card has a dedicated resource. EISA and PCI add a tricky issue — although the hardware may be able to share interrupts between cards, the drivers may not. In such cases, try to give each card dedicated resources.

- Check that adapters don't share I/O addresses. Some adapters restrict the combination of resources that they can use. For example, the older Adaptec 1540A and B models could set different I/O addresses, but the BIOS worked only with I/O address 330 hex.

**Problem 4:** Confirm that correct slots have been used. EISA, VLB, and PCI systems have both busmaster-capable and non-busmaster–capable slots available. Because nearly all SCSI host adapters for these bus systems use bus mastering, ensure that you select the correct slot type when you install the adapter.

**Problem 5:** Check that option settings are compatible with the host adapter's setting. In some cases, where the SCSI device offers a data transfer option, like parity, that option has been set but it is incompatible with the host adapter's setting (not all host adapters will support parity checking, for example). This incompatibility could lock up the SCSI controller chip on the host adapter, thus causing the BIOS or driver to think the adapter is defective.

**Finally, consider the worst case:** The host adapter may be defective.

### Hints

After ensuring that the board is seated properly and that there are no resource conflicts, disconnect the bus cables from the host adapter to see if the adapter is recognized. If it is, your problem is caused by something related to the SCSI bus.

If you inserted a new board or changed the setup of another board, the affected board may now have a resource conflict. For example, some sound boards' MIDI addresses conflict with those of certain SCSI host adapters.

**NOTE** *When you encounter errors like those listed above, always remember that the BIOS and the SCSI controller are independent components on the board. Just because one of them works doesn't necessarily mean that the other one also works.*

## Problem: One Device Not Found

### Symptom

A device isn't found on startup.

### Possible Causes/Problems

1.  There is a power failure in this component or its power connector.

2.  There are conflicting SCSI ID settings.

3.  Termination is incorrect.

4.  Cabling is incorrect. A connector plugged in the wrong way may be very dangerous! Incorrect connections can cause short circuits.

5.  The cables are too long.

6.  There is a bad cable(s).

7.  An external device was turned on after the SCSI bus scan.

### Explanations and Possible Remedies

**Problem 1:** Check to see that the device power's on. Make sure that the connector is seated correctly, that the device spins up, or that the device accepts a tape or CD-ROM, and so on. If not, attach another power cable and check the voltage on the device's connector to ensure that power is available at the device.

**Problem 2:** Check all new or external device settings. If a new or external device is connected to the bus, its SCSI ID may conflict with that of a device already on the bus. This conflict may cause the device(s) sharing this ID to malfunction and may even cause the entire bus to fail.

**Problem 3:** Make sure that the bus is terminated properly. Make sure that you didn't add a terminated device in the middle of the bus or an unterminated device at the end of the bus. Be sure that you correctly enabled or disabled the host adapter's termination.

**Problem 4:** Check that connectors, particularly non-keyed connectors, are oriented properly. It is sometimes the case (though usually only with cheap host adapters or devices with non-keyed connectors) that an internal connector is plugged in the wrong way. The shrouded (keyed) connectors, found on better host adapters and devices, prevent you from plugging a connector in the wrong way. Incorrectly inserted connectors may be hazardous to the SCSI bus itself because termination power may be connected to ground, thereby causing a short circuit.

**Problem 5:** Check cable lengths. Your cables may be too long. External devices, especially scanners, sometimes come with a cable two or three meters long, which results in an overall bus length that exceeds the SCSI limitation.

**Problem 6:** Check cable specs. Your external device may have a cheap cable that doesn't meet the SCSI specifications. It is especially important to use high-quality cables when using Fast SCSI and beyond.

**Problem 7:** If the device is external, see that it was powered on soon enough to be recognized by the SCSI bus scan. Some drivers don't recognize devices that are turned on after they have scanned the bus for devices. If you turn on your system and then turn on your external device — a CD-ROM drive, for example — the external device may take too long to react to inquiry commands from the SCSI bus, such that the host adapter thinks it isn't present. As a result, the device's driver fails to install. To see whether this is your problem, try a warm reboot.

### Hint

If you have a working setup and suddenly a device isn't recognized, then a power failure or a termination problem are the most likely causes. However, incorrect setups can continue working for some time and then fail without an obvious reason, so it's best to check all possible causes.

### Problem: No Device Found

#### Symptom

The host adapter seems to work, but it can't find any devices on the bus.

#### Possible Causes/Problems

1. The bus cable may have lost its connection.

2. Termination power may have failed.

3. Termination is incorrect.

4. Device IDs are conflicting.

5. Cabling is incorrect or bad.

6. Cables are too long.

7. There's a bad cable on the bus.

#### Explanations and Possible Remedies

**Problem 1:** Make sure that the cable is still connected properly. If the SCSI cable was under tension, it may have lost contact with the host adapter's connector.

**Problem 2:** The TERMPWR fuse may be blown.

**Problem 3:** Check the termination. You should have terminators only on the ends of the bus and no terminators on any other devices.

**Problem 4:** Check that the SCSI IDs of new or external devices do not conflict with that of a device already on the bus. Such a conflict will cause the device(s) with this ID to malfunction and may cause the entire bus to fail.

**Problem 5:** Check that connectors, particularly un-keyed connectors, are oriented properly. If you have internal devices, a connector may have been plugged in the wrong way, which may either blow the termination power fuse or simply draw most signals to ground. Either way, the bus won't work. The recommended shrouded header connectors prevent this by a mechanical key (a slot in the connector that requires that the cable be inserted only one way), but some devices use only simple connectors that may be plugged in backward.

**Problem 6:** Although cable length is very seldom the cause of a complete bus failure, check to see that the length of your cables doesn't exceed the maximum allowable.

**Problem 7:** Check the external chain for a bad cable. Try disconnecting a device or two and swap cables to see if there's a bad one. The same might apply if you connected a device by an adapter connector, as is usual for cheap SCA disk drives. Many of these adapters don't have a complete pinning and so might miss or short one or more signals. Also, you might keep in mind that SCA doesn't have a TERMPWR line — if you rely on an adapter or a combination of adapters related to SCA, there is no termination power from this point on.

### Hints

- Check for power failure with a voltmeter: If you have a working setup and suddenly a device isn't recognized, then a power failure is the most likely cause. Note that some setups may continue working for some time before failing for no apparent reason.

- If you have a new setup and the devices aren't recognized, turn the system off immediately and double-check the complete setup. The fault may involve terminators on the host adapter and/or devices. Also, some older host adapters have pluggable fuses for termination power that may have blown.

## Problem: System Can't Boot from SCSI Hard Disk

### Symptom

Although the host adapter seems to work and recognizes all devices, the system either won't boot from a SCSI hard disk or it locks up when booting.

### Possible Causes/Problems

1. You have a non-SCSI (ATA/IDE, ESDI, etc.) hard disk in the system.

2. The hard disk has an ID higher than that supported for booting. Some adapters only boot from a particular ID or range of IDs.

3. There is no active partition on the SCSI disk.

4. A DOS memory manager overwrites the SCSI BIOS.

5. Your SCSI host adapter has no BIOS or its BIOS is disabled.

6. Your SCSI adapter may need an entry for the disk in the computer's setup.

### Explanations and Possible Remedies

**Problems 1 and 2:** If a non-SCSI hard disk (IDE, EIDE, ESDI, or ST506) is in the system, it has boot priority in the system BIOS. Some PC motherboard BIOSes offer a "SCSI first" entry for the boot-up sequence, but this may not be reliable. So, if you have a non-SCSI disk, booting from SCSI may not work until you disable the non-SCSI hard disk. Many host adapters will only boot from devices with an ID of 0 or 1, so if your disk is set on ID 6, booting either isn't possible or you need to set a parameter in the SCSI host adapter's settings or a jumper to allow it to boot. (It's best to set the hard disks to lower IDs to prevent this sort of problem.)

**Problem 3:** As with any other disk drive, you need a bootable and active primary partition to boot from a SCSI hard disk drive. Use **FDISK** to set the primary partition to bootable.

**Problem 4:** If your system boots from the SCSI hard disk, but then locks up, the DOS memory manager may be overwriting the SCSI BIOS when it is started in CONFIG.SYS. To see if this is the case, make a backup copy of your CONFIG.SYS file and then remove the line for the memory manager. Now try booting the system again to see if it boots from the SCSI hard disk.

- With more advanced operating systems like Windows NT or Unix/Linux, the initialization of other peripheral's drivers may conflict with the SCSI host adapter's resources and so render the system unstable or dead from a specific point in the startup process. In this case, most operating systems support the troubleshooting with a boot-up setting that allows tracing of the driver loading.

**Problem 5:** If you get "no boot device" or similar error messages, see if your SCSI BIOS is enabled. Sometimes people try to run a hard disk from a sound card's SCSI port. While this usually works, the hard disk isn't bootable if the sound card's embedded SCSI host adapter doesn't have a SCSI BIOS, and most do not.

**Problem 6:** Some older SCSI host adapters (older DPT models, for example) emulate a WD1003 hard disk interface and need a CMOS entry for the bootable hard disk. (This is so unusual for SCSI, that it's easy to forget — so check your manual.)

### Problem: Intermittent Lockups and Communication Errors

#### Symptom

The SCSI system usually works but shows intermittent lockups.

#### Possible Causes/Problems

1. Termination is incorrect.

2. Termination power is too low and/or noisy.

3. You may have folded your internal cable into a tight, neat package, and as a result, created an R-C (resistor-capacitor) network that has unforeseeable side effects under dynamic load.

4. Cables are too long. This often happens with external devices, especially scanners, which sometimes come with a cable two or three meters long.

5. One of your devices, adapter connectors, or cables is bad.

#### Explanations and Possible Remedies

**Problem 1:** Check the termination thoroughly. Did you obey all the rules? Remember, termination occurs only at both ends of the bus.

**Problem 2:** When using internal devices with resistor *SIPs* (single inline packages), be sure that they are inserted facing in the right direction. Pin 1 is usually marked with a colored spot or line. An incorrectly inserted passive terminator for example, because it has TERMPWR and ground on the opposite ends, shifts the voltage bias point of the terminator. The bus may continue to work but will be unreliable.

- Passive termination is particularly vulnerable to low termination power voltage. If you follow the specs, TERMPWR should be between 4.25 and 5.25 volts. However, most manufacturers start with the +5 volts DC (VDC) from the PC's power supply and connect a silicone rectifier for protection. Now, if the +5VDC is really only 4.85 volts—definitely in the legal range—and we lose about 0.6 to 0.7 volts across the rectifier, we're below spec. If you add the loss on the SCSI cable, we're clearly under spec. (Active termination is far less vulnerable here because it works with a voltage regulator, and a good voltage regulator needs only about 0.5 to 1 volt over the needed 2.85 volts.)

- The same applies for noisy TERMPWR. The basic voltage supply for the termination power isn't very clean, which may cause some systems to hiccup. Noise might get through the termination network to the signal lines. As just stated, active termination is less vulnerable because the voltage regulator suppresses the noise to some degree. If noisy TERMPWR is your problem, you will need an oscilloscope or transient recorder to find it—and then you'll need even more good ideas to get rid of it.

**Problem 3:** Sometimes, people fold all their internal cables in neat packages, securing them with cable fasteners or plastic belts. This may or may not work. When you fold the cables, you create a very complex R-C network, which may cause the bus to fail at certain dynamic situations under load. So, even if you're an order fanatic or neat-nick, resist this temptation! Let the cables flow freely in the case.

**Problem 4:** Keep the bus length inside the computer at a minimum. The maximum bus lengths are defined for an ideal setup, and a real-world setup is never an ideal one. Also, each connector, each cable change, and each device introduces impedance changes; so, if possible, keep the cables shorter than the specified maximum length as a security margin.

**Problem 5:** If you get a bad cable, replace it. When you identify a cable that gives you trouble, you may find a cable sequence that works, but it will always be a suspicious point. So, if possible, replace it right away. When you buy a cable, especially an external one, don't get the cheapest — get one that adheres to the specs.

**NOTE** *SCSI vendors with a good reputation tend to have good quality cables, so their cables are usually a good choice.*

## How to Check Typical Issues

### Two Devices with the Same ID

If one or more installed devices do not work, but one of them is recognized by a tool like SHOWSCSI or the host adapter is not able to detect one of them during the boot phase, you may have two devices at the same ID.

Let's create a scenario for this situation: You have a setup with hard disk drives at IDs 0 and 1, a tape drive at ID 2, and a CD-ROM drive at ID 3. Now you add an external device, say, a CD-ROM drive, configured also for ID 3.

This change in your setup could cause various error situations:

- The two devices at ID 3 may simply not work, but the system works with the remaining devices;

- The CD-ROM driver may lock up on initializing its device; or

- The host adapter hangs at the bus scan.

With similar device types as in this example, the CD-ROM driver may even load, but later the CD-R driver may drive the system nuts. . . .

Whatever happens, check all IDs carefully. If you don't know your IDs or aren't able to find out easily, use this quick-and-dirty approach:

1. Power up the system and note which devices are found on what IDs during bootup.

2. Turn off the system and disconnect/power down the devices that were recognized—these are the ones that the system knows about.

3. Turn the system on again and watch, during bootup, for devices to show up that weren't present before you disconnected the known devices.

4. Add these devices to the list of known devices, and note their IDs to resolve a possible conflict later in the process.

5. Repeat these steps until no device is left on your system.

After following these steps, you may be surprised to discover as many as three devices at the same ID (it happened to me . . .), and you'll have a list of all attached devices and their IDs. Now, armed with your list, change the conflicting device ID(s) so that there are no longer conflicts, and everything should be OK.

Remember, ID 0 and ID 1 are usually used for hard disks, and ID 7 should remain reserved for the host adapter. Do not try to attach more devices than the host adapter is able to handle. A special case of this problem is if you set a peripheral device to the host adapter's ID. Usually, on a bus scan, this device shows up on all IDs except the host adapter's ID (because the host's ID isn't checked). The problematic part of this situation is that such a single-device configuration sometimes works, but if you connect a second peripheral device, you won't get it to show up during the bootup of your system.

**NOTE** *Some devices MAY have incomplete implementations of the SCSI interface, and some older devices have fixed IDs (though a device with an ID fixed at 7 is unheard of). See the "Tricky Devices" section later in this chapter for more information on how to handle these devices.*

### Dead Devices

Electronic devices have many ways of dying, and heaven only knows which path your device will choose. Usually, if the SCSI electronics are OK, the system finds the device, the device will react to inquiry commands, but on accesses or tests you get a "device not ready" or similar message. This is very common for defective disk drives or tape devices. If the device is electronically dead, it won't react at all—which is the easiest symptom to detect.

### Termination

First, some rules for termination:

1.  Bus termination should only be applied at the physical ends of the SCSI bus. This is the most basic rule of termination, and the one that causes the most intermittent trouble.

2.  From a practical point of view, use active terminators only—passive terminators were never really a good choice, and the introduction of higher transfer rates outlawed them years ago. But passive terminators are still sold and, because they are cheaper than even the cheapest active ones, are sometimes used even though they're inferior. Occasionally I've seen people using single-ended FTP terminators on an LVD setup—not that it worked, but they were always sure that they had done the best thing. If you need to buy a terminator block, get an active one, and if possible one compatible with active negation and LVD. With this type, you're on the safest side for whatever situation may occur.

If the termination rules are violated, the violation may not show up at once. Errors may happen infrequently and unexpectedly, often specifically linked to one device, leading you to think that that device might be defective. This impression might be further strengthened when some commands work while others, possibly including synchronous data transfers, don't.

For example, a one-sided termination (only one terminator on the bus) usually won't work with multiple devices or a longer bus cable. Some companies (for example, Apple in some older systems and NEC with some of their OEM CD-ROMs) claim that the SCSI bus in their configuration will work even with only one terminator. Although this may be true under some circumstances, (just through good karma), it isn't generally true and is definitely *not* recommended. Incorrect termination has essentially one result: The system won't work correctly. "Not correctly" can range from "sometimes works, sometimes doesn't" to "definitely dead."

### Measuring Passive Terminators

There are two ways to estimate the number of passive terminators installed. First, count them. This can be a time-consuming job, especially if you have to open your computer, remove the drives to look at them, and so on. But if you do, you can check to see that all terminators are installed correctly and all other device issues are set accordingly. Pay attention to the correct orientation of internal terminators also.

Second, use your multi-meter. Take appropriate diagrams of the connector layouts (see Appendix A) and note the position of the following signals:

- Termination power (TERMPWR)

- Ground (GND)

- One of the data lines

Then power down your computer and all devices attached to it. You can now either replace one of the SCSI cables with your diagnostic cable or you can remove one of the SCSI devices, preferably an external one. If you remove a device, don't forget to see whether it's terminated.

Using this second method, detecting passive terminators is fairly easy. With your multi-meter, you only have to measure three resistances. If the termination is correct, your measurement will match those listed in Table 6.1. (Resistances may differ within a range of approximately 5 percent.)

### Table 6.1: Termination Measurements

|  | Any Signal to GROUND | Any Signal to TERMPWR | TERMPWR to GROUND |
|---|---|---|---|
| No terminator | — | — | — |
| 1 passive terminator * | 143 ohms | 136.8 ohms | 30.5 ohms |
| 2 passive terminators | 71.5 ohms | 68.4 ohms | 15.25 ohms |
| 3 passive terminators | 47.6 ohms | 45.6 ohms | 10.2 ohms |
| More than 2 passive terminators | < 71.5 ohms | < 136.8 ohms | < 30.5 ohms |
| 1 passive and 1 active terminator * | 143 ohms | 136.8 ohms | 30.5 ohms |

*The active terminator we used in our first try didn't show up when not powered, so this was an unlucky case. Other active terminators behaved differently, depending on their internal circuitry. If the readings change when you switch your multi-meter probes, at least one active terminator is somewhere in the system.

### Measuring Active Terminators

Measuring active terminators is difficult and unpredictable. Active terminators may respond like the example in Table 6.1 (our specific model didn't show up when not powered on), but they don't necessarily react this way. (Some may be identified because they yield different readings when the multi-meter probes are interchanged.)

Because an active terminator's output resistors are clamped directly to the signal, without the simple pull-up and pull-down resistors, active terminators affect only the signal-to-TERMPWR reading, if at all — not the signal-to-ground and TERMPWR-to-ground measurements.

If you find that there are too many terminators in the bus, your only choice is to remove the additional terminators.

### Termination Power: Active versus Passive

Passive termination is especially vulnerable to low or noisy termination power voltage. The SCSI specification states very clearly that TERMPWR should be between 4.25 and 5.25 volts. Although the minimal voltage drops to 3.0 volts in SE/LVD multi-mode setups, let's stick with the SCSI specifications for the moment. In their board designs, many manufacturers start with the +5VDC level from the systems' power supply and have a silicone diode in the line as a protection diode. Now, if the +5VDC is just 4.85 volts and we lose about 0.6 to 0.7 volts across the diode, it's below spec. If you add the loss on the SCSI cable, it's clearly under spec.

### What Not to Do with Your Power Supply

If this low voltage appears in your system, you might be inclined to try adjusting the voltage of your power supply — *don't do it!* In today's systems, a power supply design with test pins and voltage adjustments is so rare that you will rarely see one — most are sealed boxes. If you open the box, you not only lose your warranty, but you may also lose your life by touching the wrong part! We don't recommend that you play with *any* power supply. (An alternative to monkeying with the power supply might be replacing the standard diode with a Schottky type that loses only about 0.3 volts or less.)

Active termination is far less vulnerable to low or noisy termination power voltage because it uses a voltage regulator, and a good voltage regulator needs an input of about 0.5 to 1 volt over its 2.85 volt output.

Noise on the TERMPWR line, especially noise in the frequency range used by SCSI data, can be even more of a nightmare and can lead to all sorts of unpredictable behavior. The supply voltage for termination power isn't always clean, and its noise might get through the termination network to the signal lines. If you encounter strange lockups after you've sorted out the basics, and if you can get access to an oscilloscope, use the oscilloscope to check the signal condition on the TERMPWR line. There shouldn't be more than about 100 mV of noise.

Here again, active termination is far less vulnerable to noise on the TERMPWR line, because virtually all voltage regulators used in active termination have very good noise and ripple rejection circuitry. This is another reason to prefer active termination over the passive variant.

Placing the computer near a high-voltage wire may also cause strange behavior. If you encounter this sort of noise, try changing the computer's orientation relative to the wire.

If noisy TERMPWR is your problem, you will need an oscilloscope or a transient recorder to find it. If you find noise in the terminator power, look at the +5V pins from the power supply and see if they show the same noise. If they do, replace the power supply with a better-quality model and add a good surge suppressor (the latter often works wonders for this problem). If the noise is only on TERMPWR, it may be due to poor quality cables causing crosstalk between SCSI signals.

### Cables

In general, do not exceed the maximum bus length. When making this calculation, remember that the maximum length varies depending on the bus transfer rate of the fastest device on the bus, and the number of devices on the bus. As a rule of thumb, the faster the SCSI bus, the shorter the maximum length. Also, don't underestimate the length of the internal cable—a typical internal four-device cable is between 2.5 feet and 4 feet (76 cm and 122 cm) in length.

Because cable quality is a critical issue, keep on hand spare internal and external cables of good quality, especially if you troubleshoot often. This way, if you suspect a cable, you can change it to see if the behavior changes.

With external cables, the better the quality of the cable, the better its shielding should be, both against external RF noise and between the signals. So, a better cable typically is less vulnerable to a noisy environment. It's sometimes worth swapping all cables for better ones, especially if you can't stabilize the system. (Sadly, though, this is not a feasible alternative to try at home, considering the price of multiple high-quality cables.)

Changing cable types is always a potential source of trouble. If, for example, your system has an external 50-pin cable connected to a disk drive, then a scanner with a 25-pin connector, and this connects to another disk drive with a 50-pin cable, you're probably in trouble. If I cannot avoid a 25-pin connector, I always make sure it is the *last* device in the chain and use a 50-pin cable with a pass-through terminator. This way, at least I ensure correct bus termination, and the few centimeters to the device count as a legal "stub" length.

## Connectors

Check all connectors for good contact—one or more may have lost contact on some pins. External cables are rather easy to check—if the security clamps or screws are OK, everything should be OK. However, this should not keep you from disconnecting and reconnecting the cable. If the cable is older or was used in a harsh environment (high humidity, for example) try using a contact cleaning spray. If this is not handy, a few disconnects and reconnects may do the trick too. Home-made cables are susceptible to the common "I needed one more connector and so I just squeezed it on" (the wrong way) error.

## Tricky Devices

Some devices can cause grief because of their particular SCSI implementation. For example, most parallel-to-SCSI adapters draw their supply power from the TERMPWR line, so if your external device(s) doesn't supply termination power to the SCSI bus, these adapters won't work.

Some older devices can create strange situations because of limited SCSI implementations. For example, the old NEC CDR-35 and CDR-36 portable CD-ROM drives don't have termination, and they have only one SCSI connector. Thus they can only be used on the end of the chain, and they must be connected via a pass-through terminator. In addition, the CDR-35 is fixed to SCSI ID 1 and can't be changed.

On some older devices, you may not find a switch to change the ID. This may be the case for two reasons: Either the device really is fixed to a specific ID (the Siemens HighScan 800 scanner, for example), or the switch is hidden somewhere inside the device. The second case occurs primarily on devices that have SCSI as an option only, like some older Epson scanners. (These came by default with special serial and parallel interfaces only, and the SCSI interface card was an option, with the ID switch on the PCB deep inside the scanner.)

If you encounter strange problems and can't find a logical explanation, it's probably time to give the manuals a look. Most of the time, these troubleshooting issues are addressed somewhere in the manual.

## Driver Problems

### Plug & Play–Related

When you install a plug & play device in a PC system, the BIOS supplies resources to the new device and sometimes remaps the resources to fit the new situation. If something goes wrong in this process—and believe me, it does sometimes—you may be able to force the system to redistribute its resources through a BIOS option called **Reset Configuration Data**, **Reset ESCD Configuration**, or similar. Before doing this, you might want to write down the current settings just in case things get worse instead of better.

This can solve many hardware conflicts, but afterward you may need to check all hardware-based configuration settings—for example those of network cards and other peripherals—because the drivers may not find the hardware at its new settings.

### Windows (All Versions)

In today's systems, drivers typically aren't an issue—but add PCI, Plug-and-Play, and autoconfiguration into the mix and you can be in deeper trouble than before: You can't even be sure that the system will repeat its configuration from one time to the next! Still, here are a few rules of thumb.

Although your Windows version may have drivers for your host adapter, check whether your adapter came with newer drivers or whether there are newer ones on the vendor's web site. Window's built-in drivers are often early releases and don't support the newer adapter models. This is normal, because the adapter vendors refine their adapters rather often, and the drivers included with the O/S often don't know how to handle the newer adapter models. Therefore, it's usually better to use the drivers supplied with the adapter or an even newer version from the vendor's support web site.

**NOTE** *Before you install a new device, be it a SCSI adapter, a network card, or whatever, try to save the system configuration. In Windows NT, this is easily done with the RDISK command. This way, if a problem arises, you can fall back to the old configuration at startup.*

### DOS

Sometimes, the SCSI device drivers for DOS can be real troublemakers. They may conflict with memory managers, be incompatible with each other, be buggy, or who knows. However, when you install them correctly and use the few hints that follow, you'll usually be able to avoid these troubles.

Let's look at a sample configuration, taken from a real support case, that shows the problems you, or the Install program, might run into (this is for an ISA PC with an Adaptec 1540 host adapter):

```
device=c:\dos\himem.sys
devicehigh=c:\dos\scsi\aspicd.sys /d:aspicd
device=c:\dos\emm386.exe ram
devicehigh=c:\dos\scsi\aspi4dos.sys /d
shell=c:\dos\command.com c:\dos\ /e:256 /p
dos=high,umb
lastdrive =f
devicehigh=c:\dos\scsi\aspidisk.sys
```

This configuration has one error and two features that may cause problems:

1. The first error is that the CD-ROM device driver (ASPICD.SYS) is started before the low-level driver (ASPI4DOS.SYS) so that, at the device driver's loading time, no ASPI interface is present. The driver will refuse to load and the CD-ROM won't work.

2. One potential problem is that EMM386.EXE is loaded with the RAM parameter without excluding the SCSI BIOS area. This may or may not work, depending on the memory manager and its version; but it's usually the case that, on loading the EMM386.EXE driver, the SCSI BIOS address range is overwritten with RAM to gain upper memory blocks (UMBs) for drivers and resident programs.

3. The other potential problem may occur because many SCSI device drivers cannot (or should not) be loaded high. In general, the basic ASPI or CAM shell drivers for SCSI adapters should be placed before all memory manager commands, because virtually all those drivers do more than just the ASPI layer. They either provide additional services and/or they provide bug fixes for the BIOS and other things.

A working configuration would look like this:

```
device=c:\dos\scsi\aspi4dos.sys /d
device=c:\dos\himem.sys
device=c:\dos\emm386.exe ram x=dc00-dfff
dos=high,umb
devicehigh=c:\dos\scsi\aspicd.sys /d:aspicd
devicehigh=c:\dos\scsi\aspidisk.sys
shell=c:\dos\command.com c:\dos\ /e:256 /p
lastdrive=f
```

Of course, the possibility for further optimization always exists, but the changes to the configuration are fairly straightforward. In this working configuration, the following are true:

- The ASPI driver is loaded before the memory manager, so as not to interfere with it.

- EMM386.EXE excludes the BIOS address range — in this case DC00 to DFFF, the 1540's default.

- All ASPI-dependent drivers are loaded after the ASPI low-level driver so that they will be able to communicate with the ASPI driver.

### General Rules for Troubleshooting Drivers

- If you suspect driver problems or the system locks up when initializing the SCSI drivers, try a clean boot with only the SCSI drivers to see if you have a memory conflict or similar problem. Then add in the other drivers one by one.

- If one or multiple devices are found by the bus scan but won't operate later, check the order of the drivers in CONFIG.SYS.

- Avoid loading the SCSI drivers in upper memory unless you've tested that configuration thoroughly.

- Check memory manager address ranges for proper exclusions.

### Driver Combinations

Combinations of different ASPI drivers may cause big trouble. By definition, ASPI drivers should be cascadable—one manufacturer's ASPI extensions should work on another's low-level driver—but this is in theory only. Virtually every manufacturer makes their own (read "incompatible") extensions to the drivers. As an example, older Adaptec and Buslogic ASPI drivers don't cooperate. Either the Buslogic driver kicks the Adaptec driver out, or the Adaptec driver refuses to load after the Buslogic driver. Ironically, both adapters (in this case, a 1740A and a Buslogic BT-742) work together at BIOS level without any hassles, but only one ASPI driver can be used. No possible combination gives you both adapters with full ASPI support, and nearly the same applies for all other combinations we tried.

**NOTE** *Different drivers from the same vendor usually don't share this problem. The manufacturers are definitely interested in making their own adapters work together, but don't even count on that before you've tried it!*

### Useful Tools

#### SCSI Sniffer

A SCSI sniffer is a pass-through connector that is plugged between the SCSI bus and the device. Some of these connectors are also a terminator and should therefore be used on the bus ends only. "Sniffer" means that the connector is equipped with LEDs that show activity or the status of various SCSI signals. The most common display LED is for Termination Power, where the simpler version shows only that there is a voltage present on the TERMPWR line. There are also versions that show the validity of the TERMPWR level with the LED color or multiple LEDs.

Table 6.2 shows typical signals from these devices.

**Table 6.2: Diagnostic LED meanings**

| Signal | LED Active Means . . . |
| --- | --- |
| I/O | The initiator reads data from the bus. |
| C/D | A command is transferred (LED inactive means data is transferred). |
| SEL | The initiator selects a target device. |
| PWR | There is power present at the TERMPWR line. |
| ACK | The initiator acknowledges a target request. |
| REQ | A target requests data from the initiator. |
| BSY | The bus is busy. |

Taking the bus phase description from Chapter 7, you can see the system's bus phase at any point in time (though this only makes sense when the system is locked up, of course). Interpreting this is not easy and, even if you can interpret it, you probably won't help yourself. In most cases it is enough to see that there is no ongoing bus activity to know it's reboot time. If your bus is hung with a certain combination of LEDs on, and you're diligent about scrutinizing the meaning of each from the protocol discussions in Chapter 7, you can probably figure out whether it was the host adapter or target device that dropped the ball.

In a case where the system is locked up, the BSY LED is active, and SEL, C/D, I/O, and MSG are not active. If we avoid a disconnect/reconnect scenario, the active device may be defective or too slow, but we don't know for sure. Interesting, but not really helpful.

However, a very active MSG LED might hint at too many transfer errors and retransmits, which in turn might point to a cabling or mis-termination issue.

### Oscilloscope

An oscilloscope is a very useful tool. The major disadvantages are that you must have one, and you must know how to use it, or it's just an expensive toy. The big advantage is that signal-dependent problems are easy to detect with an oscilloscope.

One case in which an oscilloscope might come in handy is where termination power is OK without activity and, during bus activity, the TERMPWR level drops sharply. One possible explanation for such an effect could be that a "Forced Perfect" terminator draws higher current than the drivers can deliver. With this knowledge, changing the terminator to a standard active one might correct the problem in seconds.

Another case in which an oscilloscope would be useful would be where there are strong overshoots of a signal because of a missing or defective terminator. The upper oscilloscope trace in Figure 6.1 shows these overshoots on the unterminated side of the bus. The lower oscilloscope trace shows the same

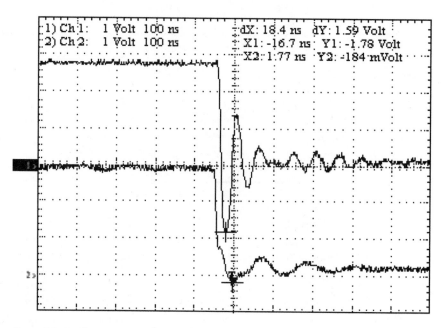

*Figure 6.1: Oscilloscope View of a Signal*

pulse on the other side of the bus (which is equipped with an active negation terminator).

Also, the signal is very noisy, because of the cheap ribbon cable used for the test setup. With clear pictures of the signals, most types of errors — or at least hints about their causes—can be found.

Amusingly, in this test setup, the single active terminator managed to keep the system working with the devices "on its side" of the bus, while a device on the unterminated side of the bus locked up on every request. Of course, this is only a side effect of a good terminator.

During our troubleshooting exercises in this chapter we've pointed you to some of the detailed information in Chapter 7, where we explain exactly how the SCSI protocol works; let's move on and find out more about it. It won't hurt!

# 7

## HOW THE BUS WORKS

As we all know by now, SCSI is an acronym for the small computer systems interface. That is all fine and dandy, but what exactly is SCSI? This chapter goes beyond where the rest of the book has been to look at the way the SCSI bus really works. So if you're running into problems that will require some analysis, you're just the curious type, or even if you're a hopeless geek who has to know how everything works, this chapter may interest you.

### An Intelligent Interface

SCSI is an intelligent interface that hides a device's physical format from the software layers above it. Each SCSI device attaches to the SCSI bus in the same manner, and the host computer's only concern is what type of device is attached (e.g., disk, tape, and so on). Information is retrieved from a SCSI device via logical *block addressing*, a scheme that hides the device's physical configuration. This is beneficial, because the host is not required to know the head, cylinder, sector, and so on where information is stored. If a host needs a file from a device, it requests the data in the form of logical block numbers from zero to the maximum address available on the device.

## SCSI Supports Generic Software

SCSI uses device-generic commands, which, in standardized system software, support many devices. In most systems, the host computer requires special software, known as a *device driver*, to properly format the command for each specified device type. There is usually a separate device driver for each device type attached to the SCSI bus.

## A True Peripheral Interface

SCSI is a true peripheral interface that allows up to 8 devices (SCSI-2) or 16 devices (SCSI-3) to be attached to a single bus/cable. These devices can be any combination of peripherals or hosts, but there must be at least one host. SCSI protocol is device-independent. The user can attach disk drives, tape drives, optical disks, and other devices (printers, scanners, and the like) to the same port.

In addition, SCSI is a buffered interface where all activities involve *handshakes* so that all devices operate properly with slower and faster devices and hosts. SCSI's handshaking allows devices of various communication speeds to coexist on the same cable. (We talk more about handshaking later in this chapter, in the section titled "Handshaking of Information.")

SCSI is also a peer-to-peer interface, where communication can take place from one host to another, one peripheral device to another, or, most commonly, a host to a peripheral device.

## Initiators, Targets, and Logical Units

To understand how SCSI works, you must first know some definitions. For each communication (I/O process) that occurs between two devices, each device involved assumes a particular role. One device assumes the role of an initiator and is responsible for starting or initiating the I/O process. The other device acts as the target and is responsible for managing or controlling the I/O process. *Logical units* are physical peripheral devices that are addressable through a target or peripheral controller (i.e., sub-address of the target). The operational diagram in Figure 7.1 shows a host-to-peripheral device connection.

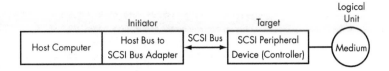

Figure 7.1: Diagram of the Host-to-Peripheral Device Connection

### What Is an I/O Process?

In SCSI, the term *I/O process* defines a particular method of doing something with an input/output device. The I/O process generally involves numerous steps. In most cases an I/O process consists of all the steps required to perform a single SCSI command, such as read or write a block of data. Figure 7.2 shows what an I/O process might look like if we were to model it.

The illustration in Figure 7.3 is an example of a SCSI transfer at its simplest. You'll find more detail in the section titled "The SCSI Protocol" later in this chapter.

## SCSI Configurations

A SCSI system can have many different configurations, including a single initiator and single target, single initiator and multiple targets, and multiple initiators and multiple targets. The diagrams in Figure 7.4 show how the SCSI standard defines each of these different bus configurations.

## Bus and Device Characteristics

A SCSI device can be a host adapter or target controller attached to the SCSI bus. Each device usually has a fixed role as an initiator or target, but some may assume either role. The host adapter is a device that connects the host system to the SCSI bus and performs the lower layers of protocol when accessing the SCSI bus. Host adapters usually act as initiators.

**NOTE** *SCSI is an "interlocked interface," which means that only two devices can communicate at any given time. When these two devices are communicating, all other devices must wait for the bus to free up before they can access the bus.*

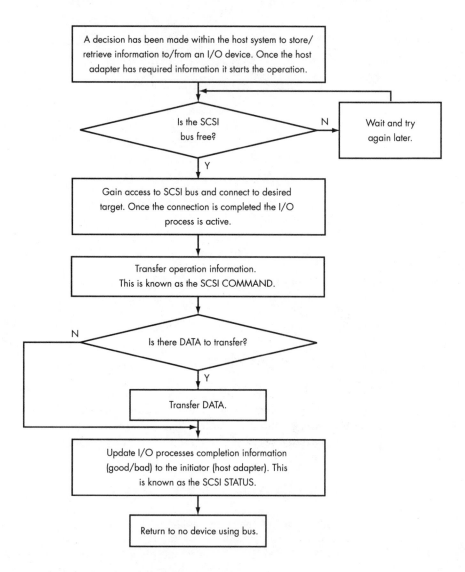

Figure 7.2: Model of the I/O Process

| Bus Connection | COMMAND | DATA | STATUS | Bus Disconnection |

Figure 7.3: A Simple SCSI Transfer

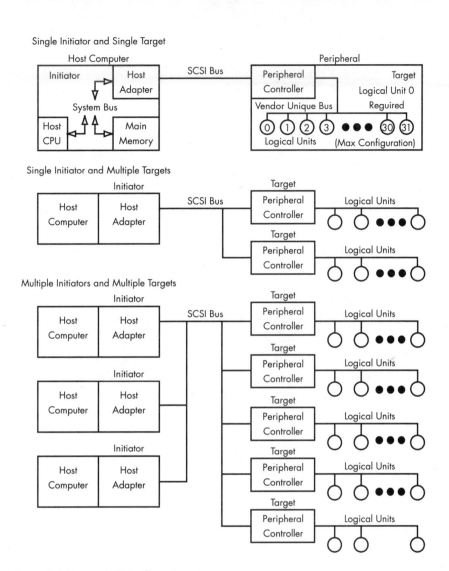

*Figure 7.4: Various SCSI Configurations*

When two devices are talking to one another, they are performing an I/O process, as briefly described later in this chapter. The detailed functions of each device are listed below.

### Initiators

When a device is acting as an initiator, it does the following:

- Originates operations.

- Determines what task needs to be executed and which target will perform the desired task.

- Delegates authority to the target device to control the I/O process.

- Controls certain bus functions, like arbitrating and target selection.

- Confirms that the target performed the task assigned to it.

### Targets

When a device is acting as a target, it does the following:

- Waits to be selected by an initiator.

- Upon selection, controls the data transfer process, by requesting that COMMAND, DATA, STATUS, or MESSAGE information be sent across the data bus.

- May arbitrate and reselect an initiator for the purpose of continuing an operation that was previously suspended because the device disconnected.

### SCSI IDs

Each device has a SCSI ID that uniquely identifies it among all other devices on a particular SCSI bus. When an initiator starts a SCSI request, it sets its ID bit and the ID bit of the desired target device on the data bus simultaneously. Priority on the data bus is determined by the bit numbers 0 through 7, with 7 the highest priority and 0 the lowest. The priority on the bus is used only when multiple devices are trying to access the bus simultaneously. In this instance, the device with the higher SCSI ID will take over the bus and the other device will sit back and wait until the bus is free for communication.

A device's address is determined by jumpers or switches on the device itself (or in the case of SCA drives, on the SCA back-plane or SCA adapter), as seen in Table 7.1. Most enclosed SCSI devices come with a switch mounted on the rear of the peripheral, and newer host adapters allow you to set the host's ID via software configuration utilities. On narrow SCSI devices, jumpers A0, A1, and A2 are required to set the SCSI ID jumper settings, because only eight devices may be attached.

When SCSI-3 Wide is used, an additional 8 devices may be attached to the bus. Priority for the lower bits will stay the same, and the remaining bits will be as shown in Table 7.1. The additional addressing of all 16 devices is easily achieved by just adding a single jumper A3. If the Q-cable is implemented, then 32 devices can be attached to a single bus and a jumper A4 will have to be added.

**Table 7.1: SCSI IDs, Their Priority on the Bus, and Jumper Settings**

| SCSI ID | Priority* | Jumper A4 | Jumper A3 | Jumper A2 | Jumper A1 | Jumper A0 |
|---|---|---|---|---|---|---|
| 7 | 1 | 0 | 0 | 1 | 1 | 1 |
| 6 | 2 | 0 | 0 | 1 | 1 | 0 |
| 5 | 3 | 0 | 0 | 1 | 0 | 1 |
| 4 | 4 | 0 | 0 | 1 | 0 | 0 |
| 3 | 5 | 0 | 0 | 0 | 1 | 1 |
| 2 | 6 | 0 | 0 | 0 | 1 | 0 |
| 1 | 7 | 0 | 0 | 0 | 0 | 1 |
| 0 | 8 | 0 | 0 | 0 | 0 | 0 |
| 15 | 9 | 0 | 1 | 1 | 1 | 1 |
| 14 | 10 | 0 | 1 | 1 | 1 | 0 |
| 13 | 11 | 0 | 1 | 1 | 0 | 1 |
| 12 | 12 | 0 | 1 | 1 | 0 | 0 |
| 11 | 13 | 0 | 1 | 0 | 1 | 1 |
| 10 | 14 | 0 | 1 | 0 | 1 | 0 |
| 9 | 15 | 0 | 1 | 0 | 0 | 1 |
| 8 | 16 | 0 | 1 | 0 | 0 | 0 |
| 23 | 17 | 1 | 0 | 1 | 1 | 1 |
| 22 | 18 | 1 | 0 | 1 | 1 | 0 |
| 21 | 19 | 1 | 0 | 1 | 0 | 1 |
| 20 | 20 | 1 | 0 | 1 | 0 | 0 |
| 19 | 21 | 1 | 0 | 0 | 1 | 1 |
| 18 | 22 | 1 | 0 | 0 | 1 | 0 |
| 17 | 23 | 1 | 0 | 0 | 0 | 1 |
| 16 | 24 | 1 | 0 | 0 | 0 | 0 |
| 31 | 25 | 1 | 1 | 1 | 1 | 1 |
| 30 | 26 | 1 | 1 | 1 | 1 | 0 |
| 29 | 27 | 1 | 1 | 1 | 0 | 1 |
| 28 | 28 | 1 | 1 | 1 | 0 | 0 |
| 27 | 29 | 1 | 1 | 0 | 1 | 1 |
| 26 | 30 | 1 | 1 | 0 | 1 | 0 |
| 25 | 31 | 1 | 1 | 0 | 0 | 1 |
| 24 | 32 | 1 | 1 | 0 | 0 | 0 |

*Where 1 is the highest priority and 32 is the lowest*

In the sections that follow, you'll learn about the cables that carry the signals, and you'll go inside the SCSI bus, where you'll learn about the bus's data and control signals. You will also learn which devices drive which signals, and how these signals control the protocol.

## SCSI Cables

In order to understand how SCSI protocol works, you'll need to know what's inside the physical cable. The cables used to connect SCSI devices are generally wired the same, although the number of conductors and the cable specifications may vary.

### Cable Evolution

The A-cable is associated with both SCSI-1 and SCSI-2, B-cable with SCSI-2 only, and the P- and Q-cables with SCSI-3.

The A-cable (Figure 7.5) is a 50-conductor cable that consists of eight data signals DB(0-7) (i.e., physical transmission lines), parity (DB(P)), and nine control signals.

The B-cable (bottom of Figure 7.6) is a 68-conductor Wide bus option that has an additional 24 data lines, three parity lines, and two control signals (REQB and ACKB).

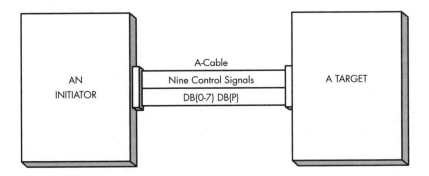

Figure 7.5: The A-Cable

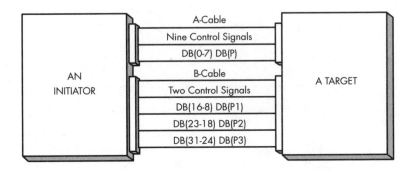

Figure 7.6: The A- and B-Cables

*The B-cable must be used in conjunction with the A-cable, as seen in Figure 7.6. But, in reality the B-cable is obsolete and the A, B combination has been replaced by the P-cable, the 16-bit wide SCSI-3 cable alternative. The B-cable was never used commercially, and the SCSI-3 alternative offers a better Wide bus solution with only one cable and up to 16 devices.*

The 16-bit Wide P-cable (Figure 7.7) is a 68-conductor bus option that has nine control signals (just like the A-cable), 16 data lines, and two parity signals. In equation form, we can look at the P-cable as follows:

P-cable = (A-cable) + (8 data lines and a parity bit)

The Q-cable option (Figure 7.8) adds full 32-bit Wide capability but must be used in conjunction with the P-cable. This option (using both P and Q)and adds two control signals (REQQ and ACKQ), 16 data lines, and two additional parity bits, for a total of 68 more conductors.

*SCSI-3 replaces the Wide A-cable / B-cable combination of SCSI-2 with the P-cable.*

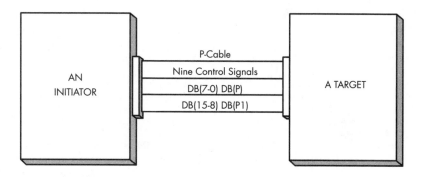

*Figure 7.7: The P-Cable*

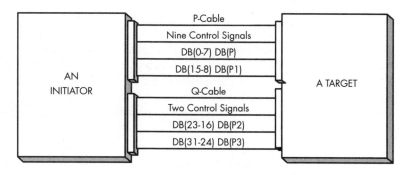

*Figure 7.8: The P- and Q-Cables*

### SCSI-1, SCSI-2, and SCSI-3 Cabling Diagram

The diagram in Figure 7.9 shows all the different cabling and bus options and what is transferred across them.

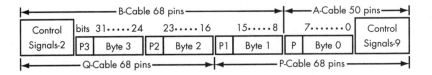

Figure 7.9: SCSI-1, SCSI-2, and SCSI-3 Signal Grouping

---

*Legend:*

| | |
|---|---|
| Control signals—9 | BSY, SEL, C/D, I/O, MSG, ATN, RST, REQ, ACK |
| Control signals—2 | B-cable—REQB/ACKB or Q-cable—REQQ/ACKQ |
| P, P1, P2, and P3 | The parity bits and byte (0 to 3) are data bus bytes. |

---

## SCSI Bus Signals

This section describes each bus signal's definition and characteristics. This information will give you a detailed description of what each transmission line is and what it does. Bus signals are either data bus or control signals. We'll address data bus signals first, because they're relatively straightforward.

**NOTE** *The device driving the signals depends upon whether the device is initiator or target. Also, note that the minus sign in front of each signal name denotes active low signals, meaning that when a device drives the signal, it goes to a 0 voltage level (on single-ended buses). When the device no longer wants to drive the signal line, it releases the signal. Now, the question is, what happens to the signal level when it is released? It goes to termination voltage (about 3 volts). This is one reason why the SCSI bus must be terminated.*

### Data Bus Signals

Data bus signals are relatively straightforward. One thing to keep in mind is your data bus width. The data bus signals are DB(31–0, P, P1, P2, and P3), and data bus signals have these five characteristics:

• Up to 32 data bus signals plus their respective parity bits (usually only 8-bit or 16-bit).

• DB7 is the Most Significant Bit (MSB) and has highest priority during ARBITRATION; DB0 is the Least Significant Bit (LSB).

- Data bit is defined as 1 when signal is true. (Asserted = 0 volts on Single Ended [S.E.] bus.)

- Data bit is defined as 0 when signal is false. (Negated = 3 volts on S.E. bus.)

- Parity is odd. (Parity bit will change to maintain an odd number of "1" bits.)

### Control Signals

The nine control signals can be split into three categories:

- Basic control signals, which are used to determine if the bus is in use, to select another device, to get the target's attention, and to reset the bus.

- Information transfer control signals, which are used by the target to control the information transfer phases. Information transfer phases are used to transmit COMMAND, MESSAGE, DATA, and STATUS information across the bus.

- Data clock signals, which are used to latch (capture) and validate the data at the receiving device.

Figure 7.10 shows all the signal names and which device can drive which signals. Notice that some signals are driven only by initiators, and others only by targets. Conversely, some signals can be driven by both initiators and targets. The control signals are used to achieve certain protocol phases, which are, in turn, used to transmit all information (including DATA) across the data bus. We'll talk about the protocol in detail in the section entitled "The SCSI Protocol." Table 7.2 shows you the actual signal name, the signal definition, whether the signal is driven by an initiator or target, and gives a brief description of the signal's function.

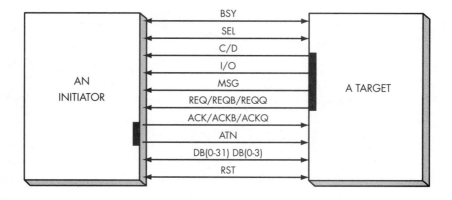

*Figure 7.10: SCSI Signal Sources*

**Table 7.2: SCSI Bus Control Signals**

| Signal | Definition | Category | Initiator | Target | Description |
|--------|-----------|----------|-----------|--------|-------------|
| BSY | Busy | Basic | Y | Y | Indicates that the bus is being used. |
| SEL | Select | Basic | Y | Y | Indicates that a SCSI device is trying to select or reselect another SCSI device. The initiator uses this signal to select a target, and the target uses it to reselect the initiator. |
| ATN | Attention | Basic | Y | N | Used by the initiator to indicate an Attention condition, marking a moment when the initiator needs to get the target's attention. |
| RST | Reset | Basic | Y | N | Indicates the Reset condition and gets everyone's attention. (Targets typically do not drive this signal, even though the SCSI standard says they could.) |
| C/D | Control/Data | Information transfer | N | Y | Indicates whether control or data information is on the bus. False indicates data information and true indicates control (COMMAND, MESSAGE, or STATUS) information on the bus. |
| I/O | Input/Output | Information transfer control | N | Y | Indicates which device is responsible for driving the datal bus and controls the direction of data movement on the data bus with respect to the initiator. False indicates the direction of data is out of the initiator and true indicates the direction of data is into the initiator. This signal is also used to distinguish between SELECTION and RESELECTION phases. |

| Signal | Definition | Category | Initiator | Target | Description |
|--------|-----------|----------|-----------|--------|-------------|
| MSG | Message | Information transfer control | N | Y | Indicates that a SCSI device has a message to transfer to another SCSI device. This signal is driven during a MESSAGE phase. |
| REQ | Request | Data clock | N | Y | Target indicates a request for an information transfer handshake. When the target is driving the data bus, this signal is used to latch the data bus into the initiator's buffer. |
| ACK | Acknowledge | Data clock | Y | N | This signal indicates the initiator's acknowledgment of an information transfer hand shake. When the initiator is driving the data bus, this signal is used to latch the data bus into the target's buffer. |

Legend:

Y   Drives signal
N   Doesn't drive signal

## The SCSI Protocol

SCSI uses a method to transfer data between devices on the bus in a circular process that starts and ends in the same layer—that is, the bus must go through specific steps in a prescribed order. From the first layer, additional layers of protocol must be executed before any data is transferred to or from another device, and layers of protocol must be completed after the data has been transferred to end the process. Figure 7.11 shows this process.

**NOTE** *The diagram in Figure 7.11 assumes no disconnection occurs (disconnection is covered in the section titled "Disconnect" in this chapter).*

The protocol layers are referred to as SCSI bus phases. Protocol layers and their SCSI bus phase equivalents can be seen in Table 7.3.

**NOTE** *In Table 7.3, the terms "In" or "Out" are based upon the initiator's perspective. The numbers next to the bus phase refer to the illustration in Figure 7.11.*

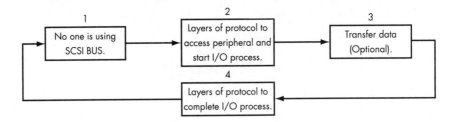

Figure 7.11: SCSI Protocol

## Table 7.3: Protocol Layers and Their SCSI Bus Phases

| Protocol Layer Characteristics | SCSI Bus Phase |
| --- | --- |
| 1. This protocol layer indicates no bus activity. <br> 2. Devices use this layer to recognize that the bus is available. <br> 3. Any time a device is not ready to transfer information, protocol reverts to this phase. <br> 4. This phase can happen many times for each I/O process. | BUS FREE 1 |
| 1. This protocol layer is used to gain control of the bus. <br> 2. Initiators or targets use this layer to resolve bus contention. <br> 3. This phase can occur many times for each I/O process. | ARBITRATION 2 |
| 1. This is the protocol layer that an initiating device uses to choose another device (a target). <br> 2. Initiators use this layer to select targets to start an I/O process. <br> 3. This phase occurs only once for each I/O process. | SELECTION 2 |
| 1. This protocol layer provides interface management to an I/O process. <br> 2. Initiators use this layer to transmit a to a target. | MESSAGE OUT 2 |

| Protocol Layer Characteristics | SCSI Bus Phase |
| --- | --- |
| 3. This phase can occur many times for message each I/O process | |
| 1. This protocol layer transfers the I/O process operation information. <br> 2. This phase tells the target which operation to perform. <br> 3. This phase occurs only once, at the beginning of each I/O process. | COMMAND OUT 2 |
| 1. This protocol layer transfers data to or from the device. <br> 2. This phase can occur many times for each I/O process. | DATA OUT 3 |
| 1. This protocol layer gives an update of the status of an operation. <br> 2. This phase occurs only once, at the end of each I/O process. | STATUS IN 4 |
| 1. This protocol layer provides interface management to an I/O process. <br> 2. Targets use this layer to transmit a message to an initiator. <br> 3. This phase may occur many times for each I/O process. | MESSAGE IN 4 |
| 1. This protocol layer is used by a target to choose an initiator. <br> 2. Targets use this layer to continue a previously disconnected I/O process. This phase can occur many times for each I/O process. | RESELECTION |

The SCSI bus can be in only one bus phase at any given time. Each phase has a predetermined set of rules, or *protocol*, that apply when the bus changes from one phase to another. The rules are part of device code, or *firmware*, that resides on all devices attached to the SCSI bus. This method of defining what can happen when is called a *state machine*. This device code makes the device intelligent by moving peripheral control operations onto the peripheral device itself.

### Phase Sequence Diagram

The sequence diagram in Figure 7.12 is taken from the SCSI-2 standard. Firmware developers, IC manufacturers, and anyone who has anything to do with SCSI all use this chart as the bible for SCSI protocol. These are the steps the bus must follow for every data transfer.

Following the diagram in Figure 7.12, the normal progression of bus phase sequencing is as follows:

1.  BUS FREE to ARBITRATION

2.  ARBITRATION to SELECTION or RESELECTION

3.  SELECTION or RESELECTION to one or more of the information transfer phases (MESSAGE, COMMAND, DATA, or STATUS)

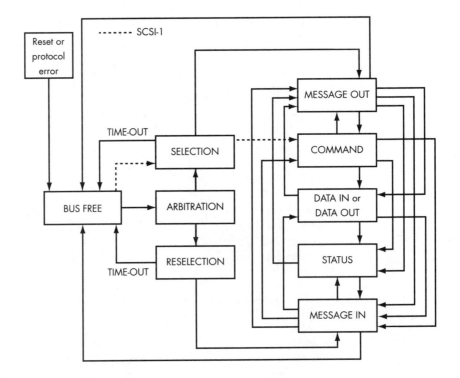

Figure 7.12: Phase Sequence Diagram

Table 7.4 is a bus phase sequence trace taken from a typical SCSI bus analyzer, which translates the bus signals into protocol phases and data information. This information is very detailed, but if you read carefully you will get a real understanding of how SCSI protocol works.

**Table 7.4: Bus Phase Sequence Trace**

| * | Timing s.mmm_μμμ_nnn | Protocol Layer or Bus Phase That Transpired | Data Bus (Single values represent SCSI IDs. Otherwise values are in hex bytes.) | | Event |
|---|---|---|---|---|---|
| 1 | 00.000_000_000 | Bus Free Detected | | | 0000 |
| 2 | 26.032_853_700 | Arbitration Start | 7 | | 0001 |
| 2 | 26.032_856_100 | Arb_win | 7 | | 0002 |
| 2 | 26.033_514_100 | | (Atn Assertion) | ATN | 0003 |
| 2 | 26.033_521_700 | Selection Start | 7 4 | ATN | 0004 |
| 2 | 26.033_522_600 | Selection Complete | | ATN | 0005 |
| 2 | 26.034_161_850 | | (Atn Negation) | ATN | 0006 |
| 2 | 26.034_833_950 | Message Out | C0 | | 0007 |
| 2 | 26.039_035_750 | Command Out | 08 00 01 00 01 00 | | 0008 |
| 3 | 26.055_860_800 | Data In | 00 00 00 00 00 00 | | 0009 |
| 3 | 26.055_862_300 | | 00 00 00 00 00 00 | | 0010 |
| 3 | 26.056_494_450 | | 00 00 00 00 00 00 | | 0011 |
| 4 | 26.056_894_350 | Status In | 00 | | 0012 |
| 4 | 26.057_852_350 | Message In | 00 | | 0013 |
| 1 | 26.058_426_300 | Bus Free Detected | | | 0014 |

*Legend:*

| | |
|---|---|
| *1 | No one using bus |
| *2 | Protocol to access peripheral and start process |
| *3 | Transfer data |
| *4 | Protocol to complete process |

Before you panic, take a look at Table 7.5, which provides a detailed description of the bus phase sequence in Figure 7.13, event by event.

**Table 7.5: Analysis of SCSI Bus Phase Sequence Diagram**

| Event | What Happened |
|-------|---------------|
| 0000 | The SCSI bus is in a BUS FREE phase. |
| 0001 | A device (initiator) with a SCSI ID=7 starts the ARBITRATION phase to gain bus access. |
| 0002 | The initiator was granted access to the bus and the ARBITRATION phase ends. |
| 0003 | The initiator asserted the ATN signal to notify the peripheral that it will have a message to transfer after the SELECTION phase is completed (Attention condition). |
| 0004 | The initiator starts the SELECTION phase and is attempting to select a peripheral (target) with a SCSI ID=4. The initiator's ID can also be seen. |
| 0005 | The SELECTION phase has ended successfully. At this point the target is in control of the bus and will continue controlling the protocol until the I/O process is complete. |
| 0006 | The initiating device drops the attention signal. |
| 0007 | The peripheral goes into the MESSAGE OUT phase and accepts the "C0" message. This is because the initiator had the ATN signal asserted during the SELECTION phase. |
| 0008 | The target enters into the COMMAND phase and requests that the command bytes be sent. |
| 0009 | The target deciphers the command code (READ command) and knows to enter the DATA IN phase. The requested data is transferred to the initiator that started the I/O process. Even though only 18 bytes of data are shown, one block (512 bytes) had been transferred. The analyzer used in the above display has a data byte filter, which causes only a few data bytes to be displayed instead of the large number actually transferred. |
| 0012 | When the target completes the DATA phase, it enters into the STATUS phase and transfers a "00" status to inform the initiating device that all went well. |
| 0013 | When the target completes the STATUS phase, it enters into the MESSAGE IN phase and transfers a "00" message to inform the initiating device that the I/O process is complete. |
| 0014 | The target disconnects from the bus and the SCSI bus returns to the BUS FREE phase. |

### Bus Phases

This section dives a little deeper into the phases of the bus and provides further examples and descriptions. Not counting the INs and OUTs, there are eight distinct bus phases, which can be divided into three categories, namely the waiting phase, bus control phases, and information transfer phases, as shown in Table 7.6.

**Table 7.6: Bus Phases**

| Waiting Phase | Bus Control Phases | Information Transfer Phases |
|---|---|---|
| BUS FREE | ARBITRATION | MESSAGE IN/OUT |
| | SELECTION | COMMAND |
| | RESELECTION | DATA IN/OUT |
| | | STATUS |

One of two types of bus operations may occur when an I/O process takes place, namely the phase sequence with no disconnection and the phase sequence with disconnection, as shown in Tables 7.7 and 7.8. The "disconnect" takes place when the second "bus free" occurs in Table 7.8. More details of each phase will be given later in this chapter.

**Table 7.7: Phase Sequence with No Disconnection**

| Phase | BSY | SEL | C/D | I/O | MSG | Data Bus |
|---|---|---|---|---|---|---|
| Bus Free | 0 | 0 | X | X | X | X |
| Arbitration Start | 1 | X | X | X | X | Init SCSI ID |
| Arb_win | 1 | X | X | X | X | Init SCSI ID |
| Selection Start | 0 | 1 | X | 0 | X | Both SCSI IDs |
| Selection Complete | 1 | 1 | X | 0 | X | Both SCSI IDs |
| Message Out | 1 | 0 | 1 | 0 | 1 | Message Byte(s) |
| Command Out | 1 | 0 | 1 | 0 | 0 | Command Bytes |
| Data In | 1 | 0 | 0 | 1 | 0 | Data Byte(s) |
| **or (Optional-data is not required for some commands.)** | | | | | | |
| Data Out | 1 | 0 | 0 | 0 | 0 | Data Byte(s) |
| Status In | 1 | 0 | 1 | 1 | 0 | Status Byte |
| Message In | 1 | 0 | 1 | 1 | 1 | Message Byte(s) |
| Bus Free | 0 | 0 | X | X | X | X |

**Table 7.8: Phase Sequence with Disconnection**

| Phase | BSY | SEL | C/D | I/O | MSG | Data Bus |
|---|---|---|---|---|---|---|
| Bus Free | 0 | 0 | X | X | X | X |
| Arbitration Start | 1 | X | X | X | X | Init SCSI ID |
| Arb_win | 1 | X | X | X | X | Init SCSI ID |
| Selection Start | 0 | 1 | X | 0 | X | Both SCSI IDs |
| Selection Complete | 1 | 1 | X | 0 | X | Both SCSI IDs |
| Message Out | 1 | 0 | 1 | 0 | 1 | Message Byte(s) |
| Command Out | 1 | 0 | 1 | 0 | 0 | Command Bytes |
| Message In | 1 | 0 | 1 | 1 | 1 | Message Byte(s) |
| Bus Free | 0 | 0 | X | X | X | X |
| Arbitration Start | 1 | X | X | X | X | Targ SCSI ID |
| Arb_win | 1 | X | X | X | X | Targ SCSI ID |
| Reselection Start | 0 | 1 | X | 1 | X | Both SCSI IDs |
| Reselection Complete | 1 | 1 | X | 1 | X | Both SCSI IDs |
| Message In | 1 | 0 | 1 | 1 | 1 | Message Byte(s) |
| Data xxx | 1 | 0 | 0 | 1 or 0 | 0 | Data Byte(s) |
| Status In | 1 | 0 | 1 | 1 | 0 | Status Byte |
| Message In | 1 | 0 | 1 | 1 | 1 | Message Byte(s) |
| Bus Free | 0 | 0 | X | X | X | X |

*Legend:*

| | | | |
|---|---|---|---|
| 1 | True | xxx | In or Out |
| 0 | False (doesn't necessarily mean driven false) | Init | Initiator |
| X | Not driven | Targ | Target |

**NOTE** *The ATN signal has been purposely omitted in Tables 7.7 and 7.8.*

## Connect, Disconnect, and Reconnect Concepts

The processes that underlie connect, disconnect, and reconnect are what make SCSI capable of multitasking. The idea behind this process is that when a device experiences some type of delay during a data transfer, mechanical or otherwise, it gets off the bus and lets another device on. Usually this is done during data transfer phases.

### Connect

The SCSI objective underlying connect is to establish a *nexus*, which is a link between initiator, target, and logical unit. The most basic SCSI nexus is called an I_T_L (initiator, target, logical unit) nexus. The nexus is used by both initiators and targets to identify an I/O process. Initiators use the nexus to ensure that the SCSI pointers in the host adapter associated with an I/O process are correctly updated when a previously disconnected I/O process resumes. That was a mouthful, but here is a translation: The nexus allows a host adapter (initiator) to keep track of multiple operations. The initiator makes sure that, for every I/O process it starts, a unique I_T_L nexus is established which is used to keep track of the progress of the I/O process within the initiator.

If an initiator is going to send multiple I/O processes to the same target and logical unit, then the initiator needs to extend the nexus to an I_T_L_Q nexus. The Q provides a command queue value that allows an initiator to queue up to 256 commands to the same target and logical unit. Targets use the nexus to differentiate I/O processes of one initiator from that of another. They also use the nexus to differentiate multiple processes from the same initiator, as in tagged command queuing (i.e., I_T_L_Q nexus).

The diagram in Figure 7.13 shows some examples of forming nexus. Here are a couple of nexus scenarios, using the devices shown in Figure 7.13.

1. Host 1 (ID=7) wants to send data to the hard disk (ID=0). Because the hard disk has only one LUN, the process is directed to LUN 0. Therefore the I_T_L nexus would be 7_0_0.

2. Host 2 (ID=6) wants to get data from the media changer (ID=5). The desired library file is on LUN 2. Therefore the I_T_L nexus will be 6_5_2.

If the bus phase sequence in Table 7.9 occurs, a nexus between the initiator, target, and logical unit will be established.

**NOTE** *In the phase sequence shown in Table 7.9, we have listed what the control signals are doing during the protocol phases. This is how an analyzer can distinguish between one bus phase and another. For example, when the BSY is asserted (true) and all other control signals are not driven (false) as shown in step 2, the bus phase is ARBITRATION.*

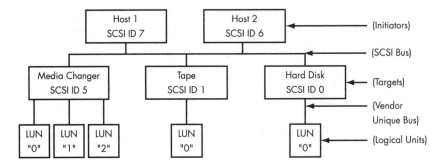

*Figure 7.13: How SCSI IDs Are Used to Form a Nexus*

**Table 7.9: Bus Phase Sequence Including Creation of I_T_L Nexus**

| | Phase | BSY | SEL | C/D | I/O | MSG | Data Bus |
|---|---|---|---|---|---|---|---|
| (1) | Bus Free | 0 | 0 | X | X | X | X |
| (2) | Arbitration Start | 1 | 0 | 0 | 0 | 0 | Initiator ID on bus |
| | Arb_win | 1 | 0 | 0 | 0 | 0 | I nexus |
| (3) | Selection Start | 0 | 1 | X | 0 | X | Both SCSI IDs on bus |
| (4) | Selection Complete | 1 | 1 | X | 0 | X | I_T nexus |
| (5) | Message Out | 1 | 0 | 1 | 0 | 1 | Identify: I_T_L nexus |

Here's a detailed description of the phase sequence shown in Table 7.9, following it step by step:

1.  Bus is free, as indicated by the simultaneously false (not driven) BSY and SEL signals.

2.  A device, in this instance an initiator, arbitrates for the bus by asserting the BSY signal and its SCSI ID via a data bus bit. The initiator wins the ARBITRATION phase and proceeds to the SELECTION phase.

3.  The SELECTION phase is used to transfer control of the I/O process from the initiator to the target. The initiator starts the SELECTION phase by driving (asserting) SEL and its SCSI ID as well as that of the target it wants to talk to. It also asserts the ATN signal (not shown in Table 7.9) to indicate that it wants the target to follow SELECTION phase with MESSAGE OUT phase. Next, the initiator waits a little while (at least 90 nanoseconds) for the signals to start propagating down the cable. Then the initiator releases

the BSY signal. Because the initiator drives both of the SCSI IDs on the data bus, the target can retrieve the initiator's ID from the setting of the data bus bits. The initiator will now wait for the target to drive the BSY signal or for a time-out condition to occur (i.e., the target doesn't drive BSY).

4. When the target detects that it's being selected, it drives the BSY signal. This notifies the initiator that the Selection process has completed successfully. Once the initiator detects that the target is driving the BSY signal, the initiator releases the SEL signal, thereby ending the SELECTION phase. The I_T portion of the nexus is now established

5. The target switches to the MESSAGE OUT phase because the ATN signal is asserted. The target must know the logical unit number that tells it where to direct the I/O process, and it gets this LUN from the Identify message sent by the initiator to the target. Not only does the Identify message contain the LUN, but it also carries an important data bit known as the Disconnect Privilege bit. If the initiator sets this bit in the Identify message, then the target can disconnect. The I_T_L nexus is now fully established.

**NOTE** *The use of the IDENTIFY message to specify the LUN was required in SCSI-2. In SCSI-1, the LUN was allowed to be specified in byte 1 of the CDB if the IDENTIFY message was not implemented.*

It is interesting to note that with respect to SCSI devices, targets control all I/O processes. Once a target allows itself to be selected, it controls the I/O process until its completion.

### Disconnect

The SCSI objective underlying disconnect is to temporarily terminate the link between devices so that other devices can access the bus. The reasons for terminating the link are to increase the number of I/Os per second by allowing a device to disconnect if it is not ready, whether because of *mechanical latency* (read/write heads moving into position to access requested data), or a full or empty buffer, so that another device can access the bus.

**NOTE** *Targets cannot disconnect unless the initiator has granted disconnect privilege in the Identify message during the original connection process.*

Disconnect can have two possible protocol sequences, depending on the type of operation, how much information is to be transferred, and buffer sizes. For example, if the initiator asks the target to store a file (WRITE), or to retrieve a file (READ), a different sequencing of protocol may occur. Or, if an initiator issues a command that writes more data than the target can store in its buffer, a disconnection will be required. The target disconnects from the initiator when its buffer is full and writes the data to the medium. Once the target has written the data to the medium, it will reconnect to the initiator and ask for more data, and so on, and so on, until all the data has been transferred.

An actual SCSI phase disconnection sequence can be seen in Table 7.10. The target can cause a disconnection by simply switching to the MESSAGE IN phase and sending a Disconnect message to the initiator. As soon as the initiator decodes a Disconnect message from the target, it will expect the target to go to the BUS FREE phase.

**Table 7.10: A SCSI Phase Disconnection Sequence**

| | Phase | BSY | SEL | C/D | I/O | MSG | Data Bus |
|---|---|---|---|---|---|---|---|
| (1) | Message In | 1 | 0 | 1 | 1 | 1 | 04h-disconnect |
| (2) | Bus Free | 0 | 0 | 0 | 0 | 0 | |

Another sort of disconnection sequence, which uses the Save Data Pointer message, can take place if only some of the data has been transferred and a target wants to disconnect. SCSI data pointers are special program variables that point to location in the memory of a host computer. Pointers can be either indirect or indexed and are located on the host adapter or may be internal to the actual SCSI protocol chip. The objectives of SCSI pointers are to break up large data transfers into smaller bursts and to facilitate error retry and recovery.

This Save Data Pointer message sequence acts as a placeholder to ensure that the initiator remembers where it left off in the data transfer if a disconnection occurs before all the data has been transferred. The Save Data Pointer message sent by the target device tells the initiator to copy its current SCSI pointers to a saved pointer value. A message sequence involving the Save Data Pointers message is shown in the phase sequence in Table 7.11.

**Table 7.11: A Sequence Showing "Save Data Pointers" and Disconnect Messages**

| | Phase | BSY | SEL | C/D | I/O | MSG | Data Bus |
|---|---|---|---|---|---|---|---|
| (1) | Message In | 1 | 0 | 1 | 1 | 1 | 02h-save data pointer |
| (2) | Message In | 1 | 0 | 1 | 1 | 1 | 04h-disconnect |
| (3) | Bus Free | 0 | 0 | 0 | 0 | 0 | |

### Reconnect

The SCSI objective underlying reconnect is to reestablish the I_T_L nexus. When speaking of reconnection in regard to SCSI, we're talking about a target reconnecting to an initiator. The following describes the reconnect process:

- A target reselects an initiator to continue a previously disconnected I/O process.

- The target determines when it's ready to reconnect to an initiator.

- The target and initiator resume their roles when a reconnection occurs.

- Reconnect is a series of bus phases.

Table 7.12 shows an actual SCSI phase reconnection sequence. At the end of the sequence, the I_T_L nexus is reestablished. Following is a detailed description of the phase sequence shown in Table 7.12:

**Table 7.12: A SCSI Phase Reconnection Sequence**

|     | Phase | BSY | SEL | C/D | I/O | MSG | Data Bus |
| --- | --- | --- | --- | --- | --- | --- | --- |
| (1) | Bus Free | 0 | 0 | X | X | X | X |
| (2) | Arbitration Start | 1 | 0 | 0 | 0 | 0 | Targ SCSI ID |
|     | Arb_win | 1 | 0 | 0 | 0 | 0 | T portion of nexus |
| (3) | Reselection Start | 0 | 1 | X | 1 | X | Both SCSI IDs |
| (4) | Reselection Complete | 1 | 1 | X | 1 | X | I_T nexus |
| (5) | Message In | 1 | 0 | 1 | 1 | 1 | 80h: I_T_L nexus |

1. Bus is free, indicated by the BSY and SEL signals simultaneously not being driven (i.e., false).

2. A device, in this instance a target, arbitrates for the bus by asserting the BSY signal and its own SCSI ID bit on the data bus. The target wins the ARBITRATION phase and proceeds to the RESELECTION phase.

3. The RESELECTION phase is used by the target to reconnect to a previously disconnected initiator. The target starts the RESELECTION phase by driving the SEL, I/O, and its own SCSI ID bit as well as the initiator ID bit it wants to talk to. Next the target waits at least 90 nanoseconds for the signals to start to propagate down the cable. Then the target releases the BSY signal. Because the target is driving the SCSI IDs on the data bus, the initiator can

retrieve the target's ID from the setting of the data bus bits. The target now waits for the initiator to drive the BSY signal or for a time-out condition to occur (i.e., the initiator doesn't drive BSY).

4.  Once the target detects that the initiator has driven BSY, it also drives the BSY signal and releases the SEL signal. Once the initiator detects the target's release of the SEL signal, it releases the BSY signal and the reselection is complete. As a result, the target drives the BSY signal, as it should, because targets are responsible for controlling the I/O process.

5.  The target switches to the MESSAGE IN phase. The Identify message sent from target to initiator tells the initiator the logical unit number of the I/O process. Once the initiator knows the logical unit number, it deduces the I_T_L nexus and then restores its SCSI pointers. Once the SCSI pointers are restored, the I/O process picks up where it left off.

### Tagged Command Queuing

Tagged command queuing is used when an initiator wants to send multiple I/O processes to the same target and logical unit. When tagged command queuing is used in a connection sequence, its protocol is like that found in Table 7.13. Here, a two-byte message (steps 6 and 7) follows the Identify message (step 5). The message consists of the Queue Tag Message (step 6), followed by the Q Tag nexus value. The Q Tag (step 7) value allows up to 256 commands to be queued to the same target–logical unit combination from the same initiator. As mentioned earlier, the nexus is extended to an I_T_L_Q nexus when tagged command queuing is used. A code that designates Ordered, Simple, or Head of Queue command queue type is sent as part of the Queue tag message.

When tagged command queuing is used in a reconnection sequence, its protocol is like that found in Table 7.14, where the two queue messages are used to re-establish the I_T_L_Q nexus upon reconnection (steps 5, 6, and 7).

**Table 7.13: Tagged Command Queuing Protocol in a Connection Sequence**

| | Phase | BSY | SEL | C/D | I/O | MSG | Data Bus |
|---|---|---|---|---|---|---|---|
| (1) | Bus Free   0 | 0 | X | X | X | X | |
| (2) | Arbitration Start | 1 | 0 | 0 | 0 | 0 | Initiator ID on bus |
| | Arb_win | 1 | 0 | 0 | 0 | 0 | I nexus |
| (3) | Selection Start | 0 | 1 | X | 0 | X | Both SCSI IDs on bus |
| (4) | Selection Complete | 1 | 1 | X | 0 | X | I_T nexus |
| (5) | Message Out | 1 | 0 | 1 | 0 | 1 | Identify: I_T_L nexus |
| (6) | Message Out | 1 | 0 | 1 | 0 | 1 | Queue Tag Message |
| (7) | Message Out | 1 | 0 | 1 | 0 | 1 | Q_Tag: I_T_L_Q nexus |

**Table 7.14: Tagged Command Queuing Protocol in a Reconnection Sequence**

| | Phase | BSY | SEL | C/D | I/O | MSG | Data Bus |
|---|---|---|---|---|---|---|---|
| (1) | Bus Free | 0 | 0 | X | X | X | X |
| (2) | Arbitration Start | 1 | 0 | 0 | 0 | 0 | Targ SCSI ID |
| | Arb_win | 1 | 0 | 0 | 0 | 0 | T portion of nexus |
| (3) | Reselection Start | 0 | 1 | X | 1 | X | Both SCSI IDs |
| (4) | Reselection Complete | 1 | 1 | X | 1 | X | I_T nexus |
| (5) | Message In | 1 | 0 | 1 | 1 | 1 | 80h: I_T_L nexus |
| (6) | Message In | 1 | 0 | 1 | 0 | 1 | Queue Tag Message |
| (7) | Message In | 1 | 0 | 1 | 0 | 1 | Q_Tag: I_T_L_Q nexus |

### How Disconnects and Reconnects Work

The sequence diagrams in Figure 7.14 demonstrate how disconnection and reconnection can help increase the number of I/Os per second on the SCSI bus when a target is not ready for an I/O process.

With regard to disconnections and reconnections in general, note that

- Any time the bus is disconnected, any device can start a new I/O process, or the same device can start another I/O process (as in tagged command queuing).

- There is no limit on how many disconnections and reconnections may occur for each I/O process.

- The COMMAND phase occurs only once at the beginning of the I/O process, and the STATUS phase occurs only once at the end of the I/O process.

## Information Transfer Phases

Now that you know about BUS FREE, ARBITRATION, SELECTION, and RESELECTION phases, it's time to learn about the other protocol phases. This section lists all of the information transfer phases that are controlled by the target and are used to transfer real information across the data bus. Before we get into any detail about the information transfer phases though, note that all phase directions (those containing "In" or "Out") are referenced from the initiator's point of view, as shown in Figure 7.15.

The following are descriptions of each of the information transfer phases shown in Figure 7.15 (following the phase order from top to bottom):

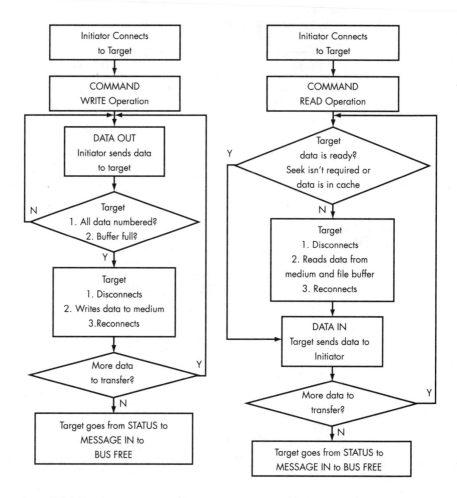

Figure 7.14: How Disconnection and Reconnection Increase I/Os

**COMMAND Phase**

- Allows the target to request command information from the initiator.

- Target asserts C/D, negates I/O and MSG during the REQ/ACK handshake.

**STATUS Phase**

- Allows the target to request that status information be sent to the initiator.

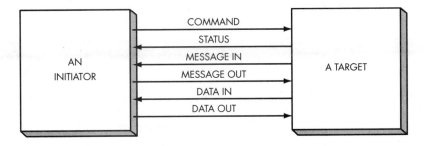

*Figure 7.15: Information Transfer Phases*

- Target asserts C/D, I/O, and negates MSG during the REQ/ACK handshake.

### MESSAGE IN Phase

- Allows the target to request that it send message(s) to the initiator.

- Target asserts C/D, I/O, and MSG during the REQ/ACK handshake.

### MESSAGE OUT Phase

- Allows the target to request that the initiator send it message(s).

- Target invokes this phase in response to the Attention condition from the initiator.

- Target asserts C/D, MSG, and negates I/O during the REQ/ACK handshake.

### DATA IN Phase

- Allows the target to request that it send data to the initiator.

- Target asserts I/O, negates C/D and MSG during the REQ/ACK handshake.

### DATA OUT Phase

- Allows the target to request that the initiator send it data.

- Target negates I/O, C/D, and MSG during the REQ/ACK handshake.

Table 7.15 lists the contents of the data bus and what is responsible for determining the information.

**Table 7.15: Contents of the Data Bus and What Is Responsible for Determining the Information**

| Information Transfer Phase | Contents of Data Bus | Device That Determines Information |
|---|---|---|
| COMMAND | CDB bytes | Initiator |
| DATA IN | Data in byte(s) | Target |
| DATA OUT | Data out byte(s) | Initiator |
| STATUS | Status byte | Target |
| MESSAGE IN | Message in byte(s) | Target |
| MESSAGE OUT | Message out byte(s) | Initiator |

### Characteristics of the Information Transfer Phases

**NOTE** *The information contained in Table 7.16 comes directly from the SCSI standard.*

**Table 7.16: Information Transfer Phases**

| Phase Name | MSG | C/D | I/O | Direction of Transfer | Comment |
|---|---|---|---|---|---|
| DATA OUT | 0 | 0 | 0 | Initiator to target | DATA phase |
| DATA IN | 0 | 0 | 1 | Target to initiator | DATA phase |
| COMMAND | 0 | 1 | 0 | Initiator to target | ——— |
| STATUS | 0 | 1 | 1 | Target to initiator | ——— |
| Reserved for future | 1 | 0 | 0 | ——— | ——— |
| Reserved for future | 1 | 0 | 1 | ——— | ——— |
| MESSAGE OUT | 1 | 1 | 0 | Initiator to target | MESSAGE phase |
| MESSAGE IN | 1 | 1 | 1 | Target to initiator | MESSAGE phase |

The characteristics of the information transfer phases shown in Table 7.16 are the following:

1. As seen in Table 7.16, three bus signals are used to distinguish the different information transfer phases, as follows:

- **MSG**  When negated, this signal says that the bus is not in a MESSAGE phase. When asserted, the bus is in a MESSAGE phase.

- **C/D**  When negated, this signal says that the bus is in a DATA phase. When asserted, the bus is in a COMMAND, STATUS, or MESSAGE phase.

- **I/O**  When negated, this signal says that the direction of transfer is from the initiator to the target. When asserted, the direction of transfer is from the target to the initiator.

2.  The target drives all three of these signals and therefore controls all changes from one information transfer phase to another. Once the target is selected, it is in control of the bus.

3.  The initiator can request a MESSAGE OUT phase by asserting ATN (not shown in table).

4.  The target can cause BUS FREE by releasing MSG, I/O, C/D, and BSY.

5.  During information transfer phases, BSY remains asserted and SEL remains de-asserted.

6.  Information transfer phases use one or more REQ/ACK handshakes to control the transfer of information.

7.  Each REQ/ACK handshake transfers one byte of information (except for wide DATA phase transfers).

8.  The target continuously envelopes the REQ/ACK handshake(s) with the C/D, I/O, and MSG signals so that these signals are valid for a bus settle delay (400 ns) before the assertion of REQ, and they remain valid until the negation of the ACK signal at the end of the handshake of the last transfer of the phase, as shown in Figure 7.16. This is necessary to prevent the initiator from thinking that the current phase has ended.

### MESSAGE Phase and Code Descriptions

Certain interface functions must be managed in order for SCSI to work properly. These functions include error recovery, synchronous negotiations, and the Identify message, which we discussed in the "Connect" section of this chapter.

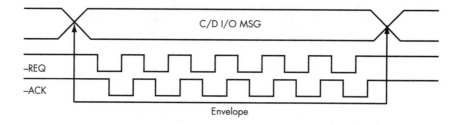

*Figure 7.16: Enveloping the REQ/ACK Handshakes Until the End of the Handshake*

Messages are used to manage the SCSI interface. Some messages are used exclusively by initiators to abort processes, reset devices, clear a target's command queue, or recover from SCSI parity errors. In order for the initiator to get the target to take a message, the initiator must assert the ATN (Attention) signal. (Remember that the target is in control of the I/O process and that the initiator must get the target's attention before it can send a message.) Once the target detects the Attention condition, it switches to the MESSAGE OUT phase and requests the message from the initiator.

Other messages are used exclusively by targets to tell the initiator that the I/O process is completed, ignore invalid data bytes, initiate a recovery procedure, or instruct the host adapter to save, restore, or modify its data pointers. Because the target is in control of the I/O process, it simply switches to the MESSAGE IN phase and requests that the initiator take the message. The initiator can tell the bus is in the MESSAGE IN phase by the state of the C/D, I/O, and MSG signals (as shown in Table 7.16).

Though most messages are a single byte long, some messages are two bytes long and require two consecutive message bytes. Single-byte messages require the transfer of a single message code from one device to another in order to perform one of the single byte message functions (such as Save Data Pointers or Disconnect).

SCSI-land is also populated with messages known as *extended messages.* These are used to negotiate for synchronous and Wide data transfers. Once power-on has completed, the SCSI interface defaults to asynchronous, narrow (8-bit) data transfers. If a device wants to transfer data using either synchronous or Wide data transfer, it must negotiate with the receiving device using an extended message before it can do so.

Probably one of the most important message functions in the SCSI interface is recovery from data bus parity errors. The message system allows two devices to recover and retry the operation without having to involve an upper-level protocol, namely the device driver. Thus, the recovery can be handled by the firmware on each device. Table 7.17 is a complete listing of all message codes by message names.

## Table 7.17: Complete Alphabetical List of All Message Codes

| Code | Support Init | Targ | Message Name | Direction | | Negate ATN Before Last ACK |
|------|------|------|--------------|-----------|-----|-----|
| 06h | O | M | ABORT | | Out | Yes |
| 0Dh* | O | O | ABORT TAG | | Out | Yes |
| 24h• | M | M | ACA TAG | | Out | No |
| 0Ch | O | M | BUS DEVICE RESET | | Out | Yes |
| 16h | M | M | CLEAR ACA | | Out | No |
| 0Eh* | O | O | CLEAR QUEUE | | Out | Yes |
| 00h | M | M | COMMAND COMPLETE | In | | — |
| 12h• | O | O | CONTINUE I/O PROCESS | | Out | Yes |
| 04h | O | O | DISCONNECT | In | | — |
| 04h | O | O | DISCONNECT | | Out | Yes |
| 01h | O | O | EXTENDED MESSAGE | In | Out | Yes |
| 80h+ | M | O | IDENTIFY | In | | — |
| 80h+ | M | M | IDENTIFY | | Out | No |
| 23h* | O | O | IGNORE WIDE RESIDUE (Two Bytes) | In | | — |
| 0Fh* | O | O | INITIATE RECOVERY | In | | — |
| 0Fh* | O | O | INITIATE RECOVERY | | Out | Yes |
| 05h | M | M | INITIATOR DETECTED ERROR | | Out | Yes |
| 0Ah | O | O | LINKED COMMAND COMPLETE | In | | — |
| 0Bh | O | O | LINKED COMMAND COMPLETE (with flag) | In | | |
| 09h | M | M | MESSAGE PARITY ERROR | | Out | Yes |
| 07h | M | M | MESSAGE REJECT | In | Out | Yes |
| *** | O | O | MODIFY DATA POINTER | In | | — |
| 08h | M | M | NO OPERATION | | Out | Yes |
| | | | QUEUE TAG MESSAGES (Two Bytes) | | | |
| 21h* | O | O | HEAD OF QUEUE TAG | | Out | No |
| 22h* | O | O | ORDERED QUEUE TAG | | Out | No |
| 20h* | O | O | SIMPLE QUEUE TAG | In | Out | No |
| 10h* | O | O | RELEASE RECOVERY | | Out | Yes |
| 03h | O | O | RESTORE POINTERS | In | | — |
| 02h | O | O | SAVE DATA POINTER | In | | — |
| *** | O | O | SYNCHRONOUS DATA TRANSFER REQUEST | In | Out | Yes |
| *** * | O | O | WIDE DATA TRANSFER REQUEST | In | Out | Yes |
| 13h | O | O | TARGET TRANSFER DISABLE | | Out | Yes |

| | Support | | | | Negate ATN Before |
|---|---|---|---|---|---|
| Code | Init | Targ | Message Name | Direction | Last ACK |
| 11h* | O | O | TERMINATE I/O PROCESS | Out | Yes |
| 15h | | | Reserved | | |
| 17h-1Fh | | | Reserved | | |
| 24h-2Fh | | | Reserved for two-byte messages | | |
| 30h-7Fh | | | Reserved | | |

*Legend:*

M    Mandatory support

In    Target to initiator

—    Not applicable

Yes    Initiator shall negate ATN before last ACK of message

\*    Messages added in SCSI-2; these messages are reserved in SCSI-1

80h+ Codes 80h through FFh are used for identify message

O    Optional support

Out    Initiator to target

\*\*\*    Extended message

No    Initiator may or may not negate ATN before last ACK of message

•    Messages added in SCSI-3; these messages are reserved in SCSI-2

### Protocol Example of a Synchronous Negotiation

Table 7.18 is a SCSI analyzer display of how messages are used to negotiate for a *synchronous data transfer request* (SDTR) between an initiator and target. The SDTR is established between devices via extended messages. Table 7.18 shows the extended message codes and their descriptions.

We don't expect you to fully comprehend the extended message scenario in Figure 7.18; this display simply shows what an extended message exchange would look like. Now that we've seen how synchronous negotiations are handled, here are the characteristics of synchronous data transfers.

1.  The synchronous negotiation is done only once, usually during initialization, because both devices have the ability to remember if an agreement had been previously established.

2.  Either initiator or target can start the negotiation process. Once the negotiation process is completed successfully, all DATA IN and DATA OUT phases will be synchronous.

3.  An initiator usually starts the negotiation process if the host adapter has a jumper installed or a software switch set to direct the host adapter to initiate the process.

4. A target may start the negotiation process if a jumper is installed or a software switch is set that directs the target to initiate the process.

5. Once an agreement is established, it can be cleared only by the following events:

- Reset, power-on reset, or a **Bus Device Reset** message.

- A re-negotiation between the same initiator and target.

- A Wide Data Transfer Request message sequence.

**Table 7.18: Protocol Example of a Synchronous Negotiation**

| Timing/Description | Phase | Data Bus | | Event # |
|---|---|---|---|---|
| 00.000_000_000 | Bus Free Detected | | | 0000 |
| 26.032_853_700 | Arbitration Start | 7 | | 0001 |
| 26.032_856_100 | Arb_win | 7 | | 0002 |
| 26.033_514_100 | | (Atn Assertion) | ATN | 0003 |
| 26.033_521_700 | Selection Start | 7  4 | ATN | 0004 |
| 26.033_522_600 | Selection Complete | | ATN | 0005 |
| 26.034_161_850 | Message Out | C0 | ATN | 0006 |
| Extended Message | Message Out | 01 | ATN | 0007 |
| Ext. Msg. Length | Message Out | 03  INITIATOR | ATN | 0008 |
| Sync Data Transfer Request | Message Out | 01  MESSAGES | ATN | 0009 |
| Transfer Period 200ns | Message Out | 32 | ATN | 0010 |
| | | (Atn Negate) | | 0011 |
| REQ/ACK Offset | Message Out | 07 | | 0012 |
| Extended Message | Message In | 01 | | 0013 |
| Ext. Msg. Length | Message In | 03  TARGET | | 0014 |
| Sync Data Transfer Request | Message In | 01  MESSAGES | | 0015 |
| Transfer Period 248ns | Message In | 3E | | 0016 |
| REQ/ACK Offset | Message In | 07 | | 0017 |
| 26.039_035_750 | Command Out | 08 00 01 00 01 00 | | 0018 |
| 26.055_860_800 | Data In | 00 00 00 00 00 00 | | 0019 |
| 26.055_862_300 | | 00 00 00 00 00 00 | | 0020 |

| Timing/Description | Phase | Data Bus | Event # |
|---|---|---|---|
| 26.056_494_450 | | 00 00 00 00 | 0021 |
| 26.056_894_350 | Status In | 00 | 0022 |
| 26.057_852_350 | Message In | 00 | 0023 |
| 26.058_426_300 | Bus Free Detected | | 0024 |

### COMMAND Phase and Code Descriptions

A command is executed when an initiator sends a *command descriptor block* (CDB) to the target during the COMMAND phase. Commands tell the target what operation to perform. The following conditions apply to each CDB:

- The first byte of the CDB is always known as the operation code.

- The last byte of the CDB is the control byte.

- The format of the operation code and control byte are identical for every SCSI command in the SCSI universe.

Table 7.19 shows an example of the basic format of a six-byte command (keep in mind, though, that many six-byte SCSI commands will differ dramatically). Here's what's shown in Table 7.19:

### Table 7.19: Basic Six-Byte CDB

| | bit 7 | bit 6 | bit 5 | bit 4 | bit 3 | bit 2 | bit 1 | bit 0 |
|---|---|---|---|---|---|---|---|---|
| byte 0 | Operation Code | | | | | | | |
| byte 1 | Logical unit number* | | | (MSB) | | | | |
| byte 2 | Logical block address (if required) | | | | | | | |
| byte 3 | | | | | | | | (LSB) |
| byte 4 | Transfer length (if required) | | | | | | | |
| byte 5 | Control byte | | | | | | | |

*Reserved in SCSI-3*

- **Operation Code**. This field tells the target how long the CDB will be and what operation the initiator wants the target to perform.

- **Logical Unit Number**. Although used in SCSI-1, this field is almost never used today, because the LUN is now determined in the Identify message.

- **Logical Block Address**. This field tells the target where the information is located on the physical medium. Logical blocks start at 0 and are contiguous to the last block location on the device's medium. Blocks, measured in bytes, are the smallest unit of measurement on a device, with a typical block size measuring 512 bytes on a hard disk. CD-ROMs have several different block sizes in the vicinity of 2K, 2048 and 2352 being the most common. It should be noted that many SCSI devices can change their logical block size. For example, if a MODE SELECT that sets the logical block size to 512 bytes is sent to a CD-ROM drive with media that has 2048 byte blocks, a future READ command asking for block 3 will return the last 512 bytes in the first physical 2048 byte block on the media, rather than the entire fourth 2048 byte block as would have happened had the MODE SELECT not been issued.

- **Transfer Length**. This field tells the target how much data to transfer, usually as an amount of blocks, with 512 bytes to each block of data. Some devices, like tape, may be able to store any number of bytes, from 1 to the maximum size of the device.

- **Control Byte**. This field is used for special operations like command linking, and it also has some bits that can be used for vendor-unique operations.

Sometimes all the information required to perform an operation cannot be squeezed into a six-byte command, and SCSI has a cure for this. The solution

**Table 7.20: Basic Ten-Byte CDB**

|        | bit 7 | bit 6 | bit 5 | bit 4 | bit 3 | bit 2 | bit 1 | bit 0 |
|--------|-------|-------|-------|-------|-------|-------|-------|-------|
| byte 0 | Operation Code ||||||||
| byte 1 | Logical unit number* ||| Reserved |||||
| byte 2 | (MSB) |||||||  |
| byte 3 | Logical block address (if required) ||||||||
| byte 4 |  |||||||  |
| byte 5 |  |||||||  (LSB) |
| byte 6 | Reserved ||||||||
| byte 7 | (MSB) | Transfer length (if required) |||||| |
| byte 8 |  |||||||  (LSB) |
| byte 9 | Control byte ||||||||

*Reserved in SCSI-3*

is to allow commands to also come in 10-, 12-, and 16-byte formats. (The 16-byte format was added in SCSI-3.) As you can see in Table 7.20 and Table 7.21, the 10-byte and 12-byte CDBs allow the initiator to address a higher logical block and transfer more blocks with a single CDB.

Some devices support different CDB sizes and others may only support six-byte CDBs. This information must be known by the device driver before it can properly format the CDBs it sends to the target. SCSI has specific commands to find out this information, which can determine the block size of the device, the maximum logical block address available, the type of device (e.g., disk or tape), and all other operational parameters that the device driver requires. Table 7.22 lists all the operation codes for the device type known as direct access (disk), which should give you an idea of the types of operations that a disk can perform. We have shown only the operation code (the first byte) of the CDB. Each command will have a specific format of all remaining bytes. It is beyond the scope of this book to completely define all the commands for all device types. If you will be writing a SCSI device driver, you will need a copy of the ANSI standard (SCSI-2 or -3) applicable to the device you're working with. Refer to the SCSI FAQ list on the accompanying CD-ROM or at http://www.scsifaq.org/ to find out how to get the standards documents.

### Table 7.21: Basic Twelve-Byte CDB

| | bit 7 | bit 6 | bit 5 | bit 4 | bit 3 | bit 2 | bit 1 | bit 0 |
|---|---|---|---|---|---|---|---|---|
| byte 0 | Operation Code | | | | | | | |
| byte 1 | Logical unit number* | | | Reserved | | | | |
| byte 2 | (MSB) | | | | | | | |
| byte 3 | Logical block address (if required) | | | | | | | |
| byte 4 | | | | | | | | |
| byte 5 | | | | | | | | (LSB) |
| byte 6 | (MSB) | | | | | | | |
| byte 7 | Transfer length (if required) | | | | | | | |
| byte 8 | | | | | | | | |
| byte 9 | | | | | | | | (LSB) |
| byte 10 | Reserved | | | | | | | |
| byte 11 | Control byte | | | | | | | |

*Reserved in SCSI-3

## Table 7.22: Direct-Access Devices Commands (Numerical Order)

| Operation Code | Command Name | Type |
|---|---|---|
| 00h | Test Unit Ready | M |
| 01h | Re-zero Unit | O |
| 03h | Request Sense | M |
| 04h | Format Unit | M |
| 07h | Re-assign Blocks | O |
| 08h | Read(6) | M |
| 0Ah | Write(6) | M |
| 0Bh | Seek(6) | O |
| 12h | Inquiry | M |
| 15h | Mode Select(6) | O |
| 16h | Reserve | M |
| 17h | Release | M |
| 18h | Copy | O |
| 1Ah | Mode Sense(6) | O |
| 1Bh | Start/Stop Unit | O |
| 1Ch | Receive Diagnostic Results | O |
| 1Dh | Send Diagnostic | M |
| 1Eh | Prevent/Allow Medium Removal | O |
| 25h | Read Capacity | M |
| 28h | Read(10) | M |
| 2Ah | Write(10) | M |
| 2Bh | Seek(10) | O |
| 2Eh | Write and Verify | O |
| 2Fh | Verify | O |
| 30h | Search Data High | O |
| 31h | Search Data Equal | O |
| 32h | Search Data Low | O |
| 33h | Set Limits | O |
| 34h | Pre-fetch | O |
| 35h | Synchronize Cache | O |
| 36h | Lock/unlock Cache | O |
| 37h | Read Defect Data | O |
| 39h | Compare | O |
| 3Ah | Copy and Verify | O |
| 3Bh | Write Buffer | O |
| 3Ch | Read Buffer | O |
| 3Eh | Read Long | O |

| Operation Code | Command Name | Type |
|---|---|---|
| 3Fh | Write Long | O |
| 40h | Change Definition | O |
| 41h | Write Same | O |
| 4Ch | Log Select | O |
| 4Dh | Log Sense | O |
| 55h | Mode Select(10) | O |
| 5Ah | Mode Sense(10) | O |

*Legend*:

M   Command implementation is mandatory.

O   Command implementation is optional.

## Status

This section explains when a status is sent and describes the status byte's format and codes. A single status byte is sent from the target to the initiator during the STATUS phase at the completion of each command, unless the command is terminated by one of the following events:

- An Abort message

- An Abort Tag message

- A Bus Device Reset message

- A Clear Queue message

- A hard reset condition

- An unexpected disconnect

The STATUS phase normally occurs at the end of an I/O process. Some status codes, like 00 = good, are easy to comprehend, whereas others, like the 02 code—which says that a CHECK CONDITION has occurred—are more difficult. (CHECK CONDITION is an error condition discussed in more detail below.) The status byte format and status byte code are shown in Tables 7.23 and 7.24, respectively.

**Table 7.23: Status Byte Format**

| bit 7 | bit 6 | bit 5 | bit 4 | bit 3 | bit 2 | bit 1 | bit 0 |
|---|---|---|---|---|---|---|---|
| Reserved | | Status byte code | | | | | Reserved |

**Table 7.24: Status Byte Codes**

| Status | Hex | Description |
|---|---|---|
| GOOD | 00 | Target has successfully completed the command. |
| CHECK CONDITION | 02 | An error or alert condition has occurred. |
| CONDITION MET | 04 | Requested operation is satisfied. |
| BUSY | 08 | The target is busy. Returned whenever a target is unable to accept a command from an otherwise acceptable initiator. |
| INTERMEDIATE | 10 | Returned for every successfully completed command in a series of linked commands (except for the last command). |
| INTERMEDIATE CONDITION MET | 14 | Combination of condition met and intermediate status. |
| RESERVATION CONFLICT | 18 | The logical unit or a portion of it is reserved for use by another initiator. |
| COMMAND TERMINATED | 22 | Target terminated current I/O process. This also indicates that a CHECK CONDITION has occurred. |
| QUEUE FULL* or TASK SET FULL** | 28 | Implemented if tagged command queuing is supported. Indicates that the target cannot accept any more commands. |
| ACA ACTIVE*** | 30 | Indicates that an Auto-Contingent Allegiance condition exists. |
| All other codes | | Reserved |

*Legend*:

*     New in SCSI-2
**    New name in SCSI-3
***   New in SCSI-3 (SAM)

# Check Condition

The CHECK CONDITION status, one of the most important, is also the status that a SCSI device driver will spend most of its code handling. In general, CHECK CONDITION status indicates that an error of some kind has occurred. To find out what type of error it is, the device driver must look at the SENSE DATA. Depending on the operating system and I/O subsystem involved, the

SENSE DATA may already be stored in the AUTOSENSE buffer, or the driver may have to issue a REQUEST SENSE command to get it.

## Contingent Allegiance Condition

A situation called "Contingent Allegiance Condition" occurs after a target returns CHECK CONDITION or COMMAND TERMINATED status. When in this condition the target must retain the SENSE DATA describing the error until one of the following occurs:

- a BUS RESET is issued

- the initiator issues a BUS DEVICE RESET

- the initiator issues an ABORT message

- the initiator issues another command (usually a REQUEST SENSE) to the target

If the target issues an INITIATE RECOVERY message, the condition is now known as extended contingent allegiance. Once in this state, the target will preserve the SENSE DATA until it receives a BUS DEVICE RESET or RELEASE RECOVERY message, or a BUS RESET occurs.

In SCSI-3 the ACA state is retained until an explicit CLEAR ACA message is received from the initiator that caused the ACA to occur. A BUS RESET will also do it.

If the NACA bit in the control byte of the CDB is set, the target will follow SCSI-3 rules; if the NACA bit isn't set, the target will follow SCSI-2 rules.

The change was deemed necessary because with the new serial SCSI buses (like Fibre Channel), several commands can be "floating around" at the time the Contingent Allegiance occurs.

## Handshaking of Information

In the previous section, we talked about how to determine which phase the bus is in. Now we'll explain how information is transferred. Handshaking is the term SCSI gurus use when they speak of transferring information across the data bus. Handshaking the information ensures that data on the bus is properly latched into the receiving device.

In Chapter 3, we told you a bit about asynchronous and synchronous transfer. These are the two methods of handshaking information. We'll take you beyond a basic understanding of these concepts in the paragraphs that follow.

*COMMAND, MESSAGE, and STATUS information can only be transferred via the asynchronous handshake method, whereas the DATA phase is the only phase that can transfer information using either the asynchronous or synchronous handshake method.*

### Asynchronous Handshake Method

*Asynchronous transfer* is characterized by the transfer of one byte of data via the following four-step process:

1. The target asserts the REQ signal.

2. The initiator asserts the ACK signal.

3. The target negates the REQ signal.

4. The initiator negates the ACK signal.

Asynchronous handshaking is shown in the diagram in Figure 7.17.

*During asynchronous transfer, the following rules apply: The ACK signal can't assert until the REQ asserts; the REQ signal can't negate until the ACK signal asserts; the ACK signal can't negate until the REQ negates.*

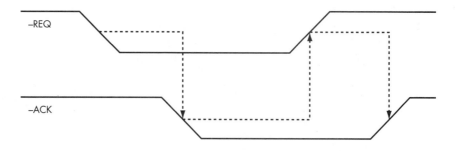

*Figure 7.17: The Four Steps of Asynchronous Transfer*

The name "asynchronous transfer" stems from the fact that this transfer method is not dependent upon any uniform timing. Asynchronous transfer rates range from 2 MB to 6 MB per second, because asynchronous data transfer is subject to a number of delays, including cable propagation delays; internal device delays between receiving a signal and responding to that signal; de-skew delays; and cable skew delays. These latter delays occur because the REQ and ACK pulses must interlock with one another and because handshake must occur for each byte of data transferred. The skew delays are required in order to compensate for small differences in the lengths of the conductors in the bus (yes, really).

### Synchronous Handshake Method

*Synchronous transfers* allow devices to transfer data more quickly. This is accomplished by allowing the target to request that the initiator either send or receive data before the initiator has to acknowledge the target's request. It is all done in hardware (thank goodness!), so you don't need to worry about it.

That's the simple explanation. Now for the more technical, detailed explanation, which sometimes takes half an hour to explain to a roomful of people during a training session.

The synchronous handshake method is optional and must be negotiated for between a target and an initiator. Synchronous transfer depends on uniform, or synchronous, timing, hence its name. The objective behind synchronous transfers is to minimize the effect of cable and device delays. Although these delays cannot be eliminated entirely, their effects can be minimized.

Synchronous handshaking can support rates of up to 10 million transfers/sec when the Fast-10 SCSI option is implemented (or 20 MHz for Fast-20, or 40 MHz for Fast-40). Synchronous protocol minimizes the effects of cable and device delays, because the REQ and ACK pulses do not have a one-to-one interlock. Synchronous transfer is commonly referred to as offset interlock.

In order to transfer one byte of data (or up to four bytes if a Wide32 transfer) via synchronous handshaking, the process is the following:

1. A REQ/ACK offset is used to establish a pacing mechanism. During the synchronous data transfer, the REQ and ACK signals are issued independent of one another. The specified offset indicates how far ahead the sender is allowed to get without seeing an ACK. At the end of the DATA phase, each device checks to ensure that the number of REQ (or ACK) pulses sent is equal to the number of ACK (or REQ) pulses received.

2. The initiator and target form a transfer period from the leading edge of a REQ/ACK signal to the leading edge of the next REQ/ACK signal. During the data transfer, the edges of the REQ and ACK signals are used to latch the information on the data bus into the receiving device. These pulses are asserted and negated for a uniform amount of time and form a transfer period from the leading edge of one pulse to the leading edge of the next in the pulse train. The width of this period dictates the speed at which data can be transferred across the bus.

If any of the foregoing makes sense to you, you're doing great. The timing diagram in Figure 7.18 may help you understand the technical side of synchronous transfers.

**NOTE** *It takes special hardware (including special ICs cables and terminators) to achieve Fast synchronous transfer rates. Other restrictions on cable length may also affect your configuration. Fast synchronous transfers are usually implemented on higher-end systems and workstations. You should be careful if you are going to use the single-ended interface option and Fast transfers, because the signal quality decreases as the cable length increases. Always make sure that the cable length does not exceed the maximum allowed for the speed selected (See Table 3.3).*

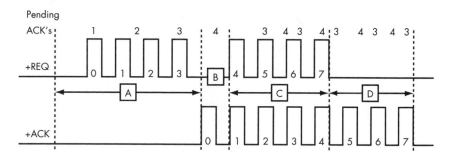

*Figure 7.18: Synchronous Offset Timing Diagram*

### Synchronous Offset Timing Diagram

Figure 7.18 demonstrates how the synchronous offset works. The "Pending ACKs" represent the number of acknowledgments that an initiator must send to the target to complete the synchronous transfer successfully.

Here's what's happening in the diagram in Figure 7.18, following along step by step, letter by letter:

A  A target issues four REQ pulses (because an offset count of four was agreed upon between the initiator and target), then the offset state machine logic in the target puts a hold on further data transfers until an ACK pulse is received from the initiator.

B  The initiator issues an ACK pulse, thereby allowing the REQ generator on the target to issue a REQ pulse. After this occurs, the REQ and ACK generators are free to issue REQ and ACK pulses independent of one another unless the data FIFOs (First In First Out memory) are full, empty, or the offset count is exceeded.

C    This represents the data transfer area. The REQ and ACK pulses form a transfer period that both the initiator and target agreed upon long before data was transferred.

D    Eventually the ACK pulses sent by the initiator must equal the REQ pulses sent by the target. Because the first ACK pulse was received at the beginning of the transfer, three more must be sent to "clean house" and complete the transfer.

## Ever Onward and Upward!

Have you had enough hardware for a while? OK, the next chapter will start to show that there's more to SCSI than the hardware. Device drivers are every bit as important!

# 8

## UNDERSTANDING DEVICE DRIVERS

There are all kinds of drivers—truck drivers, bus drivers, pile drivers, screw drivers, and many other worthy examples—but we're here to talk about device drivers.

A *device driver* is a piece of software that bridges the gap between an operating system and the computer hardware. We are going to focus on drivers that control SCSI hardware, but drivers are needed for every part of the computer except the CPU and memory. This chapter won't tell you enough to write your own drivers but will, hopefully, give you some insight into how they are structured and what functions they perform. Armed with this information, you should be better able to select the drivers you need and isolate any problems that may come up.

### In the Beginning . . .

When SCSI was first being introduced to PCs (about 1986), each host adapter manufacturer provided device drivers that supported hard disks attached to their adapter.

When CD-ROMs came on the scene, manufacturers needed to support those as well. But what if you wanted to buy a hard disk from vendor X and a CD-ROM from vendor Y? At first manufacturers tried to provide a large matrix of drivers that would cover as many combinations of devices as possible on their host adapter. They quickly (well, after about two years) realized that this was not practical and took a different approach: They divided device driver functionality into layers with standardized interfaces between the layers. This was a very important step.

Initially, each vendor defined their own interfaces, but Adaptec's ASPI interface soon emerged as the most popular choice, and the others fell by the wayside. Now it was possible to buy a device from vendor X, who would provide an ASPI (Advanced SCSI Programming Interface)-compatible driver with the device, and this driver could pass SCSI commands down to a host adapter driver layer made by vendor Y!

## The PC BIOS

Every PC contains a collection of I/O routines contained in a ROM (actually, flash RAM these days). This collection of routines is called the *BIOS*, which stands for basic input/output system. It enables the operating system code to be loaded from disk (booting), and it initializes the various chips in the system.

BIOS calls are made via software interrupts like INT 13hex (for disk-related I/O), INT 14 hex (for serial port I/O), or a whole bunch of others (each of which have their own special purpose). The BIOS routines are very simple and don't allow multiple programs to access them simultaneously (they're single-threaded). This was fine for MSDOS, because it had the same limitations. The PC BIOS on the motherboard knows how to handle only devices that are on the motherboard itself. However, IBM was farsighted enough, when defining the original PC/AT BIOS, to allow for the possibility of BIOS extensions being located on option cards. During system initialization, the motherboard BIOS looks at specific memory locations for a "BIOS extension signature" of 55AA hex. If it finds this pattern at the right location, it executes the extension at its entry point. This allows the option card BIOS to wedge itself into the interrupt it extends (INT 13hex, for example) adding its own new functionality.

The Int13 hex BIOS functions (FORMAT, READ, WRITE, etc.) provide low-level (bypassing the filesystem) access to disk devices (both floppy and hard). The parameters to these functions are in terms of CYLINDER, HEAD, and SECTOR.

## MSDOS Drivers

MSDOS is a very simple operating system. One thing to remember in MSDOS is that only one thing is going on at a time. When one I/O is started, nothing else happens until that I/O is completed. I/O is done in several different ways. I/O to very simple devices, like the keyboard, is done directly via the BIOS. If your system contains a device that is not supported by the BIOS, for example a SCSI host adapter, it must have a device driver loaded into RAM to control and provide access to it. Device drivers are loaded via a configuration file called CONFIG.SYS.

An example of one entry in such a CONFIG.SYS file would be

```
Device = c:\aspi4dos.sys /d
```

During the boot process, this line tells MSDOS to load a driver into memory and execute that driver's init routine.

This particular driver (ASPI4DOS) initializes and controls a particular type of SCSI host adapter. The next line in CONFIG.SYS might look like

```
device = c:\aspidisk.sys
```

This loads another device driver that is responsible for creating SCSI CDBs (Command Data Blocks) that will read or write the desired data to and from a SCSI disk drive. This second driver can send these CDBs to the SCSI host adapter via the ASPI interface created by the driver loaded previously (ASPI4DOS). This division of responsibility is a very important feature of device drivers, because it allows a disk from one vendor to be attached to a host adapter manufactured by a different vendor. During boot, ASPIDISK tells MSDOS how many disk drives it will support, and MSDOS assigns a drive number (80 hex through 83 hex, or in some cases 80 hex through 8F hex). These numbers are used by the BIOS to select a particular disk. If there are more than four drives, the ones beyond that cannot be accessed by the BIOS.

Each MSDOS driver has an attribute word, which indicates what type of device it supports, and two main entry points: Strategy and Interrupt. The idea was for the Strategy routine to set up an I/O transfer and the Interrupt routine to complete it. But it doesn't really matter which does what, because MSDOS just calls one then the other. The parameters to these routines are passed in the CPU registers. A set of nineteen command codes cause the driver to perform the desired operation. Some examples of the command codes are INIT, OPEN, CLOSE, INPUT, OUTPUT, IOCTL, and CHECK MEDIA. The driver interface is loosely modeled after UNIX drivers, but the similarity is purely superficial.

## Windows 3.x Drivers

Windows 3.x is really just a graphical shell running on top of MSDOS. Hence, regular MSDOS device drivers do most of the I/O under Windows 3.x. This also means that Windows 3.x doesn't do much in the way of multitasking. Applications may "give up control" for a while to let another application run, but in general, this doesn't work very smoothly.

There are also 32-bit virtual device drivers for Windows 3.x that enhance performance by operating in 32-bit mode, instead of 16-bit mode like the rest of Windows 3.x. ASPI in this environment consists of a DOS driver for the host adapter and a .vxd (virtual device driver) that handles translation from the virtual addresses used by Windows programs and the real mode addresses used by the MSDOS drivers. Also, a .dll (dynamic link library) is included that allows applications to access the driver by providing entry points that are callable from Windows programs.

A *VxD* is a special code module similar to a .dll that has a single entry point via its *device descriptor block,* or DDB. Through this single entry point, many logical entry points can be called. Some examples are event notification, virtual 86 mode services, and protected mode services. One unique thing about VxDs is that they run entirely in 386 enhanced mode with a flat memory model and not the segment:offset model used in much of the rest of Windows 3.x. A VxD is responsible for making the cooperative multitasking used in Windows 3.x work acceptably well. If not well thought out, one bad VxD can make the whole system function poorly. Another important function of a VxD is to translate the virtual addresses used by application programs into physical addresses needed to actually "touch" the hardware device.

## Windows 95/98 Drivers

Windows 95 was designed to be more of a "real" operating system, in that it contains its own device drivers and operates completely in 32-bit protected mode. It also provides true pre-emptive multitasking, which means that CPU time is divided up by the virtual machine manager (VMM32.VXD) and not by applications giving up the CPU as in Windows 3.x. Windows 98 is not a major leap forward, but it added some niceties like support for *USB* (Universal Serial Bus) devices and a *UDF* (Universal Data Format) filesystem for DVD support. A little spit and polish was put into the user interface, too.

One of the most important things about Windows 95/98 is that each application runs in its own "virtual machine." This protects each application from the transgressions of others. This also means that all devices must be virtualized. That is, when each application performs I/O to a particular device, that I/O doesn't directly affect the hardware. The VMM maintains a copy of what needs to be done to the hardware based on what each application is trying to do, and the VMM actually touches the hardware to make it happen.

Windows 95/98 uses two types of drivers: *.vxd* (virtual device drivers, explained above) and *.MPD* (miniport drivers). Miniport drivers are the lowest level of drivers in Windows 95/98. Above the miniport driver is a Microsoft-provided layer called the "SCSI'izer" ("SKUZ-ee-eye-zer"). There is a SCSI'izer for each type of SCSI device (disk, tape, CD-ROM, and so on). Above the SCSI'izer layer is another layer called the type-specific driver or TSD (also one TSD for each type of device). Like Windows 3.*x* 32-bit drivers, Windows 95 drivers are .vxd files. Note that, because of the way Windows 95/98 breaks down I/O requests into smaller requests, it doesn't use SCSI as efficiently as Windows NT does.

Another interesting thing about Windows 95/98 is that it can use MSDOS real mode drivers if necessary. This is not desirable if a Windows 95 driver can be found for your device, but it is a way to use older devices that are not supported under Windows 95/98.

## Windows NT Drivers

Windows NT is considerably more sophisticated than Windows 95/98. In addition to providing true multitasking, it is also multi-threaded. This means that not only can multiple applications run simultaneously, but multiple sub-processes within those applications can also be running simultaneously. NT is also extremely modular. Each portion of the kernel has well-defined inter-faces so that any one can be replaced without breaking the system (at least in theory). There are two basic "flavors" of NT: server and workstation. The two are very similar and for our purposes here we won't worry about the differences. In fact, much to Microsoft's chagrin, some users have found that the only real difference is a few registry key values and a few additional utilities. NT applications make requests to the WIN32 subsystem, which passes them on to the I/O Manager. The NT I/O Manager subsystem creates I/O request packets (IRPs) and passes those to a filesystem driver or possibly directly to a class driver. The class then builds a SCSI request block (SRB) and passes it to the SCSIport driver.

Windows NT uses Miniport drivers just like Windows 95/98. In fact, when Windows 95 was first being developed, Microsoft realized that they needed a new type of driver to accommodate the needs of a 32-bit operating system. Given that the drivers for Windows NT filled the bill, they adopted the Miniport Driver Model. If only they had also adopted some of the other driver layers from NT, things would be a lot simpler now! In my opinion, one of the major things preventing NT from catching on faster is the lack of suitable device drivers for many devices. When building a system to run NT, you need to be careful to select hardware that is supported by NT drivers. Many devices, especially low-end stuff, don't include drivers for NT, which can be a particularly big problem with laptops, because individual devices within the computer aren't separately replaceable. Miniport drivers initialize the host adapter, send command requests to the adapter, handle interrupts, and perform all the other babysitting that the SCSI hardware requires.

The next layer above the Miniport driver is the SCSIPort driver. The SCSIPort driver is the equivalent of the CAM XPT. It acts as a single entry point for all the SCSI requests generated by the class drivers.

**NOTE**  *CAM XPT is the transport function of the ANSI Common Access Method SCSI driver architecture defined in the T10/792-M specification. See ftp://ftp.t10.org/t10/drafts/cam/cam-r12b.pdf.*

The disk class driver gets requests from the filesystem and builds disk requests to send down to the SCSI class driver. The SCSIPort driver takes these system I/O requests, translates them into SCSI CDBs, and sends them down to the specified miniport adapter driver.

A tape class driver, also included with Windows NT, performs a translation from sequential (rather than random) system I/O requests into a form that is acceptable to the SCSIPort driver.

Although it's not included as part of the operating system, an ASPI class driver is also available for Windows NT. This separate driver accepts ASPI requests from an application (like an image scanner utility, for example) and converts it into SCSIPort driver requests.

As you can see, ASPI is not the native SCSI subsystem in any of the Windows operating systems, but is layered on top to provide compatibility with existing applications.

## UNIX Drivers

There are many flavors of UNIX. To keep things simple, I'm going to discuss UNIX drivers in general enough terms that it won't matter much exactly which UNIX I'm talking about. UNIX application programs are protected from each other by a portion of the operating system called the kernel. Applications run at user privilege level, and the kernel runs at system privilege level. UNIX applications cannot access system hardware directly; they can only talk to the kernel. To perform I/O applications, users must call device drivers via the kernel.

UNIX device drivers come in two basic types, character and block. Character drivers are used for devices like keyboards, serial ports, parallel ports, and really, almost anything except disks. Disk drivers are always block-type drivers.

Character drivers have at least the following entry points:

- Init

- Open

- Close

- Read

- Write

- Ioctl

Block drivers have these entry points:

- Init

- Open

- Close

- Strategy

These entry points are an application program's only way to access the device directly. When I refer to these entry points (which are actually C language functions [subroutines]) I will use the notation "foo()" which would be formally read as "The function named foo." Each device driver has a *device special file* (usually in the /dev directory). The purpose of these special files is to allow applications to communicate with the desired driver. Associated with each special file is a major number and minor number. The major number provides a way for the kernel to know where the driver's entry points are. It's an index into a kernel table called the *devswitch table,* which has pointers to each of the above-mentioned entry points.

The minor number can be used in any way desired by the driver writer, most often to specify parameters to the driver. For example, SCSI drivers often use the minor number to specify the bus, target, and LUN that the user is referring to.

For disk access, most applications will simply make operating system calls to read data from a file. The filesystem code within the UNIX kernel will figure out which driver supports the disk where the requested data is stored.

Because this is a book about SCSI, allow me to explain the typical UNIX method of handling SCSI commands. For the sake of example, let's assume that four requests come in via the filesystem. As each process makes its request, the filesystem figures out what disk that data is on and opens that device special file. The minor number decodes to a particular bus/target/LUN nexus. Each open() creates an instance of the responding driver's strategy() routine. The strategy routine creates a SCSI CDB that requests the data be read from the particular SCSI device. These CDBs are queued to the SCSI host adapter by a lower layer (the *SIM* [SCSI Interface Module] in CAM systems).

When the first command is sent to the disk, the disk will look at the block being requested. If the block is not one that's in the device's buffer cache, the device will disconnect from the bus and start the heads seeking to that block. The host adapter, seeing that the bus is now free, will get the next command in the queue and select the proper device to send it to. Let's say the next command targets a different device from the first. That second device is available to take the command, and it does the same as the first (looks at the block, checks its own buffer, and perhaps disconnects from the bus while it seeks the data). This continues for all four disks. Remember that disk seek times are still quite slow relative to the CPU, so all four commands will likely be sent to the disks before any data is ready to be transferred.

The disk that finds its data first will reconnect to the initiator. This tells the host adapter to find the request for that drive in its queue, set up the DMA for the data, and turn control over to the hardware. That data will transfer and the command will complete.

Immediately, the next drive that finds the requested data will reconnect to the initiator and do the same thing and so on until all the requests are satisfied. So, the arms on each disk may all be seeking at the same time, but the bus can only be doing one thing at a time. The goal is to fully utilize every cycle of the bus, and SCSI allows that to be done very efficiently. Of course, this also depends upon the device drivers doing things cleverly — which is why Win95/98 systems may not take full advantage of SCSI. Windows NT is much more efficient.

IDE is not capable of this type of overlapping, however. Once the first drive is told to get the data, that drive has the bus until it finds and transfers the data. Then the next command is sent, and so on — each drive remaining on the bus until the data is transferred. Also, only two disks are allowed per bus. No overlapping is possible.

## Enough Already!

I realize this wasn't an in-depth description of device drivers (even though I'm equally sure it was more than some of you wanted to read), but I hope it left you with a better understanding of how important device drivers are, as part of a SCSI subsystem. Without them, all that fancy hardware just sits there!

# 9

## PERFORMANCE TUNING YOUR SCSI SUBSYSTEM

 SCSI has become the interface of choice for high-performance storage subsystems, and for good reason! The original SCSI specification envisioned transfer rates of up to 5 MHz. The SCSI-2 specification allows faster rates of up to 10 MHz. And now SCSI-3 allows operation at 40 MHz! However, by pushing these original SCSI standards to their limits, system integrators have seen reliability problems mount.

A number of factors contribute to delivering the highest SCSI bus performance:

The four factors that most *directly* affect SCSI performance are:

- Selection of the fastest devices in the price range you can afford

- Selection of the most appropriate host adapter for the chosen devices

- Isolation of slower devices onto buses (or bus segments) of their own

- Setting all device parameters correctly

These factors can *indirectly* affect SCSI performance by causing errors, which then result in retries, and lost performance:

- Cable type, quality, and length

- Use of proper terminators

- Terminator power quality

- Connector adapter quality

The optimization process actually starts before you even buy the hardware. You need to think about what peripherals you want to attach and how much room for expansion you want to allow for later on.

To a large degree, the performance you get will be directly related to how much you spend. The amount of bus bandwidth you need depends upon how many devices you will attach and how fast each of them is. For example, if you want two fast hard disks that can each transfer data at 20 MB/sec, you need at least a Fast-20 Wide host adapter. Even in this case, the host adapter will be maxed out during heavy I/O. This setup also lacks headroom for other devices on the bus, so you might opt for a Fast-40 LVD (also called Ultra-2 Wide or U2W) host adapter, and LVD drives, so that you'll be able to add other devices without slowing things down.

However, even before optimizing your system hardware, you should first take care of the indirect factors listed above. Before you can speed things up, they need to operate as free from error as possible, because the very act of increasing the performance will most likely also increase the error rate unless everything is perfect in cable- and terminator-land.

The dilemma is that signal quality problems, which have been present from the start, become more apparent as buses become more heavily loaded and are operated at faster data rates.

The SCSI electrical specification has several transceiver specifications:

1. Differential RS-485 transceivers that allow for up to 10 MHz data transfer at a maximum cable length of 25 meters (82 feet).

2. Single-ended TTL transceivers, which allow

   - Synchronous data transfer of up to 5 MHz at a maximum cable length of 6 meters (20 feet).

   - Fast-10 synchronous data transfer up to 10 MHz at a maximum cable length of 3 meters (10 feet).

- Fast-20 synchronous data transfer up to 20 MHz at a maximum cable length of 1.5 meters (5 feet).

- Asynchronous data transfer (no maximum transfer rate is given, but typical rates are about 1.5 MHz to 2 MHz) at a maximum cable length of 6 meters (20 feet).

3. Low voltage differential (LVD) transceivers that allow synchronous operation at up to 40 MHz (soon up to 80 MHz) with up to 12 meters (about 39 feet) of cable.

Each transfer may consist of one, two, or four bytes, depending on the bus width option implemented. Today, though most implementations utilize 16-bit Wide data for hard disks, most other device types are only 8 bits (narrow). At this writing, at least one 16-bit Wide CD-ROM drive is available.

When 10 MHz Fast SCSI was first proposed, only differential SCSI transceivers were envisioned. However, many drive manufacturers have chosen to implement Fast SCSI with single-ended drivers because of savings in cost, size, and power consumption. This presents several problems to integrators, especially as systems increase in speed and size. A very common symptom of an unreliable single-ended interface is bus errors following the addition of devices or cabling to the system. The failures increase as the number of devices and length of the cable grow. The failures are also unpredictable and are not necessarily the same from system to system.

Most data reliability problems stem from signal reflections and noise that are read by SCSI receivers as incorrect data or false SCSI bus phases. The SCSI cable is a transmission line that has a characteristic impedance whose value depends upon the type of cable used. Discontinuities in this impedance can cause signal reflections to occur. These impedance variations can be the result of extra capacitance due to any or all of the following; chips internal to SCSI devices, connectors, improper terminators, mixing of different cable types, cable stubs, and so on. At Fast-10 SCSI rates, these reflections are much more prevalent than at the slower 5 MHz SCSI rates. Additional noise picked up from external devices, as well as from other signals on the SCSI cable, can add to these false signals. Unfortunately, a 10 MHz Fast SCSI bus is a more efficient transmitter of noise than a slower 5 MHz SCSI bus. In general, most systems become more prone to noise problems as clock speeds increase.

A carefully configured, single-ended SCSI bus can reliably transfer data at 10 MHz without a problem. However, good engineering practices should be followed in order to guarantee success:

**Use the shortest cable length possible.** The SCSI-3 SPI working group recommends that, for 10 MHz data transfers, the total cable length should not exceed 3 meters (10 feet).

**Avoid stub clustering.** Space SCSI devices on the cable *at least* 0.3 meter (12 inches) apart. When devices are clustered closely together on the SCSI cable, their capacitances add together to create an impedance discontinuity and thus reflections.

**Cable stub length should not exceed 0.1 meter (4 inches).** Some SCSI devices may create stubs internal to the device that exceed this value, resulting in excessive capacitive loading and signal reflections. This parameter is under the control of the SCSI device (e.g., tape drive or disk drive) manufacturer. The SCSI cabling itself should include no stubs.

**Watch out for capacitance.** As devices are added to a SCSI bus, capacitance is introduced to each signal from the connectors, receivers, and PC board traces. The SCSI-2 specification limits this capacitance to 25pF; this number will probably be lowered to 20pF in SCSI-3. The reason for this limit is that the added capacitance lowers the impedance of the section of cable to which these devices are added as well as adding delay. Both of these effects can be highly detrimental to a Fast SCSI bus. Look for input filters that may be attached to the SCSI front end of the printed circuit board. These filters add capacitance which as we've seen isn't a good thing on SCSI buses.

**Avoid connector adapters.** They are just another source of capacitance and signal degradation.

**Route cable with care.** Avoid practices such as rolling the cable up on itself, running the cable alongside metal for long lengths, or routing the cable past noise generators (such as power supplies). Placing the cable near ground planes created by grounded metal cabinetry reduces its impedance. For example, the free air impedance of an unshielded 28 AWG, 0.05-inch center-ribbon cable is about 105 ohms, but direct contact with a metal ground plane cuts that by 61 ohms. Such an impedance discontinuity will cause signal reflections. The SCSI-3 working group suggests that, in order to minimize discontinuities due to local impedance variation, a flat cable should be spaced at least 1.3mm (0.05 inch) from other cables, any other conductor, or the cable itself when the cable is folded.

**Use 90 to 95 ohm impedance cables wherever possible.** This will allow for closer termination impedance matching.

**Avoid mixing cable types**. Select either flat or round, shielded or non-shielded. Typically, mixing cables mixes impedances. Cable impedance mismatch is a common problem resulting in signal reflections. If cable types must be mixed, use of 26 AWG wire in 1.3mm (0.05 inch) pitch-flat cable will more closely match impedances of many round-shielded cables, resulting in fewer impedance discontinuities and therefore improved signal quality. Internal cables are typically flat-ribbon cables, whereas external cables should be shielded. Where they offer easier routing, size advantages, and better air flow, round cables can be used internally as well. This, in fact, may be desirable if it allows for better impedance matching to the external cable.

Ribbon cable shows fairly good cross talk rejection characteristics for single-ended buses, because of the Ground-signal-Ground layout. However, more care needs to be taken to ensure adequate performance when round, shielded cable is employed.

When round cable is used, select a cable that uses a wise placement of key lines within the cable. The following is suggested: In the case of a standard 25-pair round construction, pairs are arranged inside the cable in three layers. The closer the pair is to the outside shield, the lower the impedance. Conversely, pairs located closer to the center of the cable have higher impedances. Using centrally located high-impedance pairs for speed-critical signals such as REQ and ACK is desirable. By locating data pairs in the outermost layer of the cable, cross talk between REQ, ACK, and the data lines is minimized. The middle layer might contain status lines such as C/D, I/O, MSG, ATN, and so on. Another thing to look for in a round-shielded cable is to make sure that the lowest impedance wire in the cable is used for TERMPOWER to minimize transmission line effects on what is meant to be a voltage supply line. Some SCSI cable vendors have put a low-impedance conductor into the cable specifically for this purpose. Typically, a larger wire gauge along with a high dielectric constant insulation is used on this conductor.

## SCSI Cable Types

SCSI systems can utilize cabling both inside and outside the cabinet. Internal cables are typically flat unshielded ribbon cables, whereas external cables are generally round and shielded. The most common internal cable is the 50-conductor flat-ribbon cable, which typically uses 28 AWG conductors on 0.05-inch centers. Typical free air characteristic impedances for this type of cable run about 105 ohms. Good success can be had with the 3365 round conductor flat-ribbon cable manufactured by 3M Corp. It uses 28 AWG stranded wire on 0.05-inch centers and has a nominal free air characteristic impedance of 108 ohms.

External shielded 8-bit SCSI cables typically contain 25 twisted pairs (50-conductor) with an overall foil/braid composite shield. Typical free air characteristic impedances for this type of cable have run about 65 to 80 ohms. Single-ended round shielded cable impedances of 90 to 100 ohms are available and should be used where appropriate.

The SPI-2 specification requires that systems employing the fast synchronous data transfer option shall use cables consisting of 26 AWG or 28 AWG conductor s. Characteristic impedance is specified as between 90 and 95 ohms. In addition, signal attenuation should be 0.095 dB maximum per meter at 5 MHz. The pair-to-pair propagation delay delta (difference) should not exceed 0.2 ns per meter. Finally, the DC resistance is specified as 0.23 ohms maximum per meter at 20 degrees C.

## Passive Termination

Passive termination (called Alternative-1 in the SCSI-2 specification) was the most common form of termination in use a few years ago. A typical single-ended SCSI passive terminator will employ 18 sets of 220-ohm pull-up and 330-ohm pull-down, thick film resistors to equalize impedance and to absorb reflected signals. The Thevenin equivalent impedance for this type of termination is 132 ohms.

In order to maintain the largest possible high-level noise margin, it is advisable to use resistors with a maximum tolerance of 2 percent rather that 10 percent. In worst-case conditions, the difference could easily add up to 140 mV. Worst case occurs when the pull-up resistor is high and the pull-down resistor is low.

Consider the situation where TERMPWR is being driven across a 6-meter (19-foot) cable. Due to power supply tolerances and to the 15 or so SCSI bus signals that may be drawing current simultaneously, it is possible for the remote end TERMPWR to be sitting at 3.65 volts (see the "Where to Terminate" section for more details). If 2 percent resistors are used, the worst-case termination voltage divider will have a divider ration of 0.588, and the quiescent signal bias will be 2.15 V. If 10 percent resistors are used, the worst-case termination voltage divider will have a divider ratio of 0.551, and the quiescent signal bias will be 2.01 V. In this worst-case example, given the SCSI-mandated minimum logic high voltage of 2.0 V, only 10 mV of high-end noise margin will remain.

## Active Termination

The preferred termination for 10 MHz and faster SCSI buses is active termination. This type of termination is known as Alternative-2 and uses only one 110-ohm resistor per signal per bus end pulled up to locally supplied, voltage-regulated 2.85 V. Features of this termination include the following:

- Termination voltages, and therefore the currents flowing through the 110-ohm termination resistors, are at least partly immune to IR voltage drops on the TERMPWR line until TERMPWR minus 2.85 V equals the dropout voltage of the voltage regulator, or about 1.1 V.

- Closer match to the characteristic impedance of the cable (110 versus 132 for passive as compared to the typical 105–108 ohms free air impedance of the cable) minimizes reflections.

- Increased high-level noise margin of de-asserted signals.

- Higher pull-down currents avoid rising "staircase" waveforms seen on weakly driven transmission lines.

Wherever possible, place SCSI devices that employ active termination at the ends of the bus or plug active terminators onto the connectors at the ends of the cable.

## Where to Terminate

Termination should be installed only at the far ends of the cable. If the host adapter is at one end of the bus and a SCSI device is at the other end, the host adapter's terminator should be enabled. If the host adapter is supporting both internal and external SCSI devices and thus is located in the middle of the bus, its terminator must be disabled. In both cases, disable the termination of any SCSI devices that are not located at the cable ends. This can usually be done by jumper configuration, removal of resistor packs, or both. Another approach is to plug a terminator module onto the end connector of the cable and not enable any of the drive terminators.

Ideally, TERMPWR should be located at the terminations, not in the middle of the cable. Interface error rates are lower if the termination voltage is maintained at the extreme ends of the cable. From strictly a signal-quality perspective, it is best if terminators get power only from the device to which they attach, and not over the bus. Unfortunately, cable end devices may be powered-down and the bus would then be inoperative unless the terminators are supplied from the other voltage sources along the bus. This fact must be balanced against desired signal quality.

Most drives provide jumpers to select the manner in which TERMPWR is supplied to their on-board termination. Having drives configured to supply their own isolated TERMPWR can help solve problems in noisy systems, but the flexibility of being able to power down individual devices shouldn't be given up lightly. TERMPWR should be applied near terminations because TERMPWR is a transmission line that shares many of the same characteristics as the signal lines. Current surges entering this line at the terminators will propagate and reflect exactly as they would on any signal line, except where there is a low-impedance voltage source. It follows, then, that current surge waveforms propagating down the bus, from a point where many data lines are changing simultaneously, will couple into other signals through the pull-up termination resistors if the TERMPWR voltage source impedance isn't low enough right at the terminator to absorb or provide the current surge needed.

For this reason, plug-on terminators often include a large capacitor (1 to 10 uF) on TERMPWR to lower the AC impedance.

The worst real-life case is one in which data lines along with MSG, C/D, and I/O all change at the same time, causing noise on signals of *opposite polarity* (several signals going low causing a de-asserted signal to also go low, or signals going high causing an asserted signal to also go high). This phenomenon has nothing to do with cross talk or driver skew rate, but is instead a function of where TERMPWR is applied and where the drivers are located.

Another reason to supply TERMPWR locally is to prevent the loss of receiver noise margin caused by TERMPWR DC voltage drop across the cable. It is not uncommon to find TERMPWR resistances of 2 ohms or more on maximally configured systems. When 15 to 18 signals conduct, the TERMPWR line will carry nearly 300 mA to the far terminators, which would cause a voltage drop across the cable of about 0.6 V during these periods. This can cause TERMPWR to drop below the specified minimum voltage, causing bus errors.

Modern host adapters drive TERMPWR onto the cable through a self-healing polymer fuse and a Schottky diode (these have only .3 V forward drop where ordinary silicon diodes drop .6 V). Taking into account power supply tolerances, it is not inconceivable that under maximum loading conditions, TERMPWR at the controller connector may be lowered to 4.25 V. Subtract 0.6 V caused by TERMPWR DC resistance, and far-end TERMPWR ends up at 3.65 V. This would bias a quiescent signal to 2.19 V ((330 / 220 + 330) * 3.65). Comparing this to the SCSI-specified minimum V(ih) of 2.0 V for single-ended inputs leaves a high-end noise margin of only 190 mV which is too close for comfort. This quick and dirty worst-case analysis does not even include termination resistor tolerances that could exacerbate the problem. It's a good thing that TTL receivers typically switch near 1.4 V to 1.5 V (the middle of the V[ih] range) rather than at 2.0 V; otherwise, most SCSI implementations would not work reliably.

For all the reasons discussed above, it is advised that TERMPWR be maintained as close to nominal voltage as possible.

### TERMPWR Bypassing

The SCSI-3 Technical Committee SPI working group recommends that all TERMPWR lines be decoupled at each terminator to minimize TERMPWR glitch coupling.

The minimum recommended values are a 2.2 uF solid tantalum capacitor along with .01 uF ceramic capacitor in parallel to help with high-frequency, low-voltage noise. These capacitors, when utilized, will supply the high-frequency, low-impedance path to ground necessary to filter out glitches. Without the capacitors, TERMPWR acts simply as a high-impedance node and couples noise from signal to signal. With the capacitors, an "AC ground" exists that filters this noise.

For cables of significant length and configurations without TERMPWR at each terminator, there is a high probability of signal corruption without adequate decoupling. Therefore, the system integrator should inspect the chosen devices to ensure that all SCSI devices provide proper decoupling capacitors on TERMPWR.

However, it is important to keep in mind that decoupling in the middle of the bus is not sufficient. If the host adapter is supporting both the internal and external SCSI buses simultaneously, then the SCSI devices at the ends of the cable need to be bypassed at their terminations. This requirement applies to both passive and active termination.

## High Voltage Differential SCSI

When the total length of a Fast-10, synchronous SCSI bus cable must exceed 3 meters (10 feet), the use of a differential SCSI interface may be indicated. With Fast-20, the decision point is 1.5 meters (5 feet).

An important concern is cable selection. When twisted-pair cable is used, differential SCSI buses provide greater signal integrity over longer distances than do single-ended, because noise coupled into a twisted-pair generally appears equally on both wires. Because differential receivers respond to differences between the conductors of the twisted-pair, rather than to their absolute Voltage, the coupled common-mode noise is rejected.

On the other hand, the signal positioning of a differential SCSI on a flat non-twisted ribbon cable causes two problems. First, noise introduced into parallel conductors tends not to be common mode. Second, whereas the single-ended conductor arrangement naturally interleaves ground wires between signal wires, there are not enough conductors to interleave grounds between each differential signal pair. These factors lead to increased cross talk between adjacent conductors on a ribbon cable.

The use of twisted-pair cable (either twisted-flat or discrete wire twisted-pairs) for differential-ended SCSI interfaces is highly recommended.

The maximum cumulative cable length permitted is 25 meters (82 feet) with devices not to be spaced any closer then 0.3 meter apart (12 inches) and stub lengths not to exceed 0.2 meter (8 inches). As in single-ended, SCSI bus terminators should be installed only at each end of the cable.

## Low Voltage Differential

For the highest performance disk drives, you'll want to use LVD drives. Because only hard disks are currently manufactured with LVD interfaces, you'll need to keep these devices isolated on their own host adapter or their own bus segment. This is because the presence of a single-ended device on the bus will prevent the LVD devices from operating in LVD mode. Certain motherboards with on-board host adapters provide bus conditioner chips that create separate LVD and single-ended segments, thus allowing the LVD drives to run at full speed without the added expense of a second host adapter.

## Tricks

One of the major parameters that affects I/O performance is *seek time*. This includes the rotational latency of waiting for the proper sector to fly under the heads. One way of minimizing this is a trick called striping or RAID0, which means instead of writing all data to one drive and incurring all the latency involved in doing that, the data will be divided into odd and even stripes (usually track-sized pieces) and written to two identical drives. The odd-numbered stripes go to one drive and the even stripes to the other. This takes advantage of the SCSI disconnect/reconnect protocol by keeping both drives busy seeking and not having to wait to write/read our data. There's more about these techniques in the Chapter 10 introduction to RAID. Striping can also be done with more than two drives, but this requires a more complicated algorithm than odd/even to distribute the data.

## How Daring Are You?

There is another trick that can be done which will increase the write performance of your system. But as with many tricks, you need to be careful or you might get hurt! The trick is to enable the "write cache" on your drives. This increases performance because the drive doesn't wait until the data is written to the magnetic media before telling the system that it's "done." Normally, this is not a problem because shortly the drive will write the data to the medium and it will be safe. But what happens if there is a power failure before the data gets written to the media? You could lose some of the data that you were writing, or even worse, the entire filesystem could be corrupted by losing blocks containing metadata like directories or FATs.

For this reason, we recommend that you only enable write caching on systems that have a UPS for power backup.

## Let's See How We Did

Now that we've applied all we know about improving SCSI performance, it's time to see how well we accomplished that task. We need to select a benchmark utility and run it to measure the transfer rate, average seek time, and CPU consumption. Some of these tools are included on the CD-ROM that comes with this book, and many others are available from various Internet sources.

## Keep Your Expectations Realistic

It's easy to get caught up in the quest for speed. When you see specifications that say "This host adapter has an 80 MB/second transfer rate!," you might tend to take this at face value and expect that running a benchmark on a disk attached to one of these host adapters will yield a result equal to or close to that number. This is *not* the case!

Did the host adapter manufacturer lie? No, not at all. You need to understand the difference between maximum transfer rate and the real data rate coming off the disk media. The host adapter is specifying the maximum speed it can move bytes across the SCSI bus. A single disk, however, cannot supply data at 80 MB/sec. A more realistic expectation would be 15 MB/sec for a single disk. This means that the Fast-40 Wide host adapter we're talking about here can handle the data from four or five such disks before it becomes the bottleneck.

Once you've eked out all the speed you can from your system, if you're still not satisfied and your wallet's not yet empty, you might be ready for RAID (coming right up. . .).

# 10

## RAID: REDUNDANT ARRAY OF INDEPENDENT DISKS

*RAID* (Redundant Array of Independent Disks) is a technology to combine multiple small, independent disk drives into an array that looks like a single, big disk drive to the system. In 1987, David A. Patterson, Garth Gibson, and Randy H. Katz at the University of California Berkeley published a study entitled "A Case for Redundant Arrays of Inexpensive Disks (RAID)."

Aside from the basic theory to replace a single big disk drive called *SLED* (Single Large Expensive Disk) with an array, the Berkeley paper defined five types of array architectures, called *RAID levels*—each providing disk fault tolerance and each offering different feature sets and performance trade-offs. To differentiate among the RAID levels, each was assigned a number from 1 to 5, where each RAID level number stands for an array architecture concept, not a quality level.

(Fault tolerance features had to be a main part of the concept, simply because in a configuration of *n* disk drives, a failure of one disk drive is about the factor *n* more likely to happen than for a single drive.)

Data is distributed over the disks of an array in blocks called *stripes*. The stripe size may range from the size of a single sector (typically 512 bytes) to several megabytes, depending on the application and its I/O requirements. A stripe is always confined to a single disk.

While it is possible to implement RAIDs using ATA drives, SCSI's parallel processing nature is of great benefit in the application.

### Name Games

After the term "RAID" was introduced, "RAID 0" was quickly adopted to describe non-redundant disk arrays, wherein the data striping was used only to increase capacity and performance of the storage system.

Around RAID 0 and the five "official" array definitions, some proprietary models were created by vendors that mostly used their own (typically high-level) numbers, to appear superior. Storage Computer's RAID 7 is such an example, although it's basically a RAID 4 system with multiple caches. Combinations of levels also get high numbers that are mostly a combination of the used levels — RAID 10, for example, mostly is used for the combination of the levels 0 and 1.

However, the practice of calling any proprietary method of array or non-array techniques "RAID level something" leads to confusion. RAID 7, for example, means typically Storage Computer's proprietary approach, whereas Mylex, one of the biggest RAID adapter manufacturers, uses the term "Mylex RAID 7" for JBOD (Just a Bunch Of Disks) configurations, where no RAID-like technology is used. Also, Mylex calls the aforementioned combination of RAID level 0 and 1 not Level 0+1 or 10, but "Mylex RAID 6."

Now, before listing the RAID levels, just a couple more definitions you'll need later: A disk drive that is part of a disk array is typically called a *member disk,* and the group of member disks that are related to a logical disk drive is called a *rank.* A RAID array may have multiple ranks.

### RAID Levels

#### RAID Level 0: Block Striping

As noted above, RAID level 0 is not a "real" RAID in the Berkeley paper sense, but it is listed here because the data striping technology it uses is the base for all RAID levels. RAID level 0 breaks data down into stripes and distributes them over the member drives of the array. While this method doesn't provide any redundancy, it does provide high I/O performance and a resulting capacity consisting of the sum of all drives. RAID level 0 is typically called *striping* and shouldn't be used in an application where data availability matters. Figure 10.1

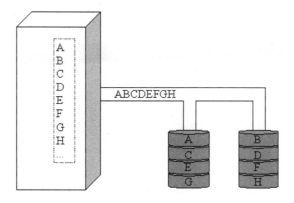

*Figure 10.1: RAID 0—Block Striping*

shows how a stream of data is broken down into stripes ABCDEFGH and then shuffled between the two ranks in the stripe set.

An even simpler method of combining multiple disk drives, called *disk spanning*, just adds the drives one after the other to a big logical drive without striping data. This also was sometimes called RAID 0 in the early days of RAID technology.

All RAID 0 arrays have one major flaw—if one drive fails, the whole array's data are gone. Therefore, RAID 0 is typically used only to achieve high capacity and performance as cheaply as possible.

### RAID Level 1: Drive Mirroring or Duplexing

RAID level 1, or *mirroring*, was used long before the RAID definitions were published. Mirroring provides redundancy by writing the same data to both sides of the mirror—i.e., to both ranks of the array, therefore leaving a "mirrored" copy on each disk. This is shown in Figure 10.2: The data ABCD are written to both disks of the array.

Level 1 is rather simple to implement, provides very good data reliability, and improves read performance of the array, but the capacity/cost ratio is unfavorable—you have to buy twice the capacity you need. To enhance reliability even more, many RAID level 1 solutions also can use mirrored disk controllers, which eliminates the disk controller as a single point of failure and is typically called *duplexing*. Even though this system requires purchasing double your capacity needs, today's disk space is cheap, and the cost of downtime is rising, so RAID level 1 is definitely worth considering for applications where data availability matters.

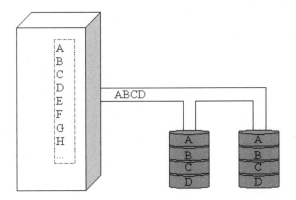

Figure 10.2: RAID 1 — Mirroring

## RAID Level 2: Striping with ECC

RAID level 2 distributes data in single bits over the member drives and uses an algorithm called Hamming Code to generate *ECC* (error correction code) checksum bits that are stored on multiple dedicated ECC disk drives (shown in Figure 10.3). At the time the RAID definitions were written, this made sense — but because most disk drives today embed ECC information in each sector, and RAID level 2 shares all disadvantages of RAID level 3 without the additional benefits, level 2 isn't used any more. (The biggest disadvantage was the high number of drives needed for ECC generation. According to the theory, you'd need four ECC drives for ten data drives and so on.)

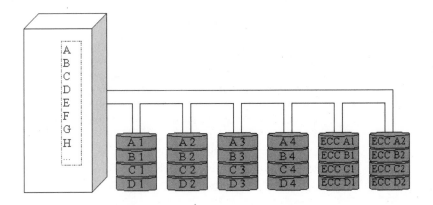

Figure 10.3: RAID 2 — Striping with ECC Stored on Dedicated Drives

### RAID Level 3: Byte Striping with Parity

RAID level 3 uses the same striping method as RAID level 2, but instead of calculating ECC information over the whole data set, level 3 generates parity information over the data on a dedicated parity disk (see Figure 10.4).

If a disk drive fails, the data can be restored on the fly by calculating the *exclusive OR* (XOR) of the data from the remaining drives. RAID level 3 provides high data transfer rates and high data availability and is cheaper than mirroring.

The major drawback to level 3 is that every read or write operation needs to access all drives of a rank, so only one request can be pending at a time and the transaction rate is limited to the transaction rate of a single drive. Also, the block size depends on the number of disks—with the practical stripe size of one sector (512 bytes) per drive, if you want to add a drive to a set of four disk drives and a parity drive, the request block size of the array would be 2.5K (kilobytes). This is very unusual block size and hard to handle for most operating systems. So, RAID level 3 arrays typically work only with an even number of data drives to achieve more normal block sizes.

RAID level 3 is bad for a "standard" system with multiple I/O transactions at any time but, on the other hand, a single read transaction performs very well with the cumulative bandwidth of all drives of the rank.

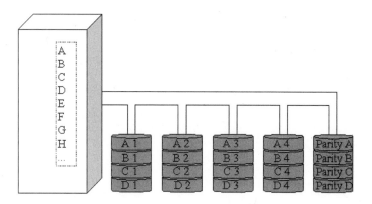

*Figure 10.4: RAID 3—Byte Striping with Parity*

### RAID Level 4: Block Striping with Parity Drive

RAID level 4 is somewhat similar to level 3, but where level 3 distributes data bit or byte oriented over the drives of a rank, level 4 uses larger stripe sizes—various vendors offer data block sizes between 8K and 128K. Therefore, small (≤ stripe size) data blocks can be read asynchronously from multiple drives of the rank, giving a very good read transaction rate.

For example, using Figure 10.5, the Parity 1 block (P1) would contain the XOR of blocks A, B, C, and D, but each of these blocks is separately accessible. So, if data records fit into the logical block size, multiple records can be read from the drives in a quasi-parallel manner.

On the other hand, every write access has to wait until the writing of the parity data on the parity drive is completed. When re-writing block C, both C and P1 have to be read then re-written; the other three drives do not have to be accessed. The parity drive therefore becomes a bottleneck because it has to be accessed for all writes, and write performance is identical to that of a single drive — the parity drive.

With this in mind, RAID level 4 performs best with parallel read accesses to several logical blocks. However, because RAID level 5 shares the advantages of level 4, but avoids the single parity drive, it is the better choice in such a system. Possibly for that reason, we don't know of any commercial RAID 4 implementation.

### RAID Level 5: Block Striping with Distributed Parity

RAID level 5 is identical to level 4 in all but one aspect: It reduces the write bottleneck by distributing the parity data across all member drives of the rank.

Figure 10.6 shows how the parity drives are re-arranged for RAID level 5. As with RAID level 4, read performance is very good, whereas write performance is substantially less so — although not as troublesome as in level 4. Because the combination of performance, data availability, and cost/capacity ratio is the best compromise of all Berkeley RAID levels, RAID level 5 is the most used level today.

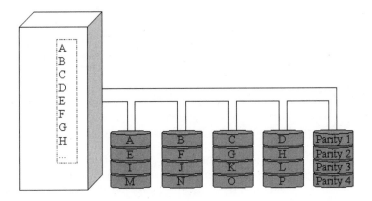

Figure 10.5: RAID 4 — Block Striping with Parity

Parity 1: blocks ABC
Parity 2: blocks DEF
Parity 3: blocks GHI
Parity 4: blocks JKL

*Figure 10.6: RAID 5 — Block Striping with Distributed Parity*

## RAID Level 6: Block Striping with Two Distributed Parities

RAID level 6 is a RAID level 5 array with an additional parity generated over all drives, including the RAID 5 parity. This gives one additional level of data availability, because this scheme can compensate for the loss of two drives — an improvement over RAID 5's one-drive fault tolerance. Figure 10.7 shows the arrangement of a level 7 system.

Although level 6 was later established as one additional "official" RAID level, no one has implemented it yet. It would be the perfect RAID for mission-critical applications; its downsides are the cost of a very complex controller design and very bad write performance because of the two-stage parity generation.

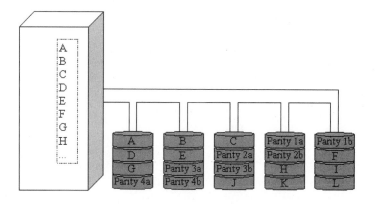

*Figure 10.7: RAID 6 — Block Striping with Two Distributed Parities*

### RAID Level 7: Storage Computer Proprietary

Storage Computer's RAID 7 system is simply a RAID 4 system with fully asynchronous I/O transfers and big caches (see Figure 10.8). Each disk drive has its own SCSI disk controller that caches all read and write transfers. The system controller accesses these SCSI disk controllers asynchronously via a proprietary high-speed bus called *X-Bus*. Additionally, the system controller has a very big cache and confirms write operations while they are stored in the cache only.

RAID 7's main advantage over the "standard" RAID levels is extremely high performance for both read and write operations due to the larger number of disk drives. The major disadvantage is extremely high cost per megabyte.

### RAID Level 0+1 or Level 10: Mirrored Striping Array

RAID level 0+1 or 10 is a combination of the levels 0 (striping) and 1 (mirroring) and has the same advantages and disadvantages as a standard RAID 1 solution (shown in Figure 10.9).

The additional advantage of RAID level 0+1 is performance — read performance goes up because of the parallel access over multiple drives, and because no parity needs to be calculated, write operations are very fast. RAID 0+1 is usually considered the fastest of the available RAID implementations.

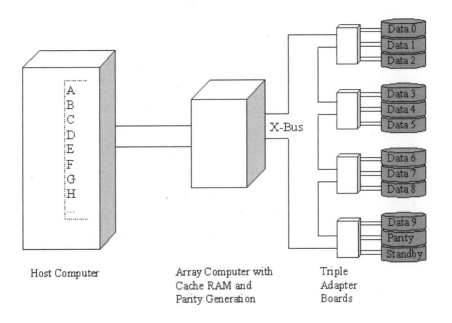

*Figure 10.8: RAID 7 — Storage Computer*

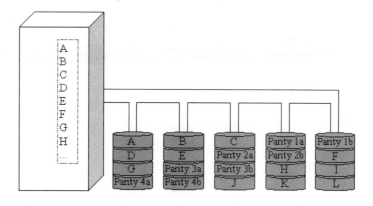

Figure 10.9: RAID 0+1 — Mirrored Striping Array

## Analyze Your Needs

The advantages and disadvantages of the RAID levels vary depending on the system architecture of the RAID adapter and the disk drives. If an intelligent RAID controller with big memory caches can be used, the write performance hit of, for example, RAID 5, is not really noticeable. If, on the other hand, RAID 5 is done in software, the XOR calculation draws noticeable resources from your main CPU(s). Selection of a RAID system should be done only after careful analysis of your needs.

## RAID and the RAB

In 1992, eight RAID manufacturers and consultants founded the *RAB* (RAID Advisory Board) to present a podium for RAID and to achieve better market presence for the RAID idea and their products. The RAB (www.raid advisory. com) offers the RAIDBook, which describes all RAID and EDAP issues in great detail.

Since then, the RAB has grown to include all major players in the RAID field and has extended the fault tolerance aspect of RAID to a broader view called *EDAP* (Extended Data Availability and Protection). The idea behind EDAP is that a storage system with EDAP capability can protect its data and provide online access to its data despite failures within the disk system, attached units, or its environment. This is a major extension of the RAID concept. Specifically, RAID is the part that addresses failures in the disk system on the lowest level.

### Extended Data Availability and Protection (EDAP)

The original definition of EDAP is the ability of a storage system to provide reliable online access to data even under abnormal conditions. These conditions are clearly specified as shown in Table 10.1.

**Table 10.1: Types of Failures and Their Conditions**

| Failure Type | Example |
| --- | --- |
| Internal Failures | Failures within the disk system. |
| External Failures | Failures of equipment attached to the disk system, including host I/O buses and host computers. |
| Environmental Failures | Failures resulting from abnormal environmental conditions, from a power outage or over-temperature to flood, earthquake, terrorism, or sabotage. |
| Replacement Periods | Replacement periods means the time needed to do maintenance, for example to replace a disk drive. Typically, in a good RAID setup with hot standby disks and hot-swap support, this means only some time in "reduced mode," where the next failing disk drive could mean disaster. (Note that if hot swap is not supported by the disk system, then the component replacement period is identical to down time.) |
| Vulnerable Periods | Vulnerable period, or reduced mode time, means that the disk system has to work around a failing component, that the system is vulnerable to additional (possibly disastrous) failures, and that the system operates at reduced performance until the fault is corrected. |

EDAP now certifies whether a storage system or component fulfills specific EDAP criteria called *EDAP attributes*. The EDAP attribute range of a disk system may include providing EDAP capability in case of an internal disk failure to providing EDAP capability against any internal, external, or environmental failure.

RAID denotes the lowest level of EDAP capability—prevention of online data access because of a disk failure—whereas the highest levels include things like remote mirroring to protect data access in case of catastrophes like earthquakes.

### EDAP Criteria

EDAP uses seven base classifications for disk systems. Each EDAP classification level supercedes the previous level. To meet the criteria for a classification, the listed EDAP attributes must be fulfilled.

**Failure Resistant Disk System**, FRDS, criteria are:

- Protection against data loss and loss of access to data due to disk failure

- Reconstruction of failed disk contents to a replacement disk

- Protection against data loss due to a "write hole"

- Protection against data loss due to host and host I/O bus failures

- Protection against data loss due to component failure

- FRU monitoring and failure indication

**Failure Resistant Disk System Plus**, FRDS+, does everything an FRDS does and adds the following criteria:

- Disk hot swap

- Protection against data loss due to cache component failure

- Protection against data loss due to external power failure

- Protection against data loss due to a temperature-out-of-operating-range condition

- Component and environmental failure warning

**Failure Tolerant Disk System**, FTDS, adds the following criteria:

- Protection against loss of access to data due to device channel failure

- Protection against loss of access to data due to controller failure

- Protection against loss of data access due to cache component failure

- Protection against loss of data access due to power supply failure

**Failure Tolerant Disk System Plus**, FTDS+, meets all previous criteria and additionally offers:

- Protection against loss of access to data due to host and host I/O bus failures

- Protection against loss of access to data due to external power failure

- Protection against loss of data access due to FRU replacement

- Disk hot spare

**Failure Tolerant Disk System Plus Plus**, FTDS++, meets all previous criteria and adds:

- Protection against data loss and loss of access to data due to multiple disk failures in an FTDS+

**Disaster Tolerant Disk System**, DTDS, adds the term "zone," meaning a geographic zone. Being an FTDS+ array by definition, the DTDS adds mainly:

- Protection against loss of data access due to zone failure

This means that if, for example, a building is flooded, the DTDS has some provision to offer online data access by a backup unit in a different building that's definitely not affected by this flood.

**Disaster Tolerant Disk System Plus**, DTDS+, uses bigger zones to guarantee online data access, as follows:

- Long distance protection against loss of data access due to zone failure

As you might expect, the higher the EDAP classification, the higher the price of a complete solution—to fulfill the DTDS criteria, you need to set up two data centers in two separate buildings or at least building parts that may not be vulnerable to the same fire, for example. If you're really serious about disaster tolerance you'll want the two locations in separate cities, or counties—preferably on separate tectonic plates!

## How Does All This Stuff Connect to My System?

There are three basic types of RAID implementations, internal hardware, external hardware, and software only. Internal RAID controllers consist of an intelligent multi-channel host adapter card (usually PCI). The card contains a CPU (usually a RISC processor) and a large amount of memory as well as several SCSI bus channels (usually three).

An external RAID unit consists of a cabinet with a controller card and a bunch of bays to mount drives in. The controller card is similar to the one in internal RAIDs, but also provides another SCSI bus to act as the "front side" connection (from the host to the RAID). More sophisticated external RAIDs provide a second "front side" bus to remove the possibility of this being a single point of failure. When all is said and done the entire RAID looks to the host like one giant SCSI disk drive!

### Software RAID

The software approach is certainly the least expensive, but also the most limited way to implement RAID. Software RAID0 or RAID1 are fairly practical, but going beyond this incurs a substantial performance hit. Windows NT Server and Linux have software RAID capability. Remember, though, that you can't boot from a software RAID.

RAID can be a topic for an entire book, but I think we've gone far enough to inform the typical user or system integrator of what this RAID stuff is all about.

# 11

# A PROFILE OF ASPI
# PROGRAMMING

ASPI stands for advanced SCSI programming interface. ASPI is an Adaptec-developed interface specification for sending commands to SCSI host adapters that most hardware manufacturers have adopted today. The interface provides an abstraction layer that insulates the programmer from considerations of the particular host adapter used. With ASPI, software drivers can be broken into two components: the low-level ASPI manager, which is operating system and hardware dependent, and the ASPI module. The ASPI manager accepts ASPI commands and performs the steps necessary to send the SCSI command to the target. For example, although the Adaptec AHA-152x and AHA-294x host adapters have very different hardware, the ASPI interface to these boards is the same. (Obviously, the driver module that implements the ASPI interface for the particular host adapter, e.g., ASPI2DOS.SYS, is different for each board.)

The ASPI module is tailored to the command set of a particular peripheral, such as CD-ROM. Although an ASPI-based CD-ROM driver would have to handle the differences between different CD-ROM drives, it would not have to handle host adapter differences.

## I. ASPI Developer Information

In response to widespread demand for ASPI software, Adaptec provides the ASPI Software Developer's Kit (SDK), a complete toolkit for developing SCSI drivers for PC peripherals. This kit is designed to help you write your own ASPI device module that will work with any ASPI-compliant host adapter. The following sections describe the ASPI specifications for DOS, Windows, and OS/2. Updated information can be downloaded from the Adaptec FTP site: ftp://ftp.adaptec.com/pub/BBS/adaptec/.

The ASPI Software Developer Kit contains the following documentation and tools.

- A copy of the ASPI specification document and programming guides for four major operating systems: DOS, Windows, OS/2, and NetWare.

- Sample assembler source code for DOS.

- A SCSI DOS disk driver, which can handle at most one SCSI partition on one SCSI drive.

- An ASPI demo program, which provides examples of how to use the ASPI programming interface.

- Sample C source code for Windows.

- An ASPI for Windows utility, which constantly scans the SCSI bus and displays the name of a device, if it finds one.

- A debugging utility for ASPI for Windows development.

- An ASPI demo utility for OS/2, which scans the SCSI bus and displays information about the targets it finds. It is a 32-bit application created with Borland C++ for OS/2. A project file and makefile are included.

- Sample C source code for OS/2.

- An ASPI device driver for OS/2. This driver is intended for simple, single-threaded applications. If you need to support multitasking, you need to make your own modifications.

- A complimentary copy of Adaptec EZ-SCSI, the latest version of DOS/Windows software managers, plus an installation program, CD-ROM drivers, and other utilities.

To use this kit, it is assumed that you have a solid understanding of system-level programming and are familiar with at least device driver development for the operating system you are targeting. Prior to getting this kit, you should get the device driver kit from the appropriate operating system vendor.

To order in the U.S. and Canada, call 800-442-7274. To order internationally, call 408-957-7274. Price is US $150.00.

**NOTE** *Numerous tables of information appear throughout this chapter. For convenience, we have abbreviated certain column headings as R/W. In cases where R/W appears as a heading, the entries in that column indicate whether the field is sent to ASPI (W), returned from ASPI (R), or reserved (—).*

## II. ASPI for DOS Specification

Two steps are involved in order for a driver to make use of ASPI: obtain the ASPI entry point, and call the ASPI driver. Typically, the entry point is obtained once, and then ASPI calls are made multiple times within a device driver. ASPI function calls are used to return data about the ASPI manager, host adapter, and SCSI devices, but they are mainly used to execute SCSI I/O requests. The ASPI layer is re-entrant and can accept function calls before previous calls have completed. A call will normally return immediately with zero status, indicating that the request has been successfully queued. In order to continue program flow after the function completes, the driver either polls ASPI status or enables the post bit, which turns control over to a specified routine upon completion of the ASPI call.

**NOTE** *When a program makes a call to an ASPI manager, the manager uses the caller's stack. It is therefore necessary for the program to allocate enough stack memory for itself as well as the ASPI manager. There is no fixed amount of stack needed by all ASPI managers; a programmer needs to be aware of this constraint and test code with individual managers for compatibility.*

## Accessing ASPI

Device drivers wishing to access ASPI must open the driver by performing a DOS Int 21h function call OPEN A FILE as follows:

### On Entry:

AX = 3D00h
DS:DX = Pointer to SCSIMGR$, 0

### On Return:

AX = File handle if carry flag is not set
Error code if carry flag is set

## Getting the ASPI Entry Point

Device drivers can get the entry point to ASPI by performing a DOS Int 21h function call IOCTL READ as follows:

### On Entry:

AX = 4402h
DS:DX = Pointer to data returned (4 bytes)
CX = 4
BX = File handle

### On Return:

AX = Nothing
Data returned in DS:DX contains the ASPI entry point:
Byte 0–1: ASPI Entry Point Offset
Byte 2–3: ASPI Entry Point Segment

## Closing ASPI

Device drivers wishing to close ASPI must do it by performing a DOS Int 21h function call CLOSE A FILE as follows:

### On Entry:

AH = 3Eh
BX = File handle

### On Return:

AX = Error code if carry flag is set
Nothing if carry flag is not set

## Calling ASPI

The following is an example of how to call the ASPI manager:

```
                .MODEL SMALL
                .STACK 100h                     ;100h byte stack


                .DATA
SCSIMgrString   db "SCSIMGR$"
                dw 0                            ;NULL-terminate string
ASPI_Entry      db 4 dup (?)
SRB             db 58 dup (0)                   ;Initialize SRB for Host
                                                ;Adapter Inquiry

                .CODE
start:          mov   ax,@DATA
                mov   ds,ax                     ;Init DS
                mov   ax,03D00h
                lea   dx,SCSIMgrString
                int   21h                       ;Open ASPI Manager
                jc    NoASPIManager             ;Branch if none found
                push  ax                        ;Save ASPI File Handle

                mov   bx,ax                     ;BX = File Handle
                mov   ax,4402h
                lea   dx,ASPI_Entry             ;Store entry point here
                mov   cx,4                       ;Four bytes to transfer
                int   21h                       ;Get ASPI entry point

                mov   ah,03Eh
                pop   bx                        ;BX = ASPI File Handle
                int   21h                       ;Close ASPI Manager

                push  ds                        ;Push SRB's segment
                lea   bx,SRB
                push  bx                        ;Push SRB's offset
                lea   bx,ASPI_Entry
                call  DWORD PTR [bx]            ;Call ASPI
                add   sp,4                       ;Restore the stack

ASPI_Exit:      mov   ax,4C00h                  ;Exit to DOS
                int   21h
                ret


NoASPIManager:                                  ;No ASPI Manager found!!
                jmp   ASPI_Exit                 ;Handle it.
                END
```

As shown in the preceding sample code, the SRB's segment is first pushed onto the stack followed by its offset. ASPI is then called directly.

## SCSI Request Block (SRB)

A SCSI request block (SRB) (see Table 11.1) contains the command to be executed by the ASPI manager and is used by both drivers and application programs. An SRB consists of an SRB header followed by additional fields dependent on the command code. All request blocks have an 8-byte header.

**Table 11.1: SCSI Request Block**

| Offset | #Bytes | Description | R/W |
|--------|--------|-------------|-----|
| 00h (00) | 01h (01) | Command Code | W |
| 01h (01) | 01h (01) | Status | R |
| 02h (02) | 01h (01) | Host Adapter Number | W |
| 03h (03) | 01h (01) | SCSI Request Flags | W |
| 04h (04) | 04h (04) | Reserved for Expansion = 0 | — |

### Command Codes

The Command Code field is used to indicate which of the ASPI services is being accessed. Refer to Valid ASPI Command Codes in Table 11.2.

**Table 11.2: Valid ASPI Command Codes**

| Command Code | Description |
|--------------|-------------|
| 00h | Host Adapter Inquiry |
| 01h | Get Device Type |
| 02h | Execute SCSI I/O Command |
| 03h | Abort SCSI I/O Command |
| 04h | Reset SCSI Device |
| 05h | Set Host Adapter Parameters |
| 06h | Get Disk Drive Information |
| 07h–7Fh | Reserved for Future Expansion |
| 80h–FFh | Reserved for Vendor Unique |

### Status

The Status Byte field is used to post the status of the command. Refer to ASPI Status Bytes in Table 11.3.

### Host Adapter Number

The Host Adapter Number field specifies which installed host adapter the request is intended for. Host adapter numbers are always assigned by the SCSI manager layer beginning with zero.

### SCSI Request Flags

The SCSI Request Flags field definition is command code-specific.

### Reserved for Expansion

The last 4 bytes of the header are reserved and must be zero.

## ASPI Command Codes

**Table 11.3: ASPI Status Bytes**

| Status Byte | Description |
| --- | --- |
| 00h | SCSI Request in Progress |
| 01h | SCSI Request Completed Without Error |
| 02h | SCSI Request Aborted by Host |
| 04h | SCSI Request Completed With Error |
| 80h | Invalid SCSI Request |
| 81h | Invalid Host Adapter Number |
| 82h | SCSI Device Not Installed |

### ASPI Command Code = 0: Host Adapter Inquiry

The status byte (defined in Table 11.3) will always return with a nonzero status. A SCSI Request Completed Without Error (01h) status indicates that the remaining fields are valid. An Invalid Host Adapter Number (81h) status indicates that the specified host adapter is not installed. This function (as shown in Table 11.4) is used to get information on the installed host adapter hardware, including number of host adapters installed. It can be issued once with host adapter zero specified to get the number of host adapters. If further information is desired, it can be issued for each individual host adapter.

The SCSI Request Flags field is currently undefined for this command and should be zeroed.

**Table 11.4: ASPI Command Code = 0: Host Adapter Inquiry**

| Offset | # Bytes | Description | R/W |
|--------|---------|-------------|-----|
| 00h (00) | 01h (01) | Command Code = 0 | W |
| 01h (01) | 01h (01) | Status | R |
| 02h (02) | 01h (01) | Host Adapter Number | W |
| 03h (03) | 01h (01) | SCSI Request Flags | W |
| 04h (04) | 04h (04) | Reserved for Expansion = 0 | — |
| 08h (08) | 01h (01) | Number of Host Adapters | R |
| 09h (09) | 01h (01) | ID of Host Adapter | R |
| 0Ah (10) | 10h (16) | SCSI Manager ID | R |
| 1Ah (26) | 10h (16) | Host Adapter ID | R |
| 2Ah (42) | 10h (16) | Host Adapter Unique Parameters | R |

The SCSI Manager ID field contains a 16-byte ASCII string describing the SCSI manager.

The Host Adapter ID field contains a 16-byte ASCII string describing the SCSI host adapter.

The definition of the Host Adapter Unique Parameters field is left to implementation notes specific to a particular host adapter.

### ASPI Command Code = 1: Get Device Type

This command (defined in Table 11.5) will always return with nonzero status.

A SCSI Request Completed Without Error (01h) status indicates that the specified device is installed and the peripheral device type field is valid. A SCSI Device Not Installed Error (82h) indicates that the peripheral device type field is not valid.

This command is intended for use by various drivers, during initialization, for identifying the targets that they need to support. A CD-ROM driver, for example, can scan each target/LUN on each installed host adapter looking for the device type corresponding to CD-ROM devices. This eliminates the need for each driver to duplicate the effort of scanning the SCSI bus for devices.

The peripheral device type is determined by sending a SCSI Inquiry command to the given target. Refer to any SCSI specification to learn more about the Inquiry command.

The SCSI Request Flags field is currently undefined for this command and should be zeroed.

**Table 11.5: ASPI Command Code = 1: Get Device Type**

| Offset | # Bytes | Description | R/W |
|---|---|---|---|
| 00h (00) | 01h (01) | Command Code = 1 | W |
| 01h (01) | 01h (01) | Status | R |
| 02h (02) | 01h (01) | Host Adapter Number | W |
| 03h (03) | 01h (01) | SCSI Request Flags | W |
| 04h (04) | 04h (04) | Reserved for Expansion = 0 | — |
| 08h (08) | 01h (01) | Target ID | W |
| 09h (09) | 01h (01) | LUN | W |
| 0Ah (10) | 01h (01) | Peripheral Device Type of Target/LU | R |

## ASPI Command Code = 2: Execute SCSI I/O Command

This command (defined in Table 11.6) will usually return with zero status indicating that the request was queued successfully. Command completion can be determined by polling for nonzero status or through the use of the Post Routine Address field (discussed later in the section "ASPI Command Posting"). Keep in mind that if you are going to use polling, interrupts must be enabled.

**Table 11.6: ASPI Command Code = 2: Execute SCSI I/O Command**

| Offset | # Bytes | Description | R/W |
|---|---|---|---|
| 00h (00) | 01h (01) | Command Code = 2 | W |
| 01h (01) | 01h (01) | Status | R |
| 02h (02) | 01h (01) | Host Adapter Number | W |
| 03h (03) | 01h (01) | SCSI Request Flags | W |
| 04h (04) | 04h (04) | Reserved for Expansion = 0 | — |
| 08h (08) | 01h (01) | Target ID | W |
| 09h (09) | 01h (01) | LUN | W |
| 0Ah (10) | 04h (04) | Data Allocation Length | W |

| Offset | # Bytes | Description | R/W |
|---|---|---|---|
| OEh (14) | 01h (01) | Sense Allocation Length (N) | W |
| OFh (15) | 02h (02) | Data Buffer Pointer (Offset) | W |
| 11h (17) | 02h (02) | Data Buffer Pointer (Segment) | W |
| 13h (19) | 02h (02) | SRB Link Pointer (Offset) | W |
| 15h (21) | 02h (02) | SRB Link Pointer (Segment) | W |
| 17h (23) | 01h (01) | SCSI CDB Length (M) | W |
| 18h (24) | 01h (01) | Host Adapter Status | R |
| 19h (25) | 01h (01) | Target Status | R |
| 1Ah (26) | 02h (02) | Post Routine Address (Offset) | W |
| 1Ch (28) | 02h (02) | Post Routine Address (Segment) | W |
| 1Eh (30) | 22h (34) | Reserved for ASPI Workspace | — |
| 40h (64) | _____ | SCSI Command Descriptor Block (CDB) | W |
| 40h+M | N | Sense Allocation Area | R |

### The SCSI Request Flags Byte Is Defined As Follows:

| 7 | 6 | 5 | 4 | 3 | 2 | 1 | 0 |
|---|---|---|---|---|---|---|---|
| Rsvd | Rsvd | Rsvd | Direction Bits | | Rsvd | Link | Post |

The Post bit specifies whether posting is enabled (bit 0 = 1) or disabled (bit 0 = 0).

The Link bit specifies whether linking is enabled (bit 1 = 1) or disabled (bit 1 = 0).

The Direction bits specify which direction the transfer is:

00      Direction determined by SCSI command. Length not checked.

01      Transfer from SCSI target to host. Length checked.

10      Transfer from host to SCSI target. Length checked.

11      No data transfer.

The Target ID and LUN fields are used to specify the peripheral device involved in the I/O.

The Data Allocation Length field indicates the number of bytes to be transferred. If the SCSI command to be executed does not transfer data (i.e., Rewind, Start Unit, etc.) the Data Allocation Length must be set to zero.

The Sense Allocation Length field indicates, in bytes, the number of bytes allocated at the end of the SRB for sense data. A request sense is automatically generated if a check condition is presented at the end of a SCSI command.

The Data Buffer Pointer field is a pointer to the I/O data buffer. You place the logical address here. ASPI will convert it to the physical address in the case of a bus master or DMA transfer.

The SRB Link Pointer field is a pointer to the next SRB in a chain. See the discussion on linking for more information.

The SCSI CDB Length field establishes the length, in bytes, of the SCSI command descriptor block (CDB).

The Host Adapter Status field is used to report the host adapter status as follows:

| | |
|---|---|
| 00h | Host adapter did not detect any error |
| 11h | Selection timeout |
| 12h | Data overrun/underrun |
| 13h | Unexpected bus free |
| 14h | Target bus phase sequence failure |

The Target Status field is used to report the target's SCSI status including:

| | |
|---|---|
| 00h | No target status |
| 02h | Check status (sense data is in sense allocation area) |
| 08h | Specified target/LUN is busy |
| 18h | Reservation conflict |

The Post Routine Address field, if specified, is called when the I/O is completed. See the discussion on posting for more information.

The SCSI command descriptor block (CDB) field contains the CDB as defined by the target's SCSI command set. The length of the SCSI CDB is specified in the SCSI Command Length field.

The sense allocation area is filled with sense data on a check condition. The maximum length of this field is specified in the Sense Allocation Length field. Note that the target can return fewer than the number of sense bytes requested.

## SCSI Command Linking with ASPI

ASPI provides the ability to use SCSI linking to guarantee the sequential execution of several commands. Note that the use of this feature requires the involved target(s) to support SCSI linking.

To use SCSI linking, a chain of SRBs is built with the SRB link pointer used to link the elements together. The link bit should be set in the SCSI request flags byte of all SRBs except the last in the chain. When a SCSI target returns indicating that the linked command is complete, the next SRB is immediately processed, and the appropriate CDB is dispatched. When using SCSI linking, make sure that the linking flags in the SCSI CDB agree with the link bit in the SCSI request flags. Inconsistencies can cause unpredictable results. For example, setting the CDB up for linking but failing to set the link bit may result in a random address being used for the next SRB pointer.

Any error returned from the target on a linked command will break the chain. Note that if linking without tags is used, as defined in SCSI, posting may not occur on any elements in the chain until the chain is complete. If you have the post bit set in each SRB's SCSI request flags byte, then each SRB's post routine will be called.

**NOTE** *It is strongly recommended that you do not use SCSI linking. There are many SCSI targets, as well as SCSI host adapters, which do not handle SCSI linking and will not work with your ASPI module.*

### ASPI Command Posting

To use posting, the post bit must be set in the SCSI request flags. Posting refers to the SCSI manager making a FAR call to a post routine as specified in the SRB. The post routine is called to indicate that the SRB is complete. The specific SRB completed is indicated by a 4-byte SRB pointer on the stack. It is assumed that all registers are preserved by the post routine.

The ASPI manager will first push the completed SRB's 2-byte segment onto the stack followed by its 2-byte offset. The following is a sample ASPI post handler:

```
ASPI_Post    proc far
             push bp
             mov  bp,sp

             pusha                  ;Save all registers
             push ds
             push es

             mov  bx,[bp+6]         ;BX = SRBs offset
             mov  es,[bp+8]         ;ES = SRBs segment
                .                   ;ES:BX points to SRB
                .
                .

             pop  es
             pop  ds
             popa
             pop  bp                ;Restore all registers
             retf                   ;and return to ASPI
ASPI_Post    endp
```

When your post routine is first entered, the stack will look as follows:

Top of Stack     [SP+0] —>     Return Address (Offset)

                 [SP+2] —>     Return Address (Segment)

                 [SP+4] —>     SRB Pointer (Offset)

                 [SP+6] —>     SRB Pointer (Segment)

                 ...

                 ...

                 ...

You may issue any ASPI command from within your post routine except for an Abort command. Your post routine should get in and out as quickly as possible.

Posting can be used by device drivers and terminate and stay resident (TSR) programs, which need to operate in an interrupt-driven fashion.

### ASPI Command Code = 3: Abort SCSI I/O Command

This command (defined in Table 11.7) is used to request that an SRB be aborted. It should be issued on any I/O request that has not completed if the driver wishes to timeout on that request. Success of the Abort command is never assured.

**Table 11.7: ASPI Command Code = 3: Abort SCSI I/O Command**

| Offset | # Bytes | Description | R/W |
|--------|---------|-------------|-----|
| 00h (00) | 01h (01) | Command Code = 3 | W |
| 01h (01) | 01h (01) | Status | R |
| 02h (02) | 01h (01) | Host Adapter Number | W |
| 03h (03) | 01h (01) | SCSI Request Flags | W |
| 04h (04) | 04h (04) | Reserved for Expansion = 0 | — |
| 08h (08) | 02h (02) | SRB Pointer to Abort (Offset) | W |
| 0Ah (10) | 02h (12) | SRB Pointer to Abort (Segment) | W |

This command always returns with SCSI Request Completed Without Error, but the actual failure or success of the abort operation is indicated by the status eventually returned in the SRB specified.

The SCSI Request Flags field is currently undefined for this command and should be zeroed.

The SRB Pointer to Abort field contains a pointer to the SRB that is to be aborted.

**NOTE** *An Abort command should not be issued during a post routine.*

### ASPI Command Code = 4: Reset SCSI Device

This command (defined in Table 11.8) is used to reset a specific SCSI target. Note that the structure passed is nearly identical to the execute SCSI I/O SRB except that some of the fields are not used.

This command usually returns with zero status indicating that the request was queued successfully. Command completion can be determined by polling for nonzero status or through the use of posting.

**Table 11.8: ASPI Command Code = 4: Reset SCSI Device**

| Offset | # Bytes | Description | R/W |
|--------|---------|-------------|-----|
| 00h (00) | 01h (01) | Command Code = 4 | W |
| 01h (01) | 01h (01) | Status | R |
| 02h (02) | 01h (01) | Host Adapter Number | W |
| 03h (03) | 01h (01) | SCSI Request Flags | W |
| 04h (04) | 04h (04) | Reserved for Expansion = 0 | — |
| 08h (08) | 01h (01) | Target ID | W |
| 09h (09) | 01h (01) | LUN | W |
| 0Ah (10) | 0Eh (14) | Reserved | — |
| 18h (24) | 01h (01) | Host Adapter Status | R |
| 19h (25) | 01h (01) | Target Status | R |
| 1Ah (26) | 02h (02) | Post Routine Address (Offset) | W |
| 1Ch (28) | 02h (02) | Post Routine Address (Segment) | W |
| 1Eh (30) | 02h (02) | Reserved for ASPI Workspace | — |

### The SCSI Request Flags Byte Is Defined As Follows:

| 7 | 6 | 5 | 4 | 3 | 2 | 1 | 0 |
|---|---|---|---|---|---|---|---|
| Rsvd | | | | | | | Post |

The Post bit specifies whether posting is enabled (bit 0 = 1) or disabled
(bit 0 = 0).

## ASPI Command Code = 5: Set Host Adapter Parameters

The definition of the host adapter unique parameters (shown in Table 11.9)
is left to implementation notes specific to a particular host adapter.

**Table 11.9: ASPI Command Code = 5: Set Host Adapter Parameters**

| Offset | # Bytes | Description | R/W |
| --- | --- | --- | --- |
| 00h (00) | 201h (01) | Command Code = 5 | W |
| 01h (01) | 01h (01) | Status | R |
| 02h (02) | 01h (01) | Host Adapter Number | W |
| 03h (03) | 01h (01) | SCSI Request Flags | W |
| 04h (04) | 04h (04) | Reserved for Expansion = 0 | — |
| 08h (08) | 10h (16) | Host Adapter Unique Parameters | W |

ASPI managers that support this command code always return with a status
of SCSI Request Completed Without Error (01h). ASPI managers that do
not support this command code always return with a status of Invalid SCSI
Request (80h).

## ASPI Command Code = 6: Get Disk Drive Information

This command (defined in Table 11.10) is intended for use by SCSI disk drivers
that need to determine which disk drives are already being controlled by some
BIOS/DOS and which disk drives are available for use by the disk driver. It also
provides a means to determine which drives are not under control of the BIOS/
DOS yet are still accessible via Int 13h. This is useful because many disk caching
utilities will cache Int 13h requests but not any disk driver requests. There are
also some disk utility programs that will allow the user to access physical sectors
on a disk via Int 13h.

**Table 11.10: ASPI Command Code = 6: Get Disk Drive Information**

| Offset | # Bytes | Description | R/W |
| --- | --- | --- | --- |
| 00h (00) | 01h (01) | Command Code = 6 | W |
| 01h (01) | 01h (01) | Status | R |
| 02h (02) | 01h (01) | Host Adapter Number | W |

| Offset | # Bytes | Description | R/W |
|--------|---------|-------------|-----|
| 03h (03) | 01h (01) | SCSI Request Flags | W |
| 04h (04) | 04h (04) | Reserved for Expansion = 0 | — |
| 08h (08) | 01h (01) | Target ID | W |
| 09h (09) | 01h (01) | LUN | W |
| 0Ah (10) | 01h (01) | Drive Flags | R |
| 0Bh (11) | 01h (01) | Int 13h Drive | R |
| 0Ch (12) | 01h (01) | Preferred Head Translation | R |
| 0Dh (13) | 01h (01) | Preferred Sector Translation | R |
| 0Eh (14) | 0Ah (10) | Reserved for Expansion = 0 | — |

The SCSI Requests Flags field is currently undefined for this command and should be zero.

## The Drive Flags Byte Is Defined As Follows:

| 7 | 6 | 5 | 4 | 3 | 2 | 1 | 0 |
|---|---|---|---|---|---|---|---|
| Rsvd | Rsvd | Rsvd | Rsvd | Rsvd | Rsvd | Int 13 Info | |

*All reserved (Rsvd) bits will return zeroed.*

The Int 13 Info bits return information pertaining to the Int 13h drive field:

00      The given drive (HA #/target/LUN) is not accessible via Int 13h. If you wish to read/write to this drive, you will need to send ASPI read/write requests to the drive. The Int 13h Drive field is invalid.

01      The given drive (HA #/target/LUN) is accessible via Int 13h. The Int 13h Drive field contains the drive's Int 13h drive number. This drive is under the control of DOS.

10      The given drive (HA #/target/LUN) is accessible via Int 13h. The Int 13h Drive field contains the drive's Int 13h drive number. This drive is not under control of DOS and can be used, for example, by a SCSI disk driver.

11      Invalid.

The Int 13h Drive field returns the Int 13 drive number for the given host adap-ter number, target ID, and LUN. Valid Int 13 drive numbers range for 00-FFh. The Preferred Head Translation field indicates the given host adapter's/ disk drive's preferred head translation method. A typical value will be 64 heads. The Preferred Sector Translation field indicates the given host adapter's/disk drive's preferred sector translation method. A typical value will be 32 sectors per track.

## ASPI for DOS under Windows 3.x

Windows is a graphical user interface that runs under DOS, but writing a device driver or application capable of making ASPI calls in a Windows environment is not as simple as in the strictly DOS case. The problem is that ASPI for DOS uses a real mode interface and Windows uses the DOS protected mode interface (DPMI). ASPI expects a real mode segment and offset for the SRB and the entry point of ASPI, while Windows uses a selector and offset to address data and code. To program correctly in this environment, a consortium of companies (including Microsoft and Intel) have written the DOS Protected Mode Interface Specification. The details are too complex to go into detail here, but a copy should be obtained from the DPMI committee for programming purposes. Two steps need to be followed to access ASPI for DOS from a Windows application:

1. Allocate all SRBs and buffers down in real mode memory. This can be accomplished using Windows' GlobalDosAlloc routine or using DPMI interrupt 31h, function 100h. This allows the ASPI module and manager to locate the SRB and data buffers using segments and offsets.

2. Call the real mode procedure with Far Return Frame Function (interrupt 31h, function 0301h). This makes it possible to call the ASPI manager, which is a real mode procedure.

## III. ASPI for Windows Specification

ASPI for Windows is implemented as a dynamic link library (DLL). The name of this file is called winaspi.dll. ASPI function calls (shown in Table 11.11) are used to return information about the ASPI manager, host adapter, and SCSI devices, but they are mainly used to execute SCSI I/O requests. The ASPI for Windows layer is fully multitasking and can accept function calls before previous calls have completed. There are two functions that need to be imported from winaspi.dll into your Windows application.

**Table 11.11: Description of ASPI for Windows Functions**

| Function | Description |
|---|---|
| GetASPISupportInfo | This function returns the number of host adapters installed and other miscellaneous information. You should call this function to make sure that ASPI is properly initialized before calling the SendASPICommand function. |
| SendASPICommand | This function allows you to send an ASPI for Windows command. All of your SRBs and data buffers must be in locked memory before being passed to ASPI. |

## ASPI Managers for Windows

It is not the intent of this specification to define the protocol between winaspi.dll and any DOS ASPI managers that may be loaded. There are many reasons for this, including the following:

- Some hardware companies may decide to write an ASPI for Windows manager without concurrent ASPI for DOS support.

- Some may decide to have winaspi.dll communicate with a Windows 386 enhanced mode virtual device driver (VxD).

- Some may decide to only support Windows 3.1, which may or may not have improved hardware support.

It is also not the intent of this specification to define which modes of Windows need to be supported. We anticipate that most hardware companies will support ASPI for Windows in standard and 386 enhanced modes, and forego real mode support.

## GetASPISupportInfo

**WORD GetASPISupportInfo(VOID)**
The GetASPISupportInfo function returns the number of host adapters installed and other miscellaneous information. It is recommended that this function be called first before issuing an ASPI command to ensure ASPI has been properly initialized. This function call does not perform any initialization itself, but rather confirms that everything is ready for processing.

This function has no parameters.

### Returns

The return value specifies the outcome of the function. The LOBYTE returns the number of host adapters installed if the HIBYTE value equals SS_COMP. The HIBYTE returns whether ASPI for Windows is ready to accept ASPI commands. Refer to the sample code. The HIBYTE is defined as shown in Table 11.12.

**Table 11.12: HIBYTE Return Values for GetASPISupportInfo**

| Value | Meaning |
| --- | --- |
| SS_COMP | SCSI/ASPI request has completed without error. |
| SS_OLD_MANAGER | One or more ASPI for DOS managers are loaded that do not support ASPI for Windows. |

| Value | Meaning |
|---|---|
| SS_ILLEGAL_MODE | This ASPI manager does not support this mode of Windows. You will typically see this error code when running Windows in real mode. |
| SS_NO_ASPI | No ASPI managers are loaded. This is typically caused by a DOS ASPI manager not being resident in memory. |
| SS_FAILED_INIT | For some reason, other than SS_OLD_MANAGER, SS_ILLEGAL_MODE, or SS_NO_ASPI, ASPI for Windows could not properly initialize itself. This may be caused by a lack of system resources. |

### *Example*

The following example returns the current status of ASPI for Windows:

```
WORD ASPIStatus;
BYTE NumAdapters;
HWND hwnd;

       .
       .

ASPIStatus = GetASPISupportInfo();
switch ( HIBYTE(ASPIStatus) )
{
  case SS_COMP:
    //ASPI for Windows is properly initialized
    NumAdapters = LOBYTE(ASPIStatus);
    break;
  case SS_NO_ASPI:
    MessageBox( hwnd, "No ASPI managers were found!!", NULL, MB_ICONSTOP );
    return 0;
  case SS_ILLEGAL_MODE:
    MessageBox( hwnd, "ASPI for Windows does not support this mode!!", NULL, MB_ICONSTOP );
    return 0;
  case SS_OLD_MANAGER:
    MessageBox( hwnd, "An ASPI manager which does not support Windows is resident!!",
      NULL, MB_ICONSTOP );
    return 0;
  default:
  MessageBox( hwnd, "ASPI for Windows is not initialized!!",
   NULL, MB_ICONSTOP );
   return 0;
}
       .
       .
```

# SendASPICommand—SC_HA_INQUIRY

**WORD SendASPICommand(lpSRB)**
    **LPSRB lpSRB;**

The SendASPICommand function with command code SC_HA_INQUIRY (defined in Table 11.13) is used to get information on the installed host adapter hardware, including the number of host adapters installed.

| Parameter | Description |
|-----------|-------------|
| lpSRB | Points to the following SCSI request block: |

```
typedef struct
{
  BYTE  SRB_Cmd;              // ASPI command code = SC_HA_INQUIRY
  BYTE  SRB_Status;           // ASPI command status byte
  BYTE  SRB_HaId;             // ASPI host adapter number
  BYTE  SRB_Flags;            // ASPI request flags
  DWORD SRB_Hdr_Rsvd;         // Reserved, MUST = 0
  BYTE  HA_Count;             // Number of host adapters present
  BYTE  HA_SCSI_ID;           // SCSI ID of host adapter
  BYTE  HA_ManagerId[16];     // String describing the manager
  BYTE  HA_Identifier[16];    // String describing the host adapter
  BYTE  HA_Unique[16];        // Host Adapter Unique parameters
} SRB_HAInquiry;
```

**Table 11.13: SRB_HAInquiry Structure Definition**

| Member | Description | R/W |
|--------|-------------|-----|
| SRB_Cmd | This field must contain SC_HA_INQUIRY. | W |
| SRB_Status | On return, this field will be the same as the return status defined below. | R |
| SRB_HaId | This field specifies which installed host adapter the request is intended for. Host adapter numbers are always assigned by the SCSI manager layer beginning with zero. | W |
| SRB_Flags | The SRB Flags field is currently reserved for this function and must be zeroed before passed to the ASPI manager. | W |
| SRB_Hdr_Rsvd | This DWORD field is currently reserved for this function and must be zeroed before passed to the ASPI manager. | — |

| Member | Description | R/W |
|---|---|---|
| HA_Count | The ASPI manager will set this field with the number of host adapters installed under ASPI. For example, a return value of 2 indicates that host adapters #0 and #1 are valid. To determine the total number of host adapters in the system, the SRB_Hald field should be set to zero, or GetASPISupportInfo can be used. | R |
| HA_SCSI_ID | The ASPI manager will set this field with the SCSI ID of the given host adapter. | R |
| HA_ManagerId[..] | The ASPI manager will fill this 16-character buffer with an ASCII string describing the ASPI manager. | R |
| HA_Identifier[..] | The ASPI manager will fill this 16-character buffer with an ASCII string describing the SCSI host adapter. | R |
| HA_Unique[..] | The ASPI manager will fill this 16-byte buffer with host adapter unique parameters. The definition is left to implementation notes specific to a particular host adapter. | R |

### Returns

The return value specifies the outcome of the function. One of the values shown in Table 11.14 will be returned by ASPI for Windows.

**Table 11.14: Values Returned by ASPI for Windows**

| Value | Meaning |
|---|---|
| SS_COMP | SCSI/ASPI request has completed without error |
| SS_INVALID_HA | Invalid host adapter number |
| SS_INVALID_SRB | The SCSI request block (SRB) has one or more parameters set incorrectly |

### Example

The following example retrieves host adapter hardware information from adapter #0:

```
SRB_HAInquiry MySRB;
WORD ASPI_Status;
        .
        .
MySRB.SRB_Cmd = SC_HA_INQUIRY;
```

```
MySRB.SRB_HaId = 0;
MySRB.SRB_Flags = 0;
MySRB.SRB_Hdr_Rsvd = 0;
ASPI_Status = SendASPICommand ( (LPSRB) &MySRB );
                .
                .
```

## SendASPICommand—SC_GET_DEV_TYPE

**WORD SendASPICommand(lpSRB)**
    **LPSRB lpSRB;**

The SendASPICommand function with command code SC_GET_DEV_TYPE
(defined in Table 11.15) is intended for use by Windows applications for identifying the targets they need to support. For example, a Windows tape backup
package can scan each target/LUN on each installed host adapter looking for
the device type corresponding to sequential access devices. This eliminates the
need for each Windows application to duplicate the effort of scanning the SCSI
bus for devices.

**NOTE** *Rather than use this command, some Windows applications may favor scanning the
SCSI bus themselves in case a SCSI device was not present during ASPI initialization
but was rather powered up after ASPI initialization.*

| Parameter | Description |
|-----------|-------------|
| lpSRB | Points to the following SCSI request block: |

```
typedef struct
{
  BYTE  SRB_Cmd;               // ASPI command code = SC_GET_DEV_TYPE
  BYTE  SRB_Status;            // ASPI command status byte
  BYTE  SRB_HaId;              // ASPI host adapter number
  BYTE  SRB_Flags;             // ASPI request flags
  DWORD SRB_Hdr_Rsvd;          // Reserved, MUST = 0
  BYTE  SRB_Target;            // Target's SCSI ID
  BYTE  SRB_Lun;               // Target's LUN number
  BYTE  SRB_DeviceType;        // Target's peripheral device type
} SRB_GDEVBlock;
```

### Returns

The return value specifies the outcome of the function. One of the values
shown in Table 11.16 will be returned by ASPI for Windows.

## Table 11.15: SRB_GDEVBlock Structure Definition

| Member | Description | R/W |
|---|---|---|
| SRB_Cmd | This field must contain SC_GET_DEV_TYPE. | W |
| SRB_Status | On return, this field will be the same as the return status defined below. | R |
| SRB_HaId | This field specifies which installed host adapter the request is intended for. Host adapter numbers are always assigned by the SCSI manager layer beginning with zero. | W |
| SRB_Flags | The SRB Flags field is currently reserved for this function and must be zeroed before passed to the ASPI manager. | W |
| SRB_Hdr_Rsvd | This DWORD field is currently reserved for this function and must be zeroed before passed to the ASPI manager. | — |
| SRB_Target | Target ID of device. | W |
| SRB_Lun | Logical unit number (LUN) of device. | W |
| SRB_DeviceType | The ASPI manager will fill this field with the peripheral device type. Refer to any SCSI specification to learn more about the SCSI Inquiry command. | R |

## Table 11.16: Return Values for SendASPI Command SC_GET_DEV_TYPE

| Value | Meaning |
|---|---|
| SS_COMP | SCSI/ASPI request has completed without error. |
| SS_INVALID_HA | Invalid host adapter number. |
| SS_NO_DEVICE | SCSI device not installed. |
| SS_INVALID_SRB | The SCSI request block (SRB) has one or more parameters set incorrectly. |

### *Example*

The following example retrieves the peripheral device type from host adapter #0, target ID #4, and LUN #0.

```
SRB_GDEVBlock MySRB;
WORD ASPI_Status;

          .

MySRB.SRB_Cmd = SC_GET_DEV_TYPE;
MySRB.SRB_HaId = 0;
MySRB.SRB_Flags = 0;
MySRB.SRB_Hdr_Rsvd = 0;
MySRB.SRB_Target = 4;
MySRB.SRB_Lun = 0;
ASPI_Status = SendASPICommand ( (LPSRB) &MySRB );

          .

/***************************************************/
/* If ASPI_Status == SS_COMP, MySRB.SRB_DeviceType */
/* will contain the peripheral device type.        */
/***************************************************/

          .

          .
```

## SendASPICommand—SC_EXEC_SCSI_CMD

**WORD SendASPICommand(lpSRB)**
**LPSRB lpSRB;**

The SendASPICommand function with command code SC_EXEC_SCSI_CMD (defined in Table 11.17) is used to execute a SCSI command, for example, send a SCSI Test Unit Ready command to a tape drive, etc.

### Returns

The return value specifies the outcome of the function. One of the values shown in Table 11.18 will be returned by ASPI for Windows.

**Table 11.17: ExecSCSICmd Structure Definition**

| Member | Description | R/W |
|--------|-------------|-----|
| SRB_Cmd | This field must contain SC_EXEC_SCSI_CMD. | W |
| SRB_Status | On return, this field will be the same as the return status defined below. | R |

| Member | Description | R/W |
|---|---|---|
| SRB_Hald | This field specifies which installed host adapter the request is intended for. Host adapter numbers are always assigned by the SCSI manager layer beginning with zero. | W |
| SRB_Flags | The SRB Flags field is defined as follows: | W |

| Value | Meaning |
|---|---|
| SRB_DIR_SCSI | Direction determined by SCSI command. Length not checked. |
| SRB_DIR_IN | Transfer from SCSI target to host. Length checked. |
| SRB_DIR_OUT | Transfer from host to SCSI target. Length checked. |
| SRB_POSTING | If this value is ORed in with one of the previous three values, posting will be enabled. Refer to the section on ASPI posting. |

| Member | Description | R/W |
|---|---|---|
| SRB_Hdr_Rsvd | This DWORD field is currently reserved for this function and must be zeroed before passed to the ASPI manager. | — |
| SRB_Target | Target ID of device. | W |
| SRB_Lun | Logical unit number (LUN) of device. | W |
| SRB_BufLen | This field indicates the number of bytes to be transferred. If the SCSI command to be executed does not transfer data (i.e., est Unit Ready, Rewind, etc.), this field must be set to zero. | W |
| SRB_SenseLen | This field indicates the number of bytes allocated at the end of the SRB for sense data. A request sense is automatically generated if a check condition is presented at the end of a SCSI command. | W |
| SRB_BufPointer | This field is a pointer to the data buffer. | W |
| SRB_CDBLen | This field establishes the length, in bytes, of the SCSI command descriptor block (CDB). This value will typically be 6 or 10. | W |

| Member | Description | R/W |
|---|---|---|
| SRB_HaStat | Upon completion of the SCSI command, the ASPI manager will set this field with the host adapter status as follows: | |

| Value | Meaning |
|---|---|
| HASTAT_OK | Host adapter did not detect an error |
| HASTAT_SEL_TO | Selection timeout |
| HASTAT_DO_DU | Data overrun/underrun |
| HASTAT_BUS_FREE | Unexpected bus free |
| HASTAT_PHASE_ERR | Target bus phase sequence failure |

| Member | Description | R/W |
|---|---|---|
| SRB_TargStat | Upon completion of the SCSI command, the ASPI manager will set this field with the target status as follows: | R |

| Value | Meaning |
|---|---|
| STATUS_GOOD | No target status |
| STATUS_CHKCOND | Check status (sense data is in Sense Area) |
| STATUS_BUSY | Specified target/LUN is busy |
| STATUS_RESCONF | Reservation conflict |

| Member | Description | R/W |
|---|---|---|
| SRB_PostProc | If posting is enabled, ASPI for Windows will post completion of an ASPI request to this function pointer. Refer to the section on ASPI Posting. | W |
| CDBByte[..] | This field contains the CDB as defined by the target's SCSI command set. The length of the SCSI CDB is specified in the SRB_CDBLen field. | W |
| SenseArea[..] | The SenseArea is filled with the sense data on a check condition. The maximum length of this field is specified in the SRB_SenseLen field. Note that the target can return fewer than the number of sense bytes requested. | R |

**NOTE** *You can easily create a new structure for nonstandard CDB lengths.*

| Parameter | Description |
|---|---|
| lpSRB | Points to one of the following SCSI request blocks: |

```
typedef struct
{                                      // Structure for 6-byte CDBs
  BYTE   SRB_Cmd;                      // ASPI command code = SC_EXEC_SCSI_CMD
  BYTE   SRB_Status;                   // ASPI command status byte
  BYTE   SRB_HaId;                     // ASPI host adapter number
  BYTE   SRB_Flags;                    // ASPI request flags
  DWORD  SRB_Hdr_Rsvd;                 // Reserved, MUST = 0
  BYTE   SRB_Target;                   // Target's SCSI ID
  BYTE   SRB_Lun;                      // Target's LUN number
  DWORD  SRB_BufLen;                   // Data Allocation LengthPG
  BYTE   SRB_SenseLen;                 // Sense Allocation Length
  BYTE   far *SRB_BufPointer;          // Data Buffer Pointer
  DWORD  SRB_Rsvd1;                    // Reserved, MUST = 0
  BYTE   SRB_CDBLen;                   // CDB Length = 6
  BYTE   SRB_HaStat;                   // Host Adapter Status
  BYTE   SRB_TargStat;                 // Target Status
  FARPROC SRB_PostProc;                // Post routine
  BYTE   SRB_Rsvd2[34];                // Reserved, MUST = 0
  BYTE   CDBByte[6];                   // SCSI CDB
  BYTE   SenseArea6[SENSE_LEN];        // Request Sense buffer
} SRB_ExecSCSICmd6;


typedef struct
{                                      // Structure for 10-byte CDBs
BYTE    SRB_Cmd;                       // ASPI command code = SC_EXEC_SCSI_CMD
BYTE    SRB_Status;                    // ASPI command status byte
BYTE    SRB_HaId;                      // ASPI host adapter number
BYTE    SRB_Flags;                     // ASPI request flags
DWORD   SRB_Hdr_Rsvd;                  // Reserved, MUST = 0
BYTE    SRB_Target;                    // Target's SCSI ID
BYTE    SRB_Lun;                       // Target's LUN number
DWORD   SRB_BufLen;                    // Data Allocation Length
BYTE    SRB_SenseLen;                  // Sense Allocation Length
BYTE    far *SRB_BufPointer;           // Data Buffer Pointer
DWORD   SRB_Rsvd1;                     // Reserved, MUST = 0
BYTE    SRB_CDBLen;                    // CDB Length = 10
BYTE    SRB_HaStat;                    // Host Adapter Status
BYTE    SRB_TargStat;                  // Target Status
FARPROC SRB_PostProc;                  // Post routine
```

```
BYTE  SRB_Rsvd2[34];           // Reserved, MUST = 0
BYTE  CDBByte[10];             // SCSI CDB
BYTE  SenseArea10[SENSE_LEN];  // Request Sense buffer
} SRB_ExecSCSICmd10;
```

**Table 11.18: Return Values for SendASPI Command SC_EXEC_SCSI_CMD**

| Value | Meaning |
| --- | --- |
| SS_PENDING | SCSI request is in progress. |
| SS_COMP | SCSI/ASPI request has completed without error. |
| SS_ABORTED | SCSI command has been aborted. |
| SS_ERR | SCSI command has completed with an error. |
| SS_INVALID_SRB | SCSI request block (SRB) has one or more parameters set incorrectly. |
| SS_ASPI_IS_BUSY | ASPI manager cannot handle the request at this time. This error will generally occur if the ASPI manager is already using up all of its resources to execute other requests. You should try resending the command later. |
| SS_BUFFER_TO_BIG | ASPI manager cannot handle the given transfer size. Please refer to the "Miscellaneous" section for more information. |

### Example

The following example sends a SCSI Inquiry command to host adapter #0, target #0, and LUN #0:

```
SRB_ExecSCSICmd6 MySRB;
char InquiryBuffer[32];
FARPROC lpfnPostProcedure;
        .
        .
        .
lpfnPostProcedure = MakeProcInstance (PostProcedure, hInstance);
        .
        .
        .
MySRB.SRB_Cmd = SC_EXEC_SCSI_CMD;
MySRB.SRB_HaId = 0;
MySRB.SRB_Flags = SRB_DIR_SCSI | SRB_POSTING;
MySRB.SRB_Hdr_Rsvd = 0;
MySRB.SRB_Target = 0;
MySRB.SRB_Lun = 0;
MySRB.SRB_BufLen = 32;
MySRB.SRB_SenseLen = SENSE_LEN;
MySRB.SRB_BufPointer = InquiryBuffer;
```

```
MySRB.SRB_CDBLen = 6;
MySRB.SRB_PostProc = lpfnPostProcedure;
MySRB.CDBByte[0] = SCSI_INQUIRY;
MySRB.CDBByte[1] = 0;
MySRB.CDBByte[2] = 0;
MySRB.CDBByte[3] = 0;
MySRB.CDBByte[4] = 32;
MySRB.CDBByte[5] = 0;

        .

/***************************************************/
/* Make sure all other reserved fields are zeroed */
/* before passing the SRB to ASPI for Windows      */
/***************************************************/

SendASPICommand ( (LPSRB) &MySRB );

        .

        .
```

## SendASPICommand—SC_ABORT_SRB

**WORD SendASPICommand(lpSRB)**
    **LPSRB lpSRB;**

The SendASPICommand function with command code SC_ABORT_SRB (defined in Table 11.19) is used to request that an SRB be aborted. It should be issued on any I/O request that has not completed if the application wishes to timeout on that request. Success of the Abort command is never ensured.

**Table 11.19: SRB_Abort Structure Definition**

| Member | Description | R/W |
|---|---|---|
| SRB_Cmd | This field must contain SC_ABORT_SRB. | W |
| SRB_Status | On return. | R |
| SRB_Hald | This field specifies which installed host adapter the request is intended for. Host adapter numbers are always assigned by the SCSI manager layer beginning with zero. | W |
| SRB_Flags | The SRB flags field is currently reserved for this function and must be zeroed before passed to the ASPI manager. | W |
| SRB_Hdr_Rsvd | This DWORD field is currently reserved for this function and must be zeroed before passed to the ASPI manager. | — |
| SRB_ToAbort | This field contains a pointer to the SRB that is to be aborted. The actual failure or success of the abort operation is indicated by the status eventually returned in this SRB. | W |

| Parameter | Description |
|-----------|-------------|
| lpSRB | Points to the following SCSI request block: |

```
typedef struct
{
  BYTE    SRB_Cmd;                    // ASPI command code = SC_ABORT_SRB
  BYTE    SRB_Status;                 // ASPI command status byte
  BYTE    SRB_HaId;                   // ASPI host adapter number
  BYTE    SRB_Flags;                  // ASPI request flags
  DWORD   SRB_Hdr_Rsvd;               // Reserved, MUST = 0
  LPSRB   SRB_ToAbort;                // Pointer to SRB to abort
} SRB_Abort;
```

### Returns

The return value specifies the outcome of the function. One of the values shown in Table 11.20 will be returned by ASPI for Windows.

### Table 11.20: Return Values for SendASPICommand SC_ABORT_SRB

| Value | Meaning |
|-------|---------|
| SS_COMP | SCSI/ASPI request has completed without error. |
| SS_INVALID_HA | Invalid host adapter number. |
| SS_INVALID_SRB | SCSI request block (SRB) has one or more parameters set incorrectly. |

### Example

The following example shows how to abort a stuck SCSI I/O:

```
SRB_ExecSCSICmd6 StuckSRB;
SRB_Abort AbortSRB;
WORD ASPI_Status;
       .
       .
       .
AbortSRB.SRB_Cmd = SC_ABORT_SRB;
AbortSRB.SRB_HaId = 0;
AbortSRB.SRB_Flags = 0;
AbortSRB.SRB_Hdr_Rsvd = 0;
AbortSRB.SRB_ToAbort = (LPSRB) &StuckSRB;
ASPI_Status = SendASPICommand ( (LPSRB) &AbortSRB );
       .
       .
       .
while (StuckSRB.SRB_Status==SS_PENDING);
       .
       .
```

```
/**********************************************/
/* This sample code has no error handling, time-  */
/* out code, nor does it free up the processor.   */
/* Your application should be more robust.        */
/**********************************************/
```

## SendASPICommand—SC_RESET_DEV

**WORD SendASPICommand(lpSRB)**
   **LPSRB lpSRB;**
The SendASPICommand function with command code SC_RESET_DEV
(defined in Table 11.21) is used to send a SCSI bus device reset to the specified target.

### Table 11.21: SRB_BusDeviceReset Structure Definition

| Member | Description | R/W |
|--------|-------------|-----|
| SRB_Cmd | This field must contain SC_RESET_DEV. | W |
| SRB_Status | On return, this field will be the same as the return status defined below. | R |
| SRB_HaId | This field specifies which installed host adapter the request is in-tended for. Host adapter numbers are always assigned by the SCSI manager layer beginning with zero. | W |
| SRB_Flags | The SRB Flags field is currently reserved for this function and must be zeroed before passed to the ASPI manager. | W |
| SRB_Hdr_Rsvd | This DWORD field is currently reserved for this function and must be zeroed before passed to the ASPI manager. | — |
| SRB_Target | Target ID of device. | W |
| SRB_Lun | Logical unit number (LUN) of device. This field is ignored by ASPI for Windows since SCSI bus device resets are done on a per tar-get basis only. | W |
| SRB_HaStat | Upon completion of the SCSI command, the ASPI manager will set this field with the host adapter status as follows: | R |

| Member | Description | R/W |
|---|---|---|

| Value | Meaning |
|---|---|
| HASTAT_OK | Host adapter did not detect an error |
| HASTAT_SEL_TO | Selection timeout |
| HASTAT_DO_DU | Data overrun/underrun |
| HASTAT_BUS_FREE | Unexpected bus free |
| HASTAT_PHASE_ERR | Target bus phase sequence failure |

**SRB_TargStat** — Upon completion of the SCSI command, the ASPI manager will set this field with the target status as follows: — R

| Value | Meaning |
|---|---|
| STATUS_GOOD | No target status |
| STATUS_CHKCOND | Check status (sense data is in SenseArea) |
| STATUS_BUSY | Specified target/LUN is busy |
| STATUS_RESCONF | Reservation conflict |

**SRB_PostProc** — If posting is enabled, ASPI for Windows will post completion of an ASPI request to this function pointer. Refer to the section on ASPI Posting. — W

| Parameter | Description |
|---|---|
| lpSRB | Points to the following SCSI request block: |

```
typedef struct
{
  BYTESRB_Cmd;                    // ASPI command code = SC_RESET_DEV
  BYTE   SRB_Status;              // ASPI command status byte
  BYTE   SRB_HaId;                // ASPI host adapter number
  BYTE   SRB_Flags;               // ASPI request flags
  DWORD  SRB_Hdr_Rsvd;            // Reserved, MUST = 0
  BYTE   SRB_Target;              // Target's SCSI ID
  BYTE   SRB_Lun;                 // Target's LUN number
  BYTE   SRB_ResetRsvd1[14];      // Reserved, MUST = 0
  BYTE   SRB_HaStat;              // Host Adapter Status
  BYTE   SRB_TargStat;            // Target Status
  FARPROC SRB_PostProc;           // Post routine
  BYTE   SRB_ResetRsvd2[34];      // Reserved, MUST = 0
} SRB_BusDeviceReset
```

### Returns

The return value specifies the outcome of the function. One of the values shown in Table 11.22 will be returned by ASPI for Windows. Refer to each ASPI command code definition for information on which ASPI commands return which errors.

**Table 11.22: Return Values for SendASPICommand SC_RESET_DEV**

| Value | Meaning |
| --- | --- |
| SS_COMP | SCSI/ASPI request has completed without error. |
| SS_INVALID_HA | Invalid host adapter number. |
| SS_INVALID_SRB | SCSI request block (SRB) has one or more parameters set incorrectly. |
| SS_ASPI_IS_BUSY | ASPI manager cannot handle the request at this time. This error will generally occur if the ASPI manager is already using up all of his resources to execute other requests. You should try resending the command later. |

### Example

The following example issues a SCSI bus device reset to host adapter #0, target #5:

```
SRB_BusDeviceReset MySRB;
WORD ASPI_Status;
        .
        .
        .
MySRB.SRB_Cmd = SC_RESET_DEV;
MySRB.SRB_HaId = 0;
MySRB.SRB_Flags = 0;
MySRB.SRB_Hdr_Rsvd = 0;
MySRB.SRB_Target = 5;
MySRB.SRB_Lun = 0;
ASPI_Status = SendASPICommand ( (LPSRB) &MySRB );
        .
        .
/************************************************/
/* Make sure all other reserved fields are zeroed */
/* before passing the SRB to ASPI for Windows    */
/************************************************/
        .
while (MySRB.SRB_Status==SS_PENDING);
        .
        .
```

```
/**************************************************/
/* This sample code has no error handling, time-  */
/* out code, nor does it free up the processor.   */
/* Your application should be more robust.        */
/**************************************************/
```

## ASPI Polling

Once you send an ASPI for Windows SCSI request, you have two ways of being notified that the SCSI request has completed. The first and simplest method is called polling. After the command is sent, and ASPI for Windows returns control back to your program, you can poll the status byte waiting for the command to complete. For example, the following code segment sends a SCSI Inquiry command to target #2.

```
SRB_ExecSCSICmd6 MySRB;
char InquiryBuffer[32];

          .
          .

/**************************************************/
/* Code is entered with 'MySRB' zeroed.           */
/**************************************************/
MySRB.SRB_Cmd = SC_EXEC_SCSI_CMD;
MySRB.SRB_Flags = SRB_DIR_SCSI;
MySRB.SRB_Target = 2;
MySRB.SRB_BufLen = 32;
MySRB.SRB_SenseLen = SENSE_LEN;
MySRB.SRB_BufPointer = InquiryBuffer;
MySRB.SRB_CDBLen = 6;
MySRB.CDBByte[0] = SCSI_INQUIRY;
MySRB.CDBByte[4] = 32;

          .
          .

SendASPICommand ( (LPSRB) &MySRB );               // Send Inquiry command
while ( MySRB.SRB_Status == SS_PENDING );         // Wait till it's finished
/**************************************************/
/* At this point, the SCSI command has completed  */
/* with or without an error.                      */
/**************************************************/
if ( MySRB.SRB_Status == SS_COMP )
        ;                                         // Command completed without error
else
        ;                                         // Command completed with error
```

Since Windows is currently a nonpreemptive multitasking operating system, you should use polling with caution. The example above is not very good about freeing up the processor, nor does it have any timeout handler. Later in this specification, you will find sample code that does free up the processor while using polling.

## ASPI Posting

Most applications will use posting, rather than polling, to be notified that a SCSI request has completed. When posting is enabled, ASPI for Windows will post completion by calling your callback function. For example, the following code segment will send a SCSI Inquiry command to target #2 during the WM_CREATE message.

```
long FAR PASCAL WndProc (HWND, WORD, WORD, LONG);
void FAR PASCAL ASPIPostProc ( LPSRB );
HWND PostHWND;
HANDLE hInstance;

            .
            .
            .

//*************************************************************************
// ASPIPostProc - ASPI for Windows will post completion of a SCSI
//                request to this function. Note that this is most
//                likely during interrupt time so you can only use
//                a few Windows functions like 'PostMessage.' This
//                example post procedure is very simple. It will
//                wake up your application by posting a WM_ASPIPOST
//                message to your window handle.
//*************************************************************************
void FAR PASCAL ASPIPostProc ( LPSRB DoneSRB )
{
  PostMessage (PostHWND, WM_ASPIPOST,
   (WORD) ((SRB_ExecSCSICmd6 far *)DoneSRB)->SRB_Status,
   (DWORD) DoneSRB );
  return;
}
//*************************************************************************
// WndProc - Window message handler
//*************************************************************************
long FAR PASCAL WndProc ( HWND hwnd, WORD message, WORD wParam, LONG lParam)
{
  static SRB_ExecSCSICmd6 MySRB;
  static char InquiryBuffer[32];
  switch (message)
```

```
{
  case WM_CREATE:
    /***************************************************/
    /* Code is entered with 'MySRB' zeroed.            */
    /***************************************************/
    lpfnASPIPostProc = MakeProcInstance (ASPIPostProc, hInstance);
    PostHWND = hwnd;
    MySRB.SRB_Cmd = SC_EXEC_SCSI_CMD;
    MySRB.SRB_Flags = SRB_DIR_SCSI|SRB_POSTING;
    MySRB.SRB_Target = 2;
    MySRB.SRB_BufLen = 32;
    MySRB.SRB_SenseLen = SENSE_LEN;
    MySRB.SRB_BufPointer = InquiryBuffer;
    MySRB.SRB_CDBLen = 6;
    ExecSRB.SRB_PostProc = lpfnASPIPostProc;
    MySRB.CDBByte[0] = SCSI_INQUIRY;
    MySRB.CDBByte[4] = 32;

        .
        .
    if ( SendASPICommand ( (LPSRB) &MySRB ) != SS_PENDING )
    {
        ;                       // Check return status for cause of failure!
        ;                       // Posting will NOT occur due to failure
    }
    else
    {
        ;                       // ASPI for Windows will post completion to
        ;                       // 'lpfnASPIPostProc' when command has completed.
    }
    return 0;
  case WM_ASPIPOST:
                                // Return status is in 'wParam'
                                // SRB Pointer is in 'lParam'
                                // We might want to send another ASPI request here.
                                // Look at 'ASPIPostProc' for more information.

    return 0;
  case WM_DESTROY:
    PostQuitMessage(0);
    return 0;
}
return DefWindowProc ( hwnd, message, wParam, lParam );
}

        .
        .
        .
```

When the post routine gets called, the sample post handler will fill the wParam field and will contain the status of ASPI command (SRB_Status) while the lParam field will contain a far pointer to the SRB that has completed.

## Miscellaneous

- Your ASPI for Windows program should never exit with pending SCSI I/Os. Doing so could lead to system instability. Send an ASPI Abort command if you need to.

- Your SRBs and data buffers must be in page-locked memory. Most SCSI host adapters are bus masters. This means that the data buffer must not move while the transfer is taking place. We recommend that you allocate your buffers using GlobalAlloc and then locking it first with GlobalLock and then with GlobalPageLock. This technique has been used to over-come some of the quirks that Windows 3.x seems to have with locking down buffers.

- It is a minimal requirement that all ASPI for Windows managers support transfers of 64K (64 kilobytes) or less. It is not possible for all SCSI host adapters to transfer data larger than this size. If the ASPI manager is unable to support your requested transfer size, you will be returned the SS_BUFFER_TO_BIG error from the SendASPICommand routine. No posting will occur. If this occurs, you should break the transfer down into 64K transfers or less. For maximum compatibility, it is recommended that you do not request transfer sizes larger than 64K if you do not need to.

- Do not forget to support the SS_ASPI_IS_BUSY return status when sending a SCSI command. Under extreme loads, some ASPI for Windows managers may not have enough resources to service each request.

- If you send an ASPI request with posting enabled, and the return value is not equal to SS_PENDING (in other words, the request is not in progress), then ASPI for Windows will not post completion to your specified window handle. (Refer to the specific return value for more information as to why the request is not in progress.)

- ASPI for Windows is fully multitasking. You can send a request to ASPI while another request is executing. Make sure you use a separate SRB for each ASPI request. It is also recommended that you only send one SRB at a time per target.

- If using posting, your post routine will most likely be called during inter-rupt time. Since most Windows routines are non-reentrant, you should call Windows routines with caution. One function you can call is PostMessage, which can be called during interrupt time.

- Make sure that you zero out all reserved fields before passing the SRB to ASPI for Windows.

# Error Codes and Messages

All ASPI for Windows calls can fail. This specification has already defined which error codes can be returned by each ASPI routine. Table 11.23 summarizes all of the error codes returned by ASPI routines.

**Table 11.23: ASPI for Windows Error Codes**

| Error Code | Value | Meaning |
|------------|-------|---------|
| 0x0000 | SS_PENDING | SCSI request is in progress. |
| 0x0001 | SS_COMP | SCSI/ASPI request has completed without error. |
| 0x0002 | SS_ABORTED | SCSI command has been aborted. |
| 0x0004 | SS_ERR | SCSI command has completed with an error. |
| 0x0080 | SS_INVALID_CMD | Invalid ASPI command code. |
| 0x0081 | SS_INVALID_HA | Invalid host adapter number. |
| 0x0082 | SS_NO_DEVICE | SCSI device not installed. |
| 0x00E0 | SS_INVALID_SRB | SCSI request block (SRB) has one or more parameters set incorrectly. |
| 0x00E1 | SS_OLD_MANAGER | One or more ASPI for DOS managers are loaded that do not support Windows. |
| 0x00E2 | SS_ILLEGAL_MODE | This ASPI manager does not support this mode of Windows. You will typically see this error code when running Windows in real mode. |
| 0x00E3 | SS_NO_ASPI | No ASPI managers are loaded. This is typically caused by a DOS ASPI manager not being resident in memory. |
| 0x00E4 | SS_FAILED_INIT | For some reason, other than SS_OLD_MANAGER, SS_ILLEGAL_MODE, or SS_NO_ASPI, ASPI for Windows could not properly initialize itself. This may be caused by a lack of system resources. |
| 0x00E5 | SS_ASPI_IS_BUSY | ASPI manager cannot handle the request at this time. This error will generally occur if the ASPI manager is already using up all of his resources to execute other requests. You should try resending the command later. |
| 0x00E6 | SS_BUFFER_TO_BIG | ASPI manager cannot handle this larger than 64K transfer. You'll need to break up the SCSI I/O into smaller 64K transfers. |

## IV. ASPI for Win32 Specification

ASPI for Win32 is rather similar to ASPI for Windows, but has a few issues to keep in mind:

- If you are using explicit dynamic linking, remember that the ASPI for Win32 DLL is named WNASPI32.DLL and not WINASPI.DLL. Make sure to call LoadLibrary appropriately. Similarly, make sure to use WNASPI32.LIB instead of WINASPI.LIB when using implicit dynamic linking.

- ASPI for Win32 is fully reentrant and permits overlapped, asynchronous I/O. ASPI modules can send additional ASPI requests while others are pending completion. Be sure to use separate SRBs for each ASPI request.

- SRB structure definitions are different in ASPI for Win32 from those in ASPI for Win16; however, structure names are consistent with those used in ASPI for Win16. If you would like to use one source base for both 16- and 32-bit applications, make sure that you conditionally compile with the appropriate include files for each programming model. Include files are available in the ASPI developer's kit.

- For requests requiring data transfers, the direction bits in the SRB_Flags field must be set correctly. Direction bits are no longer optional for data transfers. This means that SRB_DIR_SCSI is no longer a valid setting. For requests not requiring data transfers, the direction bits are ignored.

- Be sure that buffers are aligned according to the buffer alignment mask returned by the SC_HA_INQUIRY command. An alignment of at least a double word is recommended.

- ASPI SCSI Request Blocks (SRBs) and data buffers do not need to be in page-locked memory. The ASPI manager takes care of locking buffers and SRBs. This is different from previous versions of ASPI for Win16 which required the application to page lock both the SRB and the data buffer.

- If an error SS_BUFFER_TO_BIG is returned by the SendASPI32Command routine, you should break the transfer down into multiple 64K-byte transfers or less. Another alternative is to use the GetASPI32Buffer/ FreeASPI32Buffer calls to allocate large transfer buffers. For maximum compatibility, however, we strongly recommend that you do not request transfer sizes larger than 64K bytes.

- If you send an ASPI request with posting (callbacks) enabled, the post procedure will always be called. This is different from previous versions of ASPI for DOS and ASPI for Win16 which only performed the callback if SS_PENDING was returned from SendASPI32Command.

- The CDB area has been fixed in length at 16. Therefore, the sense data area no longer shifts location depending on command length as in ASPI for Win16. If you are developing an application targeted only at Win32, you no longer need to account for the "floating" sense buffer.

- When scanning for devices, the SendASPI32Command may also return the status SS_NO_DEVICE in the SRB_Status field. Check for this exception in addition to the host adapter status HASTAT_SEL_TO.

## Programming Conventions

This specification contains function prototypes and structure definitions with the following data types (Table 11.24):

**Table 11.24: Data Types for ASPI for Win32**

| Type | Size (Bytes) | Description |
|---|---|---|
| VOID | N/A | Indicates lack of a return value or lack of function arguments. |
| BYTE | 1 | Unsigned 8-bit value. |
| WORD | 2 | Unsigned 16-bit value. |
| DWORD | 4 | Unsigned 32-bit value. |
| LPVOID | 4 | Generic pointer. Used in SRB fields which require either a pointer to a function or a Win32 handle (for example, SRB_PostProc). |
| LPBYTE | 4 | Pointer to an array of BYTEs. Mainly used as a buffer pointer. |
| LPSRB | 4 | Generic pointer to one of the SRB_* structures defined below. |

Unless otherwise noted, all multibyte fields follow Intel's byte order of low byte first and end with the high byte. For example, if there is a 2-byte offset field, the first byte is the low byte of the offset while the second byte is the high byte of the offset.

All structure fields marked reserved *must be set to zero,* and structures *must be packed!* Packed means that byte alignment is used on all structure definitions. Microsoft compilers allow byte packing to be set through the use of "#pragma pack(1)" while Borland compilers allow packing to be set with "#pragma option -a1." See your compiler documentation for more information. Failure to pack structures and zero reserved fields can cause system instability, including crashes.

All ASPI for Win32 functions are exported from WNASPI32.DLL using the 'C' calling convention (specifically, __cdecl as implemented by Microsoft's compilers). With the 'C' calling convention the caller pushes the last function argument on the stack first (the first argument has the lowest memory address), and the caller is responsible for popping arguments from the stack.

## Calling ASPI Functions

Applications which utilize ASPI for Win32 are known as ASPI modules. ASPI modules interact with ASPI through WNASPI32.DLL which is a dynamic link library with five entry points (Table 11.25):

**Table 11.25: ASPI for Win32 functions**

| Entry Point | Description |
|---|---|
| GetASPI32SupportInfo | Initializes ASPI and returns basic configuration information. |
| SendASPI32Command | Submits SCSI Request Blocks (SRBs) for execution by ASPI. |
| GetASPI32Buffer | Allocates buffers which meet Win95/WinNT large transfer requirements. |
| FreeASPI32Buffer | Releases buffers previously allocated with GetASPI32Buffer. |
| TranslateASPI32Address | Translates ASPI HA/ID/LUN address triples to/from Win95 DEVNODEs. |

Note that three of these functions — GetASPI32Buffer, FreeASPI32Buffer, and TranslateASPI32Address — did not become a part of ASPI for Win32 until version 4.01 of EZ-SCSI.

In order to access these five functions, they must be resident in memory. Dynamic linking is the process by which Windows 95 and Windows NT loads dynamic link libraries (DLLs) into memory and then resolves application references to functions within those DLLs. There are two ways in which this load/ resolve sequence is handled: explicitly or implicitly.

### Explicit Dynamic Linking

Explicit dynamic linking occurs when applications or other DLLs *explicitly* load a DLL using LoadLibrary and then manually resolve references to individual DLL functions through calls to GetProcAddress. This is the preferred method for loading and calling ASPI for Win32. Explicit dynamic linking allows complete control over when ASPI is loaded and how load errors are handled. It also is the only way to detect if the three new ASPI functions are available for use in an application.

The following block of code is all that is required to load ASPI:

```
HINSTANCE hinstWNASPI32;
hinstWNASPI32 = LoadLibrary( "WNASPI32" );
if( !hinstWNASPI32 )
{
// Handle ASPI load error here. Usually this involves the display of an
// informative message based on the results of a call to GetLastError().
}
```

Once a valid instance handle for ASPI is obtained, GetProcAddress is used to obtain addresses for each of the ASPI for Win32 entry points:

```
DWORD (*pfnGetASPI32SupportInfo)( void );
DWORD (*pfnSendASPI32Command)( LPSRB );
BOOL (*pfnGetASPI32Buffer)( PASPI32BUFF );
BOOL (*pfnFreeASPI32Buffer)( PASPI32BUFF );
BOOL (*pfnTranslateASPI32Address)( PDWORD, PDWORD );
pfnGetASPI32SupportInfo = GetProcAddress( hinstWNASPI32, "GetASPI32SupportInfo"
);
pfnSendASPI32Command = GetProcAddress( hinstWNASPI32, "SendASPI32Command" );
pfnGetASPI32Buffer = GetProcAddress( hinstWNASPI32, "GetASPI32Buffer" );
pfnFreeASPI32Buffer = GetProcAddress( hinstWNASPI32, "FreeASPI32Buffer" );
pfnTranslateASPI32Address = GetProcAddress(
hinstWNASPI32,"TranslateASPI32Address" );
```

At this point there should be a valid address for each of the five functions. If you have an old version of ASPI then the last three function addresses will be NULL. This case should be handled by disabling all use of new features in your ASPI module. It is also good practice to check pfnGetASPI32SupportInfo and pfnSendASPI32Command for NULL as well. These variables will be NULL if there is an error accessing the DLL. If either of these two functions have NULL addresses your application should cease its use of ASPI and unload WNASPI32.DLL with a call to FreeLibrary.

Using the addresses returned from GetProcAddress is very simple. Just use the variable name wherever you would normally use the function name. For example,

```
DWORD dwASPIStatus = pfnGetASPI32SupportInfo();
```

will call the GetASPI32SupportInfo and place the result in dwASPIStatus. Of course, if one of these function pointers is NULL and you make a call to it, your application will crash.

### Implicit Dynamic Linking

Implicit dynamic linking occurs when a dependent DLL is loaded as a result of loading another module. This dependency can be established either by listing exported functions from the DLL in the IMPORTS section of a ".DEF" file linked with the application, or by including the WNASPI32.LIB file (from the ASPI SDK) on the linker command line of the calling application.

Implicit dynamic linking is not recommended for three reasons:

* You cannot control when ASPI is loaded. Like anything else, ASPI consumes system resources. When you use implicit dynamic linking those resources are allocated as soon as the application starts, and they remain allocated until the application shuts down. With explicit dynamic linking the application controls when (and if) ASPI is loaded.

* You have no control over how load errors are reported to users. If ASPI is not found during an implicit load a fairly ugly error message (sometimes two) is displayed by the operating system. If you use explicit loading in conjunction with a call to SetErrorMode( SEM_NOOPENFILEERRORBOX ) then your application can fully handle any load errors on its own.

* Your application cannot recover if it relies on new ASPI features and it is run with an older version of ASPI. If your application relies on GetASPI32Buffer, FreeASPI32Buffer, or TranslateASPI32Address, and then that function is not found in the loaded version of WNASPI32.DLL, then the load fails. By using explicit dynamic linking the application can alter its behavior so that the functions are not used. For example, an application which "relies" on TranslateASPI32Address could simply disable Plug and Play support if the function is not found in the DLL.

## GetASPI32SupportInfo

The GetASPI32SupportInfo function returns the number of host adapters installed and ensures that the ASPI manager is initialized properly. This function must be called once at initialization time, before SendASPI32Command is accessed.

```
DWORD GetASPI32SupportInfo( VOID );
```

### Parameters

None.

### Return Values

The DWORD return value is split into three pieces. The high order WORD is reserved and shall be set to 0. The two low order bytes represent a status code (bits 15-8) and a host adapter count (bits 7-0).

If the call to GetASPI32SupportInfo is successful, then the status byte is set to either SS_COMP or SS_NO_ADAPTERS. If set to SS_COMP then the host adapter status will be non-zero. An error code of SS_NO_ADAPTERS indicates that ASPI initialized successfully, but that it could not find any SCSI host adapters to manage.

If the function fails the status byte will be set to one of SS_ILLEGAL_MODE, SS_NO_ASPI, SS_MISMATCHED_COMPONENTS, SS_INSUFFICIENT_RESOURCES, SS_FAILED_INIT. See the table of ASPI errors later in this chapter for more information on each of the errors.

### Remarks

The number of host adapters returned represents the logical bus count, not the true physical adapter count. For host adapters with a single bus, the host adapter count and logical bus count are identical.

### Example

This example returns the current status of ASPI for Win32.

```
BYTE byHaCount;
BYTE byASPIStatus;
DWORD dwSupportInfo;
dwSupportInfo = GetASPI32SupportInfo();
byASPIStatus = HIBYTE(LOWORD(dwSupportInfo));
byHaCount = LOBYTE(LOWORD(dwSupportInfo));
if( byASPIStatus != SS_COMP && byASPIStatus != SS_NO_ADAPTERS )
{
// Handle ASPI error here. Usually this involves the display
// of a dialog box with an informative message.
}
```

# SendASPI32Command

The SendASPI32Command function handles all SCSI I/O requests. Each SCSI I/O request is handled through a SCSI Request Block (SRB) which defines the exact ASPI operation to be performed.

```
DWORD SendASPI32Command( LPSRB psrb );
```

### Parameters

*psrb:*

All SRBs have a standard header, and the header contains a command code which defines the exact type of SCSI I/O being requested.

```
typedef struct
{
BYTE SRB_Cmd;        // ASPI command code
BYTE SRB_Status;     // ASPI command status byte
BYTE SRB_HaId;       // ASPI host adapter number
BYTE SRB_Flags;      // ASPI request flags
DWORD SRB_Hdr_Rsvd;  // Reserved, MUST = 0
}
SRB_Header;
```

The SRB_Cmd field contains the command code for the desired SCSI I/O operation. This field can be set to one of the values from Table 11.26.

### Table 11.26: ASPI Commands

| Symbol | Value | Description |
|---|---|---|
| SC_HA_INQUIRY | 0x00 | Queries ASPI for information on specific host adapters. |
| SC_GET_DEV_TYPE | 0x01 | Requests the SCSI device type for a specific SCSI target. |
| SC_EXEC_SCSI_CMD | 0x02 | Sends a SCSI command (arbitrary CDB) to a SCSI target. |
| SC_ABORT_SRB | 0x03 | Requests that ASPI cancel a previously submitted request. |
| SC_RESET_DEV | 0x04 | Sends a BUS DEVICE RESET message to a SCSI target. |
| SC_GET_DISK_INFO | 0x06 | Returns BIOS information for a SCSI target (Win95 only). |
| SC_RESCAN_SCSI_BUS | 0x07 | Requests a rescan of a host adapter's SCSI bus. |
| SC_GETSET_TIMEOUTS | 0x08 | Sets SRB timeouts for specific SCSI targets. |

The use of the remaining header fields varies according to the command type. Each of the commands along with their associated SRBs is described in detail in the following sections.

### Return Values

The above ASPI commands may be broken into two categories: synchronous and asynchronous. All of the SRBs are synchronous except for SC_EXEC_SCSI_CMD and SC_RESET_DEV, which are asynchronous.

Calls to SendASPI32Command with synchronous SRBs will not return until execution of that SRB is complete. Upon return the SRB_Status field will be set to the same value which is returned from SendASPI32Command.

Calls to SendASPI32Command with asynchronous SRBs may return control to the caller before the submitted SRB has completed execution. In this case the return value from this function is SS_PENDING, and the caller will have to use polling, posting, or event notification to wait for SRB completion. Once completed, the SRB_Status field contains the true completion status. Remember that while waiting for SRB completion, it is always safe to submit additional SRBs to ASPI for execution.

See the "Waiting for Completion" and "ASPI for Win32 Errors" sections for more information on synchronous/asynchronous SRBs and the various error codes which can be returned either from this function or within an SRB_Status field.

## SC_HA_INQUIRY

The SendASPI32Command function with command code SC_HA_INQUIRY is used to get information on the installed host adapter hardware, including the number of host adapters installed.

```
typedef struct
{
BYTE  SRB_Cmd;                // ASPI command code = SC_HA_INQUIRY
BYTE  SRB_Status;             // ASPI command status byte
BYTE  SRB_HaId;               // ASPI host adapter number
BYTE  SRB_Flags;              // Reserved, MUST = 0
DWORD SRB_Hdr_Rsvd;           // Reserved, MUST = 0
BYTE  HA_Count;               // Number of host adapters present
BYTE  HA_SCSI_ID;             // SCSI ID of host adapter
BYTE  HA_ManagerId[16];       // String describing the manager
BYTE  HA_Identifier[16];      // String describing the host adapter
BYTE  HA_Unique[16];          // Host Adapter Unique parameters
WORD  HA_Rsvd1;               // Reserved, MUST = 0
}
SRB_HAInquiry, *PSRB_HAInquiry;
```

### SRB Fields

**SRB_Cmd (Input)** This field must contain SC_HA_INQUIRY (0x00).

**SRB_Status (Output)** SC_HA_INQUIRY is a synchronous SRB. On return, this field is the same as the SendASPI32Command return value and is set to either SS_COMP or SS_INVALID_HA.

**SRB_HaId (Input)** This field specifies which installed host adapter the request is intended for. Host adapter numbers are always assigned by the ASPI manager, beginning with zero. To determine the total number of host adapters in the system set this field to 0 and then check the HA_Count value on return. GetASPI32SupportInfo can also be used.

**HA_Count (Output)** The number of host adapters detected by ASPI. For example, a return value of 2 indicates that host adapters #0 and #1 are valid. The number of host adapters returned represents the logical bus count instead of the true physical adapter count. For host adapters that support single bus only, the host adapter count and logical bus count are identical. For host adapters that support multiple buses, the host adapter count represents the total logical bus count.

**HA_SCSI_ID (Output)** The SCSI ID of the host adapter on the SCSI bus. SCSI adapters usually use ID 7 as their SCSI ID.

**HA_ManagerId (Output)** The ASCII string "ASPI for Win32." The string is padded with spaces to the full width of the buffer, and it is not null terminated.

**HA_Identifier (Output)** An ASCII string describing the host adapter. The string is padded with spaces to the full width of the buffer, and it is not null terminated.

**HA_Unique (Output)** Host adapter unique parameters as defined in Table 11.27.

**Table 11.27: Host Adapter Unique Parameters**

| Size | Offset | Description |
|------|--------|-------------|
| WORD | 0 | Buffer alignment mask. The host adapter requires data buffer alignment specified by this 16-bit value. A value of 0x0000 indicates no boundary requirements (e.g., byte alignment), 0x0001 indicates word alignment, 0x0003 indicates double-word, 0x0007 indicates 8-byte alignment, etc. The 16-bit value allows data buffer alignments of up to 65536-byte boundaries. Alignment of buffers can be tested by logical ANDing ('&' in 'C') this mask with the buffer address. If the result is 0 the buffer is properly aligned. |

| Size | Offset | Description |
|------|--------|-------------|
| BYTE | 2 | Residual byte count. Set to 0x01 if residual byte counting is supported, 0x00 if not. See "Remarks" below for more information. |
| BYTE | 3 | Maximum SCSI targets. Indicates the maximum number of targets (SCSI IDs) the adapter supports. If this value is not set to 8 or 16, then it should be assumed by the application that the maximum target count is 8. |
| DWORD | 4 | Maximum transfer length. DWORD count indicating the maximum transfer size the host adapter supports. If this number is less than 64KB then the application should assume a maximum transfer count of 64KB. |

### Remarks

Residual byte length is the number of bytes not transferred to, or received from, the target SCSI device. For example, if the ASPI buffer length for a SCSI INQUIRY command is set for 100 bytes, but the target only returns 36 bytes; the residual length is 64 bytes. If the ASPI buffer length for a SCSI WRITE command is set for 514 bytes but the target only takes 512 bytes, the residual length is 2 bytes. ASPI modules can determine if the ASPI manager supports residual byte length by checking byte 1 of the HA_Unique field. See SC_EXEC_SCSI_CMD for more information on enabling residual byte counting.

### Example

This example sends an SC_HA_INQUIRY to host adapter #1, and, if successful, records the maximum transfer length supported by the host adapter.

```
DWORD dwMaxTransferBytes;
SRB_HAInquiry srbHAInquiry;
memset( &srbHAInquiry, 0, sizeof(SRB_HAInquiry) );
srbHAInquiry.SRB_Cmd = SC_HA_INQUIRY;
srbHAInquiry.SRB_HaId = 1;
SendASPI32Command( (LPSRB)&srbHAInquiry );
if( srbHAInquiry.SRB_Status != SS_COMP )
{
// Error in HAInquiry. Most likely SS_INVALID_HA.
Return FALSE;
}
dwMaxTransferBytes = *(DWORD *)(srbHAInquiry.HA_Unique + 4);
```

# SC_GET_DEV_TYPE

The SendASPI32Command function with command code SC_GET_DEV_TYPE enables you to identify the devices available on the SCSI bus. A Win32 tape backup package, for example, can scan each target/LUN on each installed host adapter looking for a device type corresponding to sequential access devices. This eliminates the need for each Win32 application to duplicate the effort of scanning the SCSI bus for devices.

```
typedef struct
{
BYTE SRB_Cmd;                   // ASPI command code = SC_GET_DEV_TYPE
BYTE SRB_Status;                // ASPI command status byte
BYTE SRB_HaId;                  // ASPI host adapter number
BYTE SRB_Flags;                 // Reserved, MUST = 0
DWORD SRB_Hdr_Rsvd;             // Reserved, MUST = 0
BYTE SRB_Target;                // Target's SCSI ID
BYTE SRB_Lun;                   // Target's LUN number
BYTE SRB_DeviceType;            // Target's peripheral device type
BYTE SRB_Rsvd1;                 // Reserved, MUST = 0
}
SRB_GDEVBlock, *PSRB_GDEVBlock;
```

## *SRB Fields*

**SRB_Cmd (Input)** This field must contain SC_GET_DEV_TYPE (0x01).

**SRB_Status (Output)** SC_GET_DEV_TYPE is a synchronous SRB. On return, this field is the same as the SendASPI32Command return value and is set to SS_COMP, SS_INVALID_HA, or SS_NO_DEVICE.

**SRB_HaId (Input)** This field specifies which installed host adapter the request is intended for.

**SRB_Target (Input)** SCSI ID of target device.

**SRB_Lun (Input)** Logical Unit Number (LUN) of target device.

**SRB_DeviceType (Output)** The peripheral device type. The value is one of the codes defined by the SCSI specification (see Table 11.28).

## Table 11.28: Peripheral Device Types

| Symbol | Value | Description |
|---|---|---|
| DTYPE_DASD | 0x00 | Direct-access device (e.g. magnetic disk). |
| DTYPE_SEQD | 0x01 | Sequential-access device (e.g. magnetic tape). |
| DTYPE_PRNT | 0x02 | Printer device. |
| DTYPE_PROC | 0x03 | Processor device. |
| DTYPE_WORM | 0x04 | Write-once device (e.g. some optical disks). |
| DTYPE_CDROM | 0x05 | CD-ROM device. |
| DTYPE_SCAN | 0x06 | Scanner device. |
| DTYPE_OPTI | 0x07 | Optical memory device (e.g. some optical disks). |
| DTYPE_JUKE | 0x08 | Medium changer device (e.g. jukeboxes). |
| DTYPE_COMM | 0x09 | Communication device. |
| N/A | 0x0A-0x0B | Defined by ASC IT8 (Graphic arts pre-press devices). |
| N/A | 0x0C-0x1E | Reserved. |
| DTYPE_UNKNOWN | 0x1F | Unknown or no device type. |

### *Example*

This example scans the system for all **CD-ROM** drives (all targets must be at LUN #0). Please note that **MAX_HA_ID** and **MAX_TARGET_ID** should be replaced with a host adapter count returned by GetASPI32SupportInfo and a target count retrieved from a **SC_HA_INQUIRY** SRB performed within the host adapter loop.

```
BYTE byHaId;
BYTE byTarget;
SRB_GDEVBlock srbGDEVBlock;
for( byHaId = 0; byHaId < MAX_HA_ID; byHaId++ )
{
for( byTarget = 0; byTarget < MAX_TARGET_ID; byTarget++ )
{
memset( &srbGDEVBlock, 0, sizeof(SRB_GDEVBlock) );
srbGDEVBlock.SRB_Cmd = SC_GET_DEV_TYPE;
srbGDEVBlock.SRB_HaId = byHaId;
srbGDEVBlock.SRB_Target = byTarget;
SendASPI32Command( (LPSRB)&srbGDEVBlock );
if( srbGDEVBlock.SRB_Status != SS_COMP ) continue;
if( srbGDEVBlock.SRB_DeviceType == DTYPE_CDROM )
```

```
{
    // A CD-ROM exists at HA/ID/LUN = byHaId/byTarget/0.
    // Do whatever you want with it from here!
    }
  }
}
```

## SC_EXEC_SCSI_CMD

The SendASPI32Command function with command code SC_EXEC_
SCSI_CMD is used to execute a SCSI I/O command. Once an ASPI
client has initialized, virtually all I/O is performed with this command.

```
typedef struct
{
BYTE SRB_Cmd;                  // ASPI command code = SC_EXEC_SCSI_CMD
BYTE SRB_Status;               // ASPI command status byte
BYTE SRB_HaId;                 // ASPI host adapter number
BYTE SRB_Flags;                // ASPI request flags
DWORD SRB_Hdr_Rsvd;            // Reserved, MUST = 0
BYTE SRB_Target;               // Target's SCSI ID
BYTE SRB_Lun;                  // Target's LUN number
WORD SRB_Rsvd1;                // Reserved for Alignment
DWORD SRB_BufLen;              // Data Allocation Length
LPBYTE SRB_BufPointer;         // Data Buffer Pointer
BYTE SRB_SenseLen;             // Sense Allocation Length
BYTE SRB_CDBLen;               // CDB Length
BYTE SRB_HaStat;               // Host Adapter Status
BYTE SRB_TargStat;             // Target Status
LPVOID SRB_PostProc;           // Post routine
BYTE SRB_Rsvd2[20];            // Reserved, MUST = 0
BYTE CDBByte[16];              // SCSI CDB
BYTE SenseArea[SENSE_LEN+2];   // Request Sense buffer
}
SRB_ExecSCSICmd, *PSRB_ExecSCSICmd;
```

### SRB Fields

**SRB_Cmd (Input)** This field must contain SC_EXEC_SCSI_CMD (0x02).

**SRB_Status (Output)** SC_EXEC_SCSI_CMD is an asynchronous SRB. This field
should not be examined until after the caller has waited for proper completion
of the SRB (see "Waiting for Completion"). Once completed, this field may be
set to a number of different values. The most common values are SS_COMP or
SS_ERR.

**SS_COMP** indicates successful completion while SS_ERR indicates the caller should examine the SRB_HaStat and SRB_TargStat fields for more information. See "ASPI for Win32 Error" for a complete description of possible error codes.

**SRB_HaId (Input)** This field specifies which installed host adapter the request is intended for. Host adapter numbers are always assigned by the SCSI manager layer beginning with zero.

**SRB_Flags (Input)** One or more of the following flags (see Table 11.29—note restrictions where they apply):

**Table 11.29: SRB Flags**

| Symbol | Value | Description |
|---|---|---|
| SRB_POSTING | 0x01 | Enable posting. See "Waiting for Completion" for more information. This flag and SRB_EVENT_NOTIFY are mutually exclusive. |
| SRB_ENABLE_RESIDUAL_COUNT | 0x04 | Enables residual byte counting assuming it is supported. Whenever a data under-run occurs the SRB_BufLen field is updated to reflect the remaining bytes to transfer. |
| SRB_DIR_IN | 0x08 | Data transfer is from SCSI target to host. Mutually exclusive with SRB_DIR_OUT. |
| SRB_DIR_OUT | 0x10 | Data transfer is from host to SCSI target. Mutually exclusive with SRB_DIR_IN. |
| SRB_EVENT_NOTIFY | 0x40 | Enable event notification. See "Waiting for Completion" for more information. This flag and SRB_POSTING are mutually exclusive. |

**SRB_Target (Input)** SCSI ID of target device.

**SRB_Lun (Input)** Logical Unit Number (LUN) of target device.

**SRB_BufLen (Input)** This field indicates the number of bytes to be transferred. If the SCSI command to be executed does not transfer data (e.g., Test Unit Ready, Rewind, etc.), this field *must* be set to zero. If residual byte length is supported (see "SC_HA_INQUIRY") and selected (see SRB_Flags above), this field is returned with the residual number of bytes (usually 0).

**SRB_BufPointer (Input)** This field is a pointer to the data buffer. If there is no data to be transfered this field should be NULL.

**SRB_SenseLen (Input)** This field indicates the number of bytes allocated at the end of the SRB for sense data. A request sense is automatically generated if a check condition is presented at the end of a SCSI command. Please note that under Windows NT it is not possible to reliably request more than 18 bytes of sense data.

**SRB_CDBLen (Input)** This field establishes the length, in bytes, of the SCSI Command Descriptor Block (CDB). This value is typically 6, 10, or 12. See the SCSI specification for more information on valid CDBs.

**SRB_HaStat (Output)** Upon completion of the SCSI command, this field is set to the host adapter status as defined in Table 11.30. Do not examine this status byte if SRB_Status is set to SS_COMP. It is only to be considered valid if there is unsuccessful completion of the SRB.

### Table 11.30: Host Adapter Status

| Symbol | Value | Description |
|---|---|---|
| HASTAT_OK | 0x00 | Host adapter did not detect an error. |
| HASTAT_TIMEOUT | 0x09 | The time allocated for a bus transaction ran out. |
| HASTAT_COMMAND_TIMEOUT | 0x0B | SRB expired while waiting to be processed. |
| HASTAT_MESSAGE_REJECT | 0x0D | MESSAGE REJECT received while processing SRB. |
| HASTAT_BUS_RESET | 0x0E | A bus reset was detected. |
| HASTAT_PARITY_ERROR | 0x0F | A parity error was detected. |
| HASTAT_REQUEST_SENSE_FAILED | 0x10 | The adapter failed in issuing a Request Sense after a check condition was reported by the target device. |
| HASTAT_SEL_TO | 0x11 | Selection of target timed out. |
| HASTAT_DO_DU | 0x12 | Data overrun. |
| HASTAT_BUS_FREE | 0x13 | Unexpected Bus Free. |
| HASTAT_PHASE_ERR | 0x14 | Target Bus phase sequence failure. |

**SRB_TargStat (Output)** Upon completion of the SCSI command, this field is set to the final SCSI target status. Do not examine this status byte if SRB_Status is set to SS_COMP. It is only to be considered valid if there is unsuccessful completion of the SRB. Note that Table 11.31 only covers the most common result codes. Check the SCSI specification for more information on these and other status byte codes.

**Table 11.31: SCSI Target Status**

| Symbol | Value | Description |
| --- | --- | --- |
| STATUS_GOOD | 0x00 | No target status. |
| STATUS_CHKCOND | 0x02 | Check status (sense data is in SenseArea). |
| STATUS_BUSY | 0x08 | Specified Target/LUN is busy. |
| STATUS_RESCONF | 0x18 | Reservation conflict. |

**SRB_PostProc (Input)** If posting is enabled (SRB_POSTING) this field contains a pointer to a function. The ASPI manager calls this function upon completion of the SRB. If event notification is enabled (SRB_EVENT_NOTIFY) this field contains a handle to an event. The ASPI manager signals this event upon completion of the SRB. See "Waiting for Completion" for more information.

**CDBByte (Input)** This field contains the CDB as defined by the target's SCSI command set. The length of the SCSI CDB is specified in the SRB_CDBLen field.

**SenseArea (Output)** The SenseArea is filled with the sense data after a check condition (SRB_Status == SS_ERR and SRB_TargStat == STATUS_CHKCOND). The maximum length of this field is specified in the SRB_SenseLen field.

### Example

This example sends a SCSI INQUIRY command to host adapter #0, target #5, LUN #0. When examining the code, please note the following:

Manual-reset events are used. The ResetEvent is not needed in this particular sample because we just created the event, but it is good practice to put the reset immediately before every SendASPI32Command call to make sure you don't enter the routine with an event signalled.

Because this is an asynchronous SRB, we fully wait for completion before checking the SRB_Status byte. Also, we use dwASPIStatus instead of SRB_Status to check for a SS_PENDING return for the same reason.

There is an INFINITE timeout on the WaitForSingleObject because SRB timeouts are *not* the same as event timeouts. Use SC_GETSET_TIMEOUT to associate a timeout with an SRB.

```
BYTE byInquiry[32];
DWORD dwASPIStatus;
HANDLE heventSRB;
SRB_ExecSCSICmd srbExec;
heventSRB = CreateEvent( NULL, TRUE, FALSE, NULL );
if( !heventSRB )
{
// Couldn't get manual reset event, put error handling code here!
}
memset( &srbExec, 0, sizeof(SRB_ExecSCSICmd) );
srbExec.SRB_Cmd = SC_EXEC_SCSI_CMD;
srbExec.SRB_Flags = SRB_DIR_IN | SRB_EVENT_NOTIFY;
srbExec.SRB_Target = 5;
srbExec.SRB_BufLen = 32;
srbExec.SRB_BufPointer = byInquiry;
srbExec.SRB_SenseLen = SENSE_LEN;
srbExec.SRB_CDBLen = 6;
srbExec.SRB_PostProc = (LPVOID)heventSRB;
srbExec.CDBByte[0] = SCSI_INQUIRY;
srbExec.CDBByte[4] = 32;
ResetEvent( hevenSRB );
dwASPIStatus = SendASPI32Command( (LPSRB)&srbExec );
if( dwASPIStatus == SS_PENDING )
{
WaitForSingleObject( heventSRB, INFINITE );
}
if( srbExec.SRB_Status != SS_COMP )
{
// Error processing the SRB, put error handling code here.
```

## SC_ABORT_SRB

The SendASPI32Command function with command code SC_ABORT_SRB is used to request that a pending SRB be aborted. It should be issued on any I/O request that has not completed if the application wishes to halt execution of that request. Success of the abort command is *never* assured.

```
typedef struct
{
BYTE SRB_Cmd;                       // ASPI command code = SC_ABORT_SRB
BYTE SRB_Status;                    // ASPI command status byte
BYTE SRB_HaId;                      // ASPI host adapter number
BYTE SRB_Flags;                     // Reserved, MUST = 0
DWORD SRB_Hdr_Rsvd;                 // Reserved, MUST = 0
LPSRB SRB_ToAbort;                  // Pointer to SRB to abort
}
SRB_Abort, *PSRB_Abort;
```

### SRB Fields

**SRB_Cmd (Input)** This field must contain SC_ABORT_SRB (0x03).

**SRB_Status (Output)** SC_ABORT_SRB is a synchronous SRB. On return, this field is the same as the SendASPI32Command return value and is set to SS_COMP, SS_INVALID_HA, or SS_INVALID_SRB. Remember that a return of SS_COMP does *not* indicate that the SRB to be aborted has been halted. Instead, it indicates that *an attempt* was made at aborting that SRB. If the SRB to be aborted completes with SS_ABORTED then there is positive indication that the original SC_ABORT_SRB worked.

**SRB_HaId (Input)** This field specifies which installed host adapter the request is intended for. Host adapter numbers are always assigned by the ASPI manager layer beginning with zero.

**SRB_ToAbort (Input)** This field contains a pointer to the SRB which is to be aborted. The actual failure or success of the abort operation is indicated by the status eventually returned in this SRB.

### Remarks

As stated above, the success of an SC_ABORT_SRB command is *never* guaranteed. As a matter of fact, the situations in which ASPI is capable of aborting an SRB already sent to the system are few and far between. The original use for SC_ABORT_SRB was to terminate I/O which had timed out under ASPI for DOS and ASPI for Win16. The nature of SC_ABORT_SRB under Win32 greatly reduces its usefulness. It is recommended that the SC_GETSET_TIMEOUTS SRB be used to manage SRB timeouts in all new ASPI modules.

## SC_RESET_DEV

The SendASPI32Command function with command code SC_RESET_DEV is used to send a SCSI Bus Device reset to the specified target.

```
typedef struct
{
BYTE SRB_Cmd;                   // ASPI command code = SC_RESET_DEV
BYTE SRB_Status;                // ASPI command status byte
BYTE SRB_HaId;                  // ASPI host adapter number
BYTE SRB_Flags;                 // Reserved, MUST = 0
DWORD SRB_Hdr_Rsvd;             // Reserved, MUST = 0
BYTE SRB_Target;                // Target's SCSI ID
BYTE SRB_Lun;                   // Target's LUN number
BYTE SRB_Rsvd1[12];             // Reserved, MUST = 0
BYTE SRB_HaStat;                // Host Adapter Status
BYTE SRB_TargStat;              // Target Status
LPVOID SRB_PostProc;            // Post routine
BYTE SRB_Rsvd2[36];             // Reserved, MUST = 0
}
SRB_BusDeviceReset, *PSRB_BusDeviceReset;
```

### SRB Fields

**SRB_Cmd (Input)** This field must contain SC_RESET_DEV (0x04).

**SRB_Status (Output)** SC_RESET_DEV is an asynchronous SRB. This field should not be examined until *after* the caller has waited for proper completion of the SRB (see "Waiting for Completion"). Once completed, this field may be set to a number of different values. The most common values are SS_COMP or SS_ERR. SS_COMP indicates successful completion while SS_ERR indicates the caller should examine the SRB_HaStat and SRB_TargStat fields for more information. See "ASPI for Win32 Error" for a complete description of possible error codes.

**SRB_HaId (Input)** This field specifies which installed host adapter the request is intended for. Host adapter numbers are always assigned by the SCSI manager layer beginning with zero.

**SRB_Target (Input)** SCSI ID of target device.

**SRB_Lun (Input)** Logical Unit Number (LUN) of target device. This field is ignored by ASPI for Win32, since SCSI BUS DEVICE RESET is done on a per-target basis only.

**SRB_HaStat (Output)** Upon completion of the SCSI command, this field is set to the host adapter status as defined in Table 11.32. Do not examine this status byte if SRB_Status is set to SS_COMP. It is only to be considered valid if there is unsuccessful completion of the SRB.

**Table 11.32: Host Adapter Status**

| Symbol | Value | Description |
|---|---|---|
| HASTAT_OK | 0x00 | Host adapter did not detect an error. |
| HASTAT_TIMEOUT | 0x09 | The time allocated for a bus transaction ran out. |
| HASTAT_COMMAND_TIMEOUT | 0x0B | SRB expired while waiting to be processed. |
| HASTAT_MESSAGE_REJECT | 0x0D | MESSAGE REJECT received while processing SRB. |
| HASTAT_BUS_RESET | 0x0E | A bus reset was detected. |
| HASTAT_PARITY_ERROR | 0x0F | A parity error was detected. |
| HASTAT_REQUEST_SENSE_FAILED | 0x10 | The adapter failed in issuing a Request Sense after a check condition was reported by the target device. |
| HASTAT_SEL_TO | 0x11 | Selection of target timed out. |
| HASTAT_DO_DU | 0x12 | Data overrun. |
| HASTAT_BUS_FREE | 0x13 | Unexpected Bus Free. |
| HASTAT_PHASE_ERR | 0x14 | Target Bus phase sequence failure. |

**SRB_TargStat (Output)** Upon completion of the SCSI command, this field is set to the final SCSI target status. Do not examine this status byte if SRB_Status is set to SS_COMP. It is only to be considered valid if there is unsuccessful completion of the SRB. Note that Table 11.33 only covers the most common result codes. Check the SCSI specification for more information on these and other status byte codes.

### Table 11.33: SCSI Target Status

| Symbol | Value | Description |
|--------|-------|-------------|
| STATUS_GOOD | 0x00 | No target status. |
| STATUS_CHKCOND | 0x02 | Check status (sense data is in SenseArea). |
| STATUS_BUSY | 0x08 | Specified Target/LUN is busy. |
| STATUS_RESCONF | 0x18 | Reservation conflict. |

**SRB_PostProc (Input)** If posting is enabled (SRB_POSTING) this field contains a pointer to a function. The ASPI manager calls this function upon completion of the SRB. If event notification is enabled (SRB_EVENT_NOTIFY) this field contains a handle to an event. The ASPI manager signals this event upon completion of the SRB. See "Waiting for Completion" for more information.

### Remarks

The Windows 95 and Windows NT operating systems do not handle BUS DEVICE RESET properly at the current time. For this reason, SC_RESET_DEV calls are not guaranteed to function properly. The command is present mainly to keep older code ported from Win16 from failing.

## SC_GET_DISK_INFO

The SendASPI32Command function with command code SC_GET_DISK_INFO is used to obtain information about a disk type SCSI device. The information returned includes BIOS Int 13h control and accessibility of the device, the drive's Int 13h physical drive number, and the geometry used by the Int 13h services for the drive.

**NOTE** *This command is not valid for Windows NT, which does not use the Int 13 interface.*

```
typedef struct
{
BYTE SRB_Cmd;                // ASPI command code = SC_GET_DISK_INFO
BYTE SRB_Status;             // ASPI command status byte
BYTE SRB_HaId;               // ASPI host adapter number
BYTE SRB_Flags;             // Reserved
DWORD SRB_Hdr_Rsvd;          // Reserved
BYTE SRB_Target;             // Target's SCSI ID
BYTE SRB_Lun;                // Target's LUN number
BYTE SRB_DriveFlags;         // Driver flags
BYTE SRB_Int13HDriveInfo;    // Host Adapter Status
```

```
BYTE SRB_Heads;              // Preferred number of heads translation
BYTE SRB_Sectors;            // Preferred number of sectors translation
BYTE SRB_Rsvd1[10];          // Reserved
}
SRB_GetDiskInfo, *PSRB_GetDiskInfo;
```

### SRB Fields

**SRB_Cmd (Input)** This field must contain SC_GET_DISK_INFO (0x06).

**SRB_Status (Output)** SC_GET_DISK_INFO is a synchronous SRB. On return, this field is the same as the SendASPI32Command return value and is set to SS_COMP, SS_INVALID_HA, or SS_NO_DEVICE, or SS_INVALID_SRB.

**SRB_HaId (Input)** This field specifies which installed host adapter the request is intended for. Host adapter numbers are always assigned by the ASPI manager layer beginning with zero.

**SRB_Target (Input)** SCSI ID of target device.

**SRB_Lun (Input)** Logical Unit Number (LUN) of target device.

**SRB_DriveFlags (Output)** Upon completion of the SCSI command this field is set according to Table 11.34.

**Table 11.34: Drive Flags**

| Symbol | Value | Description |
| --- | --- | --- |
| DISK_NOT_INT13 | 0x00 | Device is not controlled by Int 13h services. |
| DISK_INT13_AND_DOS | 0x01 | Device is under Int 13h control and is claimed by DOS. |
| DISK_INT13 | 0x02 | Device is under Int 13h control but not claimed by DOS. |

**SRB_Int13DriveInfo (Output)** Upon completion of the SCSI command, the ASPI manager sets this field with the physical drive number that Int 13h services assigned to the device. The valid drive numbers are 0x00 to 0xFF. This field is only valid if SRB_DriveFlags is set to DISK_INT13_AND_DOS or DISK_INT13.

**SRB_Heads (Output)** Upon completion of the SCSI command, the ASPI manager sets this field to the number of heads the Int 13h services is using for this device's geometry. The valid drive numbers are 0x00 to 0xFF. This field is only valid if SRB_DriveFlags is set to DISK_INT13_AND_DOS or DISK_INT13.

**SRB_Sectors (Output)** Upon completion of the SCSI command, the ASPI manager sets this field to the number of sectors the Int 13h services is using for this device's geometry. The valid drive numbers are 0x00 to 0xFF. This field is only valid if SRB_DriveFlags is set to DISK_INT13_AND_DOS or DISK_INT13.

### Example

This example obtains disk information from device LUN 0, SCSI ID 2, attached to host adapter 0.

```
SRB_GetDiskInfo srbGetDiskInfo;
memset( &srbGetDiskInfo, 0, sizeof(SRB_GetDiskInfo) );
srbGetDiskInfo.SRB_Header.SRB_Cmd = SC_GET_DISK_INFO;
srbGetDiskInfo.SRB_Target = 2;
SendASPI32Command( (LPSRB)&srbGetDiskInfo );
if( srbGetDiskInfo.SRB_Status != SS_COMP )
{
// Error handling GetDiskInfo SRB. Error handling code goes here!
```

## SC_RESCAN_SCSI_BUS

The SendASPI32Command function with command code SC_RESCAN_SCSI_BUS is used to rescan the SCSI bus specified by the host adapter number in the SRB. It will instruct the I/O subsystem to rescan the SCSI bus and update both the system device map and the ASPI manager device tables.

```
typedef struct
{
BYTE SRB_Cmd;              // ASPI command code = SC_RESCAN_SCSI_BUS
BYTE SRB_Status;           // ASPI command status byte
BYTE SRB_HaId;             // ASPI host adapter number
BYTE SRB_Flags;            // Reserved, MUST = 0
DWORD SRB_Hdr_Rsvd;        // Reserved, MUST = 0
}
SRB_RescanPort, *PSRB_RescanPort;
```

### SRB Fields

**SRB_Cmd (Input)** This field must contain SC_RESCAN_SCSI_BUS (0x07).

**SRB_Status (Output)** SC_RESCAN_SCSI_BUS is a synchronous SRB. On return, this field is the same as the SendASPI32Command return value and is set to SS_COMP, or SS_INVALID_HA.

**SRB_HaId (Input)** This field specifies which installed host adapter the request is intended for. Host adapter numbers are always assigned by the ASPI manager layer beginning with zero.

### Remarks

Under Windows NT, the I/O subsystem does not rescan devices/IDs it already knows about. The impact of this is that it will detect new devices but will not detect removal of devices or exchanging of devices.

Under Windows 95, there can be a substantial delay between the time a rescan is initiated with this command and the time at which new devices are added or old devices are removed from the device map. The best way deal with this is to rely on the Plug and Play messages in conjunction with TranslateASPI32Address, or to simply perform your own refresh five or ten seconds after the rescan command is issued.

There is no way to force a rescan of the entire system. It is up to the operating system to detect the arrival of new host adapters (for example, PCMCIA) through Plug and Play, if it is available.

### Example

The following example forces a rescan of the SCSI bus attached to host adapter #0:

```
SRB_RescanPort srbRescanPort;
memset( &srbRescanPort, 0, sizeof(SRB_RescanPort) );
srbRescanPort.SRB_Cmd = SC_RESCAN_SCSI_BUS;
SendASPI32Command( (LPSRB)&srbRescanPort );
if( srbRescanPort.SRB_Status != SS_COMP )
{
// Error issuing port rescan. Error handling code goes here.
```

## SC_GETSET_TIMEOUTS

The SendASPI32Command function with command code SC_GETSET_TIMEOUTS enables you to set target specific timeouts in 1/2 second increments. Once set, a timeout applies to all SCSI commands sent through the SC_EXEC_SCSI_CMD command. Timeouts are process specific, so two different applications may set different timeouts for the same target. The SRB_HaId, SRB_Target, and SRB_Lun fields may be set to a wildcard value to ease the setting of timeouts on multiple targets. Note that by default, all target timeouts are set to 30 hours (the maximum allowed).

```
typedef struct
{
BYTE SRB_Cmd;                  // ASPI command code = SC_GETSET_TIMEOUTS
BYTE SRB_Status;               // ASPI command status byte
BYTE SRB_HaId;                 // ASPI host adapter number
BYTE SRB_Flags;                // ASPI request flags
DWORD SRB_Hdr_Rsvd;            // Reserved
BYTE SRB_Target;               // Target's SCSI ID
BYTE SRB_Lun;                  // Target's LUN number
DWORD SRB_Timeout;             // Timeout in half seconds
}
SRB_GetSetTimeouts, *PSRB_GetSetTimeouts;
```

### SRB Fields

**SRB_Cmd (Input)** This field must contain SC_GETSET_TIMEOUTS (0x08).

**SRB_Status (Output)** SC_GETSET_TIMEOUTS is a synchronous SRB. On return, this field is the same as the SendASPI32Command return value and is set to SS_COMP, SS_INVALID_HA, SS_NO_DEVICE, or SS_INVALID_SRB (bad flags, invalid timeout, etc.).

**SRB_HaId (Input)** This field specifies which installed host adapter the request is intended for. If SRB_DIR_OUT is set in SRB_Flags then this value may be a wildcard (0xFF) indicating that the SRB_Target/SRB_Lun combination on ALL host adapters should get a new timeout.

**SRB_Flags (Input)** May be set to one and only one of the two constants from Table 11.35.

**Table 11.35: SRB Flags for SC_GETSET_TIMEOUTS**

| Symbol | Value | Description |
|---|---|---|
| SRB_DIR_IN | 0x08 | SRB is being used to retrieve current timeout setting. Wildcards are not allowed in the ASPI address fields. |
| SRB_DIR_OUT | 0x10 | SRB is being used to change the current timeout setting. Wildcards are valid in the ASPI address fields. |

**SRB_Target (Input)** This field indicates the SCSI ID of the target device. If SRB_DIR_OUT is set in SRB_Flags then this value may be a wildcard (0xFF) indicating that ALL SCSI IDs of the passed SRB_HaId/SRB_Lun combination should get a new timeout.

**SRB_Lun (Input)** This field indicates the Logical Unit Number (LUN) of the device. If SRB_DIR_OUT is set in SRB_Flags then this value may be a wildcard (0xFF) indicating that ALL LUNs of the passed SRB_HaId/SRB_Target combination should get a new timeout.

**SRB_Timeout (Input)** Target's timout in half seconds. If SRB_DIR_OUT then this value holds the new timeout for the specified target(s). If SRB_DIR_IN then the value is set by ASPI to the current timeout for the specified target. The timeout can be from 0-108000 (30 hours) with 0 being an easier way of saying "max timeout" (again, 30 hours).

### Remarks

Once a timeout is set for a target, that timeout will be used on all SRBs passed to SendASPI32Command with SC_EXEC_SCSI_CMD. If one of these SRBs actually times out, then the SCSI bus will be reset (this is NOT a bus device reset, but a full SCSI bus reset). This causes all of the SRBs executing on the bus to be cancelled, and the miniport will set error codes in the SRBs as appropriate. It is up to the code which originally submitted these SRBs to retry the commands as necessary (for example, if an ASPI request times out and the bus is reset, a file system command to another target could be cancelled, and it is up to the file system to retry the command).

In addition, the result placed in the SRB which times out depends on the error codes which the miniport places in the SRB. In the case of Adaptec controllers, the result code is SS_ABORT. In other miniports, the result may be SS_ERR with a host adapter status set to HASTAT_TIMEOUT or HASTAT_COMMAND_TIMEOUT, or it may be some new error result not yet encountered. Suffice it to say that the SRB which times out should return with an error, and it is up to the higher-level applications to perform retries of the SRB and any other SRB which may have been affected by the associated bus reset.

When using event notification with timeouts, it is important to remember that the HEVENT used in the SRB_PostProc field has an ENTIRELY SEPERATE timeout associated with it. In other words, the timeout associated with an event is seperate from the timeout associated with an SRB. If you set a timeout on an SRB and then set an infinite timeout in WaitForSingleObject on the SRB event, then the SRB will STILL TIMEOUT and signal completion of the SRB. Conversely, if you set a 30-hour timeout on the SRB and a 5-second timeout on the event, the event will always go signaled before the SRB completes, and no cleanup of the SRB on the bus will take place.

### Examples

The first example (Table 11.36) illustrates how wildcards work with set timeout. The main point here is that the wildcards are specific. In other words, setting the HaId to 0xFF does not make SRB_Target / SRB_Lun "don't cares."

## Table 11.36: Wildcard Validity for SC_GETSET_TIMEOUTS

| HA | ID | LN | Affected Device |
|----|----|----|-----------------|
| 00 | 01 | FF | All of target 1's luns on host adapter 0. |
| FF | 00 | FF | All luns on targets with ID 0 on any host adapter. |
| FF | FF | 00 | Lun 0 of all targets on any host adapter. |
| FF | FF | FF | All targets on any host adapter with any lun number (everything). |

Next is an example in which all LUNs on target 5, host adapter 0 are set to 10 seconds:

```
SRB_GetSetTimeouts srbGetSetTimeouts;
memset( &srbGetSetTimeouts, 0, sizeof(SRB_GetSetTimeouts) );
srbGetSetTimeouts.SRB_Cmd = SC_GETSET_TIMEOUTS
srbGetSetTimeouts.SRB_Flags = SRB_DIR_OUT;
srbGetSetTimeouts.SRB_Target = 0x05;
srbGetSetTimeouts.SRB_Lun = 0xFF;
srbGetSetTimeouts.SRB_Timeout = 10*2;
SendASPI32Command( (LPSRB)&srbGetSetTimeouts );
if( srbGetSetTimeouts.SRB_Status != SS_COMP )
{
// Error setting timeouts. Put error handling code here.
```

# GetASPI32Buffer

GetASPI32Buffer allocates blocks of memory (up to 512KB) which are "safe" for use in ASPI modules. Under normal circumstances memory buffers from the stack or allocated with VirtualAlloc will be too physically fragmented to allow a transfer greater than 64KB on bus-mastering host adapters. For those rare instances where a large transfer is required, GetASPI32Buffer allows a buffer to be allocated which will pass all operating system requirements for physical continuity.

```
BOOL GetASPI32Buffer( PASPI32BUFF pab );
```

### Parameters

*pab:*
Pointer to a filled out ASPI32BUFF structure.

```
typedef struct
```

```
{
LPBYTE AB_BufPointer;        // Pointer to the ASPI allocated buffer
DWORD AB_BufLen;             // Length in bytes of the buffer
DWORD AB_ZeroFill;           // Flag set to 1 if buffer should be zeroed
DWORD AB_Reserved;           // Reserved, MUST = 0
}
ASPI32BUFF, *PASPI32BUFF;
```

**AB_BufPointer (Output)** After a successful call (return value TRUE) this field contains the address of the large transfer buffer which has been allocated for the application.

**AB_BufLen (Input)** Set to the size, in bytes, desired for the transfer buffer. This must be less than or equal to 512KB and should be greater than 64KB (although there are no requirements on the low end).

**AB_ZeroFill (Input)** Set this flag to 1 if ASPI should clear the transfer buffer after allocation but before returning to the caller. Leave the flag set to 0 if the memory can remain uninitialized.

### Return Values

This function returns TRUE if it successfully allocates a large transfer buffer, and FALSE otherwise. The caller should assume that this call can fail, and should allow the code to work with smaller transfer buffers allocated from VirtualAlloc (if at all possible).

### Example

The following example allocates a 128KB buffer for use with ASPI.

```
ASPI32BUFF ab;
memset( &ab, 0, sizeof(ASPI32BUFF) );
ab.AB_BufLen = 131072lu;
ab.AB_ZeroFill = 1;
if( !GetASPI32Buffer( &ab ) )
{
// Unable to allocate buffer. Error handling code goes here!
```

# FreeASPI32Buffer

FreeASPI32Buffer releases memory previously allocated by a successful call go **GetASPI32Buffer**.

```
BOOL FreeASPI32Buffer( PASPI32BUFF pab );
```

*pab:*

Pointer to a filled out ASPI32BUFF structure.

```
typedef struct
{
LPBYTE AB_BufPointer;        // Pointer to the ASPI allocated buffer
DWORD AB_BufLen;             // Length in bytes of the buffer
DWORD AB_ZeroFill;           // Reserved, MUST = 0
DWORD AB_Reserved;           // Reserved, MUST = 0
}
ASPI32BUFF, *PASPI32BUFF;
```

**AB_BufPointer (Input)** Pointer to the buffer previously returned from a successful call to GetASPI32Buffer. The address must match exactly for the free to occur.

**AB_BufLen (Input)** Set to the original size, in bytes, of the buffer allocated by a call to GetASPI32Buffer. The size must match exactly for the free to occur.

### Return Values

This function returns TRUE if the memory allocated to the buffer has been released. FALSE is returned if there is an error freeing the memory or if the passed in AB_BufPointer/AB_BufLen fields don't match those of a previously allocated buffer.

## TranslateASPI32Address

TranslateASPI32Address provides translation between Windows 95 DEVNODEs and ASPI HA/ID/LUN triples (or vice versa). Because DEVNODEs are associated with WM_DEVICECHANGE messages, it is possible to use this function to associate ASPI target addresses with Plug and Play events.

**NOTE** *This command is not valid for Windows NT, which does not currently have Plug and Play capabilities.*

```
BOOL TranslateASPI32Address( PDWORD pdwPath, PDWORD pdwDEVNODE );
```

### Parameters

**pdwPath** Pointer to a ASPI address "path." The path is simply a packed version of an ASPI address triple. Every target address in ASPI consists of a host adapter identifier, a SCSI ID, and a SCSI LUN. Each of these values consists of a BYTE, so an ASPI address "path" is a DWORD encoded as 0x00HHIILL where HH is the host adapter identifier, II is the SCSI ID, and LL is the SCSI LUN. Note that if II and LL are both 0xFF then the path represents a host adapter. This is necessary because host adapters have their own DEVNODEs in the Plug and Play subsystem.

**pdwDEVNODE** Pointer to a DWORD which contains a Windows 95 DEVNODE ID. This parameter controls the direction of translation. If the DWORD contains a 0 (note that this does *not* mean that pdwDEVNODE is NULL) then translation is from the ASPI triple to the DEVNODE. If the DEVNODE is non-zero then translation is from the DEVNODE to an ASPI triple.

### Return Values

TRUE if there is a successful translation. FALSE is returned if the parameters are invalid or if there is no translation between ASPI path and Windows 95 DEVNODE.

### Remarks

In order for this scheme to work properly, applications should pay attention to WM_DEVICECHANGE messages which utilize DBT_DEVTYP_DEVNODE device change data. The device change data type can be detected by checking the dcbh_devicetype field in the DEV_BROADCAST_HEADER associated with device change events. Review the Plug and Play documentation in Win32 for more information.

### Example

The function below checks broadcast data from a WM_DEVICECHANGE message to see if the device change message is related to an ASPI target (but not host adapter).

```
BOOL CheckForASPITargetBroadcast( PDEV_BROADCAST_HDR pHeader )
{
BOOL bStatus;
DWORD dwTargetPath;
DWORD dwDEVNODE;
PDEV_BROADCAST_DEVNODE pDevnodeData
```

```
if( pHeader->dbch_devicetype != DBT_DEVTYP_DEVNODE )
{
return FALSE;
}
pDevnodeData = (PDEV_BROADCAST_DEVNODE)pHeader;
dwDEVNODE = pDevnodeData->dbcd_devnode;
bStatus = TranslateASPI32Address( &dwTargetPath, &dwDEVNODE );
if( !bStatus || ((dwTargetPath & 0xFFFFlu) == 0xFFFFlu) )
{
return FALSE;
}
return TRUE;
}
```

## Waiting for Completion

There are two types of SRBs sent to SendASPI32Command: synchronous
and asynchronous. Synchronous SRBs are always complete when the call
to SendASPI32Command returns. Asynchronous SRBs, however, may or
may not be complete upon return from the SendASPI32Command call.

When called with an asynchronous SRB, the status return from
SendASPI32Command should be checked for a value of SS_PENDING. If
the status code *is not* SS_PENDING then the SRB is complete and it is safe
to look at its status codes, etc. If SS_PENDING *is* returned then the SRB is still
under the control of ASPI, and the caller needs to wait for the SRB to
complete before doing anything else with that SRB.

There are three ways of being notified that an asynchronous SRB has
completed. The first and recommended method uses event notification. The
second method uses posting (a callback), and the third method uses polling.
All three completion methods are illustrated below using a simple INQUIRY
command to host adapter #0, SCSI ID #5, LUN #0.

### Event Notification

Event notification is an ideal mechanism for notifying ASPI clients of the completion of an ASPI request. ASPI clients may efficiently block on this event until
completion. Upon completion of a request, the ASPI for Win32 manager will
set the event to the signaled state. The ASPI client is responsible for making
sure that the event is a manual-reset style event which is not in a signaled state
when an ASPI request is submitted.

```
BYTE byInquiry[32];
DWORD dwASPIStatus;
HANDLE heventSRB;
SRB_ExecSCSICmd srbExec;
heventSRB = CreateEvent( NULL, TRUE, FALSE, NULL );
if( !heventSRB )
{
// Couldn't get manual reset event, put error handling code here!
}
memset( &srbExec, 0, sizeof(SRB_ExecSCSICmd) );
srbExec.SRB_Cmd = SC_EXEC_SCSI_CMD;
srbExec.SRB_Flags = SRB_DIR_IN | SRB_EVENT_NOTIFY;
srbExec.SRB_Target = 5;
srbExec.SRB_BufLen = 32;
srbExec.SRB_BufPointer = byInquiry;
srbExec.SRB_SenseLen = SENSE_LEN;
srbExec.SRB_CDBLen = 6;
srbExec.SRB_PostProc = (LPVOID)heventSRB;
srbExec.CDBByte[0] = SCSI_INQUIRY;
srbExec.CDBByte[4] = 32;
ResetEvent( hevenSRB );
dwASPIStatus = SendASPI32Command( (LPSRB)&srbExec );
if( dwASPIStatus == SS_PENDING )
{
WaitForSingleObject( heventSRB, INFINITE );
}
if( srbExec.SRB_Status != SS_COMP )
{
// Error processing the SRB, put error handling code here.
}
```

### Posting

Posting (or callbacks) may be used to receive notification that a SCSI request has completed. When posting is used, ASPI for Win32 posts completion by passing control to a callback function. If you send an ASPI request with posting enabled, the callback procedure will always be called. The post or callback routine is called as a standard C function. The caller (in this case, the ASPI manager) cleans up the stack. The prototype for the callback is below in the sample.

```
BYTE byInquiry[32];
SRB_ExecSCSICmd srbExec;
memset( &srbExec, 0, sizeof(SRB_ExecSCSICmd) );
srbExec.SRB_Cmd = SC_EXEC_SCSI_CMD;
srbExec.SRB_Flags = SRB_DIR_IN | SRB_POSTING;
```

```
srbExec.SRB_Target = 5;
srbExec.SRB_BufLen = 32;
srbExec.SRB_BufPointer = byInquiry;
srbExec.SRB_SenseLen = SENSE_LEN;
srbExec.SRB_CDBLen = 6;
srbExec.SRB_PostProc = ASPIInquiryCallback;
srbExec.CDBByte[0] = SCSI_INQUIRY;
srbExec.CDBByte[4] = 32;
SendASPI32Command( (LPSRB)&srbExec );
. . .
/**
*** The code above is a separate thread of execution from
*** the code below which handles the inquiry callback. Note that
*** the callback usually signals the main thread of execution that
*** the an SRB it submitted has completed. In this case we aren't
*** doing anything but checking for errors.
**/
VOID ASPIInquiryCallback( SRB_ExecSCSICmd psrbExec )
{
if( psrbExec->SRB_Status != SS_COMP )
{
// Error processing the SRB, put error handling code here.
}
}
```

### Polling

Polling is another method of determining SCSI request completion. This method is not recommended because of the large number of CPU cycles consumed while checking the status byte. After the command is sent and ASPI for Win32 returns control back to the calling application, you can then poll the status byte waiting for the command to complete. Note that this completion method is the only one to "break" the rule of not touching an SRB's data until after completion. With polling you must look at the SRB_Status byte in order to tell when the SRB is complete. You are still prohibited from accessing any other fields of the SRB.

```
BYTE byInquiry[32];
SRB_ExecSCSICmd srbExec;
memset( &srbExec, 0, sizeof(SRB_ExecSCSICmd) );
srbExec.SRB_Cmd = SC_EXEC_SCSI_CMD;
srbExec.SRB_Flags = SRB_DIR_IN;
srbExec.SRB_Target = 5;
srbExec.SRB_BufLen = 32;
srbExec.SRB_BufPointer = byInquiry;
```

```
srbExec.SRB_SenseLen = SENSE_LEN;
srbExec.SRB_CDBLen = 6;
srbExec.CDBByte[0] = SCSI_INQUIRY;
srbExec.CDBByte[4] = 32;
SendASPI32Command( (LPSRB)&srbExec );
while( srbExec.SRB_Status == SS_PENDING );
if( srbExec.SRB_Status != SS_COMP )
{
// Error processing the SRB, put error handling code here.
}
```

## ASPI for Win32 Errors

Each of these errors can be returned by ASPI for Win32 on either Windows 95 or Windows NT. The ASPI header files included with the ASPI SDK may have codes defined which cannot be returned by an actual ASPI implementation. These codes are in the header file to serve as placeholders for other ASPI managers. They are not documented in this table (Table 11.37).

**Table 11.37: ASPI for Win32 Errors**

| Symbol | Value | Description |
| --- | --- | --- |
| SS_PENDING | 0x00 | Returned from SendASPI32Command on SC_EXEC_SCSI_CMD and SC_RESET_DEV SRBs to indicate that the command is in progress. Use polling, posting, or event-notification (preferred) to wait for completion. |
| SS_COMP | 0x01 | Either returned from SendASPI32Command, or set in the SRB_Status field of the SRB header. This value indicates successful completion of an SRB. |
| SS_ABORTED | 0x02 | The current SRB was aborted either by the operating system directly (for example, a third party does a hard reset of the SCSI bus) or through a SC_ABORT_SRB. |
| SS_ERR | 0x04 | Returned on SC_EXEC_SCSI_CMD calls if there is a host adapter, SCSI bus, or SCSI target error. It indicates that the caller should examine SRB_TargStat and SRB_HaStat for additional information. |
| SS_INVALID_CMD | 0x80 | The SRB_Cmd passed in an SRB is invalid. |

| Symbol | Value | Description |
|---|---|---|
| SS_INVALID_HA | 0x81 | The SRB_Hald passed in an SRB is invalid. Call GetASPI32SupportInfo to determine the valid range of host adapters identifiers. |
| SS_NO_DEVICE | 0x82 | Returned from calls to SendASPI32Command, or set in the SRB_Status field of the SRB header. This value indicates that there is no target present at the SCSI address indicated in the SRB. Note that this is not a selection timeout. The operating system keeps a table of known devices and does not permit commands to "non-existent" devices. This code could be returned if an operating system rescan of the SCSI bus is required to detect a newly powered-on device. |
| SS_INVALID_SRB | 0xE0 | An SRB sent to ASPI had a valid address and a valid command byte, but it was somehow faulty in another way. The exact cause of the failure is dependent on the SRB type. For example, an SC_EXEC_SCSI_CMD SRB may fail if an invalid flag is set in the SRB_Flags word, if a buffer length is specified but there is a NULL buffer pointer, or if ASPI detects an SRB has been reused. In any case, the code creating the SRB is faulty and needs to be analyzed. |
| SS_BUFFER_ALIGN | 0xE1 | SRB data buffers must meet alignment requirements as returned by SC_HA_INQUIRY SRBs. If a transfer buffer does not meet those requirements, this error is returned. |
| SS_ILLEGAL_MODE | 0xE2 | An attempt was made to start ASPI for Win32 from Win32s. ASPI for Win32 is a pure Win32 component and cannot be run under the Windows 3.1x Win32 subsystem. |
| SS_NO_ASPI | 0xE3 | WNASPI32.DLL is present on the system, but it could not find its helper driver. Under Windows 95 APIX.VXD is the helper driver, and under Windows NT ASPI32.SYS is the helper driver. Either the ASPI installation is invalid, or there are resource conflicts preventing ASPI from starting. |

| Symbol | Value | Description |
| --- | --- | --- |
| SS_FAILED_INIT | 0xE4 | A general internal failure has occurred within ASPI. This can occur during initialization or at run-time. This error should only occur if basic Windows operating services begin to fail, in which case the whole system is unstable. |
| SS_ASPI_IS_BUSY | 0xE5 | Returned either from SendASPI32Command, or set in the SRB_Status field of the SRB header. This code indicates that ASPI did not have enough resources to complete the requested SRB at the present time. This is different from SS_INSUFFICIENT_RESOURCES in that it is usually a temporal condition, and the failed SRB may be retried at a later time. |
| SS_BUFFER_TO_BIG | 0xE6 | Returned in the SRB_Status field of a failing SRB. The code indicates that the buffer associated with the SRB did not meet internal operating system constraints for a valid transfer buffer. For example, a buffer >64KB on a bus-mastering controller will usually fail with this error because it is not physically contiguous enough to be described by a scatter/gather list. |
| SS_MISMATCHED_COMPONENTS | 0xE7 | ASPI for Win32 consists of three components under Windows 95: WNASPI32.DLL, APIX.VXD, and ASPIENUM.VXD. It consists of two components under Windows NT: WNASPI32.DLL, ASPI32.SYS. Each of these components has a version number, and all the version numbers on a particular platform must agree for ASPI to function. This error will only occur if the installation has been corrupted, and components with different version numbers have been installed on the system. The only fix for this is to remove all of the ASPI components for that operating system, and then reinstall a full, consistent set of ASPI drivers. |

| Symbol | Value | Description |
|--------|-------|-------------|
| SS_NO_ADAPTERS | 0xE8 | Returned from GetASPI32SupportInfo if ASPI has initialized successfully, but there are no host adapters on the system. It is still possible that an adapter may become active through Plug and Play, so a lack of manageable host adapter is no longer considered an error as it was in previous versions of ASPI. |
| SS_INSUFFICIENT_RESOURCES | 0xE9 | The error occurs only during initialization if there are not enough system resources (memory, event handles, critical sections, etc.) to fully initialize ASPI. If this error occurs it is likely that the system is critically low on memory. |

# V. ASPI for OS/2 Specification

Device drivers wishing to access ASPI must determine the address of the ASPI entry point through an OS/2 Attach Device Help call as follows:

```
SCSIMGR$            DB `SCSIMGR$´,0
Return_Data_Buffer  DB 12 DUP(?)
                    MOV BX,OFFSET SCSIMGR
                    MOV DI,OFFSET Return_Data_Buffer
                    MOV DL,DevHlp_AttachDD

                    CALL [DevHlp]
```

On return from the Attach Device Help call, a clear carry flag indicates that the SCSI manager SCSIMGR$ was found and that the return data is valid. A set carry flag indicates that the SCSI manager was not found.

The return data buffer has the following format:

```
ASPI_Real  DW Real Mode offset of ASPI entry point
           DW Real Mode CS segment of ASPI entry point
Real_DS    DW Real Mode DS of ASPI entry point
ASPI_Prot  DW Protected Mode offset of ASPI entry point
           DW Protected Mode CS selector of ASPI entry point
Prot_DS    DW Protected Mode DS of ASPI entry point
```

*ASPI_Real and Real_DS are used by OS/2 1.x only. Information returned under OS/2 2.x is irrelevant.*

## Calling ASPI

Once the ASPI entry point parameters have been successfully determined, calling ASPI is a matter of using the values appropriate to the mode of the processor. The address of the ASPI request block and the DS of the ASPI entry point must be pushed onto the stack before making a FAR call.

The following is an example of how to call ASPI:

```
              PUSH AX                  ;Save AX
              PUSH @ASPI_SRB           ;Push pointer to ASPI SRB
              SMSW AX                  ;Check mode of processor
              TEST AX,PROTECT_MODE
              JNZ  PROT_CALL
              PUSH Real_DS
              CALL [ASPI_REAL]
              JMP  CALL_DONE

PROT_CALL:    PUSH Prot_DS
              CALL [ASPI_PROT]

CALL_DONE:    ADD  SP,6                ;Restore the stack
              POP  AX
```

## Accessing ASPI at Initialization Time

At initialization time, an OS/2 device driver lacks the privilege level for making a FAR call to the ASPI interface. To circumvent this restriction, the SCSI manager provides a special IOCTL that can be used by a driver to pass an ASPI request. To use the IOCTL, the driver must first use a DOSOPEN call to get a file handle for the SCSI manager. Having completed this successfully, the driver can call ASPI at initialization time as follows:

```
              PUSH @DATA_BUFFER        ;Not Applicable
              PUSH @REQUEST_BLOCK      ;Parameter List = SRB
              PUSH 40H                 ;Function Code
              PUSH 80H                 ;Function Category
              PUSH ASPI_Handle         ;File handle from DosOpen
              CALL DOSDEVIOCTL
```

Once the driver has returned from initialization, this access method is no longer valid.

## ASPI and OS/2 2.x

The device driver architecture for OS/2 2.x is divided into several basic layers. Device manager drivers (DMDs) receive requests from the file systems and other device drivers. These requests are passed on to an adapter device driver (ADD), which sends the appropriate command to the host adapter.

ASPI for OS/2 2.x is a translation layer, and it has been implemented as a device driver (os2aspi.dmd). An application can send SRBs to any SCSI adapter that has an ADD installed. It is no longer possible to set host adapter parameters, because OS2ASPI has no direct control over the host adapter.

## Target Allocation with OS/2 2.x

The device driver architecture for OS/2 2.x is structured so that targets controlled by an ADD must be allocated to an individual DMD. For example, when the system boots, os2dasd.dmd is normally the first device manager loaded, and it will automatically search for all available hard drives and permanently allocate them for use by the file systems. Other DMDs usually do something similar with targets that they assume should be controlled by them.

The standard method for preventing a DMD from allocating a particular target is through the use of command line switches on the ADD that handles the device. If you are planning on using ASPI to control a device that may be allocated by a DMD that loads before os2aspi.dmd, be sure to specify that the device manager in question is not allowed access to it.

- If you are writing an ASPI application for a magneto-optical drive (target 6 on an AHA-1540) that returns device type 0 (DASD) in the Inquiry data, you must be sure to prevent OS2DASD from accessing it:

  ```
  BASEDEV=AHA154X.ADD /A:0 /!DM:6
  ```

- If you are writing an ASPI application for a device that also may be controlled by a device driver through os2scsi.dmd (target 6 on an AHA-1540), you can also prevent OS2SCSI from accessing it:

  ```
  BASEDEV=AHA154X.ADD /A:0 /!SM:6
  ```

Currently, only os2dasd.dmd and os2scsi.dmd can be controlled in this manner, because they are the only DMDs mentioned in IBM's specification for ADDs. For a complete explanation of command line switches supported by the ADD that are provided with OS/2 2.1, consult the online help for SCSI.

The current ASPI specification does not provide a method for allocating targets, and there are no command line switches for os2aspi.dmd that can be used with the current ADD. The target for each SRB will be allocated and deallocated on a command basis until the first Execute I/O SRB is sent. At this point, the target will be permanently allocated to os2aspi.dmd and other DMDs will no longer have access to the target.

## Sample Code for OS/2 2.x

The SDK (ASPI Software Developer's Kit) includes sample code for designing ASPI applications and device drivers to be used with OS/2 2.x.

ASPIAPP is a simple program that scans the SCSI bus and displays information about any targets that it finds on adapters in the system. This application is a single-threaded, character-based application intended to show you how ASPI can be used.

ASPIDRV is a simple device driver that passes requests from ASPIAPP to os2aspi.dmd after converting any virtual addresses to physical addresses. This driver is intended for handling single-threaded requests that are small enough not to require a scatter/gather list. If you are transferring large blocks of data, you may have to convert the virtual address of the buffer into a page table that can be used as a scatter/gather list.

## SCSI Request Block (SRB)

A SCSI request block (SRB), defined in Table 11.38, contains the command to be executed by the ASPI manager and is used by both drivers and application programs. An SRB consists of an SRB header followed by additional fields dependent on the command code. All request blocks have an 8-byte header.

**Table 11.38: SCSI Request Block Header**

| Offset | # Bytes | Description | R/W |
| --- | --- | --- | --- |
| 00h (00) | 01h (01) | Command Code | W |
| 01h (01) | 01h (01) | Status | R |
| 02h (02) | 01h (01) | Host Adapter Number | W |
| 03h (03) | 01h (01) | SCSI Request Flags | W |
| 04h (04) | 04h (04) | Reserved for Expansion = 0 | — |

### Command Code

The Command Code field is used to indicate which of the ASPI services is being accessed. Refer to Table 11.39 for a description of valid ASPI command codes.

### Status

The Status Byte field is used to post the status of the command. Refer to Table 11.40 for a description of ASPI status bytes.

### Host Adapter Number

The Host Adapter Number field specifies which installed host adapter the request is intended for. Host adapter numbers are always assigned by the SCSI manager layer beginning with zero.

### SCSI Request Flags

The SCSI Request Flags field definition is command code–specific.

### Reserved for Expansion

The last 4 bytes of the header are reserved and must be zero.

## ASPI Command Codes

### Valid ASPI Command Codes

See Table 11.39 for a list of valid ASPIcommand codes, and their descriptions.

**Table 11.39: Valid ASPI Command Codes**

| Command Code | Description |
|---|---|
| 00h | Host Adapter Inquiry |
| 01h | Get Device Type |
| 02h | Execute SCSI I/O Command |
| 03h | Abort SCSI I/O Command |
| 04h | Reset SCSI Device |
| 05h | Set Host Adapter Parameters |
| 06h-7Fh | Reserved for Future Expansion |
| 80h-FFh | Reserved for Vendor Unique |

### ASPI Status Bytes

See Table 11.40 for a list of ASPI status bytes, and their descriptions.

**Table 11.40: ASPI Status Bytes**

| Status Byte | Description |
| --- | --- |
| 00h | SCSI Request In Progress |
| 01h | SCSI Request Completed Without Error |
| 02h | SCSI Request Aborted By Host |
| 04h | SCSI Request Completed With Error |
| 80h | Invalid SCSI Request |
| 81h | Invalid Host Adapter Number |
| 82h | SCSI Device Not Installed |

### ASPI Command Code = 0: Host Adapter Inquiry

The status byte (defined in Table 11.41) always returns with a nonzero status. A SCSI Request Completed Without Error (01h) status indicates that the remaining fields are valid. An Invalid Host Adapter Number (81h) status indicates that the specified host adapter is not installed.

**Table 11.41: ASPI Command Code = 0: Host Adapter Inquiry**

| Offset | # Bytes | Description | R/W |
| --- | --- | --- | --- |
| 00h (00) | 01h (01) | Command Code = 0 | W |
| 01h (01) | 01h (01) | Status | R |
| 02h (02) | 01h (01) | Host Adapter Number | W |
| 03h (03) | 01h (01) | SCSI Request Flags | W |
| 04h (04) | 04h (04) | Reserved for Expansion = 0 | — |
| 08h (08) | 01h (01) | Number of Host Adapters | R |
| 09h (09) | 01h (01) | Target ID of Host Adapter | R |
| 0Ah (10) | 10h (16) | SCSI Manager ID | R |
| 1Ah (26) | 10h (16) | Host Adapter ID | R |
| 2Ah (42) | 10h (16) | Host Adapter Unique Parameters | R |

This function is used to get information on the installed host adapter hardware, including number of host adapters installed. It can be issued once with host adapter zero specified to get the number of host adapters. If further information is desired, it can be issued for each individual host adapter.

The SCSI Request Flags field is currently undefined for this command and should be zeroed.

The SCSI Manager ID field contains a 16-byte ASCII string describing the SCSI manager.

The Host Adapter ID field contains a 16-byte ASCII string describing the SCSI host adapter.

The definition of the Host Adapter Unique Parameters field is left to implementation notes specific to a particular host adapter.

### ASPI Command Code = 1: Get Device Type

This command (defined in Table 11.42) always returns with a nonzero status.

**Table 11.42: ASPI Command Code = 1: Get Device Type**

| Offset | # Bytes | Description | R/W |
|--------|---------|-------------|-----|
| 00h (00) | 01h (01) | Command Code = 1 | W |
| 01h (01) | 01h (01) | Status | R |
| 02h (02) | 01h (01) | Host Adapter Number | W |
| 03h (03) | 01h (01) | SCSI Request Flags | W |
| 04h (04) | 04h (04) | Reserved for Expansion = 0 | — |
| 08h (08) | 01h (01) | Target ID | W |
| 09h (09) | 01h (01) | LUN | W |
| 0Ah (10) | 01h (01) | Peripheral Device Type of Target/LUN | R |

A SCSI Request Completed Without Error (01h) status indicates that the specified device is installed and the peripheral device type field is valid. A SCSI Device Not Installed Error (82h) indicates that the peripheral device type field is not valid.

This command is intended for use by various drivers, during initialization, for identifying the targets they need to support. A CD-ROM driver, for example, can scan each target/LUN on each installed host adapter looking for the device type corresponding to CD-ROM devices. This eliminates the need for each driver to duplicate the effort of scanning the SCSI bus for devices.

The peripheral device type is determined by sending a SCSI Inquiry command to the given target. Refer to any published SCSI specification to learn more about the Inquiry command.

The SCSI Request Flags field is currently undefined for this command and should be zeroed.

### ASPI Command Code = 2: Execute SCSI I/O Command

This command (defined in Table 11.43) usually returns with zero status indicating that the request was queued successfully. Command completion can be determined by polling for nonzero status or through the use of the Post Routine Address field in the ASPI Command Posting section (discussed later). Keep in mind that if you are going to use polling, interrupts must be enabled.

**Table 11.43: ASPI Command Code = 2: Execute SCSI I/O Command**

| Offset | # Bytes | Description | R/W |
|--------|---------|-------------|-----|
| 00h (00) | 01h (01) | Command Code = 2 | W |
| 01h (01) | 01h (01) | Status | R |
| 02h (02) | 01h (01) | Host Adapter Number | W |
| 03h (03) | 01h (01) | SCSI Request Flags | W |
| 04h (04) | 02h (02) | Length of Scatter/Gather List | W |
| 06h (06) | 02h (02) | Reserved for Expansion = 0 | — |
| 08h (08) | 01h (01) | Target ID | W |
| 09h (09) | 01h (01) | LUN | W |
| 0Ah (10) | 04h (04) | Data Allocation Length | W |
| 0Eh (14) | 01h (01) | Sense Allocation Length (N) | W |
| 0Fh (15) | 04h (04) | Data Buffer Pointer | W |
| 13h (19) | 04h (04) | SRB Link Pointer | W |
| 17h (23) | 01h (01) | SCSI CDB Length (M) | W |
| 18h (24) | 01h (01) | Host Adapter Status | R |
| 19h (25) | 01h (01) | Target Status | R |
| 1Ah (26) | 02h (02) | Real Mode Post Routine Offset* | W |
| 1Ch (28) | 02h (02) | Real Mode Post Routine CS* | W |
| 1Eh (30) | 02h (02) | Real Mode Post Routine DS* | W |
| 20h (32) | 02h (02) | Protected Mode Post Routine Offset | W |
| 22h (34) | 02h (02) | Protected Mode Post Routine CS | W |

| Offset | # Bytes | Description | R/W |
|--------|---------|-------------|-----|
| 24h (36) | 02h (02) | Protected Mode Post Routine DS | W |
| 26h (38) | 04h (04) | Physical Address of SRB | W |
| 2Ah (42) | 16h (22) | Reserved for ASPI Workspace | — |
| 40h (64) | M | SCSI Command Descriptor Block (CDB) | W |
| 40h+M | N | Sense Allocation Area | R |

*Used by OS/2 1.x only. Fields are not used under OS/2 2.x.*

### The SCSI Request Flags Byte Is Defined as Follows:

| 7 | 6 | 5 | 4 | 3 | 2 | 1 | 0 |
|---|---|---|---|---|---|---|---|
| Rsvd | Rsvd | SGE | Direction Bit | | Rsvd | Link | Post |

The Post bit specifies whether posting is enabled (bit 0 = 1) or disabled (bit 0 = 0).

The Link bit specifies whether linking is enabled (bit 1 = 1) or disabled (bit 1 = 0).

The Direction Bits specify which direction the transfer is:

00      Direction determined by SCSI command. Length not checked.

01      Transfer from SCSI target to host. Length checked.

10      Transfer from host to SCSI target. Length checked.

11      No data transfer.

The Scatter/Gather Enable (SGE) bit specifies whether scatter/gather is enabled (bit 5=1) or disabled (bit 5=0).

The Target ID and LUN fields are used to specify the peripheral device involved in the I/O.

The Data Allocation Length field indicates the number of bytes to be transferred. If the SCSI command to be executed does not transfer data (i.e., Rewind, Start Unit, etc.), the data allocation length must be set to zero.

The Length of Scatter/Gather List field is valid only when the scatter/gather enable bit in the flags is set. It contains the number of descriptors in the array pointed by the Data Buffer Pointer field.

The Sense Allocation Length field indicates, in bytes, the number of bytes allocated at the end of the SRB for sense data. A request sense is automatically generated if a check condition is presented at the end of a SCSI command.

The Data Buffer Pointer field is a pointer to the I/O data buffer. When scatter/gather is enabled, this field is a physical pointer to a scatter/gather list. A scatter/gather list is made up of one or more descriptors of the following format:

DWORD Buffer Pointer

DWORD Buffer Size

The SRB Link Pointer field is a pointer to the next SRB in a chain. See the section "SCSI Command Linking with ASPI" for more information.

The SCSI CDB Length field establishes the length, in bytes, of the SCSI command descriptor block (CDB).

The Host Adapter Status field is used to report the host adapter status as follows:

| | |
|---|---|
| 00h | Host adapter did not detect any error |
| 11h | Selection timeout |
| 12h | Data overrun/underrun |
| 13h | Unexpected bus free |
| 14h | Target bus phase sequence failure |

The Target Status field is used to report the target's SCSI status, including:

| | |
|---|---|
| 00h | No target status |
| 02h | Check status (sense data is in sense allocation area) |
| 08h | Specified target/LUN is busy |
| 18h | Reservation conflict |

**NOTE** *The host adapter status and the target status are valid only when the status byte is either 2 or 4.*

The Post Routine Address field, if specified, is called when the I/O is completed. See the section "ASPI Command Posting" for more information.

The SCSI command descriptor block (CDB) field contains the CDB as defined by the target's SCSI command set. The length of the SCSI CDB is specified in the SCSI Command Length field.

The sense allocation area is filled with sense data on a check condition. The maximum length of this field is specified in the Sense Allocation Length field. Note that the target can return fewer than the number of sense bytes requested.

### SCSI Command Linking with ASPI

ASPI provides the ability to use SCSI linking to guarantee the sequential execution of several commands. Note that the use of this feature requires the involved target(s) to support SCSI linking.

To use SCSI linking, a chain of SRBs is built with the SRB link pointer used to link the elements together. The link bit should be set in the SCSI request flags byte of all SRBs except the last in the chain. When a SCSI target returns indicating that the linked command is complete, the next SRB is immediately processed and the appropriate CDB is dispatched. When using SCSI linking, make sure that the linking flags in the SCSI CDB agree with the link bit in the SCSI request flags. Inconsistencies can cause unpredictable results. For example, setting the CDB up for linking but failing to set the link bit may result in a random address being used for the next SRB pointer.

Any error returned from the target on a linked command will break the chain. Note that if linking without tags is used, as defined in SCSI, posting may not occur on any elements in the chain until the chain is complete. If you have the post bit set in each SRB's SCSI request flags byte, then each SRB's post routine will be called.

**NOTE** *It is strongly recommended that you do not use SCSI linking. There are many SCSI targets, as well as SCSI host adapters, that do not handle SCSI linking and will not work with your ASPI module.*

### ASPI Command Posting

Posting refers to the SCSI manager making a FAR call to a post routine as specified in the SRB. This can be used by a driver much like a hardware interrupt might be used. Post routines have all the same privileges and restrictions as a hardware interrupt service routine in OS/2. Posting is optional but should almost always be used in OS/2. To use posting, the post bit must be set in the SCSI request flags. The post routine is called to indicate that the requested I/O is complete. The specific SRB completed is indicated by the 4-byte SRB pointer on the stack. The DS of the post routine as specified in the SRB is also passed to the stack.

The post routine will be called with interrupts enabled. It is assumed that all registers are preserved by the post routine.

```
ASPI_Post   proc far
            push bp                         ;Use bp as a reference
            mov  bp,sp
            pusha                           ;Save all registers
            push es                         ;Save ES
            mov  bx,[bp+6]                  ;Load DS of POST routine
            mov  ax,[bp+10]                 ;Physical address of SRB->AX:BX
            mov  ax,[bp+8]
```

```
                    .
                    .
                    .
            pop  es                    ;Restore registers
            popa
            pop  ds
            pop  bp
            retf
ASPI_Post  endp
```

When your post routine is first entered, the stack will look as follows:

```
Top of Stack [SP+0] —> Return Address (Offset)
             [SP+2] —> Return Address (Segment)
             [SP+4] —> SRB Pointer (Offset)
             [SP+6] —> SRB Pointer (Segment)
             . . .
             . . .
             . . .
```

You may issue any ASPI command from within your post routine except for an abort command. Your post routine should get in and out as quickly as possible.

### ASPI Command Code = 3: Abort SCSI I/O Request

This command (defined in Table 11.44) is used to request that an SRB be aborted. It should be issued on any I/O request that has not completed if the driver wishes to timeout on that request. Success of the Abort command is never assured.

**Table 11.44: ASPI Command Code = 3: Abort SCSI I/O Request**

| Offset | # Bytes | Description | R/W |
|--------|---------|-------------|-----|
| 00h (00) | 01h (01) | Command Code = 3 | W |
| 01h (01) | 01h (01) | Status | R |
| 02h (02) | 01h (01) | Host Adapter Number | W |
| 03h (03) | 01h (01) | SCSI Request Flags | W |
| 04h (04) | 04h (04) | Reserved for Expansion = 0 | — |
| 08h (08) | 04h (04) | Physical SRB Pointer | W |

This command always returns with SCSI Request Completed Without Error, but the actual failure or success of the abort operation is indicated by the status eventually returned in the SRB specified.

The SCSI Request Flags field is currently undefined for this command and should be zeroed.

The SRB Pointer to Abort field contains a pointer to the SRB that is to be aborted.

**NOTE** *An Abort command should not be issued during a post routine.*

### ASPI Command Code = 4: Reset SCSI Device

This command (defined in Table 11.45) is used to reset a specific SCSI target. Note that the structure passed is nearly identical to the execute SCSI I/O SRB except that some of the fields are not used.

**Table 11.45: ASPI Command Code = 4: Reset SCSI Device**

| Offset | # Bytes | Description | R/W |
|---------|---------|-------------|-----|
| 00h (00) | 01h (01) | Command Code = 4 | W |
| 01h (01) | 01h (01) | Status | R |
| 02h (02) | 01h (01) | Host Adapter Number | W |
| 03h (03) | 01h (01) | SCSI Request Flags | W |
| 04h (04) | 04h (04) | Reserved for Expansion = 0 | — |
| 08h (08) | 01h (01) | Target ID | W |
| 09h (09) | 01h (01) | LUN | W |
| 0Ah (10) | 0Eh (14) | Reserved | — |
| 18h (24) | 01h (01) | Host Adapter Status | R |
| 19h (25) | 01h (01) | Target Status | R |
| 1Ah (26) | 02h (02) | Real Mode Post Routine Offset* | W |
| 1Ch (28) | 02h (02) | Real Mode Post Routine CS* | W |
| 1Eh (30) | 02h (02) | Real Mode Post Routine DS* | W |
| 20h (32) | 02h (02) | Protected Mode Post Routine Offset | W |
| 22h (34) | 02h (02) | Protected Mode Post Routine CS | W |
| 24h (36) | 02h (02) | Protected Mode Post Routine DS | W |
| 26h (38) | 16h (22) | Reserved for ASPI Workspace | — |

*Used by OS/2 1.x only. Fields are not used under OS/2 2.x.*

This command usually returns with zero status indicating that the request was queued successfully. Command completion can be determined by polling for nonzero status or through the use of posting.

### The SCSI Request Flags Byte Is Defined as Follows:

| 7 | 6 | 5 | 4 | 3 | 2 | 1 | 0 |
|---|---|---|---|---|---|---|---|
| Rsvd | | | | | | | Post |

The Post bit specifies whether posting is enabled (bit 0 = 1) or disabled (bit 0 = 0).

### ASPI Command Code = 5: Set Host Adapter Parameters

The definition of the host adapter unique parameters (defined in Table 11.46) is left to implementation notes specific to a particular host adapter.

**Table 11.46: ASPI Command Code = 5: Set Host Adapter Parameters**

| Offset | # Bytes | Description | R/W |
|--------|---------|-------------|-----|
| 00h (00) | 01h (01) | Command Code = 5 | W |
| 01h (01) | 01h (01) | Status | R |
| 02h (02) | 01h (01) | Host Adapter Number | W |
| 03h (03) | 01h (01) | SCSI Request Flags | W |
| 04h (04) | 04h (04) | Reserved for Expansion = 0 | — |
| 08h (08) | 10h (16) | Host Adapter Unique Parameters | W |

# VI. ASPI for NetWare Specification

Before creating your NetWare loadable module (NLM), you must first create the object file and a definition file. In the definition file, you tell NetWare® what routines you wish to export to the operating system and what routines you wish to import into your NLM. You will need to import one ASPI routine. Sample definition file:

```
        .
        .
        .
    IMPORT
        .
        .
        .
    ASPI_Entry
        .
        .
        .
```

Using the Novell linker, the object and definition files are linked together to create your NLM.

During load time, if NetWare 386 does not find this imported routine, it will not load your NLM. You must load the ASPI module before the other modules can access it.

## ASPI Routine: ASPI_Entry

This routine allows you to pass a SCSI request block (SRB) to ASPI.

### Syntax

Void ASPI_Entry ( void *ASPIRequestBlock )

### Return Values

Returns nothing

### Parameters

| Parameter | Description |
| --- | --- |
| ASPIRequestBlock | This field contains a pointer to your SRB. |

### Assembly Example

```
push OFFSET ASPI_ReqBlock      ;Push SRB onto the stack
call ASPI_Entry                ;Call ASPI
lea  esp,[esp+(1*4)]           ;Restore the stack
```

### Remarks

On entry, interrupts should be disabled. Returns with interrupts disabled.

## SCSI Request Block (SRB)

A SCSI request block (SRB) contains the command to be executed by the ASPI manager and is used by both drivers and application programs. An SRB consists of an SRB header (shown in Table 11.47) followed by additional fields dependent on the command code. All request blocks have an 8-byte header.

**Table 11.47: SCSI Request Block Header**

| Offset | # Bytes | Description | R/W |
|--------|---------|-------------|-----|
| 00h (00) | 01h (01) | Command Code | W |
| 01h (01) | 01h (01) | Status | R |
| 02h (02) | 01h (01) | Host Adapter Number | W |
| 03h (03) | 01h (01) | SCSI Request Flags | W |
| 04h (04) | 04h (04) | Reserved for Expansion = 0 | — |

### Command Code

The Command Code field indicates which ASPI service is being accessed. Table 11.48 lists the valid ASPI command codes.

### Status

The Status Byte field is used to post the status of the command. Refer to Table 11.49 for a description of ASPI status bytes.

### Host Adapter Number

The Host Adapter Number field specifies which installed host adapter the request is intended for. Host adapter numbers are always assigned by the SCSI manager layer beginning with zero.

### SCSI Request Flags

The SCSI Request Flags field definition is command code–specific.

### Reserved for Expansion

The last 4 bytes of the header are reserved and must be zero.

## ASPI Command Codes

### Valid ASPI Command Codes

Table 11.48 lists the valid ASPI command codes and their descriptions.

**Table 11.48: Valid ASPI Command Codes**

| Command Code | Description |
| --- | --- |
| 00h | Host Adapter Inquiry |
| 01h | Get Device Type |
| 02h | Execute SCSI I/O Command |
| 03h | Abort SCSI I/O Command |
| 04h | Reset SCSI Device |
| 05h | Set Host Adapter Parameters |
| 06h-7Fh | Reserved for Future Expansion |
| 80h-FFh | Reserved for Vendor Unique |

### ASPI Status Bytes

Table 11.49 lists the ASPI status bytes and their descriptions.

**Table 11.49: ASPI Status Bytes**

| Status Byte | Description |
| --- | --- |
| 00h | SCSI Request in Progress |
| 01h | SCSI Request Completed Without Error |
| 02h | SCSI Request Aborted by Host |
| 04h | SCSI Request Completed With Error |
| 80h | Invalid SCSI Request |
| 81h | Invalid Host Adapter Number |
| 82h | SCSI Device Not Installed |

### ASPI Command Code = 0: Host Adapter Inquiry

The status byte (defined in Table 11.50) always returns with a nonzero status. A SCSI Request Completed Without Error (01h) status indicates that the remaining fields are valid. An Invalid Host Adapter Number (81h) status indicates that the specified host adapter is not installed.

**Table 11.50: ASPI Command Code = 0: Host Adapter Inquiry**

| Offset | # Bytes | Description | R/W |
|--------|---------|-------------|-----|
| 00h (00) | 01h (01) | Command Code = 0 | W |
| 01h (01) | 01h (01) | Status | R |
| 02h (02) | 01h (01) | Host Adapter Number | W |
| 03h (03) | 01h (01) | SCSI Request Flags | W |
| 04h (04) | 04h (04) | Reserved for Expansion = 0 | — |
| 08h (08) | 01h (01) | Number of Host Adapters | R |
| 09h (09) | 01h (01) | Target ID of Host Adapter | R |
| 0Ah (10) | 10h (16) | SCSI Manager ID | R |
| 1Ah (26) | 10h (16) | Host Adapter ID | R |
| 2Ah (42) | 10h (16) | Host Adapter Unique Parameters | R |

This function is used to get information on the installed host adapter hardware, including number of host adapters installed. It can be issued once with host adapter zero specified to get the number of host adapters. If further information is desired, it can be issued for each individual host adapter.

The SCSI Request Flags field is currently undefined for this command and should be zeroed.

The SCSI Manager ID field contains a 16-byte ASCII string describing the SCSI manager.

The Host Adapter ID field contains a 16-byte ASCII string describing the SCSI host adapter.

The definition of the Host Adapter Unique Parameters field is left to implementation notes specific to a particular host adapter.

### ASPI Command Code = 1: Get Device Type

This command (defined in Table 11.51) always returns with nonzero status.

A SCSI Request Completed Without Error (01h) status indicates that the specified device is installed and the peripheral device type field is valid. A SCSI Device Not Installed Error (82h) indicates that the peripheral device type field is not valid.

**Table 11.51: ASPI Command Code = 1: Get Device Type**

| Offset | # Bytes | Description | R/W |
|--------|---------|-------------|-----|
| 00h (00) | 01h (01) | Command Code = 1 | W |
| 01h (01) | 01h (01) | Status | R |
| 02h (02) | 01h (01) | Host Adapter Number | W |
| 03h (03) | 01h (01) | SCSI Request Flags | W |
| 04h (04) | 04h (04) | Reserved for Expansion = 0 | — |
| 08h (08) | 01h (01) | Target ID | W |
| 09h (09) | 01h (01) | LUN | W |
| 0Ah (10) | 01h (01) | Peripheral Device Type of Target/LUN | R |

This command is intended for use by various drivers during initialization for identifying the targets that they need to support. A CD-ROM driver, for example, can scan each target/LUN on each installed host adapter looking for the device type corresponding to CD-ROM devices. This eliminates the need for each driver to duplicate the effort of scanning the SCSI bus for devices.

The peripheral device type is determined by sending a SCSI Inquiry command to the given target. Refer to any SCSI specification to learn more about the Inquiry command.

The SCSI Request Flags field is currently undefined for this command and should be zeroed.

### ASPI Command Code = 2: Execute SCSI I/O Command

This command (defined in Table 11.52) usually returns with zero status indicating that the request was queued successfully. Command completion can be determined by polling for nonzero status or through the use of the Post Routine Address field (discussed later in the section ASPI Command Posting). Keep in mind that if you are going to use polling, interrupts must be enabled.

## Table 11.52: ASPI Command Code = 2: Execute SCSI I/O Command

| Offset | # Bytes | Description | R/W |
|--------|---------|-------------|-----|
| 00h (00) | 01h (01) | Command Code = 2 | W |
| 01h (01) | 01h (01) | Status | R |
| 02h (02) | 01h (01) | Host Adapter Number | W |
| 03h (03) | 01h (01) | SCSI Request Flags | W |
| 04h (04) | 04h (04) | Reserved for Expansion = 0 | W |
| 08h (08) | 01h (01) | Target ID | — |
| 09h (09) | 01h (01) | LUN | W |
| 0Ah (10) | 04h (04) | Data Allocation Length | W |
| 0Eh (14) | 01h (01) | Sense Allocation Length (N) | W |
| 0Fh (15) | 04h (04) | Data Buffer Pointer | W |
| 13h (19) | 04h (04) | SRB Link Pointer | W |
| 17h (23) | 01h (01) | SCSI CDB Length (M) | W |
| 18h (24) | 01h (01) | Host Adapter Status | R |
| 19h (25) | 01h (01) | Target Status | R |
| 1Ah (26) | 04h (04) | Post Routine Address | W |
| 1Eh (30) | 22h (34) | Reserved for ASPI Workspace | — |
| 40h (64) | M | SCSI Command Descriptor Block (CDB) | W |
| 40h+M | N | Sense Allocation Area | R |

## The SCSI Request Flags Byte Is Defined as Follows:

| 7 | 6 | 5 | 4 | 3 | 2 | 1 | 0 |
|---|---|---|---|---|---|---|---|
| Rsvd | Rsvd | Rsvd | Direction Bits | | Rsvd | Link | Post |

- The Post bit specifies whether posting is enabled (bit 0 = 1) or disabled (bit 0 = 0).

- The Link bit specifies whether linking is enabled (bit 1 = 1) or disabled (bit 1 = 0).

- The Direction bits specify which direction the transfer is.

| 00 | Direction determined by SCSI command. Length not checked. |
| 01 | Transfer from SCSI target to host. Length checked. |
| 10 | Transfer from host to SCSI target. Length checked. |
| 11 | No data transfer. |

The Target ID and LUN fields are used to specify the peripheral device involved in the I/O.

The Data Allocation Length field indicates the number of bytes to be transferred. If the SCSI command to be executed does not transfer data (i.e., Rewind, Start Unit, etc.) the Data Allocation Length must be set to zero.

The Sense Allocation Length field indicates, in bytes, the number of bytes allocated at the end of the SRB for sense data. A request sense is automatically generated if a check condition is presented at the end of a SCSI command.

The Data Buffer Pointer field is a pointer to the I/O data buffer. You place the logical address here. ASPI will convert it to the physical address in the case of a bus master or DMA transfer.

The SRB Link Pointer field is a pointer to the next SRB in a chain. See the discussion on linking for more information.

The SCSI CDB Length field establishes the length, in bytes, of the SCSI command descriptor block (CDB).

The Host Adapter Status field is used to report the host adapter status as follows:

| 00h | Host adapter did not detect any error. |
| 11h | Selection timeout. |
| 12h | Data overrun/underrun. |
| 13h | Unexpected bus free. |
| 14h | Target bus phase sequence failure. |

The Target Status field is used to report the target's SCSI status, including:

| 00h | No target status. |
| 02h | Check status (sense data is in sense allocation area). |
| 08h | Specified target/LUN is busy. |
| 18h | Reservation conflict. |

The Post Routine Address field, if specified, is called when the I/O is completed. See the section ASPI Command Posting for more information.

The SCSI command descriptor block (CDB) field contains the CDB as defined by the target's SCSI command set. The length of the SCSI CDB is specified in the SCSI Command Length field.

The Sense Allocation Area is filled with sense data on a check condition. The maximum length of this field is specified in the Sense Allocation Length field. Note that the target can return fewer than the number of sense bytes requested.

### SCSI Command Linking with ASPI

ASPI provides the ability to use SCSI linking to guarantee the sequential execution of several commands. Note that the use of this feature requires the involved target(s) to support SCSI linking.

To use SCSI linking, a chain of SRBs is built with the SRB link pointer used to link the elements together. The link bit should be set in the SCSI request flags byte of all SRBs except the last in the chain. When a SCSI target returns indicating that the linked command is complete, the next SRB is immediately processed, and the appropriate CDB is dispatched. When using SCSI linking, make sure that the linking flags in the SCSI CDB agree with the link bit in the SCSI request flags. Inconsistencies can cause unpredictable results. For example, setting the CDB up for linking but failing to set the link bit may result in a random address being used for the next SRB pointer.

Any error returned from the target on a linked command will break the chain. Note that if linking without tags is used, as defined in SCSI, posting may not occur on any elements in the chain until the chain is complete. If you have the post bit set in each SRB's SCSI request flags byte, then each SRB's post routine will be called.

**NOTE** *It is strongly recommended that you do not use SCSI linking. There are many SCSI targets, as well as SCSI host adapters, that do not handle SCSI linking and will not work with your ASPI module.*

### ASPI Command Posting

To use posting, the Post bit must be set in the SCSI request flags. Posting refers to the SCSI manager making a call to a post routine as specified in the SRB. The post routine is called to indicate that the SRB is complete. The specific SRB completed is indicated by a 4-byte SRB pointer on the stack.

If your post routine is written in assembly language, it must save the C registers: EBP, EBX, ESI, and EDI. Below is a sample ASPI post handler:

```
ASPI_Post  proc near
           Cpush                          ;Push 'C' required regs
           mov  eax, [esp+20]             ;EAX points to SRB
           .
           .                              ;Handle posted SRB
           .
           CPop                           ;Restore registers and
           ret                            ;  return to ASPI
ASPI_Post  endp
```

## C example:

```
void ASPI_Post  ( SRB_Pointer )
void *SRB_Pointer;
{
        .
        .                                 /* Handle posted SRB */
        .

}
```

**NOTE** *On entry, interrupts will be disabled. You should return with interrupts disabled. You may issue any ASPI command from within your post routine except for an abort command. Your post routing should get in and out as quickly as possible.*

### ASPI Command Code = 3: Abort SCSI I/O Command

This command (defined in Table 11.53) is used to request that an SRB be aborted. It should be issued on any I/O request that has not completed if the driver wishes to timeout on that request. Success of the Abort command is never assured.

**Table 11.53: ASPI Command Code = 3: Abort SCSI I/O Command**

| Offset | # Bytes | Description | R/W |
|--------|---------|-------------|-----|
| 00h (00) | 01h (01) | Command Code = 3 | W |
| 01h (01) | 01h (01) | Status | R |
| 02h (02) | 01h (01) | Host Adapter Number | W |
| 03h (03) | 01h (01) | SCSI Request Flags | W |
| 04h (04) | 04h (04) | Reserved for Expansion = 0 | — |
| 08h (08) | 04h (04) | SRB Pointer to Abort | W |

This command always returns with SCSI Request Completed Without Error (01h), but the actual failure or success of the abort operation is indicated by the status eventually returned in the SRB specified.

The SCSI Request Flags field is currently undefined for this command and should be zeroed.

The SRB Pointer to Abort field contains a pointer to the SRB that is to be aborted.

**NOTE** *An abort command should not be issued during a post routine.*

### ASPI Command Code = 4: Reset SCSI Device

This command (defined in Table 11.54) is used to reset a specific SCSI target. Note that the structure passed is nearly identical to the execute SCSI I/O SRB except that some of the fields are not used.

This command usually returns with zero status indicating that the request was queued successfully. Command completion can be determined by polling for nonzero status or through the use of posting.

**Table 11.54: ASPI Command Code = 4: Reset SCSI Device**

| Offset | # Bytes | Description | R/W |
|---------|----------|-------------|-----|
| 00h (00) | 01h (01) | Command Code = 4 | W |
| 01h (01) | 01h (01) | Status | R |
| 02h (02) | 01h (01) | Host Adapter Number | W |
| 03h (03) | 01h (01) | SCSI Request Flags | W |
| 04h (04) | 04h (04) | Reserved for Expansion = 0 | — |
| 08h (08) | 01h (01) | Target ID | W |
| 09h (09) | 01h (01) | LUN | W |
| 0Ah (10) | 0Eh (14) | Reserved | — |
| 18h (24) | 01h (01) | Host Adapter Status | R |
| 19h (25) | 01h (01) | Target Status | R |
| 1Ah (26) | 02h (02) | POST Routine Address | W |
| 1Eh (30) | 02h (02) | Reserved for ASPI Workspace | — |

## The SCSI Request Flags Byte Is Defined as Follows:

| 7 | 6 | 5 | 4 | 3 | 2 | 1 | 0 |
|---|---|---|---|---|---|---|---|
| Rsvd | Rsvd | Rsvd | Direction Bits | | Rsvd | Link | Post |

The Post bit specifies whether posting is enabled (bit 0 = 1) or disabled (bit 0 = 0).

### ASPI Command Code = 5: Set Host Adapter Parameters

The definition of the host adapter unique parameters (defined in Table 11.55) is left to implementation notes specific to a particular host adapter.

#### Table 11.55: ASPI Command Code = 5: Set Host Adapter Parameters

| Offset | # Bytes | Description | R/W |
|--------|---------|-------------|-----|
| 00h (00) | 01h (01) | Command Code = 5 | W |
| 01h (01) | 01h (01) | Status | R |
| 02h (02) | 01h (01) | Host Adapter Number | W |
| 03h (03) | 01h (01) | SCSI Request Flags | W |
| 04h (04) | 04h (04) | Reserved for Expansion = 0 | — |
| 08h (08) | 10h (16) | Host Adapter Unique Parameters | W |

# Handling Greater than 16 MB

Bus master ISA SCSI host adapters have a restriction in that they cannot perform DMA above 16MB of RAM. This is because the ISA bus only receives 2 bits of the address bus ($2^{24}$ = 16 MB). Thus, if you pass a buffer pointer above 16MB to an ASPI manager/hardware that cannot handle it, you will most likely crash the file server. For these host adapters, you must make sure that both the ASPI SRBs and data buffers are below the first 16MB of RAM. Adaptec's current host adapters handle this situation as detailed:

### Host Adapters Handling > 16MB

- AHA-1510
- AHA-1520
- AHA-1522
- AIC-6260
- AIC-6360

### Host Adapters Handling PIO or Second-Party DMA Host Transfers

When in PIO mode, there is no restriction. When in second-party DMA mode, all ASPI SRBs and all data buffers must be below the first 16MB of RAM.

- AHA-1540
- AHA-1542

### Host Adapters Handling Bus Mastering ISA Mode Host Transfers

All ASPI SRBs and all data buffers must be below the first 16MB of RAM.

- AHA-1640
- AHA-1740 (standard mode)
- AHA-1740 (enhanced mode)
- AHA-2740 series

### Host Adapters Handling EISA or PCI Mode Host Transfers

Host adapters with no restrictions are the EISA adapters AHA-1740 in enhanced mode and the AHA-2740 series, and all PCI adapters.

For the AHA-1540/1542/1640/1740 (standard mode), you will need to run with an ASPI manager that can run with more than 16MB of RAM. You will need aha1540.dsk v2.22 or later, or aha1640.dsk v2.22 or later for this.

NetWare 386 v3.11 (and above) has defined some new routines you can use to force a buffer allocation below the first 16MB of RAM. Refer to the NetWare 386 Technical Specification for more information.

## Scanning for New Devices

Most ASPI managers will not immediately scan the SCSI bus when first loaded. Rather, ASPI managers will wait for NetWare 386 to call its Scan for New Devices routine before the ASPI manager will scan the bus and update its internal ASPI device table. There may be some cases where you use ASPI's Get Device Type routine and your device does not appear although it is really there. In this case, you may want to request NetWare Force A Scan For New Devices, or you may want to scan the SCSI bus from within your own ASPI module. Refer to the appropriate NetWare 386 Technical Specification for more information.

# VII. ASPI Specification Addendum

Adaptec has made minor additions to the ASPI specification to give greater flexibility to ASPI modules. The main addition is support for residual byte length reporting.

## What Is Residual Byte Length?

Residual byte length is the number of bytes not transferred to, or received from, the target SCSI device. For example, if the ASPI buffer length for a SCSI Inquiry command is set for 100 bytes, but the target only returns back 36 bytes, this makes for a residual length of 64 bytes. As another example, if the ASPI buffer length for a SCSI write command is set for 514 bytes, but the target only takes 512 bytes, this makes for a residual length of 2 bytes.

## How Do I Find Out If the ASPI Manager Loaded Supports This New Feature?

ASPI modules can determine if the loaded ASPI manager supports residual byte length by issuing an Extended Host Adapter Inquiry command. If you refer to the current ASPI for DOS specification, the standard Host Adapter Inquiry command is shown in Table 11.56.

**NOTE** *The following discussion assumes you are already familiar with sending an ASPI Host Adapter Inquiry command to an ASPI manager. If not, refer to the section ASPI Command Codes for the operating system you are using.*

**Table 11.56: Host Adapter Inquiry Command**

| Offset # | # Bytes | Description | R/W |
|---|---|---|---|
| 00h (00) | 01h (01) | Command Code = 0 | W |
| 01h (01) | 01h (01) | Status | R |
| 02h (02) | 01h (01) | Host Adapter Number | W |
| 03h (03) | 01h (01) | SCSI Request Flags | W |
| 04h (04) | 04h (04) | Reserved for Expansion = 0 | |
| 08h (08) | 01h (01) | Number of Host Adapters | R |
| 09h (09) | 01h (01) | Target ID of Host Adapter | R |
| 0Ah (10) | 10h (16) | SCSI Manager ID | R |
| 1Ah (26) | 10h (16) | Host Adapter ID | R |
| 2Ah (42) | 10h (16) | Host Adapter Unique Parameters | R |

The Extended Host Adapter Inquiry command is defined in Table 11.57.

**Table 11.57: Extended Host Adapter Inquiry Command**

| Offset | # Bytes | Description | R/W |
|---|---|---|---|
| 00h (00) | 01h (01) | Command Code = 0 | W |
| 01h (01) | 01h (01) | Status | R |
| 02h (02) | 01h (01) | Host Adapter Number | W |
| 03h (03) | 01h (01) | SCSI Request Flags | W |
| 04h (04) | 01h (01) | Extended Request Signature = 55h | R/W |
| 05h (05) | 01h (01) | Extended Request Signature = AAh | R/W |
| 06h (06) | 01h (01) | Length of Extended Buffer (N),Low Byte | R/W |
| 07h (07) | 01h (01) | Length of Extended Buffer (N),High Byte | R/W |
| 08h (08) | 01h (01) | Number of Host Adapters | R |
| 09h (09) | 01h (01) | Target ID of Host Adapter | R |
| 0Ah (10) | 10h (16) | SCSI Manager ID | R |
| 1Ah (26) | 10h (16) | Host Adapter ID | R |
| 2Ah (42) | 10h (16) | Host Adapter Unique Parameters | R |
| 3Ah (58) | N | Extended Buffer | R |

The user places the AA55h in bytes #4–5 of the structure. The Extended Buffer length (N) also needs to be initialized to the size of the extended buffer. A typical value would be four.

If the ASPI manager that is passed this new extended structure supports the Extended Host Adapter Inquiry command, the AA55h bytes will be flipped around to 55AAh. If this does not occur, the caller should assume that the ASPI manager does not support residual byte length or any of the other defined fields in the extended buffer. Note that it is possible to have multiple host adapters loaded where the ASPI manager loaded for one card supports this Extended call, while the ASPI manager for the other card does not. In certain situations, this could cause the Extended Host Adapter Inquiry call to fail (i.e., default back to standard Host Adapter Inquiry call).

If the signature bytes are swapped (AA55h->55AAh), the Length of Extended Buffer field will also be modified to indicate how many bytes of the extended buffer were modified. This leaves us room to expand the meaning of the extended buffer in the future. For example, if an extended buffer size of ten is passed in, though the ASPI manager loaded only supports the first 4 bytes, then the value of four will be returned in the Length of Extended Buffer field.

Currently only the first 8 bytes of the extended buffer are defined.

The extended buffer field is formatted as shown in Table 11.58.

### Table 11.58: Extended Buffer Field Definition

| Offset | # Bytes | Description | R/W |
|---|---|---|---|
| 3Ah (58) | 02h (02) | Features Word | R |
| | Bits 15-4 | Reserved | |
| | Bit 3 | 0 = Not Wide SCSI 32 host adapter <br> 1 = Wide SCSI 32 host adapter | |
| | Bit 2 | 0 = Not Wide SCSI 16 host adapter <br> 1 = Wide SCSI 16 host adapter | |
| | Bit 1 | 0 = Residual byte length not reported <br> 1 = Residual byte length reported | |
| | Bit 0 | 0 = Scatter/gather not supported <br> 1 = Scatter/gather supported | |
| 3Ch (60) | 02h (02) | Maximum Scatter/gather list length | R |
| 3Eh (62) | 04h (04) | Maximum SCSI data transfer length | R |

The Features Word bit fields defined above are self-explanatory. Note that if bit #2 is set, your ASPI module should scan SCSI IDs 0–15 on this host adapter for SCSI devices. The Scatter/Gather fields (including the scatter/gather list length) are currently only used by ASPI for OS/2.

A Maximum SCSI Data Transfer Length of zero indicates no data transfer length limitation. A nonzero value indicates the largest value you should specify in the ASPI SRB Data Allocation Length.

**IMPORTANT** *Make sure you check the return value in the Length of Extended Buffer field to make certain that the field you are looking at is valid (e.g., if 4 is returned in the Length of Extended Buffer field, you should not use the value in the Maximum SCSI Data Transfer Length field).*

## Now That I Know My ASPI Manager Supports Residual Byte Length, How Do I Make Use of It?

### The SCSI Request Flags Byte Is Currently Defined in the Various ASPI Specifications as Follows:

| 7 | 6 | 5 | 4 | 3 | 2 | 1 | 0 |
|---|---|---|---|---|---|---|---|
| Rsvd | Rsvd | S/G | Direction Bits | | Rsvd | Link | Post |

Note: The S/G (scatter/gather) bit is currently used only under ASPI for OS/2.

### The New Definition For This Byte Is as Follows:

| 7 | 6 | 5 | 4 | 3 | 2 | 1 | 0 |
|---|---|---|---|---|---|---|---|
| Rsvd | Rsvd | S/G | Direction Bits | | Residual | Link | Post |

If bit #2 (Residual) is set to 1, and the ASPI manager supports residual byte length, then the residual byte length will be reported in the Data Allocation Length field within the SRB (bytes 0Ah–0Dh). On a typical command completion with all requested data transferred and no residual bytes, the Data Allocation Length field will contain the value zero.

**NOTE** *Adaptec EZ-SCSI since v3.0 includes support for the residual byte feature.*

# 12

## THE FUTURE OF SCSI AND STORAGE IN GENERAL

Perhaps Winston Churchill best expressed the frustration involved in trying to predict what is yet to come: "The future is just one damned thing after another . . . " It hasn't gotten any easier since his day!

### If You Can't Beat 'em, Buy 'em!

That seems to be the accepted business philosophy these days. Almost every day, the business section of the newspaper describes the latest corporate merger or acquisition. The computer industry is constantly churning with such transactions, and the SCSI segment is no different.

Adaptec bought Trantor, then Future Domain, then Western Digital's host adapter product line, then Corel's CD creator product, then Incat Systems' Easy CD product. Apparently they're not done yet, because in November, 1999, they announced their intention to buy DPT for $235 million. This gives them primary control of the PC host adapter market and the CD recording software market. With the addition of DPT's resources it gives them a strong grip on the RAID market, too!

AT&T bought NCR and called it AT&T GIS. Then they sold the Microelectronics Division to Hyundai, who called it Symbios. Adaptec tried to buy Symbios, but the FTC said no (because it would give Adaptec too much control of the SCSI industry), so LSI Logic bought them instead!

It seems strange, but these days former competitors form alliances and pool their resources to withstand the market pressure of larger companies looking to take over their market. Other companies that try to go it alone often buckle and disappear — like Micropolis and many other names from the past.

Another sequence of interesting acquisitions was when Conner Peripherals bought Archive and then Seagate bought Conner. Seagate's purchase of Conner Peripherals was the final blow that killed SSA. With Conner gone, IBM had no credible second source of SSA disk drives.

All these changes can influence your decision when choosing a host adapter. For example, you look for assurance that the company will be there when you need technical support or updated drivers. Will your card be supported under the new whiz-bang operating system when it's available? All manufacturers compete to provide what their market research tells them is the best combination of price, performance, support, name recognition, and so on. If you choose the wrong product, it may become an orphan if it loses sufficient market share to keep software vendors interested in supporting it.

## Coming Down the Pike

### Ultra-3 (Fast-80) LVD

As of early 2000, manufacturers offer host adapters and disk drives that transfer data at 160 MB/sec over a parallel bus. The first implementations at this speed will be called Ultra3 160. The parallel SCSI vendors find themselves in a race with the serial SCSI vendors, and at the moment it seems that parallel is winning. They're trying to increase the performance of parallel SCSI to the point where Fibre Channel (100 MB/sec) and IEEE-1394 (50 MB/sec) will *not* be improvements and thus postpone the serial takeover as long as possible.

### IEEE 1394

This interface holds great promise and potential, but has been slow in coming to fruition. Currently, the main application for IEEE 1394 is in connecting digital cameras and camcorders to PCs for high-quality video capture and editing. Standard parallel SCSI is unsuitable for this purpose for several reasons: First, the parallel SCSI cables are just too big and thick to attach to something like a camcorder. Second, parallel SCSI lacks an isochronous (real time) transfer mode. IEEE 1394 provides this ability and is relatively inexpensive to implement as well. "Time waits for no man," and neither does video!

### Fibre Channel

This has been the "Promised Land" of heavy-duty storage users and is finally coming into popular use.

Fibre Channel comes in two interface types: copper and actual glass fibre. The copper connection is lower in cost, yet still offers many of the serial interface's advantages. A fibre connection is required to get the full benefit of Fibre Channel, though. Its long connection distances (10 km/segment for glass fibre) and high speed (100 MB/sec) make fibre channel a good choice for corporate servers, off-site backups, and redundant storage systems.

At some point, the price of fibre channel host adapters and devices may come down to the point where it will be used in PCs, but that day seems quite a ways off. See http://www.fibrechannel.com for more information.

### Device Bay

This is a proposed standard being developed by Compaq, Intel, and Microsoft to allow computer users to add peripheral devices to their system without opening the case. It can support any computer peripheral except for memory, CPUs, and video cards. The three sizes of Device Bay modules—DB13 (.5"), DB20 (.8"), and DB32 (1.3")—accommodate the different sizes of computers and devices, laptops through desktops. It combines IEEE 1394 and USB. Whether Device Bay becomes an important development remains to be seen. See http://www.devicebay.org for more information.

### SCSI Harbor

This is an attempt by the SCSI Industry to define a standard modular package for SCSI devices. This would make them more interchangeable and user installable. The current proposal consists of a "wrapper" assembly that accepts a 3.5" form factor SCA-2 drive, which plugs into a dock assembly allowing easy insertion and removal of the drive from a system.

It's a shame this wasn't standardized long ago. We're looking forward to being able to install SCSI drives without fiddling with ID switch cables and jumpers! To check on the progress of this project, go to http://www.scsita.org.

### Storage Area Networks

Corporations with vast amounts of mission-critical data want their data not only to be available quickly throughout their entire company, they demand that it also be automatically backed up in separate geographic locations so that it is protected from natural disasters, fire, and so on. Storage Area Networks are the answer to this need. They are similar in some ways to data communications networks like intranets, but they have some additional requirements because of the nature of the data they carry. Protocols for data storage must ensure that the data actually gets written onto the media even in situations where the connection is lost or hardware fails. Communications protocols like TCP/IP generally don't handle such situations well, so special protocols are being developed for this purpose. In general, Fibre Channel is the transport of choice for SANs. They may even be its raison d'etre.

Watch companies like Compaq, EMC, Adaptec and others for product announcements. Comedian Stephen Wright has been heard to say: "You can't have everything; Where would you put it?" Well, the storage industry apparently didn't realize he was joking! It seems that at the current rate of growth, before too long, there will be enough disk space to store a detailed description of every atom on the planet (well, maybe not quite). In the "Information Age," the more data you can store, the more value you provide. We don't see an end to this trend any time soon.

# ALL-PLATFORM TECHNICAL REFERENCE

Parallel SCSI contains two types of electrical interface: single-ended and differential. The single-ended interface, labeled "SE," is the standard signal-to-ground interface that came from the legacy of the SCSI predecessor SASI. Differential SCSI, which uses the voltage difference between two signal wires, came into the game as an interface for the professional market, where greater distances between the system and the peripherals were desirable and reliability requirements were higher.

With the ongoing work on SCSI-3, differential SCSI now splits into two interfaces: the old differential SCSI, now called high voltage differential or HVD, and low voltage differential, or LVD. Whereas HVD has always been more expensive to implement, LVD is comparable to single-ended SCSI in price and therefore should replace HVD in time.

Because most interface types use the same connectors, SCSI-2 introduced logos to indicate the type of interface. Figure A.1 shows these logos. If you have a system or external device that's not too old (made in 1996 or later), it should have one of these logos near the SCSI port to differentiate between the visually identical interfaces. These icons can be used on devices, cables, terminators, and connectors; they may appear with or without text labels. Also, they can be scaled as needed.

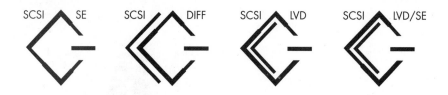

Figure A.1: SCSI Logos (left to right): Single-Ended (SE), High Voltage Differential (DIFF), Low Voltage Differential (LVD), and LVD/SE SCSI

(In Figure A.1, SCSI LVD/SE means the device is a multi-mode SCSI device that senses if it's connected to an LVD or an SE SCSI bus and switches its drivers to the correct mode.)

Now let's take a deeper look at the interfaces.

## Electrical Specs

### Single-Ended SCSI Interface

The standard electrical interface for SCSI is single-ended, which means an interface with one signal line and a corresponding ground line for each SCSI signal. All signals are active low, which means that when the voltage is high the signal is false, and when the voltage is low the signal is true. The official SCSI term for the true signal state is *signal assertion.*

To define it more technically, the single-ended SCSI interface consists of an open-collector or tri-state driver for each signal, capable of sinking at least 48 milliamps of current on signal assertion. The signal levels are listed in Table A.1.

**Table A.1: Single-Ended SCSI Signal Levels**

| Signal State | Electrical Level | Voltage |
|---|---|---|
| True (or "asserted") | Low | 0.0 to 0.5 V DC |
| False (or "deasserted") | High<br>mode (see below) | 2.5 to 5.25 V DC, 2.5 to 3.7 V DC<br>in active negation |

The single-ended SCSI interface can have a bus length of up to 6 meters (19.7 feet), when using standard 5 MB/sec SCSI-2 timing. Using higher signal frequencies makes it necessary to shorten the bus accordingly. Therefore, if you use Fast SCSI, your maximum bus length drops to 3 meters (9.8 feet). Ultra-

SCSI (Fast-20) keeps this bus length, if you attach no more than four devices on the bus. With more than four devices, UltraSCSI specifies a maximum bus length of 1.5 meters (4.9 feet).

### Active Negation

The faster UltraSCSI timing required active negation, a method to speed up the asserted/deasserted transition of the line drivers by supporting the line driver. Whereas a standard SE SCSI driver has two states, asserted and high-impedance (deasserted), an active negation driver additionally has a transitional state, wherein it actively negates (in the SCSI logical sense) the signal by pulling the signal up to about 3 V. Technically, this is done by sourcing current until the signal line has reached a safe negation level.

Active negation should be used by devices capable of higher speeds than Fast SCSI on the REQ, ACK, and data lines. Active negation cannot be used on the OR-tied signals, and it needs to be disabled while the SCAM protocol runs. You may find "Active Negation" also written on terminator packages, because newer termination chips tend to have active negation compatibility listed as a feature, but any active terminator will work fine.

### Differential SCSI Interfaces

#### "Classic" or "High Voltage" Differential (HVD)

The differential SCSI interface was defined to increase robustness and to overcome the maximum bus length limitation of single-ended SCSI. Two-wire differential signaling is an old and proven way to achieve reliable signal transmission in noisy environments and over long distances. The industry standard for HVD SCSI interfaces is ISO/IEC 8482-1993-12.

Differential SCSI's greatest advantage is its ability to use bus lengths of up to 25 meters (82 feet), regardless of the signal timing used. Also, differential SCSI is the only SCSI-2 interface that officially supports Fast SCSI timings. It's interesting to note the elegant way the SCSI-2 standard says this: "Use of single-ended drivers and receivers with the fast synchronous data transfer option is not recommended."

In differential SCSI, each signal consists of two lines called "–signal" and "+signal." A signal is true if the +signal is higher than the –signal and false if the –signal is higher than the +signal. This setup, along with twisted-pair cables, yields very good noise immunity. Also, the resultant higher voltage levels of the differential configuration make it possible to achieve a 25-meter (82-foot) bus.

The signal levels for high voltage differential SCSI are shown in Table A.2.

## Table A.2: Differential SCSI Signal Levels

| Signal State | HVD Voltage Levels |
|---|---|
| Low-level (false) output voltage | 1.7 V maximum |
| High-level (true) output voltage | 2.7 V minimum |
| Differential output voltage | 1 V minimum |
| Common mode (DC) voltage range | –7 to +12 V DC |

To avoid the risk of burning up a SCSI bus by accidentally connecting a single-ended device to a differential bus, the SCSI standard defines a protection scheme. The differential line drivers are enabled by a signal called DIFFSENS (differential sense) on the SCSI bus. If you connect a single-ended device to the bus, the DIFFSENS line is grounded and the differential drivers are disabled. However, some (fortunately only a few) older devices didn't use the DIFFSENS line, so if you have some older differential SCSI disks, be sure to find out if they are single-ended or differential before connecting them to your system. Single-ended and high voltage differential devices can't coexist on the same bus.

### Low Voltage Differential (LVD as Used in "Ultra2" and "Ultra3" SCSI)

The higher working frequencies of Fast-40 SCSI made it nearly impossible to maintain data integrity with the single-ended interface. On the other hand, the implementation cost of the classic differential SCSI interface made it too expensive for the mass market. So a new standard was born, called low voltage differential, or LVD, signaling. With LVD, the synchronous timing could be reduced to achieve an effective working frequency of 40 MHz, or an 80 MB/sec data rate for a 16-bit wide channel. Additionally, cable length could go up to 12 meters (39.4 feet). For point-to-point connections, this distance may even be extended up to 25 meters (82 feet).

Additionally, with LVD, differential technology and its advantages can be implemented into the protocol chip, eliminating the need for external drivers and high voltages on the logic board. This makes LVD competitive with the standard single-ended interface in terms of implementation cost and introduces differential signaling in the mass market.

(It's nearly impossible for a simple signal table to show the voltage levels as in SE or HVD. If you're ready to dig deeply into electrical matters, check Chapter 7 and Annex A of the actual SCSI-3 SPI standard—but this may be more than you need to know to create a robust, functional system.)

As compatibility with single-ended interfaces is built in, LVD will likely eliminate the single-ended interface in the long term,  The newer line drivers that are used in LVD devices don't turn off the interface when they sense ground on the DIFFSENS line, but switch to single-ended mode. This happens at power-on, and LVD devices on this bus react like standard single-ended UltraSCSI devices. This downward compatibility poses one potential problem, however: Imagine a typical system with, say, two LVD disks inside and one external, all attached to 4 meters (13.1 feet) of cable length—easily within the spec. Now, if for any reason you need to connect a single-ended device (with external cable) to this SCSI channel—bingo, you just exceeded the single-ended UltraSCSI spec by at least 2 meters (6.6 feet). In such cases you would have to disable all "Fast anything" support. To overcome this issue, most host adapter vendors use a two-channel solution with one LVD and one SE channel on one chip.

## Cable Specs

In SCSI, the cable is—in some ways—the most important part of the bus, because its quality directly affects the reliability of the whole system. It's important to obey SCSI's rather tight cable specifications in order to get the best performance from your SCSI system. Like everything in SCSI, the cable evolved over time. In SCSI-1, a cable impedance of 132 ohms would have been a perfect impedance match with the SE termination circuit (an HVD cable impedance should have been 122 ohms). At that time, such cables simply were not available, so this was noted in the standard. In the end, 100 ohms ± 10% were defined. SCSI-2 used the same recommendations but restated them slightly, specifying cable impedance of over 90 ohms and under 140 ohms. For Fast SCSI-2, the upper limit dropped to 132 ohms. The SCSI-3 drafts SPI-2 and SPI-3 now state minimum and maximum impedances for every speed and interface. In general, using a cable with a characteristic impedance between 84 ohms and 96 ohms meets the SE requirements for all speeds, and a cable with an impedance between 115 and 135 ohms is the perfect match for differential SCSI, be it HVD or LVD. This sounds like different cables, but because of the different measuring setups for SE and differential modes, a good quality cable typically can meet both specs. For example, a typical good ribbon SCSI cable is specified with impedance values of 90 ± 6 ohms for SE and 125 ± 10 ohms for differential SCSI mode.

### Internal Cables

The SCSI-2 standard defines 50- and 68-conductor unshielded flat-ribbon cables with an impedance between 90 and 140 ohms and a minimum conductor size of 0.080 inch (28 AWG). Also specified is a 25- or 34-pair twisted-pair cable. The twisted-pair cable is better for two reasons: First, a signal line twisted with its ground wire is less sensitive to RF (radio frequency) noise than is a flat-ribbon cable. Second, twisted-pair cables often have loose cable pairs between the connectors, making them more flexible and easier to handle than a rather stiff 50- or 68-conductor ribbon cable.

### External Cables

The electrical specifications for external cables are fundamentally identical to those of internal cables. External cables are, in virtually all cases, round shielded cables with a SCSI connector on both ends. The SCSI standard even specifies a particular layout for an external cable, wherein the signals are distributed in three layers of wire pairs with REQ and ACK, the most sensitive signals, in the center. For cables that have a third pair of wires in the center, the SCSI standard defines the third pair as ground.

Figure A.2 shows a cross section of an external SCSI cable with some of the wire pairs drawn in to indicate the layers. The REQ and ACK signals are in the very center, control signals are in the middle layer, and data lines and termination power are in the outer layer.

**NOTE** *The largest hurdle to overcome with external SCSI cabling is the numerous connections between the round external cables and ribbon cables. The junction of every connector causes impedance mismatches and signal losses. As a result, a SCSI system with many external devices is more susceptible to data errors than one with many internal devices.*

Lately, Teflon® cables have gotten a lot of attention. This refers to a standard copper cable with a PTFE (Poly Tetra Fluoro Ethylene) insulation instead of the typical polyvinyl chloride (PVC) or thermoplastic elastomer (TPE) insulation. These really are better cables—aside from better electrical specs (capacitance and cross talk are lower, insulation resistance is higher than with

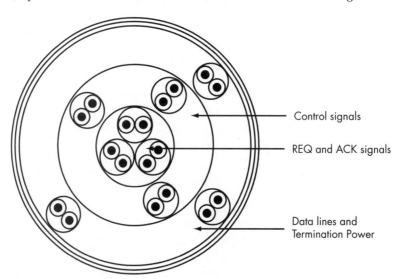

Control signals

REQ and ACK signals

Data lines and
Termination Power

*Figure A.2: Recommended SCSI Round Cable Layout*

PVC, for example), PTFE is harder and tougher than PVC—giving you a more robust cable physically and electrically.

## Connector Specs

Connectors are a continuing saga in the life of SCSI because of the various interface widths, longevity of the standards process, and manufacturer preferences. We'll look at the standard connectors first.

Since the first SCSI-2 drafts, the cables are called by one-letter names like A-cable or B-cable and so on, differentiated by bus width and cable/connector layout. You might expect that each letter would name a typical combination of cable layout and connector type, but that would be too easy. Instead, the A-cable comes in three different flavors, all three in current use, and some of the other cable connectors in both a shielded and an unshielded version.

We need to differentiate between unshielded and shielded official connectors, vendor-specific connectors, and obsolete connectors (both shielded and unshielded). To sum up, following are the connectors we'll specify later.

The *unshielded* connectors in use are:

- 50-pin flat cable connector called IDC header ("A-cable"; female configuration for cables, male for devices). This connector was defined in SCSI-1.

- 68-pin high-density connector ("P-cable" and "Q-cable"; male for cables, female for devices). This connector was introduced in SCSI-2 and is the standard connector for Wide SCSI.

- 80-pin single connector attachment (SCA-2) connector. This connector was introduced in the SCSI-3 SPI-2 standard and carries the P-cable together with device power and a few additional control signals. It is meant to be used with SCSI backplanes.

*Shielded* connectors that are common in the market are:

- 50-pin Centronics-type connector ("A-cable"; male for cables, female for devices). This connector was defined in SCSI-1.

- 50-pin high-density connector ("A-cable"; male for cables, female for devices). This connector was defined in SCSI-2 and, together with the Centronics-type connector, is the standard connector for 8-bit SCSI.

- 68-pin high-density connector ("P-cable" and "Q-cable"; male for cables, female for devices). This connector was introduced in SCSI-2 and is the standard external connector for Wide SCSI.

- 68-pin very high-density cable interconnect (VHDCI or VHD) connector ("P-cable" and "Q-cable"; male for cables, female for devices). The VHDCI connector was introduced in the SCSI-3 SPI-2 standard.

From the *vendor-specific* connectors, the following are still in use:

- 25-pin Sub-D connector (Apple defined pin wiring). Apple defined this connector and layout with the introduction of the Macintosh computer. Because of the Mac's popularity, the cable was widely used for external devices (and still haunts us to this day). This connector works only for single-ended, asynchronous signaling.

- Apple 30-pin HDI connector ("PowerBook connector"). When Apple needed a SCSI connector for their PowerBook notebooks, they defined a new compact SCSI connector instead of using the new HD connector, presumably for cost reasons.

- IBM 60-pin high-density mini Centronics connector. This connector was in discussion for SCSI-2, but then became unpopular. IBM used this connector on PS/2 and RS-6000 machines.

And last, but not least, the *obsolete* connectors:

- 68-pin high-density for the Wide SCSI B-cable. The B-cable never really appeared . . . .

- Sun 50-pin sub-D connector. This three-row sub-D connector was widely used by Sun Microsystems on their old workstations.

- Novell/Procomp DCB SCSI connector. A two-row 37-pin sub-D connector defined by Novell for their DCB controller boards.

- 25-pin sub-D connector (Future Domain pinout). At about the same time as Apple, Future Domain defined this connector and layout as a cheap SCSI connector for the emerging market of personal computers. This pinout never caught on in a big way.

All official standard connectors are available in single-ended, high voltage differential, and low voltage differential versions. Some of the vendor-specific and obsolete ones are available in single-ended and high voltage differential: In sum, this adds up to a whopping 40 connector/interface options—and you can be sure that some are missing!

*Cables designed for differential use generally can be used for single-ended operation, but be careful if you attempt to use a single-ended cable in a differential system. Aside from the connector options with less than 50 pins, some — mainly cheaper — SCSI cables use less than the required 50 conductors by combining multiple ground pins on one conductor. On a single-ended system, it's "only" the signal quality that is at risk, but using this cable in a differential setup shorts multiple signal lines and may not be healthy for the devices.*

### Unshielded Connectors

#### 50-Pin 8-Bit IDC Header Connector

The venerable 50-pin IDC header connector was the standard connector for SCSI's predecessor SASI and still is the standard device connector for 8-bit SCSI devices. Even devices with vendor-specific external connectors (Apple, Future Domain, IBM, Novell/Procomp) use this connector on the inside. Figures A.3 and A.4 show the 50-pin IDC header connector. The upper connector with the female contacts is the cable connector, and the lower male part is the connector you will see on SCSI devices. If you're unsure about the orientation or if you have a connector without the keying notch, you can generally identify pin 1 by a mark on the connector's plastic body—typically an arrow, spot, or line is used.

*Figure A.3: Female IDC Header Connector (Cable)*

*Figure A.4: Male IDC Header Connector (Device)*

The pinouts for the single-ended and differential variants of this connector are shown in Table A.3.

## Table A.3: A-Cable Pinouts (IDC Header Connector)

| Pin | Single Ended | High Voltage Differential | Low Voltage Differential | Pin | Single Ended | High Voltage Differential | Low Voltage Differential |
|-----|--------------|---------------------------|--------------------------|-----|--------------|---------------------------|--------------------------|
| 1 | SIGNAL RETURN | GROUND | +DB(0) | 26 | TERMPWR | TERMPWR | TERMPWR |
| 2 | –DB(0) | GROUND | –DB(0) | 27 | RESERVED | RESERVED | RESERVED |
| 3 | SIGNAL RETURN | +DB(0) | +DB(1) | 28 | RESERVED | RESERVED | RESERVED |
| 4 | –DB(1) | –DB(0) | –DB(1) | 29 | GROUND | +ATN | GROUND |
| 5 | SIGNAL RETURN | +DB(1) | +DB(2) | 30 | GROUND | –ATN | GROUND |
| 6 | –DB(2) | –DB(1) | –DB(2) | 31 | SIGNAL RETURN | GROUND | +ATN |
| 7 | SIGNAL RETURN | +DB(2) | +DB(3) | 32 | –ATN | GROUND | –ATN |
| 8 | –DB(3) | –DB(2) | –DB(3) | 33 | GROUND | +BSY | GROUND |
| 9 | SIGNAL RETURN | +DB(3) | +DB(4) | 34 | GROUND | –BSY | GROUND |
| 10 | –DB(4) | –DB(3) | –DB(4) | 35 | SIGNAL RETURN | +ACK | +BSY |
| 11 | SIGNAL RETURN | +DB(4) | +DB(5) | 36 | –BSY | –ACK | –BSY |
| 12 | –DB(5) | –DB(4) | –DB(5) | 37 | SIGNAL RETURN | +RST | +ACK |
| 13 | SIGNAL RETURN | +DB(5) | +DB(6) | 38 | –ACK | –RST | –ACK |
| 14 | –DB(6) | –DB(5) | –DB(6) | 39 | SIGNAL RETURN | +MSG | +RST |
| 15 | SIGNAL RETURN | +DB(6) | +DB(7) | 40 | –RST | –MSG | –RST |
| 16 | –DB(7) | –DB(6) | –DB(7) | 41 | SIGNAL RETURN | +SEL | +MSG |
| 17 | SIGNAL RETURN | +DB(7) | +DB(P) | 42 | –MSG | –SEL | –MSG |
| 18 | –DB(P) | –DB(7) | –DB(P) | 43 | SIGNAL RETURN | +C/D | +SEL |
| 19 | GROUND | +DB(P) | GROUND | 44 | –SEL | –C/D | –SEL |
| 20 | GROUND | –DB(P) | GROUND | 45 | SIGNAL RETURN | +REQ | +C/D |
| 21 | GROUND | DIFFSENS | DIFFSENS | 46 | –C/D | –REQ | –C/D |
| 22 | GROUND | GROUND | GROUND | 47 | SIGNAL RETURN | +I/O | +REQ |
| 23 | RESERVED | RESERVED | RESERVED | 48 | –REQ | –I/O | –REQ |
| 24 | RESERVED | RESERVED | RESERVED | 49 | SIGNAL RETURN | GROUND | +I/O |
| 25 | N/C | TERMPWR | TERMPWR | 50 | –I/O | GROUND | –I/O |

### 68-Pin Wide SCSI P- and Q-Cables

The P- and Q-cables use the high-density connector introduced in SCSI-2. The high-density connector was specified for multiple reasons, but one of the most pressing was that the emerging (at that time) $3\frac{1}{2}$-inch devices didn't have enough mounting space to fit an IDC connector with 68 pins. This connector is basically the same for internal and external cables — the internal version is unshielded, has a plastic body, and lacks locking mechanisms. The cable connector is the male connector (Figure A.5); the device is the female connector (Figure A.6).

Table A.4 shows the pinouts for single-ended and differential P-cables.

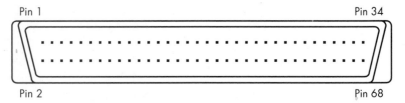

Figure A.5: SCSI-2 Wide High-Density Connector, Male (P- and Q-cable)

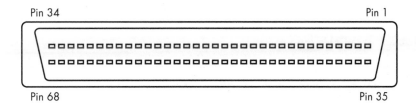

Pin 34                                 Pin 1

Pin 68                                Pin 35

*Figure A.6: SCSI-2 Wide High-Density Connector, Female (Device)*

Table A.4 shows the pinouts for single-ended and differential P-cables.

## Table A.4: P-Cable Pinouts

| Pin | SE | HVD | LVD | Pin | SE / LVD | HVD |
|-----|-----|------|------|-----|----------|------|
| 1 | SIGNAL RETURN | +DB(12) | +DB(12) | 35 | −DB(12) | −DB(12) |
| 2 | SIGNAL RETURN | +DB(13) | +DB(13) | 36 | −DB(13) | −DB(13) |
| 3 | SIGNAL RETURN | +DB(14) | +DB(14) | 37 | −DB(14) | −DB(14) |
| 4 | SIGNAL RETURN | +DB(15) | +DB(15) | 38 | −DB(15) | −DB(15) |
| 5 | SIGNAL RETURN | +DB(P1) | +DB(P1) | 39 | −DB(P1) | −DB(P1) |
| 6 | SIGNAL RETURN | GND | +DB(0) | 40 | −DB(0) | GROUND |
| 7 | SIGNAL RETURN | +DB(0) | +DB(1) | 41 | −DB(1) | −DB(0) |
| 8 | SIGNAL RETURN | +DB(1) | +DB(2) | 42 | −DB(2) | −DB(1) |
| 9 | SIGNAL RETURN | +DB(2) | +DB(3) | 43 | −DB(3) | −DB(2) |
| 10 | SIGNAL RETURN | +DB(3) | +DB(4) | 44 | −DB(4) | −DB(3) |
| 11 | SIGNAL RETURN | +DB(4) | +DB(5) | 45 | −DB(5) | −DB(4) |
| 12 | SIGNAL RETURN | +DB(5) | +DB(6) | 46 | −DB(6) | −DB(5) |
| 13 | SIGNAL RETURN | +DB(6) | +DB(7) | 47 | −DB(7) | −DB(6) |
| 14 | SIGNAL RETURN | +DB(7) | +DB(P) | 48 | −DB(P) | −DB(7) |
| 15 | GROUND | +DB(P) | GROUND | 49 | GROUND | −DB(P) |
| 16 | GROUND | DIFFSENS | DIFFSENS | 50 | GROUND | GROUND |
| 17 | TERMPWR | TRMPWR | TERMPWR | 51 | TERMPWR | TRMPWR |
| 18 | TERMPWR | TRMPWR | TERMPWR | 52 | TERMPWR | TRMPWR |
| 19 | RESERVED | RESERVED | RESERVED | 53 | RESERVED | RESERVED |
| 20 | GROUND | +ATN | GROUND | 54 | GROUND | −ATN |
| 21 | SIGNAL RETURN | GROUND | +ATN | 55 | −ATN | GROUND |
| 22 | GROUND | +BSY | GROUND | 56 | GROUND | −BSY |
| 23 | SIGNAL RETURN | +ACK | +BSY | 57 | −BSY | −ACK |
| 24 | SIGNAL RETURN | +RST | +ACK | 58 | −ACK | −RST |
| 25 | SIGNAL RETURN | +MSG | +RST | 59 | −RST | −MSG |
| 26 | SIGNAL RETURN | +SEL | +MSG | 60 | −MSG | −SEL |
| 27 | SIGNAL RETURN | +C/D | +SEL | 61 | −SEL | −C/D |
| 28 | SIGNAL RETURN | +REQ | +C/D | 62 | −C/D | −REQ |
| 29 | SIGNAL RETURN | +I/O | +REQ | 63 | −REQ | −I/O |
| 30 | SIGNAL RETURN | GROUND | +I/O | 64 | −I/O | GROUND |
| 31 | SIGNAL RETURN | +DB(8) | +DB(8) | 65 | −DB(8) | −DB(8) |
| 32 | SIGNAL RETURN | +DB(9) | +DB(9) | 66 | −DB(9) | −DB(9) |
| 33 | SIGNAL RETURN | +DB(10) | +DB(10) | 67 | −DB(10) | −DB(10) |
| 34 | SIGNAL RETURN | +DB(11) | +DB(11) | 68 | −DB(11) | −DB(11) |

Table A.5 shows the pinouts for single-ended and differential Q-cables.

**Table A.5: Q-Cable Pinouts**

| Pin | SE | LVD | HVD | Pin | SE / LVD | HVD |
|---|---|---|---|---|---|---|
| 1 | SIGNAL RETURN | +DB(28) | +DB(28) | 35 | −DB(28) | −DB(28) |
| 2 | SIGNAL RETURN | +DB(29) | +DB(29) | 36 | −DB(29) | −DB(29) |
| 3 | SIGNAL RETURN | +DB(30) | +DB(30) | 37 | −DB(30) | −DB(30) |
| 4 | SIGNAL RETURN | +DB(31) | +DB(31) | 38 | −DB(31) | −DB(31) |
| 5 | SIGNAL RETURN | +DB(P3) | +DB(P3) | 39 | −DB(P3) | −DB(P3) |
| 6 | SIGNAL RETURN | +DB(16) | GROUND | 40 | −DB(16) | GROUND |
| 7 | SIGNAL RETURN | +DB(17) | +DB(16) | 41 | −DB(17) | −DB(16) |
| 8 | SIGNAL RETURN | +DB(18) | +DB(17) | 42 | −DB(18) | −DB(17) |
| 9 | SIGNAL RETURN | +DB(19) | +DB(18) | 43 | −DB(19) | −DB(18) |
| 10 | SIGNAL RETURN | +DB(20) | +DB(19) | 44 | −DB(20) | −DB(19) |
| 11 | SIGNAL RETURN | +DB(21) | +DB(20) | 45 | −DB(21) | −DB(20) |
| 12 | SIGNAL RETURN | +DB(22) | +DB(21) | 46 | −DB(22) | −DB(21) |
| 13 | SIGNAL RETURN | +DB(23) | +DB(22) | 47 | −DB(23) | −DB(22) |
| 14 | SIGNAL RETURN | +DB(P2) | +DB(23) | 48 | −DB(P2) | −DB(23) |
| 15 | GROUND | GROUND | +DB(P2) | 49 | GROUND | −DB(P2) |
| 16 | GROUND | DIFFSENS | DIFFSENS | 50 | GROUND | GROUND |
| 17 | TERMPWRQ | TERMPWRQ | TERMPWRQ | 51 | TERMPWRQ | TERMPWRQ |
| 18 | TERMPWRQ | TERMPWRQ | TERMPWRQ | 52 | TERMPWRQ | TERMPWRQ |
| 19 | RESERVED | RESERVED | RESERVED | 53 | RESERVED | RESERVED |
| 20 | GROUND | GROUND | TERMINATED | 54 | GROUND | TERMINATED |
| 21 | GROUND | TERMINATED | GROUND | 55 | TERMINATED | GROUND |
| 22 | GROUND | GROUND | TERMINATED | 56 | GROUND | TERMINATED |
| 23 | GROUND | TERMINATED | +ACKQ | 57 | TERMINATED | −ACKQ |
| 24 | SIGNAL RETURN | +ACKQ | TERMINATED | 58 | −ACKQ | TERMINATED |
| 25 | GROUND | TERMINATED | TERMINATED | 59 | TERMINATED | TERMINATED |
| 26 | GROUND | TERMINATED | TERMINATED | 60 | TERMINATED | TERMINATED |
| 27 | GROUND | TERMINATED | TERMINATED | 61 | TERMINATED | TERMINATED |
| 28 | GROUND | TERMINATED | +REQQ | 62 | TERMINATED | −REQQ |
| 29 | SIGNAL | +REQQ | TERMINATED | 63 | −REQQ | TERMINATED |
| 30 | GROUND | TERMINATED | GROUND | 64 | TERMINATED | GROUND |
| 31 | SIGNAL RETURN | +DB(24) | +DB(24) | 65 | −DB(24) | −DB(24) |
| 32 | SIGNAL RETURN | +DB(25) | +DB(25) | 66 | −DB(25) | −DB(25) |
| 33 | SIGNAL RETURN | +DB(26) | +DB(26) | 67 | −DB(26) | −DB(26) |
| 34 | SIGNAL RETURN | +DB(27) | +DB(27) | 68 | −DB(27) | −DB(27) |

### 80-Pin Wide SCSI SCA Connector

The SCA-2 connector was specified in SCSI-3 SPI-2 for SCSI backplanes—with disk drive arrays in mind—and is a bit different from the other connectors, because it not only carries the SCSI signals, but also supplies voltage for the devices and necessary control signals for drive arrays.

The SCA-2 connector is an approved EIA standard (EIA-700A0AE) and an SFF project (SFF-8451). SCA-2 has some advantages for applications wherein drives may be swapped or lots of identical drives must be held as spare parts:

- SCA-2, together with the defined connector position, is ideal for slide-in devices. The manufacturer doesn't necessarily need to define a proprietary connector (nor do you). Of course, most manufacturers still do.

- As stated, it carries all SCSI signals and the supply power in one connector, removing the need for different connectors.

- SCA-2 is hot-pluggable. Defined lengths of the pins lead to a defined contact sequence with pre-charging of the drive's electronic circuits, enabling suppression of spikes and other signal noise while connecting. The embedded motor start control helps here and also carries the mechanism for standby drives.

- SCA-2 carries spindle synchronization. Even though spindle sync is not yet standardized over different disk drives, it remains desirable for arrays of identical drives. This signal is now considered obsolete and may be removed in new devices.

- SCA-2 devices by definition are not terminated. Therefore you can't accidentally forget to remove this jumper.

Figures A.7 and A.8 show the connectors; Table A.6 lists the pinouts.

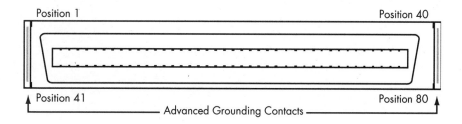

Figure A.7: SCA-2 Connector, Female (Backplane)

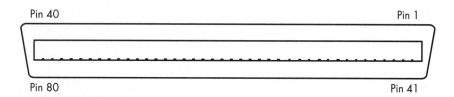

Figure A.8: SCA-2 Connector, Male (Device)

## Table A.6: SCA-2 Pinouts

| Pin | Single Ended | LVD/HVD | Pin | Single Ended | LVD/HVD |
|-----|--------------|---------|-----|--------------|---------|
| 1 (Long) | 12 V CHARGE | 12 V CHARGE | 41 (Long) | 12 V GROUND | 12 V GROUND |
| 2 | 12 V | 12 V | 42 (Long) | 12 V GROUND | 12 V GROUND |
| 3 | 12 V | 12 V | 43 (Long) | 12 V GROUND | 12 V GROUND |
| 4 | 12 V | 12 V | 44 | MATED 1 | MATED 1 |
| 5 | 3.3 V | 3.3 V | 45 (Long) | 3.3 V CHARGE | 3.3 V CHARGE |
| 6 | 3.3 V | 3.3 V | 46 (Long) | GROUND | DIFFSENS |
| 7 | –DB(11) | –DB(11) | 47 | SIGNAL RETURN | +DB(11) |
| 8 | –DB(10) | –DB(10) | 48 | SIGNAL RETURN | +DB(10) |
| 9 | –DB(9) | –DB(9) | 49 | SIGNAL RETURN | +DB(9) |
| 10 | –DB(8) | –DB(8) | 50 | SIGNAL RETURN | +DB(8) |
| 11 | –I/O | –I/O | 51 | SIGNAL RETURN | +I/O |
| 12 | –REQ | –REQ | 52 | SIGNAL RETURN | +REQ |
| 13 | –C/D | –C/D | 53 | SIGNAL RETURN | +C/D |
| 14 | –SEL | –SEL | 54 | SIGNAL RETURN | +SEL |
| 15 | –MSG | –MSG | 55 | SIGNAL RETURN | +MSG |
| 16 | –RST | –RST | 56 | SIGNAL RETURN | +RST |
| 17 | –ACK | –ACK | 57 | SIGNAL RETURN | +ACK |
| 18 | –BSY | –BSY | 58 | SIGNAL RETURN | +BSY |
| 19 | –ATN | –ATN | 59 | SIGNAL RETURN | +ATN |
| 20 | –DB(P) | –DB(P) | 60 | SIGNAL RETURN | +DB(P) |
| 21 | –DB(7) | –DB(7) | 61 | SIGNAL RETURN | +DB(7) |
| 22 | –DB(6) | –DB(6) | 62 | SIGNAL RETURN | +DB(6) |
| 23 | –DB(5) | –DB(5) | 63 | SIGNAL RETURN | +DB(5) |
| 24 | –DB(4) | –DB(4) | 64 | SIGNAL RETURN | +DB(4) |
| 25 | –DB(3) | –DB(3) | 65 | SIGNAL RETURN | +DB(3) |
| 26 | –DB(2) | –DB(2) | 66 | SIGNAL RETURN | +DB(2) |
| 27 | –DB(1) | –DB(1) | 67 | SIGNAL RETURN | +DB(1) |
| 28 | –DB(0) | –DB(0) | 68 | SIGNAL RETURN | +DB(0) |
| 29 | –DB(P1) | –DB(P1) | 69 | SIGNAL RETURN | +DB(P1) |
| 30 | –DB(15) | –DB(15) | 70 | SIGNAL RETURN | +DB(15) |
| 31 | –DB(14) | –DB(14) | 71 | SIGNAL RETURN | +DB(14) |
| 32 | –DB(13) | –DB(13) | 72 | SIGNAL RETURN | +DB(13) |
| 33 | –DB(12) | –DB(12) | 73 | SIGNAL RETURN | +DB(12) |
| 34 | 5 V | 5 V | 74 | MATED 2 | MATED 2 |
| 35 | 5 V | 5 V | 75 (Long) | 5 V GROUND | 5 V GROUND |
| 36 (Long) | 5 V CHARGE | 5 V CHARGE | 76 (Long) | 5 V GROUND | 5 V GROUND |
| 37 (Long) | SPINDLE SYNC | SPINDLE SYNC | 77 (Long) | ACTIVE LED OUT | ACTIVE LED OUT |
| 38 (Long) | RMT_START | RMT_START | 78 (Long) | DLYD_START | DLYD_START |
| 39 (Long) | SCSI ID (0) | SCSI ID (0) | 79 (Long) | SCSI ID (1) | SCSI ID (1) |
| 40 (Long) | SCSI ID (2) | SCSI ID (2) | 80 (Long) | SCSI ID (3) | SCSI ID (3) |

**NOTE** *On most of the cheap SCA connector adapters on the market, the DIFFSENS pin in the SCA connector is not connected. This leads to trouble with an SCA LVD drive on an SE bus. If you have such an adapter, you'll need to solder a short wire from the SCA connector's pin 46 to the HD connector's pin 16 to connect DIFFSENS.*

### Shielded Connectors

Shielded connectors are used generally for external cables, meaning cables that are not located in closed cases and therefore need shielding. Compared with the few standardized unshielded connectors, this is where the real mess with SCSI connectors starts. Whatever you do, be prepared for the fact that the adapter you need *now* isn't available in your favorite store.

#### 50-Pin Centronics-Style (A-Cable)

The Centronics-style connector started in SCSI-1 and is still the de facto standard for external connections—even though it is losing ground against the high-density connector. This connector is usually secured with two spring clamps. Like all other ribbon-contact connectors, it is intended to be foolproof—you virtually can't damage it or connect it incorrectly, even using force, and contact reliability is typically very high.

Table A.7 lists the pinouts for 50-pin Centronics-style connectors. Figures A.9 and A.10 show the 50-position shielded low-density cable and device connectors (A-cable).

**Table A.7: Centronics-Style Connector Pinouts**

| Pin | Single Ended | HVD | LVD | Pin | Single Ended | HVD | LVD |
|-----|--------------|-----|-----|-----|--------------|-----|-----|
| 1 | GROUND | GROUND | +DB(0) | 26 | −DB(0) | GROUND | TERMPWR |
| 2 | GROUND | +DB(0) | −DB(0) | 27 | −DB(1) | −DB(0) | RESERVED |
| 3 | GROUND | +DB(1) | +DB(1) | 28 | −DB(2) | −DB(1) | RESERVED |
| 4 | GROUND | +DB(2) | −DB(1) | 29 | −DB(3) | −DB(2) | GROUND |
| 5 | GROUND | +DB(3) | +DB(2) | 30 | −DB(4) | −DB(3) | GROUND |
| 6 | GROUND | +DB(4) | −DB(2) | 31 | −DB(5) | −DB(4) | +ATN |
| 7 | GROUND | +DB(5) | +DB(3) | 32 | −DB(6) | −DB(5) | -ATN |
| 8 | GROUND | +DB(6) | −DB(3) | 33 | −DB(7) | −DB(6) | GROUND |
| 9 | GROUND | +DB(7) | +DB(4) | 34 | −DB(P) | −DB(7) | GROUND |
| 10 | GROUND | +DB(P) | −DB(4) | 35 | GROUND | −DB(P) | +BSY |
| 11 | GROUND | DIFFSENS | +DB(5) | 36 | GROUND | GROUND | −BSY |
| 12 | RESERVED | RESERVED | −DB(5) | 37 | RESERVED | RESERVED | +ACK |
| 13 | Not connected | TERMPWR | +DB(6) | 38 | TERMPWR | TERMPWR | −ACK |
| 14 | RESERVED | RESERVED | −DB(6) | 39 | RESERVED | RESERVED | +RST |
| 15 | GROUND | +ATN | +DB(7) | 40 | GROUND | −ATN | −RST |
| 16 | GROUND | GROUND | −DB(7) | 41 | −ATN | GROUND | +MSG |
| 17 | GROUND | +BSY | +DB(P) | 42 | GROUND | −BSY | −MSG |
| 18 | GROUND | +ACK | −DB(P) | 43 | −BSY | −ACK | +SEL |
| 19 | GROUND | +RST | GROUND | 44 | −ACK | −RST | −SEL |
| 20 | GROUND | +MSG | GROUND | 45 | −RST | −MSG | +C/D |
| 21 | GROUND | +SEL | DIFFSENS | 46 | −MSG | −SEL | −C/D |
| 22 | GROUND | +C/D | GROUND | 47 | −SEL | −C/D | +REQ |
| 23 | GROUND | +REQ | RESERVED | 48 | −C/D | −REQ | −REQ |
| 24 | GROUND | +I/O | RESERVED | 49 | −REQ | −I/O | +I/O |
| 25 | GROUND | GROUND | TERMPWR | 50 | −I/O | GROUND | −I/O |

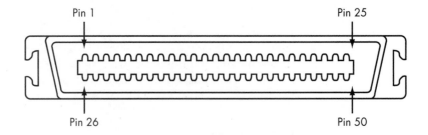

Figure A.9: Centronics-Style Low-Density Connector, Male (Cable)

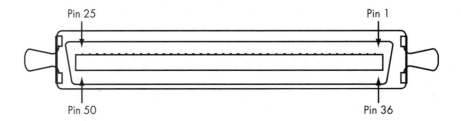

Figure A.10: Centronics-Style Low-Density Connector, Female (Device)

## 50-Pin High-Density Connector (A-cable)

Figures A.11 and A.12 show the 50-position shielded high-density cable and device connectors for the A-cable. This is the standard connector you will see as external cable connector on SCSI-2 host adapters now.

Table A.8 lists the pinouts for this connector.

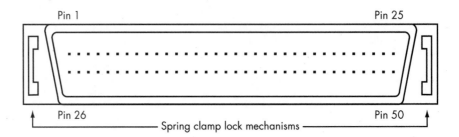

Figure A.11: Shielded High-Density Sub-D Connector, Male (Cable)

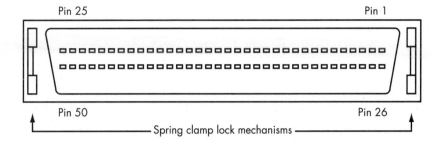

*Figure A.12: Shielded High-Density Sub-D Connector, Female (Device)*

## Table A.8: High-Density Sub-D Connector (A-Cable Pinouts)

| Pin | SE | LVD | HVD | Pin | SE / LVD | HVD |
|-----|-----|-----|-----|-----|----------|-----|
| 1 | SIGNAL RETURN | +DB(0) | GROUND | 26 | −DB(0) | GROUND |
| 2 | SIGNAL RETURN | +DB(1) | +DB(0) | 27 | −DB(1) | −DB(0) |
| 3 | SIGNAL RETURN | +DB(2) | +DB(1) | 28 | −DB(2) | −DB(1) |
| 4 | SIGNAL RETURN | +DB(3) | +DB(2) | 29 | −DB(3) | −DB(2) |
| 5 | SIGNAL RETURN | +DB(4) | +DB(3) | 30 | −DB(4) | −DB(3) |
| 6 | SIGNAL RETURN | +DB(5) | +DB(4) | 31 | −DB(5) | −DB(4) |
| 7 | SIGNAL RETURN | +DB(6) | +DB(5) | 32 | −DB(6) | −DB(5) |
| 8 | SIGNAL RETURN | +DB(7) | +DB(6) | 33 | −DB(7) | −DB(6) |
| 9 | SIGNAL RETURN | +DB(P) | +DB(7) | 34 | −DB(P) | −DB(7) |
| 10 | GROUND | GROUND | +DB(P) | 35 | GROUND | −DB(P) |
| 11 | GROUND | DIFFSENS | DIFFSENS | 36 | GROUND | GROUND |
| 12 | RESERVED | RESERVED | RESERVED | 37 | RESERVED | RESERVED |
| 13 | OPEN (1) | TERMPWR | TERMPWR | 38 | TERMPWR | TERMPWR |
| 14 | RESERVED | RESERVED | RESERVED | 39 | RESERVED | RESERVED |
| 15 | GROUND | GROUND | +ATN | 40 | GROUND | −ATN |
| 16 | SIGNAL RETURN | +ATN | GROUND | 41 | −ATN | GROUND |
| 17 | GROUND | GROUND | +BSY | 42 | GROUND | −BSY |
| 18 | SIGNAL RETURN | +BSY | +ACK | 43 | −BSY | −ACK |
| 19 | SIGNAL RETURN | +ACK | +RST | 44 | −ACK | −RST |
| 20 | SIGNAL RETURN | +RST | +MSG | 45 | −RST | −MSG |
| 21 | SIGNAL RETURN | +MSG | +SEL | 46 | −MSG | −SEL |
| 22 | SIGNAL RETURN | +SEL | +C/D | 47 | −SEL | −C/D |
| 23 | SIGNAL RETURN | +C/D | +REQ | 48 | −C/D | −REQ |
| 24 | SIGNAL RETURN | +REQ | +I/O | 49 | −REQ | −I/O |
| 25 | SIGNAL RETURN | +I/O | GROUND | 50 | −I/O | GROUND |

### 68-Pin High-Density Connector (P- and Q-Cables)

The pinouts and mechanical dimensions for the shielded P- and Q-cable connectors are the same as those of the internal connectors, except that they have a metal-shielded body and their locking mechanism uses screws instead of clamps (Figures A.13 and A.14). This is the standard connector for 16-bit SCSI interfaces since SCSI-2 Wide regardless of the electrical interface, be it Wide SCSI, Ultra Wide, or Ultra2 LVD.

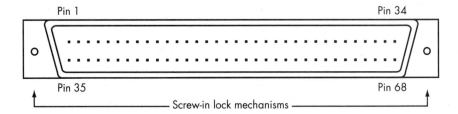

Pin 1      Pin 34

Pin 35      Pin 68

Screw-in lock mechanisms

*Figure A.13: Shielded High-Density Sub-D Connector, Male (Cable)*

Table A.9 shows the pinouts for the P-cables, Table A.10 for the Q-cable.

## Table A.9: High-Density Sub-D Connector (P-Cable Pinouts)

| Pin | SE | HVD | LVD | Pin | SE / LVD | HVD |
|-----|-----|------|------|-----|----------|------|
| 1 | SIGNAL RETURN | +DB(12) | +DB(12) | 35 | –DB(12) | –DB(12) |
| 2 | SIGNAL RETURN | +DB(13) | +DB(13) | 36 | –DB(13) | –DB(13) |
| 3 | SIGNAL RETURN | +DB(14) | +DB(14) | 37 | –DB(14) | –DB(14) |
| 4 | SIGNAL RETURN | +DB(15) | +DB(15) | 38 | –DB(15) | –DB(15) |
| 5 | SIGNAL RETURN | +DB(P1) | +DB(P1) | 39 | –DB(P1) | –DB(P1) |
| 6 | SIGNAL RETURN | GROUND | +DB(0) | 40 | –DB(0) | GROUND |
| 7 | SIGNAL RETURN | +DB(0) | +DB(1) | 41 | –DB(1) | –DB(0) |
| 8 | SIGNAL RETURN | +DB(1) | +DB(2) | 42 | –DB(2) | –DB(1) |
| 9 | SIGNAL RETURN | +DB(2) | +DB(3) | 43 | –DB(3) | –DB(2) |
| 10 | SIGNAL RETURN | +DB(3) | +DB(4) | 44 | –DB(4) | –DB(3) |
| 11 | SIGNAL RETURN | +DB(4) | +DB(5) | 45 | –DB(5) | –DB(4) |
| 12 | SIGNAL RETURN | +DB(5) | +DB(6) | 46 | –DB(6) | –DB(5) |
| 13 | SIGNAL RETURN | +DB(6) | +DB(7) | 47 | –DB(7) | –DB(6) |
| 14 | SIGNAL RETURN | +DB(7) | +DB(P) | 48 | –DB(P) | –DB(7) |
| 15 | GROUND | +DB(P) | GROUND | 49 | GROUND | –DB(P) |
| 16 | GROUND | DIFFSENS | DIFFSENS | 50 | GROUND | GROUND |
| 17 | TERMPWR | TERMPWR | TERMPWR | 51 | TERMPWR | TERMPWR |
| 18 | TERMPWR | TERMPWR | TERMPWR | 52 | TERMPWR | TERMPWR |
| 19 | RESERVED | RESERVED | RESERVED | 53 | RESERVED | RESERVED |
| 20 | GROUND | +ATN | GROUND | 54 | GROUND | –ATN |
| 21 | SIGNAL RETURN | GROUND | +ATN | 55 | –ATN | GROUND |
| 22 | GROUND | +BSY | GROUND | 56 | GROUND | –BSY |
| 23 | SIGNAL RETURN | +ACK | +BSY | 57 | –BSY | –ACK |
| 24 | SIGNAL RETURN | +RST | +ACK | 58 | –ACK | –RST |
| 25 | SIGNAL RETURN | +MSG | +RST | 59 | –RST | –MSG |
| 26 | SIGNAL RETURN | +SEL | +MSG | 60 | –MSG | –SEL |
| 27 | SIGNAL RETURN | +C/D | +SEL | 61 | –SEL | –C/D |
| 28 | SIGNAL RETURN | +REQ | +C/D | 62 | –C/D | –REQ |
| 29 | SIGNAL RETURN | +I/O | +REQ | 63 | –REQ | –I/O |
| 30 | SIGNAL RETURN | GROUND | +I/O | 64 | –I/O | GROUND |
| 31 | SIGNAL RETURN | +DB(8) | +DB(8) | 65 | –DB(8) | –DB(8) |
| 32 | SIGNAL RETURN | +DB(9) | +DB(9) | 66 | –DB(9) | –DB(9) |
| 33 | SIGNAL RETURN | +DB(10) | +DB(10) | 67 | –DB(10) | –DB(10) |
| 34 | SIGNAL RETURN | +DB(11) | +DB(11) | 68 | –DB(11) | –DB(11) |

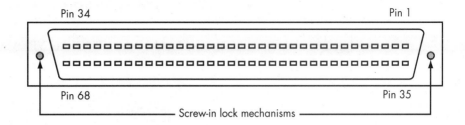

*Figure A.14: Shielded High-Density Sub-D Connector, Female (Device)*

## Table A.10: High-Density Sub-D Connector (Q-Cable Pinouts)

| Pin | SE | LVD | HVD | Pin | SE / LVD | HVD |
|-----|-----|-----|-----|-----|----------|-----|
| 1 | SIGNAL RETURN | +DB(28) | +DB(28) | 35 | –DB(28) | –DB(28) |
| 2 | SIGNAL RETURN | +DB(29) | +DB(29) | 36 | –DB(29) | –DB(29) |
| 3 | SIGNAL RETURN | +DB(30) | +DB(30) | 37 | –DB(30) | –DB(30) |
| 4 | SIGNAL RETURN | +DB(31) | +DB(31) | 38 | –DB(31) | –DB(31) |
| 5 | SIGNAL RETURN | +DB(P3) | +DB(P3) | 39 | –DB(P3) | –DB(P3) |
| 6 | SIGNAL RETURN | +DB(16) | GROUND | 40 | –DB(16) | GROUND |
| 7 | SIGNAL RETURN | +DB(17) | +DB(16) | 41 | –DB(17) | –DB(16) |
| 8 | SIGNAL RETURN | +DB(18) | +DB(17) | 42 | –DB(18) | –DB(17) |
| 9 | SIGNAL RETURN | +DB(19) | +DB(18) | 43 | –DB(19) | –DB(18) |
| 10 | SIGNAL RETURN | +DB(20) | +DB(19) | 44 | –DB(20) | –DB(19) |
| 11 | SIGNAL RETURN | +DB(21) | +DB(20) | 45 | –DB(21) | –DB(20) |
| 12 | SIGNAL RETURN | +DB(22) | +DB(21) | 46 | –DB(22) | –DB(21) |
| 13 | SIGNAL RETURN | +DB(23) | +DB(22) | 47 | –DB(23) | –DB(22) |
| 14 | SIGNAL RETURN | +DB(P2) | +DB(23) | 48 | –DB(P2) | –DB(23) |
| 15 | GROUND | GROUND | +DB(P2) | 49 | GROUND | –DB(P2) |
| 16 | GROUND | DIFFSENS | DIFFSENS | 50 | GROUND | GROUND |
| 17 | TERMPWRQ | TERMPWRQ | TERMPWRQ | 51 | TERMPWRQ | TERMPWRQ |
| 18 | TERMPWRQ | TERMPWRQ | TERMPWRQ | 52 | TERMPWRQ | TERMPWRQ |
| 19 | RESERVED | RESERVED | RESERVED | 53 | RESERVED | RESERVED |
| 20 | GROUND | GROUND | TERMINATED | 54 | GROUND | TERMINATED |
| 21 | GROUND | TERMINATED | GROUND | 55 | TERMINATED | GROUND |
| 22 | GROUND | GROUND | TERMINATED | 56 | GROUND | TERMINATED |
| 23 | GROUND | TERMINATED | +ACKQ | 57 | TERMINATED | –ACKQ |
| 24 | SIGNAL RETURN | +ACKQ | TERMINATED | 58 | –ACKQ | TERMINATED |
| 25 | GROUND | TERMINATED | TERMINATED | 59 | TERMINATED | TERMINATED |
| 26 | GROUND | TERMINATED | TERMINATED | 60 | TERMINATED | TERMINATED |
| 27 | GROUND | TERMINATED | TERMINATED | 61 | TERMINATED | TERMINATED |
| 28 | GROUND | TERMINATED | +REQQ | 62 | TERMINATED | –REQQ |
| 29 | SIGNAL RETURN | +REQQ | TERMINATED | 63 | –REQQ | TERMINATED |
| 30 | GROUND | TERMINATED | GROUND | 64 | TERMINATED | GROUND |
| 31 | SIGNAL RETURN | +DB(24) | +DB(24) | 65 | –DB(24) | –DB(24) |
| 32 | SIGNAL RETURN | +DB(25) | +DB(25) | 66 | –DB(25) | –DB(25) |
| 33 | SIGNAL RETURN | +DB(26) | +DB(26) | 67 | –DB(26) | –DB(26) |
| 34 | SIGNAL RETURN | +DB(27) | +DB(27) | 68 | –DB(27) | –DB(27) |

### 68-Pin Very High Density Cable Interconnect (VHDCI) Connector (P- and Q-Cables)

The new very high density cable interconnect (VHDCI or VHD) connector is a real godsend for RAID adapter manufacturers—with its small dimensions, two Wide SCSI bus connectors use about the same space as one HD-68 connector. The pin layout is the same as that of the high-density sub-D connector, but the VHD connector uses ribbon contacts similar to the old Centronics-type connector.

Figures A.15 and A.16 show the connectors, and Table A.11 lists the pinouts. Like the SCA-2 connector, the VHDCI connector is an approved EIA standard (EIA-700A0AF) and an SFF project(SFF-8441).

### Table A.11: VHDCI Connector (P-Cable Pinouts)

| Pin | SE | HVD | LVD | Pin | SE / LVD | HVD |
|-----|-----|-----|-----|-----|-----|-----|
| 1 | SIGNAL RETURN | +DB(12) | +DB(12) | 35 | −DB(12) | −DB(12) |
| 2 | SIGNAL RETURN | +DB(13) | +DB(13) | 36 | −DB(13) | −DB(13) |
| 3 | SIGNAL RETURN | +DB(14) | +DB(14) | 37 | −DB(14) | −DB(14) |
| 4 | SIGNAL RETURN | +DB(15) | +DB(15) | 38 | −DB(15) | −DB(15) |
| 5 | SIGNAL RETURN | +DB(P1) | +DB(P1) | 39 | −DB(P1) | −DB(P1) |
| 6 | SIGNAL RETURN | GROUND | +DB(0) | 40 | −DB(0) | GROUND |
| 7 | SIGNAL RETURN | +DB(0) | +DB(1) | 41 | −DB(1) | −DB(0) |
| 8 | SIGNAL RETURN | +DB(1) | +DB(2) | 42 | −DB(2) | −DB(1) |
| 9 | SIGNAL RETURN | +DB(2) | +DB(3) | 43 | −DB(3) | −DB(2) |
| 10 | SIGNAL RETURN | +DB(3) | +DB(4) | 44 | −DB(4) | −DB(3) |
| 11 | SIGNAL RETURN | +DB(4) | +DB(5) | 45 | −DB(5) | −DB(4) |
| 12 | SIGNAL RETURN | +DB(5) | +DB(6) | 46 | −DB(6) | −DB(5) |
| 13 | SIGNAL RETURN | +DB(6) | +DB(7) | 47 | −DB(7) | −DB(6) |
| 14 | SIGNAL RETURN | +DB(7) | +DB(P) | 48 | −DB(P) | −DB(7) |
| 15 | GROUND | +DB(P) | GROUND | 49 | GROUND | −DB(P) |
| 16 | GROUND | DIFFSENS | DIFFSENS | 50 | GROUND | GROUND |
| 17 | TERMPWR | TERMPWR | TERMPWR | 51 | TERMPWR | TERMPWR |
| 18 | TERMPWR | TERMPWR | TERMPWR | 52 | TERMPWR | TERMPWR |
| 19 | RESERVED | RESERVED | RESERVED | 53 | RESERVED | RESERVED |
| 20 | GROUND | +ATN | GROUND | 54 | GROUND | −ATN |
| 21 | SIGNAL RETURN | GROUND | +ATN | 55 | −ATN | GROUND |
| 22 | GROUND | +BSY | GROUND | 56 | GROUND | −BSY |
| 23 | SIGNAL RETURN | +ACK | +BSY | 57 | −BSY | −ACK |
| 24 | SIGNAL RETURN | +RST | +ACK | 58 | −ACK | −RST |
| 25 | SIGNAL RETURN | +MSG | +RST | 59 | −RST | −MSG |
| 26 | SIGNAL RETURN | +SEL | +MSG | 60 | −MSG | −SEL |
| 27 | SIGNAL RETURN | +C/D | +SEL | 61 | −SEL | −C/D |
| 28 | SIGNAL RETURN | +REQ | +C/D | 62 | −C/D | −REQ |
| 29 | SIGNAL RETURN | +I/O | +REQ | 63 | −REQ | −I/O |
| 30 | SIGNAL RETURN | GROUND | +I/O | 64 | −I/O | GROUND |
| 31 | SIGNAL RETURN | +DB(8) | +DB(8) | 65 | −DB(8) | −DB(8) |
| 32 | SIGNAL RETURN | +DB(9) | +DB(9) | 66 | −DB(9) | −DB(9) |
| 33 | SIGNAL RETURN | +DB(10) | +DB(10) | 67 | −DB(10) | −DB(10) |
| 34 | SIGNAL RETURN | +DB(11) | +DB(11) | 68 | −DB(11) | −DB(11) |

## Table A.12: VHDCI Connector (Q-Cable Pinouts)

| Pin | SE | LVD | HVD | Pin | SE / LVD | HVD |
|-----|-----|-----|-----|-----|----------|-----|
| 1 | SIGNAL RETURN | +DB(28) | +DB(28) | 35 | −DB(28) | −DB(28) |
| 2 | SIGNAL RETURN | +DB(29) | +DB(29) | 36 | −DB(29) | −DB(29) |
| 3 | SIGNAL RETURN | +DB(30) | +DB(30) | 37 | −DB(30) | −DB(30) |
| 4 | SIGNAL RETURN | +DB(31) | +DB(31) | 38 | −DB(31) | −DB(31) |
| 5 | SIGNAL RETURN | +DB(P3) | +DB(P3) | 39 | −DB(P3) | −DB(P3) |
| 6 | SIGNAL RETURN | +DB(16) | GROUND | 40 | −DB(16) | GROUND |
| 7 | SIGNAL RETURN | +DB(17) | +DB(16) | 41 | −DB(17) | −DB(16) |
| 8 | SIGNAL RETURN | +DB(18) | +DB(17) | 42 | −DB(18) | −DB(17) |
| 9 | SIGNAL RETURN | +DB(19) | +DB(18) | 43 | −DB(19) | −DB(18) |
| 10 | SIGNAL RETURN | +DB(20) | +DB(19) | 44 | −DB(20) | −DB(19) |
| 11 | SIGNAL RETURN | +DB(21) | +DB(20) | 45 | −DB(21) | −DB(20) |
| 12 | SIGNAL RETURN | +DB(22) | +DB(21) | 46 | −DB(22) | −DB(21) |
| 13 | SIGNAL RETURN | +DB(23) | +DB(22) | 47 | −DB(23) | −DB(22) |
| 14 | SIGNAL RETURN | +DB(P2) | +DB(23) | 48 | −DB(P2) | −DB(23) |
| 15 | GROUND | GROUND | +DB(P2) | 49 | GROUND | −DB(P2) |
| 16 | GROUND | DIFFSENS | DIFFSENS | 50 | GROUND | GROUND |
| 17 | TERMPWRQ | TERMPWRQ | TERMPWRQ | 51 | TERMPWRQ | TERMPWRQ |
| 18 | TERMPWRQ | TERMPWRQ | TERMPWRQ | 52 | TERMPWRQ | TERMPWRQ |
| 19 | RESERVED | RESERVED | RESERVED | 53 | RESERVED | RESERVED |
| 20 | GROUND | GROUND | TERMINATED | 54 | GROUND | TERMINATED |
| 21 | GROUND | TERMINATED | GROUND | 55 | GROUND | GROUND |
| 22 | GROUND | GROUND | TERMINATED | 56 | GROUND | TERMINATED |
| 23 | GROUND | TERMINATED | +ACKQ | 57 | TERMINATED | −ACKQ |
| 24 | SIGNAL RETURN | +ACKQ | TERMINATED | 58 | −ACKQ | TERMINATED |
| 25 | GROUND | TERMINATED | TERMINATED | 59 | TERMINATED | TERMINATED |
| 26 | GROUND | TERMINATED | TERMINATED | 60 | TERMINATED | TERMINATED |
| 27 | GROUND | TERMINATED | TERMINATED | 61 | TERMINATED | TERMINATED |
| 28 | GROUND | TERMINATED | +REQQ | 62 | TERMINATED | −REQQ |
| 29 | SIGNAL RETURN | +REQQ | TERMINATED | 63 | −REQQ | TERMINATED |
| 30 | GROUND | TERMINATED | GROUND | 64 | TERMINATED | GROUND |
| 31 | SIGNAL RETURN | +DB(24) | +DB(24) | 65 | −DB(24) | −DB(24) |
| 32 | SIGNAL RETURN | +DB(25) | +DB(25) | 66 | −DB(25) | −DB(25) |
| 33 | SIGNAL RETURN | +DB(26) | +DB(26) | 67 | −DB(26) | −DB(26) |
| 34 | SIGNAL RETURN | +DB(27) | +DB(27) | 68 | −DB(27) | −DB(27) |

## Vendor-Specific SCSI Connectors

Companies decide to introduce proprietary SCSI connectors for their own reasons. The most common ones still in use are Apple's 25-pin sub-D connector and their 30-pin HDI connector—used in the Macintosh computer and in PowerBook notebooks, respectively—and IBM's proprietary 60-pin mini-Centronics connector used on RS/6000 and PS/2 systems.

## 25-Pin Sub-D Connector (Apple Layout)

When Apple introduced the Macintosh computer, which used SCSI as the default bus system, it was a revolutionary event for the SCSI market: Suddenly a mass market existed for SCSI peripherals. Sadly (and possibly for space reasons) Apple did not use a standard SCSI connector—at that time, the

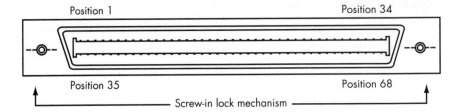

*Figure A.15: VHDCI Connector, Male (Cable)*

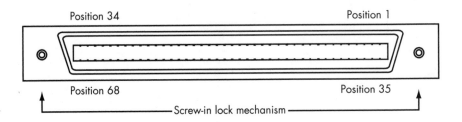

*Figure A.16: VHDCI Connector, Female (Device)*

Centronics connector would have been the logical choice, but instead of using it, Apple introduced a 25-pin sub-D connector (as Future Domain did but with a different signal layout). When it was introduced, Apple's connector/cable combination worked well with the then-current version of SCSI. However, after the introduction of Fast SCSI, the so-called "Apple SCSI" connector became the most prominent source of trouble in SCSI. Because of the lack of dedicated ground lines, signal integrity is lousy. And, because of the Mac's success, lots of peripherals still use this connector: Image scanners, ZIP drives, and similar removable media drives are good (or bad) examples of this. Figure A.17 shows the connectors and Table A.13 lists the signal pins.

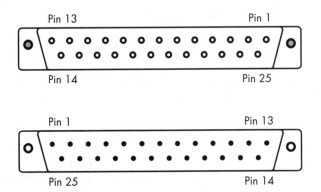

*Figure A.17: Apple Sub-D Connectors (top to bottom): Female (Device); Male (Cable)*

**Table A.13: Apple Sub-D Connector**

| Pin | Signal | | Pin | Signal |
|-----|--------|--|-----|--------|
| 1 | –REQ | | 13 | –DB7 |
| 2 | –MSG | | 14 | RESERVED/ GROUND |
| 3 | –I/O | | 15 | –C/D |
| 4 | –RST | | 16 | RESERVED /GROUND |
| 5 | –ACK | | 17 | –ATN |
| 6 | –BSY | | 18 | GROUND |
| 7 | GROUND | | 19 | –SEL |
| 8 | –DB0 | | 20 | –DBP |
| 9 | GROUND | | 21 | –DB1 |
| 10 | –DB3 | | 22 | –DB2 |
| 11 | –DB5 | | 23 | –DB4 |
| 12 | –DB6 | | 24 | GROUND |
| | | | 25 | TERMPWR* |

*\* Pin 25: Termination Power is not connected in some Mac connectors.*

### Apple PowerBook 30-Pin HDI Connector

The most recent addition to the growing list of non-standard SCSI connectors is Apple's HDI connector used in the PowerBook series of notebook computers. Its main feature is the very compact and rugged external connector shown in Figure A.18.

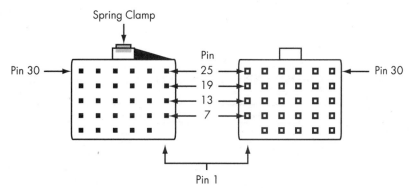

*Figure A.18: HDI-30 Connectors, Male (Cable) and Female (PowerBook). Pin 1 is reserved for special use.*

The pinout is listed in Table A.14. Pin 1 is not used and not connected in the standard cable, because it is used to select the "PowerBook Disk Mode," where the PowerBook, when connected with a special adapter cable, acts as external disk drive to a "standard" Macintosh computer.

### Table A.14: Pinout for HDI 30 External Connector (SE)

| Pin | Signal | Pin | Signal |
|-----|--------|-----|--------|
| 1 | –LINK.SEL | 16 | –DB(6) |
| 2 | –DB(0) | 17 | GROUND |
| 3 | GROUND | 18 | –DB(7) |
| 4 | –DB(1) | 19 | –DB(P) |
| 5 | TERMPWR | 20 | GROUND |
| 6 | –DB(2) | 21 | –REQ |
| 7 | –DB(3) | 22 | GROUND |
| 8 | GROUND | 23 | –BSY |
| 9 | –ACK | 24 | GROUND |
| 10 | GROUND | 25 | –ATN |
| 11 | –DB(4) | 26 | –C/D |
| 12 | GROUND | 27 | –RST |
| 13 | GROUND | 28 | –MSG |
| 14 | –DB(5) | 29 | –SEL |
| 15 | GROUND | 30 | –I/O |

### IBM 60-Pin High-Density Centronics Connector

IBM, for whatever reasons, used the 60-pin connector for their RS/6000 and early PS/2 systems. It is a high-density Centronics-style connector, and its first 50 pins are identical to the standard SCSI-2 HD connectors. The remaining 10 conductors are simply defined as "reserved" without any explanation of their purpose. (A reasonable guess would be that they're reserved for additional signals, such as spindle synchronization or a failure message bus for RAID systems.)

The connector is shown in Figures A.19 and A.20, and the pin assignments are shown in Table A.15.

### Table A.15: Pinout for IBM 60-Pin High-Density Centronics Connector (SE)

| Pin | Signal | Pin | Signal | Pin | Signal | Pin | Signal |
|-----|--------|-----|--------|-----|--------|-----|--------|
| 1 | GROUND | 16 | –DB(7) | 31 | GROUND | 46 | –C/D |
| 2 | –DB(0) | 17 | GROUND | 32 | –ATN | 47 | GROUND |
| 3 | GROUND | 18 | –DB(P) | 33 | GROUND | 48 | –REQ |
| 4 | –DB(1) | 19 | GROUND | 34 | GROUND | 49 | GROUND |
| 5 | GROUND | 20 | GROUND | 35 | GROUND | 50 | –I/O |
| 6 | –DB(2) | 21 | GROUND | 36 | –BSY | 51 | GROUND |
| 7 | GROUND | 22 | GROUND | 37 | GROUND | 52 | RESERVED |
| 8 | –DB(3) | 23 | RESERVED / GROUND | 38 | –ACK | 53 | RESERVED |
| 9 | GROUND | 24 | RESERVED / GROUND | 39 | GROUND | 54 | RESERVED |
| 10 | –DB(4) | 25 | NOT CONNECTED | 40 | –RST | 55 | RESERVED |
| 11 | GROUND | 26 | TERMPWR | 41 | GROUND | 56 | RESERVED |
| 12 | –DB(5) | 27 | RESERVED | 42 | –MSG | 57 | RESERVED |
| 13 | GROUND | 28 | RESERVED | 43 | GROUND | 58 | RESERVED |
| 14 | –DB(6) | 29 | GROUND | 44 | –SEL | 59 | RESERVED |
| 15 | GROUND | 30 | GROUND | 45 | GROUND | 60 | RESERVED |

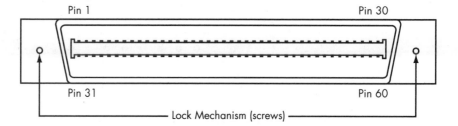

*Figure A.19: IBM 60-Pin High-Density Centronics Connector, Male (Cable)*

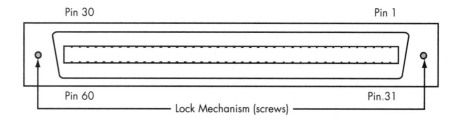

*Figure A.20: IBM 60-Pin High-Density Centronics Connector, Female (Device)*

### Obsolete Connectors

Some connectors were defined in SCSI-2 and later, but never really saw the market—the B-cable and the L-cable were such tragic cases. Just for completeness, let's have a look at them and at several other proprietary connectors that have (luckily) died since their introduction.

#### 68-pin High-Density Sub-D Connector (Wide SCSI "B-Cable")

The B-cable would have expanded the 8-bit SCSI bus of the A-cable to 32 bits. Mainly for mechanical reasons—the upcoming smaller ($3\frac{1}{2}$") disk drives didn't have the space to fit the neccessary connectors. Thus, it never appeared, and the P- and Q-cables were instead defined as one of the first tasks of the SCSI-3 committee.

#### 25-Pin Sub-D Connector (Future Domain Layout)

Very early in SCSI history, Future Domain (a major player then) created cheap (at that time) SCSI host adapters for IBM PC and clones. To reduce cost, a 25-pin sub-D connector with a proprietary layout was used. This connector is shown in Figure A.21.

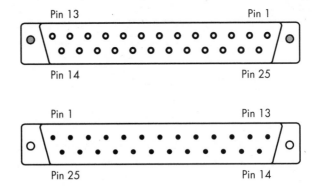

Figure A.21: 25-Pin Sub-D Connector (top to bottom): Female (Device); Male (Cable)

When Apple later introduced their own layout on the same connector, one major reason for SCSI smoke signals they also created — see for yourself in Table A.16.

**Table A.16: Future Domain and Apple Sub-D Connector Layouts**

| Future Domain | | | Apple | |
|---|---|---|---|---|
| Pin | Signal | | Pin | Signal |
| 1 | GROUND | | 1 | –REQ |
| 2 | –DB(1) | | 2 | –MSG |
| 3 | –DB(3) | | 3 | –I/O |
| 4 | –DB(5) | | 4 | –RST |
| 5 | –DB(7) | | 5 | –ACK |
| 6 | GROUND | | 6 | –BSY |
| 7 | –SEL | | 7 | GROUND |
| 8 | GROUND | | 8 | –DB0 |
| 9 | SPARE | | 9 | GROUND |
| 10 | –RST | | 10 | –DB3 |
| 11 | –C/D | | 11 | –DB5 |
| 12 | –I/O | | 12 | –DB6 |
| 13 | GROUND | | 13 | –DB7 |
| 14 | –DB(0) | | 14 | RESERVED/ GROUND |
| 15 | –DB(2) | | 15 | –C/D |
| 16 | –DB(4) | | 16 | RESERVED/ GROUND |
| 17 | –DB(6) | | 17 | –ATN |
| 18 | –DB(P) | | 18 | GROUND |
| 19 | GROUND | | 19 | –SEL |
| 20 | –ATN | | 20 | –DBP |
| 21 | –MSG | | 21 | –DB1 |
| 22 | –ACK | | 22 | –DB2 |
| 23 | –BSY | | 23 | –DB4 |
| 24 | –REQ | | 24 | GROUND |
| 25 | GROUND | | 25 | TERM. POWER |

*Virtually all signal positions are incompatible between this and the Apple connector layout, but the dangerous part is pin 25. Apple's cables don't have a connection here so there isn't a problem, but most SCSI adapters or devices with the Apple connector pinout do provide Termination Power at pin 25. So, connecting an Apple layout SCSI adapter with an old Future Domain cable will cause a short circuit that will blow the host adapter's or device's terminator power fuse. The same thing could happen with a device providing terminator power via an old Future Domain adapter. If you have an older Future Domain SCSI adapter, look for the label "Apple layout" on the cover plate and/or an "M" in the model number. If it's a Future Domain pinout type, you need a special SCSI cable — type HCA-108 — from Future Domain (now Adaptec).*

### Sun Microsystems' Sub-D Connector

Figure A.22 and Table A.17 show the Sun 50-pin sub-D connector. According to Sun's documentation, pin 1 is the pin in the upper-left corner. Remember that this means the male connector's pin 1 is on the upper-left as shown in Figure A.22. Pin 2 is the lower-left pin (in the third row of contacts, labeled pin 34). Pin 3 is the leftmost pin in the middle row (labeled pin 18). Pin 4 is the second-left pin in the upper row, and so on.

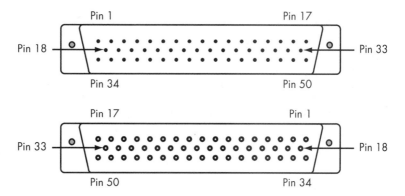

*Figure A.22: Sun 50-Pin Sub-D Connector*

Instead of Sun's pin numbering scheme, Table A.17 uses the scheme the connector manufacturers use in their documentation, because this way all sub-D connectors use a comparable numbering system. So, Table A.17 is the pinout scheme you will see if you look at a real cable, not the one shown in Sun's documentation. Beware, however, of confusing the two if you have an older Sun device.

**ALERT!** *When looking at Table A.17, keep in mind that there are two connector numbering schemes shown in the table. But the ones in Figure A.22 are the standard ones that connector manufacturers like AMP use on the connectors. These are not the numbers used by Sun. For whatever reason, Sun used an unusual numbering scheme, which differs from the counting scheme the connector manufacturers use and print on the connector bodies. So, if you use an older Sun device, be extremely careful when supplying home-made cables.*

## Table A.17: Sun 50-Pin Sub-D Connector Layouts

| | | Sun Single-Ended SCSI Pinout | | | |
|---|---|---|---|---|---|
| Standard Pin | Sun's Pin | Signal | Standard Pin | Sun's Pin | Signal |
| 1 | 1 | GROUND | 26 | 27 | RESERVED |
| 2 | 4 | −DB(1) | 27 | 30 | GROUND |
| 3 | 7 | GROUND | 28 | 33 | GROUND |
| 4 | 10 | −DB(4) | 29 | 36 | −BSY |
| 5 | 13 | GROUND | 30 | 39 | GROUND |
| 6 | 16 | −DB(7) | 31 | 42 | −MSG |
| 7 | 19 | GROUND | 32 | 45 | GROUND |
| 8 | 22 | GROUND | 33 | 48 | −REQ |
| 9 | 25 | N.C. | 34 | 2 | −DB(0) |
| 10 | 28 | RESERVED | 35 | 5 | GROUND |
| 11 | 31 | GROUND | 36 | 8 | −DB(3) |
| 12 | 34 | GROUND | 37 | 11 | GROUND |
| 13 | 37 | GROUND | 38 | 14 | −DB(6) |
| 14 | 40 | −RST | 39 | 17 | GROUND |
| 15 | 43 | GROUND | 40 | 20 | GROUND |
| 16 | 46 | −C/D | 41 | 23 | RESERVED |
| 17 | 49 | GROUND | 42 | 26 | TERMPWR |
| 18 | 3 | GROUND | 43 | 29 | GROUND |
| 19 | 6 | −DB(2) | 44 | 32 | −ATN |
| 20 | 9 | GROUND | 45 | 35 | GROUND |
| 21 | 12 | −DB(5) | 46 | 38 | −ACK |
| 22 | 15 | GROUND | 47 | 41 | GROUND |
| 23 | 18 | −DB(P) | 48 | 44 | −SEL |
| 24 | 21 | GROUND | 49 | 47 | GROUND |
| 25 | 24 | RESERVED | 50 | 50 | −I/O |

## Novell and Procomp DCB 37-Pin D-Sub Connector

Years ago, Novell designed a proprietary external connector for their DCB SCSI boards. Procomp used the same connector for their F-DCB and M-DCB host adapters to maintain 100 percent compatibility. This connection uses a

37-pin D-sub connector. Unlike the 25-pin connectors, it has enough conductors to provide discrete wire pairs for each signal. It's interesting to note that Novell's cable doesn't connect the TERMPWR line, so that the terminated device must supply its own termination power. Figure A.23 shows the connector; Table A.18 shows the pin assignments.

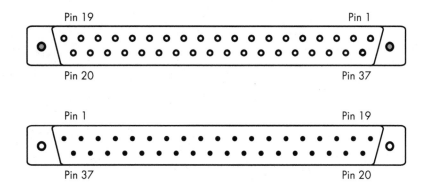

Figure A.23: Novell/Procomp 37-Pin D-Sub Connector

## Table A.18: Novell/Procomp DCB External Layout

| Pin | Signal | Pin | Signal |
|---|---|---|---|
| 1 | GROUND | 20 | –DB(0) |
| 2 | GROUND | 21 | –DB(1) |
| 3 | GROUND | 22 | –DB(2) |
| 4 | GROUND | 23 | –DB(3) |
| 5 | GROUND | 24 | –DB(4) |
| 6 | GROUND | 25 | –DB(5) |
| 7 | GROUND | 26 | –DB(6) |
| 8 | GROUND | 27 | –DB(7) |
| 9 | GROUND | 28 | –DB(P) |
| 10 | GROUND | 29 | –ATN |
| 11 | GROUND | 30 | –BSY |
| 12 | GROUND | 31 | –ACK |
| 13 | GROUND | 32 | –RST |
| 14 | GROUND | 33 | –MSG |
| 15 | GROUND | 34 | –SEL |
| 16 | GROUND | 35 | –C/D |
| 17 | GROUND | 36 | –REQ |
| 18 | GROUND | 37 | –I/O |
| 19 | TERMPWR (possibly not connected) | | |

## SCSI Bus Signals

The SCSI bus has eight (or more) data lines and a few control signals. Table A.19 shows, briefly, what the signals are and how they're used.

**Table A.19: SCSI Signals, 8- and 16-Bit**

| | |
|---|---|
| BSY (Busy) | BSY indicates that the SCSI bus is in use. |
| SEL (Select) | SEL is used in the Arbitration phase to select a target for communication. In this case, the term target could also mean an initiator, if SEL is set in a RESELECTION phase. |
| C/D (Control/Data) | C/D indicates whether control or data information is on the data bus. If C/D is set, it indicates control information. |
| I/O (Input/Output) | I/O controls the direction of data movement on the data bus, seen from the initiator. True indicates input to the initiator. I/O also distinguishes between SELECTION and RESELECTION phases. |
| MSG (Message) | MSG is used to indicate a MESSAGE phase (together with C/D). |
| REQ (Request) | REQ is used by a target to request an ACK information transfer handshake. |
| ACK (Acknowledge) | ACK is used by an initiator to acknowledge the above REQ information transfer handshake request. |
| ATN (Attention) | ATN is set by an initiator to indicate the ATTENTION condition. |
| RST (Reset) | RST indicates the RESET condition. |
| DB(0) to DB(7) | These are the data bits on the 8–bit SCSI data bus. |
| DB(P) | DB(P) is the parity bit for the first data byte. If a 16–bit bus is used, the second data byte and its parity bit are used. |
| DB(8) to DB(15) | These are the additional data bits for the 16–bit SCSI data bus. |
| DB(P1) | DB(P1) is the parity bit for the second data byte. |

Some notes about the above mentioned signals:

- BSY, SEL, and RST are OR-tied, which means they can be asserted by multiple devices simultaneously.

- ACK and ATN are used only by the initiator for control purposes.

- C/D, I/O, MSG, and REQ are driven, or controlled, by the target.

- Each data byte is accompanied by a parity bit (odd parity is used, so the parity bit is set to 1 when the number of logical 1 signals, without the parity bit, is an even number).

- If a 32-bit bus is used, additional data and control signals are needed, as shown in Table A.20. These additional signals are supplied by a second cable, the Q-cable.

## Table A.20: Additional 32-Bit SCSI Signals

| | |
|---|---|
| REQQ (RequestQ) | REQQ is the REQ signal for the Q-cable, if 32-bit data transfers are used. |
| ACKQ (AcknowledgeQ) | Similar to REQQ, ACKQ is the ACK signal for the Q-cable, if 32-bit data transfers are used. |
| DB(16) to DB(31) | These are the additional data bits for the 32-bit SCSI data bus. |
| DB(P2) and DB(P3) | DB(P2) and DB(P3) are the parity bits for the third and fourth data bytes. |

# Bus Phases and Timing Diagrams

## Bus Phases and Conditions

This section lists the bus phases defined in the SCSI standard (Tables A.21 through A.23) and provides a phase sequence diagram (Figure A.24) for quick reference.

Principally, the SCSI bus is a "state machine." This means it has a number of states, of which at any given time exactly one is active. To maintain this behavior, several states (phases) are defined, along with numerous timing parameters that are used in the state switching process.

SCSI bus states are called "phases"; the eight phases break down into two types: four phases handle the bus protocol and access control, and four phases handle information transfer. The phases handling the protocol are shown in Table A.21.

## Table A.21: Protocol Phases

| Phase | Definition |
|---|---|
| BUS FREE | The BUS FREE phase indicates that no I/O process is running and the SCSI bus is available for a connection. It is the basic state of the bus before every transfer. |
| ARBITRATION | The ARBITRATION phase allows all attached SCSI devices to announce "I need the bus" and eventually gain control over the SCSI bus so that the bus can initiate or resume an I/O process. |
| SELECTION | In the SELECTION phase, the initiator (the ARBITRATION winner) selects a target for its pending operation. When this target selection has happened, the target asserts the REQ signal to enter an information transfer phase. |
| RESELECTION | The RESELECTION phase is a special version of a SELECTION phase needed in case of an uncompleted operation. For example, if a target device disconnected itself (it allowed a BUS FREE phase by releasing the BSY and SEL signals), the RESELECTION process allows the target to reconnect to the initiator of the suspended operation. Contrary to the standard SELECTION phase, in a RESELECTION phase, the *target* of a former operation takes action to get a connection to the initiator. |

The COMMAND, DATA, STATUS, and MESSAGE phases are commonly called the information transfer phases because, in these phases, the actual data exchange between the initiator and the target happens. Their specifications are shown in Table A.22.

## Table A.22: Information Transfer Phases

| Phase | Definition |
|---|---|
| COMMAND | The COMMAND phase allows the target to request command information from the initiator. |
| DATA | DATA phase has two variants, DATA IN and DATA OUT, in which the target asks to send data to or receive data from the initiator. |
| STATUS | The STATUS phase allows the target to request that status information be sent from the target to the initiator. |
| MESSAGE | MESSAGE phase also can be a MESSAGE IN or a MESSAGE OUT phase. In the MESSAGE phase, the target can request a message to or from the initiator. A message can be either a single-byte or a multiple-byte message, but the whole message must be contained in one MESSAGE phase — that means without any change in the C/D, I/O, and MSG signals. |

Three bus signals (C/D, I/O, and MSG) are used to distinguish between the different information transfer phases and data directions.

## Table A.23: Information Transfer Phase Control Signals

| Signal* | | | Phase Name | Transfer Direction |
|---|---|---|---|---|
| MSG | C/D | I/O | | |
| 0 | 0 | 0 | DATA OUT | From Initiator to Target |
| 0 | 0 | 1 | DATA IN | To Initiator from Target |
| 0 | 1 | 0 | COMMAND | From Initiator to Target |
| 0 | 1 | 1 | STATUS | To Initiator from Target |
| 1 | 0 | 0 | RESERVED** | ———— |
| 1 | 0 | 1 | RESERVED** | ———— |
| 1 | 1 | 0 | MESSAGE OUT | From Initiator to Target |
| 1 | 1 | 1 | MESSAGE IN | To Initiator from Target |

*0 = False = Deasserted, 1 = True = Asserted
**Reserved for future standardization

During a SCSI operation, the target device controls these signals, so it has control over the changes among these information transfer phases. In these phases, REQ/ACK handshake procedures are used for each byte of information. REQ/ACK handshake means that the target asserts the REQ signal to *REQ*uest a byte of information, then the initiator sets the data bus and sets the ACK signal to *ACK*nowledge the transfer request. The target then reads the data bus and releases the REQ signal to allow the initiator to release the ACK signal. Then the next byte can be transferred with the same REQ/ACK procedure.

In addition to the bus phases are two SCSI bus "conditions": the ATTENTION and the RESET conditions.

In the ATTENTION condition, the initiator can inform a target that he has a message ready. The target then can get this message by performing a MESSAGE OUT phase. An ATTENTION condition is issued by asserting the

ATN signal; this can happen in any bus state except during the ARBITRATION or BUS FREE phases.

The RESET condition is used to immediately clear all SCSI devices from the bus. The RESET condition has absolute priority over all other phases and conditions. Any SCSI device can create the RESET condition by asserting the RST signal. On RESET, all SCSI devices release all SCSI bus signals except RST, so that a BUS FREE phase follows the reset condition.

### Phase Sequence

SCSI bus phases usually follow a defined sequence pattern. A typical phase sequence on the bus could be as follows:

- BUS FREE phase

- ARBITRATION phase

- SELECTION or RESELECTION phase

- MESSAGE OUT phase

- One or more of the information transfer phases (COMMAND, DATA, STATUS, or MESSAGE)

- MESSAGE IN phase where a DISCONNECT or COMMAND COMPLETE message is transferred, followed by the next

- BUS FREE phase

The RESET condition can abort any phase and is always followed by a BUS FREE phase. Any other phase can also be followed by the BUS FREE phase. If this happens, it's generally due to an error, but it's legal.

A complete phase model looks a bit puzzling at first, with its plentiful possible action sequences, but on second glance, it is not too difficult. See Figure A.24.

BUS FREE as the initial state can lead only into an ARBITRATION phase. ARBITRATION can lead into a SELECTION or RESELECTION phase, then either the requested Information Transfer Phase(s) are issued, until the device enters a BUS FREE phase — its idle state. The last of the information transfer phases usually is a STATUS phase for the command, followed by a MESSAGE phase with the "Command Complete" message.

To show a simple example, a typical phase sequence for the TEST UNIT READY command would have the following sequence order:

- BUS FREE idle state

- ARBITRATION data according to the IDs $90_{hex}$ would be ID7 and ID4 ($1.0.0.1.0.0.0.0_{bin}$), meaning that the devices 7 and 4 want to get the bus

- SELECTION data according to the IDs $81_{hex}$ would be ID7 and ID0 ($1.0.0.0.0.0.0.1_{bin}$), meaning that the devices at ID7 and at ID0 communicate

- MESSAGE OUT data byte $80_{hex}$ = Identify command

- COMMAND data byte $00_{hex}$ = Test Unit Ready command (The TEST UNIT READY command has 6 bytes, all 6 bytes are $00_{hex}$)

- STATUS data byte $00_{hex}$ = GOOD, which means the SCSI device is ready

- MESSAGE IN data byte $00_{hex}$ = Command Complete

- BUS FREE idle state

The "frame" (BUS FREE to MESSAGE OUT and STATUS to BUS FREE) is identical for most combinations, but the number of COMMAND phases varies with the different commands.

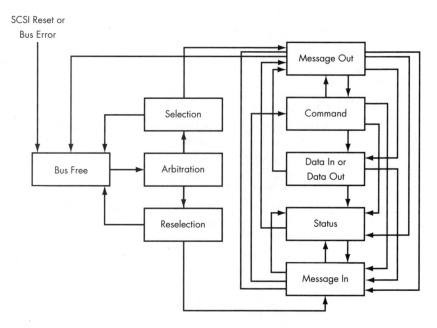

Figure A.24: SCSI Phase Sequence Model

## Bus Timing

SCSI bus timing is a very complex thing, but it can be broken down into some fundamental figures. The timing diagrams in this appendix are simplified. They do not include the various signal delays that actually occur on the SCSI bus. In reality, if an electrical signal changes its state, it never happens as cleanly as the timing diagrams would lead you to believe. To give the signals time to settle to their states, various delays are implemented. Table A.24 lists the various delays along with minimum or maximum times for defined changes to occur.

### Table A.24: SCSI Timing Elements

| Timing Element | Time | | | | Description |
|---|---|---|---|---|---|
| | SCSI-2 Syn (Fast 5) | Fast SCSI (Fast 10) | UltraSCSI (Fast-20) | Ultra2 SCSI (Fast-40) | |
| Arbitration | 2.4 µs | 2.4 µs | 2.4 µs | 2.4 µs | When a SCSI device Delay has asserted BSY during the arbitration phase, it must wait at least one Arbitration Delay before deciding that it has won the arbitration. |
| Assertion Period, Receive | 70 ns | 22 ns | 11 ns | 6.5 ns | |
| Transmit | 80 ns | 30 ns | 15 ns | 8 ns | REQ/REQB and ACK/ACKB signals must be asserted for at least one Receive Assertion period to be recognized, and the sender has to assert them for at least one transmit assertion period. |
| Bus Clear Delay | 800 ns | 800 ns | 800 ns | 800 ns | If a device detects a Bus Free phase, it has this amount of time to release all signals. |
| Bus Free Delay | 800 ns | 800 ns | 800 ns | 800 ns | After detection of a Bus Free phase, a device must wait one Bus Free Delay before starting the arbitration process. |
| Bus Set Delay | 1.6 µs | 1.6 µs | 1.6 µs | 1.6 µs | A SCSI device may assert BSY and its ID bit for an arbitration not longer than one Bus Set Delay. |
| Bus Settle Delay | 400 ns | 400 ns | 400 ns | 400 ns | After a phase change, signal levels should not be changed by devices during the Bus Settle Delay. |
| Cable Skew Delay | 4 ns (10 ns) | 4 ns (5 ns) | 3 ns | 2.5 ns | The signal run length between two SCSI signals on the bus shouldn't differ by more than a Cable Skew Delay. This is especially important when a signal is influenced by a ferrite core or similar damping measures. |
| Data Release Delay | 400 ns | 400 ns | 400 ns | 400 ns | When I/O changes its state from true to false, the initiator must release the data lines for one Data Release Delay. |
| System Deskew Delay | 45 ns | 45 ns | 45 ns | 45 ns | Time to decouple various signals. |
| Disconnection Delay | 200 µs | 200 µs | 200 µs | 200 µs | When a target gets disconnected by the initiator, the target must wait at least one Disconnection Delay before trying a new arbitration. |
| Hold Time, Receive | 25 ns | 25 ns | 11.5 ns | 4.75 ns | |
| Transmit | 53 ns | 33 ns | 16.5 ns | 9.25 ns | During a synchronous transfer, data must be asserted for at least one Hold Time to allow the receiving device to read them from the bus. |
| Negation Period | 70 ns 80 ns | 22 ns 30 ns | 11 ns 15 ns | 6.5 ns 8 ns | During a synchronous transfer, each REQ/REQB Receive Transmit or ACK/ACKB pulse must be followed by at least one Negation Period. |
| Reset Hold Time | 25 µs | 25 µs | 25 µs | 25 µs | The RST signal must be asserted for at least one Reset Hold Time before a reset is issued. |

| Timing Element | Time | | | | Description |
|---|---|---|---|---|---|
| | SCSI-2 Syn (Fast 5) | Fast SCSI (Fast 10) | UltraSCSI (Fast-20) | Ultra2 SCSI (Fast-40) | |
| Selection Abort Time | 200 μs | 200 μs | 200 μs | 200 μs | If a target doesn't react to a selection by asserting BSY during the Selection Abort Time, the initiator enforces a Bus Free phase (either through a reset condition or by releasing the data ines and then releasing SEL and ATN). |
| Setup Time Receive | 15 ns | 15 ns | 6.5 ns | 4.75 ns | |
| Transmit | 23 ns | 23 ns | 11.5 ns | 9.25 ns | |
| Transfer Period | 200 ns | 100 ns | 50 ns | 25 ns | The minimum time between two REQ/REQB or ACK/ACKB pulses. The possible Transfer Period is negotiated, between the involved devices. This is listed simply as "negotiated" in older specs, but with SCSI-3 defined timings come up. |
| Power On to Selection | 10 s | 10 s | 10 s | 10 s | A SCSI device should be able to answer to SCSI commands in this amount of time after power-on. This is only a recommendation, but a meaningful one, because most host adapter drivers consider this the maximum time for a device to respond before its ID is skipped. |
| Reset to Selection | 250 ms | 250 ms | 250 ms | 250 ms | Reset to Selection is the recommended maximum time a device is allowed to sit idle after a reset before it is able to answer to commands. |
| Selection Timeout Delay | 250 ms | 250 ms | 250 ms | 250 ms | During a Selection phase, a device should wait at least one Selection Timeout Delay for an answer before stopping the selection. This is only a recommended time, not a mandatory value. |

In the SCSI-3 drafts, new features like Quick Arbitration and Double Transition Clocking will introduce a few new variables, but the basic values are and will remain the same.

The timing diagrams included in Figures A.25 through A.30 illustrate the relationship between the various SCSI signals as follows:

- ARBITRATION and SELECTION phases (Figure A.25)

- ARBITRATION, RESELECTION, and MESSAGE IN phases (Figure A.26)

- MESSAGE OUT and COMMAND phases (Figure A.27)

- DATA I/O phases for asynchronous (Figure A.28) and synchronous (Figure A.29) transfer modes

- STATUS MESSAGE IN phase followed by a BUS FREE phase (Figure A.30)

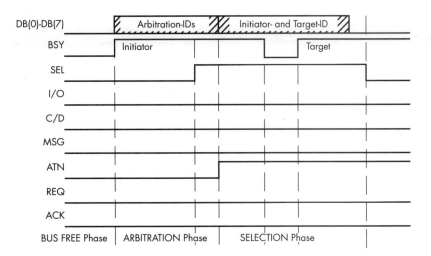

Figure A.25: ARBITRATION Followed by a SELECTION Phase

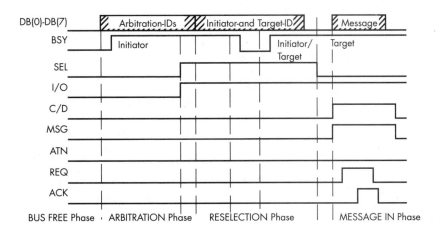

Figure A.26: ARBITRATION, RESELECTION, and MESSAGE IN Phases

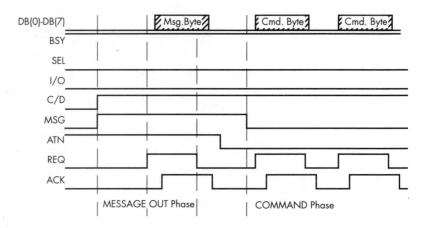

Figure A.27: MESSAGE OUT and COMMAND Phases

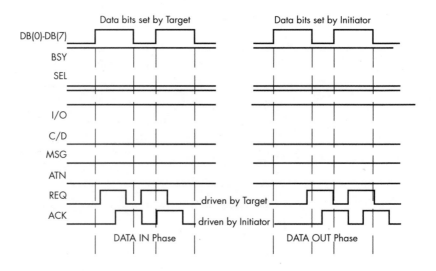

Figure A.28: Asynchronous Data Transfer

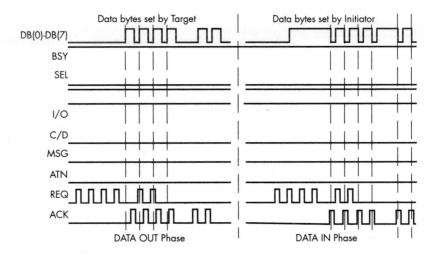

Figure A.29: Synchronous Data Transfer

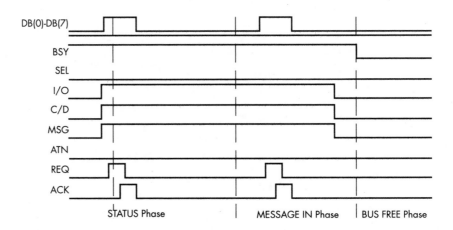

Figure A.30: MESSAGE IN Phase and BUS FREE Phase

## Termination

Next to cabling, termination is the most crucial part of SCSI. The basic rule of termination is simple: Both ends of the bus must be closed with termination circuits. Notwithstanding this simplicity, termination and termination-related issues are the cause of at least 80 percent of all SCSI problems.

To illustrate this, let's just look at three simple setups.

### Internal Devices Only

With internal devices only (Figure A.31), one cable with multiple connectors leads from the host adapter to the devices. The host adapter and the device on the last connector have to be terminated. If you don't have a device on the last connector, either move your connectors so that the last connector is used or apply a terminator to the last connector.

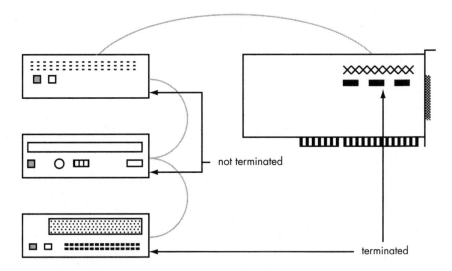

Figure A.31: Termination, Internal Devices Only

### External Devices Only

With external devices only (Figure A.32), a cable goes to the first device; from this device's second SCSI connector, a second cable goes on to the next device, and so on. The host adapter and the last device on this chain have to be terminated. On a modern host adapter, this is usually done by a jumper or by software via its SCSI BIOS. The device either has to be terminated internally *or* you have to attach a terminator plug on its second SCSI connector.

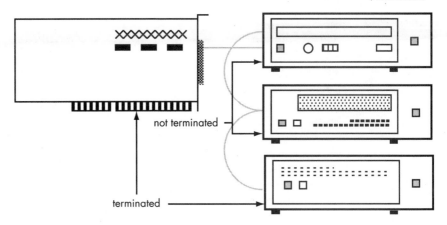

*Figure A.32: Termination, External Devices Only*

### Internal and External Devices

With both connectors on your host adapter used (Figure A.33), the same rules apply—terminate both ends only. So you disable the termination on the host adapter and terminate the last internal and the last external device.

With Wide SCSI, one new wrinkle shows up—the mix of Wide SCSI and "narrow" SCSI devices. The basic rules are the same, of course—termination on both ends of the bus. However, if you mix Wide SCSI disks and a narrow SCSI CD-ROM, the easiest setup is to have the complete SCSI bus 16 bits wide and to connect the CD-ROM in the middle of the bus with a 50-pin female

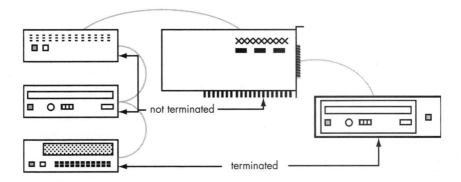

*Figure A.33: Termination, Internal and External Devices*

to 68-pin female adapter to the bus. In this configuration, you don't need termination on the CD-ROM and an adapter without high byte termination—easy and trouble-free.

With a Wide SCSI disk drive on your narrow SCSI bus, it's a bit more complex because most Wide SCSI devices need to "see" a correctly implemented Wide SCSI bus. You therefore need an adapter that terminates the high byte. This can be either a full-scale active termination circuit or a simple version that pulls up the upper byte [-DB(8) to -DB(15) and -DB(P1)] with a 4.7 kilo-ohms resistor to TERMPWR. If the adapter has no high byte termination, the drive may work or not—it depends on the drive and its abilities: Some drives won't work at all with the high byte "open," some drives can be switched to "narrow" mode and then ignore the high byte completely. It just depends on the SCSI implementation.

Some combinations may not even work when assembled correctly: An Ultra Wide SCSI host adapter with internal Ultra Wide disk drives, together with an external scanner with a 68- to 25-pin adapter and 1.5 meter cable is a nearly sure no-go case. Such an assemblage contains so many mismatches for impedance, propagation delay, grounding problems, and so on that it's pure luck if it works.

LVD is a bit different here—LVD devices typically don't have on-board termination, therefore you needn't hassle with termination settings on the devices. You just terminate the bus with a terminator plug if the cable itself is not terminated. Typically, if you buy an LVD cable or an LVD host adapter kit, you get a 16-bit LVD-compatible cable with an active LVD/SE multi-mode terminator mounted on one or on both ends.

### Termination Circuits

#### Passive Termination

When the SCSI-1 standard was published, the established standard for termination was a passive terminator for each signal. Passive means that only passive parts were used—in this case two resistors per signal line, one with 220 ohms as a pull-up resistor against the TERMPWR line and the other a 330-ohm pull-down resistor to ground (0 V). This resulted in a standby signal level of about 3 V if TERMPWR is at 5 V. Passive termination has a few drawbacks. It draws a relatively high current and, although the standard stated that using resistors with +/−1 percent tolerance improves noise margins, most passive terminators use 5 percent resistor arrays just because they're about ten cents cheaper. Figure A.34 shows a schematic of single-ended passive termination. Figure A.35 shows the schematic of the differential version of the passive terminator. Only one signal line is shown.

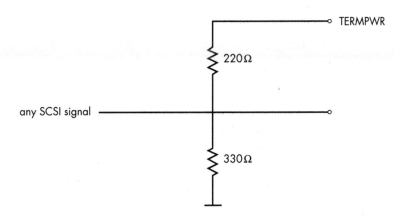

*Figure A.34: Passive Termination, Single-Ended*

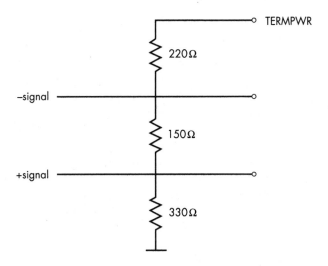

*Figure A.35: Passive Termination, High Voltage Differential*

## Active Termination

SCSI-2 introduced active termination (shown in Figure A.36), also called Boulay-Terminator after Paul Boulay, who first designed it. Even with the historic card computer buses, like S100 or the European ECB and SMP bus systems, active termination proved far superior to passive termination in signal quality and current draw. Active is far better than passive termination with respect to all signal

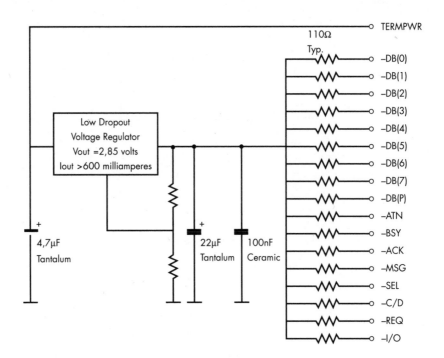

*Figure A.36: Active Termination, Single-Ended*

quality issues, and it is needed for Fast SCSI timing. However, one of active termination's biggest advantages is often underestimated: It is far more forgiving of low voltage and noise on the TERMPWR line than passive termination. Unfortunately, as with many other advances in the high-tech industry, active termination's advantages make it more complex and more expensive to use than passive termination.

The official active termination specification recommends a voltage of 2.85 V at the signal lines. Because good low-drop regulators need an input voltage of only 0.5 V above the output, the terminator could be designed to work reliably with TERMPWR as low as 3.5 V—far below the specification. To be on the safe side, however, newer devices tend to use SCSI termination ICs (integrated circuits)—like the Dallas Semiconductor DS2107A, which operates safely with TERMPWR from 4.0 to 5.25 V.

As you can see in Figure A.36, the official active termination circuit needs a voltage regulator. Although this isn't an expensive part, many vendors tend to simplify this circuit and replace the voltage regulator with a simple green LED with about 2.7 V reverse breakdown voltage. In general, these cheap terminators work, but they are a bit on the risky side.

### Forced Perfect Termination

Forced perfect termination, or FPT, is a variant of active termination. It works with a network of diodes and voltage regulators (or zener diodes acting as voltage regulators) to "force" an impedance match of the terminator to the cable. Some people recommend FPT as a means to get a critical bus to stable operation, and this sometimes even works. However, I do not recommend it in general because it draws much higher current than the SCSI spec allows (during peak surges) and so is a bit dangerous. Especially in combination with active negation drivers (see discussion earlier in this appendix) in new host adapters and devices, it is extremely dangerous for the line drivers of the negating device.

# B

## PC TECHNICAL REFERENCE

The following tables will give you a starting point for determining the possible configuration of add-on cards in your system. Due to the sheer number of add-on cards for the PC, these tables are by no means an exhaustive list of devices and their resource usage. Be sure to check the installation or user manuals for the devices in your system to ensure that you don't introduce hardware conflicts when adding new cards.

## Table B.1: I/O Port Usage

| Hex Port Range | Defined Use | Other Uses, Comments |
|---|---|---|
| 0–FF | Internal use only | Plug-in cards generally don't use I/O ports in this range. |
| 100–1EF | undefined | |
| 170h-177h | Secondary ATA hard disk controller | |
| 1F0–1F7 | Primary ATA hard disk controller | |
| 200–20F | Joystick port | Typically, only 200–207 are used. |
| 210–26F | undefined | 210, 220, 230, 240, 250, 260, 280 are typical for Sound Blaster and compatibles. |
| 270–27F | Printer port | Typically no longer used for printers. ISA Plug & Play generally uses this space. |
| 280–2AF | undefined | |
| 2B0–2DF | Alternative EGA address range | |
| 2E0–2EF | undefined | GPIB interface card at 2E0h–2Efh. |
| 2F0–2F7 | undefined | |
| 2F8–2FF | Serial port 2 (COM2:) | |
| 300–36F | undefined | This range was reserved for a prototype card, so many developers used it for their adapters. MPU-401 MIDI secondary address range at 300h–301h. MPU-401 MIDI primary addresses at 330h–331h. |
| 370–37F | Parallel port 1 | Only 370–377 are used. |
| 380–38F | undefined | SDLC or second bisync controller. |
| 390–39F | undefined | This was reserved for IBM cluster adapter. |
| 3A0–3AF | undefined | This was reserved for IBM bisync controller. |

| Hex Port Range | Defined Use | Other Uses, Comments |
|---|---|---|
| 3B0–3BF | Monochrome video card and printer port | Still needed for compatibility. Printer port on that board used 3BC–3BF. |
| 3C0–3CF | EGA vieo card | Still needed for compatibility. |
| 3D0–3DF | CGA video card | Still needed for compatibility. |
| 3E0–3EF | undefined | |
| 3F0–3F7 | Floppy disk controller | |
| 3F8–3FF | Serial port 1 (COM1:) | |
| 400–FFFF | EISA and PCI boards | In this range, addresses are typically assigned automatically by PCI. |

## Table B.2: Interrupt (IRQ) Usage

| Interrupt Number (IRQ) | Defined Use | Comments |
|---|---|---|
| 0 | Timer | Needed by the motherboard. |
| 1 | Keyboard | Needed by the motherboard. |
| 2 | Cascade for IRQ 8–15 | IRQ 2 is used for cascading the second interrupt controller. Devices on IRQ 2 are relocated to IRQ 9, so for the system, IRQ 2 = IRQ 9. This IRQ can be used for expansion boards, but is sometimes a bit tricky. |
| 3 | Serial port COM2 | |
| 4 | Serial port COM1 | |
| 5 | free | If installed, this is used by printer port LPT 2. |
| 6 | Floppy controller | |
| 7 | Printer port LPT1 | IRQ 7 can often be shared between the printer port and a sound card. |
| 8 | Real-time clock | Needed by the motherboard. |

| Interrupt Number (IRQ) | Defined Use | Comments |
| --- | --- | --- |
| 9 | IRQ 2 redirect | See IRQ 2. |
| 10 | free | |
| 11 | free | |
| 12 | free | |
| 13 | Math coprocessor | Needed by the motherboard. |
| 14 | Hard disk controller 1 | Typically IDE/ATA channel 1. Free if no IDE/ATA devices are used and the onboard controller is disabled. |
| 15 | Hard disk controller 2 | Typically IDE/ATA channel 2. Free if no IDE/ATA devices are used and the onboard controller is disabled. |

**Table B.3: DMA Channel Usage**

| DMA Channel | Defined Use | Comments |
| --- | --- | --- |
| 0 | free | 8-bit DMA |
| 1 | free | 8-bit DMA |
| 2 | Floppy controller | 8-bit DMA |
| 3 | free | 8-bit DMA |
| 4 | Cascade for DMA 0-3 | Needed by the motherboard. |
| 5 | free | 16-bit DMA |
| 6 | free | 16-bit DMA |
| 7 | free | 16-bit DMA |

Given that ISA Plug-and-Play and PCI's mostly automatic configuration are both common in today's systems, you shouldn't need to take extra care — but if your system experiences strange lockups, check anyway.

# A LOOK AT SCSI TEST EQUIPMENT

This chapter is really aimed at engineers whose job it is to bring together a set of SCSI peripherals to create a high-performance system. Also, if you're a software engineer developing SCSI device drivers, you'll find this appendix useful. If you're Joe Average-User, you can just skip this section unless your curiosity has gotten the better of you.

In SCSI, as in so many other technologies, things are great when they work, but what about when they don't? When you are responsible for deciding which devices to integrate into a system, and the ones you chose don't play happily together, what do you do? Whose fault is it? You properly terminated the bus, the IDs are all unique, but sometimes the system hangs! Now what?

If the devices are all manufactured by the same vendor, you can usually get the vendor to work it out for you. But more commonly, you'll choose a host adapter from one vendor, a disk from another vendor, and a DVD-ROM from yet another. You try to isolate the problem by removing all but one device, but find that the problem only occurs when everything is connected.

It's time to call in the big guns. Armed with some experience, the right test equipment, and your trusty SCSI standards documents, you enter the dragon's lair. When the finger-pointing starts, there just isn't any substitute for good test equipment.

## Your Mission . . .

What you need to do is capture the moment in time when things go awry and the events immediately leading up to that moment. Then, using your understanding of the SCSI protocol, you must figure out which device messed up the perfect order of things and either (1) get that vendor to fix the problem or (2) choose a different device. (Some analyzers actually minimize your own need for SCSI protocol expertise by incorporating significant intelligence of their own.)

### Rent or Buy?

These types of problems are not as common these days as they were when SCSI was new, but when they occur, you need to be able to solve them quickly. If your company is small or doesn't work with SCSI too often, renting test equipment might be the best option for you. The price tags on this stuff could scare the warts off a toad, and the SCSI standards evolve so fast that equipment can become obsolete in just a few years. You need to weigh the issues carefully and decide whether to buy or rent. Owning the equipment gives you fast access to it and — given that you own it — you use it more often and become more skilled in its use.

#### Back in the Stone Age

When I first started working with SCSI in 1986, there was no such thing as SCSI test equipment. I used a standard 16-channel logic analyzer and connected the probes to test points on a perfboard upon which I had wired SCSI connectors, some LEDs (to display the current signal state of all the SCSI signals), and a reset switch. Because the logic analyzer only had about 8K words of memory and no combination trigger, capturing exactly the part of the bus activity I wanted was no easy feat. If I set the sample rate too fast, I wouldn't capture enough. If I set it too slow, I might miss brief signal transitions (like ACK/REQ) that might be important. Developing those first device drivers was quite a challenge, because neither the host adapter hardware nor the devices I was trying to talk to had been tested, and there were no "example drivers" to give me an idea of what needed to be done!

I suppose this approach could still be used today if you're really strapped for cash or enjoy mental anguish, but I wouldn't recommend it. Today, test tools are available to help you work out problems, but the price tags pretty much restrict their purchase to professional developers. To add insult to injury, SCSI technology changes so quickly that today's state-of-the-art SCSI analyzer becomes tomorrow's doorstop very rapidly!

## Types of SCSI Analyzers

Several forms of SCSI analyzers exist. One type consists of an aluminum briefcase with a built-in data display/keyboard and several connectors (to accommodate the ever-widening selection of "standard" SCSI connectors). Switches to enable or disable internal termination or reset the bus are also present. These stand-alone units typically offer a printer connection and internal disk or other storage media. Many times you'll need to send the printed output to a device manufacturer to point out a deficiency in their device.

Another approach is to offer a small box with the SCSI connections. The box has a cable that connects to a special PCMCIA card in a notebook computer. A software analyzer application is then run on the notebook, which displays the data captured by the external module. Some analyzers allow data capture without the notebook computer attached — which helps you avoid coming back to get your results only to find that your notebook has magically vanished!

Another type consists of a special SCSI adapter in a desktop PC that, in combination with application software, performs SCSI bus analysis.

I know what you're thinking: Why doesn't someone just write software that will use my existing SCSI host adapter and let me snoop on what's happening on the SCSI bus? The answer is that SCSI controller chips, used on host adapter cards, don't provide sufficient control to allow this. So, as much as we'd all like to see it, you can't use your general-purpose host adapter as a SCSI analyzer, no matter what software you are willing to write.

### Analyzer Output

The basic function of SCSI analyzers is to display a snapshot of the sequence of bus states that were involved in a particular SCSI command execution. This may be in the form of a logic analyzer–style timing diagram or as a text listing showing which initiator selected which target and what command was sent with which parameters. The result looks similar to an assembly language program listing.

Analyzers offer so many options about what will be captured and what will cause a trigger that it generally takes longer to get things set the way you want them than to actually capture the data of interest. However, if you've decided that you've just got to have one of these, and your budget allows a $6,000 to $12,000 expenditure, here are some companies that make them:

# Manufacturers

### Ancot

115 Constitution Drive
Menlo Park, CA 94025
(650) 322-5322
http://www.ancot.com/

### Data Transit

3732-A Charter Park Drive
San Jose, CA 95136
(408) 264-4300
http://www.data-transit.com/

### Innotec Design

7035 Orangethrope Avenue, Unit I
Buena Park, CA 90621
(714) 522-1469
http://www.innotecdesign.com/

### I-Tech

10200 Valley View Road
Eden Prairie, MN 55344
(612) 941-5905
http://www.i-tech.com/

### Verisys

335-H Spreckels Drive
Aptos, CA 95003
(831) 662-7900
http://www.verisys.com

### Xyratex

U.K.:
Langstone Road
Havant
Hampshire
PO9 1SA
+44(0)23 9249 6000
http://www.xyratex.co.uk/

USA:
2151 Michelson Drive, Suite 235
Irvine, CA 92612
(949) 476-1016

# D

# ATA/IDE VERSUS SCSI

"What is better, SCSI or ATA?" is a question you may hear often these days. Usenet carries heated discussions between ATA and SCSI zealots every day (check for yourself in the comp.periphs.scsi newsgroup), and the prejudices on both sides are, in many cases, far from the technical facts.

As you might expect in a book about SCSI, the authors think SCSI is the better interface. However, the question "What is better?" usually means "What is faster?" — simply the wrong question. In fact, we have two interfaces that had (and have) rather different goals.

Because high-end systems and servers have no serious choice other than SCSI at the moment, we'll look at the issues from a small workstation's point of view.

## History

### SCSI

Historically, SCSI emerged from Shugart's SASI approach to define a universal interface for disk drives and other peripherals like tape drives, the most common peripherals at that time. Remember that we're talking about a time when CD-ROMs and other common devices used today didn't exist. The universal interface that resulted needs considerable effort to implement the hard- and software.

### ATA

ATA, the AT Attachment interface, was developed as a replacement for the ST-506 disk interface to overcome that interface's inherent limitations and yet remain as compatible as possible with old software. Therefore, all ATA disk drives still emulate the old WD-1003 controller at the I/O register level.

As the ATA specification states, "This standard defines the AT Attachment Interface. This standard defines an integrated bus interface between disk drives and host processors."

### IDE/EIDE

Whenever you see the name IDE or EIDE, the same interface is meant: When the first ATA drives came into the market, the name IDE (Integrated Drive Electronics) was used to distinguish the new ATA interface from the old ST-506 interface. When later the ATA interface was enhanced by the addition of faster transfer modes and by moving it off the slow AT bus to the faster local VLB and PCI buses, the end product was called Enhanced IDE or EIDE. ATA was the name used when formalizing the standard for this interface.

### ATAPI

Later, the ATA Packet Interface (ATAPI) was added to control additional storage devices, like CD-ROM and tape drives. From an abstract technical view, there is no SCSI storage device that couldn't be made available as an ATAPI device. After all, the ATAPI commands are just SCSI commands sent over the ATA bus.

## Speed—and Why It Isn't Everything

Data transfer rates are the feature most often compared—a silly comparison. Besides, SCSI Ultra/160 m—with bus transfer rates of up to 160 MB/sec— should settle this question for the next few years. As you'll read later, there are other considerations, but for the moment, let's have a look at the interfaces' data transfer rates shown in Table D.1.

**Table D.1: Interface Burst Transfer Rates in MB/sec**

| | SCSI | | ATA | | | |
|---|---|---|---|---|---|---|
| **Mode** | **8 Bit** | **16 Bit** | **Mode** | **PIO** | **Single-Word DMA** | **Multi-Word DMA** |
| **SCSI 1/2** | 5 | 10 | **0** | 3.3 | 2.1 | 4.2 |
| **Fast SCSI 2** | 10 | 20 | **1** | 5.2 | 4.2 | 13.3 |
| **Ultra SCSI** | 20 | 40 | **2** | 8.3 | 8.3 | 16.6 |
| **Ultra 2 LVD** | 40 | 80 | **3** | 11.1 | — | 33.3 |
| **Ultra /160 m** | 80 | 160 | **4** | 16.6 | — | 66.6 |

As you see, from a raw speed point of view, both ATA and SCSI are suitably fast for a small disk system, keeping in mind that a typical high-end disk drive still delivers under 30 MB/sec and that ATA has a limit of two devices per channel. So, at the moment, speed isn't an issue you need to consider.

What will arise isn't yet clear — IEEE 1394 should be fairly well established within a couple years, but still won't have the potential to replace ATA from a speed point of view.

## Features That Make a Difference

### I/O Device Independence and Multitasking

A big difference between SCSI and ATA is device independence and overlapping I/O capability.

#### Device Independence

A SCSI host adapter negotiates the synchronous data transfer speed independently for each device. Older, slower devices therefore limit the bus transfer speed only when they're busy transmitting data, but faster devices, in their own transmissions, use *their own* maximum transfer rate.

*ATA can do this to some extent too, but most ATA controllers and drivers don't implement this feature. So in many situations, the slowest device on an ATA channel limits the transfer mode and throttles the faster devices. Fortunately, this seems to be getting better in the newer chip sets.*

### Overlapping

Overlapping I/O is a different issue: When a command is issued in ATA, the next command can't be sent to the drive until the first command's execution has finished. This is especially ugly when a command—like Recalibrate or Seek—takes a long time. So, command tasks in ATA can only be executed in the order you send them to the device. This was not an issue in MS-DOS and similar operating systems, but given the increasing frequency of concurrent disk requests in today's operating systems, it matters now.

SCSI has two mechanisms to avoid this problem. The easiest is "Disconnect/ Reconnect"—a device receiving a command that needs some time can acknowledge the command, disconnect from the bus, execute the command, and, when it's done, reconnect to the host adapter and deliver the result.

In addition, more sophisticated SCSI devices will do *tagged command queuing*. This feature lets the device rearrange pending tasks to optimize the execution order of the commands. For example, a disk drive can reorder disk reads to optimize head movements. This was sometimes also called *elevator seeking* because the model fits perfectly—in an elevator, the door opens on the nearest selected floor, regardless of the order in which the buttons were pressed.

Sadly, because both mechanisms are only optional, you may encounter poorly designed SCSI peripherals that don't support these features.

### OS Support

Also, depending on the operating system you plan to use, you should check whether the OS supports these features. It is pointless, for example, to boast about the multitasking capabilities of the hardware if you plan to use DOS or Windows 95 on a PC. On the other hand, operating systems such as Windows NT, OS/2, and all flavors of Unix strongly benefit from these capabilities.

### *Cable Length—and What It Means in Real Life*

Cable length is always an issue. The maximum ATA cable length of 18 inches (0.5 meter) is not much, especially if you need to shorten the cable a few inches because the board vendor sacrificed maintaining short traces against a more convenient connector position. So you're nearly always on the border of the critical range with ATA systems. This poses no problem with slow transmit rates, but is a threat to system integrity with the faster ATA modes.

Compared to ATA, SCSI allows cable lengths beyond compare, even in the most limited high-speed implementations—1.5 meters (59 inches) is the shortest limitation SCSI has under most circumstances.

Mainly because of the defined bus length, external devices in ATA are dubious, even if there are some implementations of external "tabletop" cabinets for CD-ROMs.

With SCSI's bus length specifications and the definition of shielded cables, addition of external devices is not only possible but simple. SCSI is therefore still the interface of choice to attach image scanners and other external peripherals to computer systems, although USB (for low-end peripherals) and IEEE 1394 (also known as FireWire or i.Link) show some potential to compete with parallel SCSI in this area.

### Devices per Channel: Why Should You Care?

A SCSI channel allows you to attach seven to fifteen devices to a host adapter. Wide SCSI is an interesting issue for disk drives, but—aside from some high-end tape drives—non-disk peripherals are virtually unavailable as Wide SCSI. Let's therefore settle for seven devices per channel for this comparison. ATA, on the other hand, accepts only two devices per channel. Although this doesn't seem to be a big issue—you could just add channels—the reality is that in today's PC architecture, you typically need an interrupt for a channel, and interrupts are a scarce resource. In your everyday PC, you lose IRQ 14 and 15 to the two standard ATA ports.

Multi-channel adapters that overcome the IRQ issue are available for both interfaces, so all is not lost if you're out of device resources. However, with SCSI this isn't too likely at all.

This discussion is not as far-fetched as it seems. A typical home or office PC today has a disk and a CD-ROM or DVD. For such devices, distributed to both ATA channels of a system, everything should be okay. Now, if you add a CD recorder and a removable disk device like a Zip drive—two common devices—ATA's limit is reached. If you want any additional device—be it an additional disk drive, a tape drive, or something new we haven't dreamt of yet—you need to go either the SCSI route or buy a special multi-channel controller, if one is available that fits your system, and if your system has free resources (one free IRQ and a free slot) to install it. A lot of "ifs" there!

## What to Choose?

With the above said, the question is what to choose for the desired system. After the feature comparisons in Table D.2, we'll suggest a few simple rules to use as an appropriate guide.

**Table D.2: SCSI Versus ATA Design Issues**

| Feature | SCSI | ATA |
|---|---|---|
| Devices per channel | 7 (8 bit) or 15 (Wide) | 2 |
| Cable length per channel | Depending on clock rate, 1.5 m to 6 m* (4.9 ft to 19.7 ft) | 18 inches (46 cm) |
| External cabling | Yes | No |
| Independent timing per device | Yes | Sometimes |
| Data integrity mechanisms | One bit parity SCSI-3 provides ECC | None Ultra DMA provides ECC |
| Overlapping I/O (Multitasking) | Yes | No |
| Maximum Data Rate | 80 MB/sec * | 66 MB/sec |

*A few issues like LVD and Ultra/160 m are not relevant here*

### Consider Your Requirements

#### CPU Load

Note that we don't (okay, we do . . .) mention CPU load. Although SCSI tends to have lower CPU load on transfers than ATA, the introduction of busmastering DMA transfers in ATA has shifted the emphasis to exactly which devices you purchase — that is, CPU load is now more dependent on the devices and the driver quality than on the interface itself. So, for a standard system the point is moot — and where it really counts, other issues inhibit ATA.

#### Games

If you're building a standard home PC and/or a system directed at games, think about using ATA. For such systems you'd typically have one big disk drive and a fast CD-ROM, and you'd use Windows 95/98 as your operating system, which strongly limits the advantage of SCSI's device independence. The price advantage of ATA cannot be overlooked, and so you'd end up with a possibly 20 percent cheaper system to get essentially the same performance.

### Graphics, Video, or Development

If you want to do graphics, video manipulation, or development work, go SCSI. All such applications require lots of disk activity for tasks like background compiling, swapping large image files (or parts of them) in and out of memory, and generally multitasking to a high degree. With ATA's sequential tasking, timing is so much more critical that you might decide to use SCSI for that reason alone.

### External Peripherals

If you want to use external peripherals, check your requirements. Middle-quality desktop scanners are available with USB interfaces and alone are possibly not enough reason to go SCSI. Higher-end devices typically aren't available with interfaces *other* than SCSI, and then it's likely you'll be doing graphics work as discussed above. So again, it makes sense to go SCSI anyway.

### Operating Systems

If you want to use Windows NT, Windows 2000, or a flavor of UNIX, go SCSI. In operating systems like these, a lot of background processing requires disk activity, resulting in better responsiveness under load. There are profound reasons why all vendors of such operating systems recommend SCSI over ATA.

## The Bottom Line

Under most conditions, SCSI is the better—and even faster — interface. You'll have to decide for yourself if your application can use the advantages and if it's worth the price tag.

# A SMALL ASPI DEMO APPLICATION

## (OR, HOW TO USE ASPI WITHOUT DIGGING TOO DEEP)

*Source files for all the code shown in this section are included on the CD-ROM accompanying this book.*

ShowSCSI.pas is a small program that shows how to communicate with the ASPI interface. Because it concentrates strictly on communicating with the ASPI interface, there are no bells and whistles. Mostly, even error checking is simplified or omitted to keep it as small as possible. We will, however, continue developing it and extend it into a usable library with the possible add-on of a few handy tools. Check http://www.nostarch.com/scsi_updates.htm from time to time.

## Program Structure

ShowSCSI is written in Delphi and consists of mainly three components:

1.  ShowSCSI.pas, the main program. Basically, it offers the GUI and the program logic — not much in this case: It just calls the interface functions from AspiApplication.pas and offers the container lists for the results from this call.

2. AspiApplication.pas, the middle layer. AspiApplication.pas offers high level function calls for things like "Start Device" or "Eject Medium" and such. This unit doesn't know much about ASPI—it just calls a function from the "hardcore" layer ASPI_Interface.pas, submits the address of the device (host adapter, SCSI ID, LUN) and an object to hold the return value(s).

   As an example, after the completion of an issued command the list referenced by P_ASPI_DevInfo contains the result value of the command—in this case the Inquiry string of the device with list vendor name, device name, and so on.

3. ASPI_Interface.pas, the lowest layer and the only part that "talks" ASPI/SCSI to the devices. In ASPI_Interface, the ASPI/SCSI commands are defined, for example ASPI_GetDeviceType to get the device type (Disk, Optical drive, etc.) of the addressed SCSI device.

### Why Use Three Layers?

There are mainly three goals, the most important being to keep a clean structure to the code.

1. The ASPI interface should be wrapped in a layer where you can say "I want the CD-ROM tray to open" without knowing that you need to issue a Start/Stop Unit command with the right settings for the Start/Stop and Load/Eject bits in the SCSI command descriptor block. While you need to know this to implement the function in ASPI_Interface.pas, there is no need to have a SCSI CDB reference ready to use this late in your ShowSCSI application.

2. While this program and its parts are only small excerpts from the ASPI/SCSI world, the concept can be used for bigger applications, too, and we want to expand the tool chest over time. In a layered concept, it is easily possible to extend the list of SCSI functions from ASPI_Interface.pas without changing anything in other parts of the project and without the program becoming "spaghetti code." The same reason applies for the middle layer AspiApplication.pas. Therefore, if you want to add a new function, which we'll do later in this appendix, you'll stay compatible with all other parts of the old program.

3. The user interface should be strictly separated from the technical part of the program. While we have an application with a graphical user interface here, it is no problem to replace ShowSCSI.pas with a console mode part, for example, to eject a CD from the command line or a batch file.

So, using a layered concept is a key point to easy expansion of the program, and if you want to add a new function, which we'll do later in this appendix, you'll stay compatible with all other parts of the old program.

Additionally, a few files offer definitions: wnaspi32.pas for ASPI for Windows 32, SCSI.pas has some SCSI definitions, and LibUtil.pas gives us a handy conversion routine for packing option bits into bytes for the SCSI command. Please keep in mind that the separation is not complete; for clarity, some definitions are local in the sources.

What we want is a program that checks if ASPI is installed, shows us the known devices, and offers buttons to stop and start a selected device. Provided that this command (Start/Stop Unit) makes sense to the device, it should then spin down or up. A slightly extended version should have the possibility to eject and load the medium tray, for example on a CD-ROM drive.

Now let's dive a little deeper into it. On startup, ShowSCSI searches for ASPI host adapters (including the check if ASPI is installed at all) and collects the host adapter data in a list called HAList.

If a host adapter is selected, all possible device IDs are checked for a device with the SCSI Inquiry command. The inquiry data are written to a new list called DeviceList and the devices are shown in the GUI. After a device is selected, a command can be issued to it, in our case either Start or Stop. These two "high-level" commands are basically the same SCSI command with just one bit set differently.

Typically, the first thing to do is to initialize all neccessary structures of the program. This is done by the startup routine in the main program:

```
procedure TForm1.FormCreate(Sender: TObject);
    .
  ...
HAList     :=TList.Create;              // list of host adapters
   DeviceList :=TList.Create;           // list of actual devices
    .

GetHAInfos(Memo.Lines);                 // get HA's and display list in Memo
   for i:=0 to HAList.count-1 do begin  // load HA listbox with all HA's
      HAListBox.Items.Add(inttostr(PHADevices(HAList[i])^.HA)+': ' +
            PHADevices(HAList[i])^.HAName);
    .
    .
```

Of course, the ASPI parts of the program from the lower layers are responsible for their own initializing, for the code here doesn't know anything about their internals. Therefore the GetHAInfos function from AspiApplication.pas has its own housekeeping that uses the parameters from ASPI_Interface.pas. As confusing as it may sound at first, it is easier to define it this way than to have all parameters defined locally.

```
function GetHAInfos(Protokoll:TStrings):boolean;
VAR NumAdap    : Longint;
    HA_Num     : integer;
    pString    : string ;
    AktHA      : PHADevices;
    PASPI_HAInfo:P_ASPI_HAInfo ;
 begin
    GetHAInfos:=false;                          // initialise ASPI manager

    PASPI_HAInfo := New(P_ASPI_HAInfo) ;        // from ASPI_Interface ...
    ASPI_GetHANum(NumAdap) ;                    // return the number of HAs
[0..n]
    for HA_Num:=0 to NumAdap-1 do begin         // ask every found hostadapter ...
        ASPI_GetHAInfos(HA_Num, PASPI_HAInfo) ;
        AktHA:=New(PHADevices);
        AktHA^.HA:=HA_Num;
        HAList.Add(AktHA) ;                      // add one entry (hostadapter) to the
                                                 //listbox "host adapters"
        pString := format('Hostadapter ' + PASPI_HAInfo^.HaName +
            ' AspiNum: %d, SCSI-ID: %d',
            [PASPI_HAInfo^.HaAspiId,PASPI_HAInfo^.HaScsiId]);
        Protokoll.add(pString);                  // add one entry to the
                                                 // memofield "device info"

        AktHA^.HAName := PASPI_HAInfo^.HaName;
    end;
end;
```

Here, the ASPI manager is asked whether there are host adapters present, and which ones they are. If no ASPI manager is present, we can safely assume that there is no point in continuing the program. Due to the lack of an error handler here, the program just quits with an error message from Windows, while in a commercial quality program, you would include an error handler here to end the program gracefully.

Now we have a list of host adapters (in HAList) from which we can select one. This is done back in the GUI part ShowSCSI.pas in the HAListBoxClick procedure:

```
procedure TForm1.HAListBoxClick(Sender: TObject); // clicking on a HA
var
    i : integer;                                 // adapter from the list ...
    HA:integer ;                                 // Number of the selected hostadapter
begin
    HA := HAListBox.ItemIndex;                   // selected Host adapter, defined in
                                                 // the ASPIApplication unit
```

```
  // form cleanup ....
    ListBox1.Clear;                          // clear devicelist
    ListBox1.Refresh;                        // refresh devicelist
    // action ...
    GetDeviceList(HA, DeviceList);           // get devices and load memo field
    for i:=0 to DeviceList.count-1 do        // fill device listbox
      ListBox1.Items.Add(inttostr(P_ASPI_DevInfo(DeviceList[i])^.ID)+':'+
                    inttostr(P_ASPI_DevInfo(DeviceList[i])^.LUN)+': '+
                    P_ASPI_DevInfo(DeviceList[i])^.Inquiry.ProductId);
end;
```

Again, some housekeeping should be done by clearing the device list first, then GetDeviceList from AspiApplication.pas is called with the selected host adapter, and fills the list of devices called DeviceList. The GUI part then extracts the neccessary data to fill the Listbox to click on a particular device. If this click happens, the clicked device is selected and the inquiry data from this device are shown in a text box (Memo).

```
procedure TForm1.ListBox1Click(Sender: TObject);
var
   DEVINDEX  : integer ;
begin

    Memo.Clear;                              // clear memofield
    DEVINDEX := ListBox1.ItemIndex;          // selected Device (element from Listbox)

    with P_ASPI_DevInfo(DeviceList[DEVINDEX])^ do // add device information
                                            // to memolist "Devices"
    begin
        Memo.Lines.add(format('Device HA: %d : ID %d, LUN %d, Type %d = '
        +DevType,[HA,ID,LUN,TypeNum]));      // output inquiry data in
        Memo.Lines.add(InquiryString);       // memofield
    end;
end;
```

Now, any of the buttons can be pressed to submit a SCSI command to the device.

```
procedure TForm1.StopButtonClick(Sender: TObject); //Stop Button
var i:integer;
begin
  for i:=0 to ListBox1.items.count-1 do
    if Listbox1.selected[i]                  // for each selected device
    then                                     // send Start/Stop Unit command with
                                            // 'start' and 'eject' flags set false
      StartStopUnit(false,DeviceList[i]);
end;
```

This button sends a Start/Stop Unit command with the Start/Stop bit set to "Stop" to the selected device (DeviceList[i]). If we look deeper into what happens now, StartStopUnit fills the SRB structure with the neccessary parameters and calls ASPI_StartStopUnit:

```
function ASPI_StartStopUnit(HA,ID,LUN:integer; Start:boolean;
var errorcode:integer):boolean ;

var Buffer:PSRBBuf;                     // PSRBBuf from Wnaspi32
    SRB:PSRB_ExecSCSICmd;               // PSRB_ExecSCSICmd from Wnaspi32
begin
  SRB:=New(PSRB_ExecSCSICmd);          // create new SRB structures
  Buffer:=New(PSRBBuf);
  InitSRB(SRB,sizeOf(SRB^));           // initialize SRB
  SRB^.SRB_HAId:=HA;                   // fill SRB parameters ...
  SRB^.SRB_Target:=ID;
  SRB^.SRB_Lun:=LUN;
  SRB^.SRB_BufPointer:=Buffer;
  SRB^.SRB_CMD:=SC_EXEC_SCSI_CMD;
  SRB^.SRB_Flags:=0;
  SRB^.SRB_BufPointer:=nil;            // no buffer:
  SRB^.SRB_Buflen:=0;                  // buffer size 0, the Start/Stop Unit
                                       //   command doesn't transfer data...
  SRB^.SRB_SenseLen:=SENSE_LEN;        // default ASPI sense buffer length, 14 bytes
  SRB^.SRB_CDBLen:=6;                  // 6-Byte command
                                       // ---- SCSI command block parameters ----
  SRB^.CDBByte[0]:=$1B;                // Start/Stop Unit $1B
  SRB^.CDBByte[1]:=LUN*32;             // LUN shifted 5 bits to the left
                                       // where it belongs ....
  if Start then                        // set SCSI command - start bit
    SRB^.CDBByte[4]:=1
  else
    SRB^.CDBByte[4]:=0;

  SendASPI32Command(SRB);              // action!
```

Now the program polls the ASPI status until it indicates that the command has completed. Because it's pointless to poll a few million times until a start/stop unit command completes, we add 100ms pauses to release the CPU for this time.

```
while SRB^.SRB_Status=0 do begin
      sleep(100) ;                     // don't lockup the machine...
  end ;
```

If the command has completed, the SCSI target status of the device is checked. This would be the place to implement a SCSI error handler, if you want or need one. At the moment, we check only if the command succeeded or not.

```
case SRB^.SRB_TargStat of      // This handler may be used later to repeat
                               // a command based on certain conditions
    TARGSTAT_GOOD:             // All done now
    begin
        ASPI_StartStopUnit:=True ;
    end;
    TARGSTAT_CHKCOND:          // Check Condition,
    begin                      // e.g. process sense data
        ASPI_StartStopUnit:=False ;
    end;
    TARGSTAT_BUSY:             // Device is Busy
    begin
        ASPI_StartStopUnit:=False ;
    end;
    TARGSTAT_RESCONF:          // Reservation Conflict
    begin
        ASPI_StartStopUnit:=False ;
    end;
else
    begin                      // there may be very special cases...
        ASPI_StartStopUnit:=False ;
    end;
end ;
```

Finally, the data structures used for the SCSI function call are freed.

```
                               // cleanup data structures...
    dispose(SRB);
    dispose(Buffer);
end ;
```

More or less, this is it — a working program using the ASPI interface to communicate with a SCSI device. However, this code has two known problems. One lies in using the ASPI polling mechanism. As shown above in the

```
while SRB^.SRB_Status=0 do begin
        sleep(100) ;                   // don't lockup the machine...
    end ;
```

piece of code, we add a pause of 100ms after each ASPI poll for the SRB status. If this weren't there, the program would use 100 percent of CPU time until the command completes and SRB^.SRB_Status would change from 0 to another value. If you write more complex or commercial applications with ASPI, the keyword here is "ASPI posting," together with setting timeouts using the ASPI SC_GETSET_TIMEOUTS command.

The second problem is a bigger one. With the standard ASPI layer present in Windows 95, 98, or NT4, all interfaces being or mimicking a SCSI host adapter are listed as host adapters. This includes the standard ATAPI driver under the name ESDI_506 as well as special drivers like Notebook PCMCIA ATA cards and drivers like VirtualCD. Note that most of these appear only if there are non-disk devices attached to the adapter.

Now, our program sends the Inquiry command to each possible device to get a list of devices. If such a real or virtual device doesn't respond, the ASPI layer locks up waiting for a response and — usually after a few tries of the user to kill the program — takes the system with him. In general, behavior here is not really predictable; as far as the systems used in writing this demo program, some worked, and some locked up — without any possibility of recovery. A possible quick and dirty approach that even some commercial programs use is to filter the names of the host adapters and either eliminate the known names or accept only known names, but this isn't a very good solution. Here again, the keyword is setting timeouts using the ASPI SC_GETSET_TIMEOUTS command.

Enough for now with complex problems — next, we'll try to implement a new command in our program to load or eject the media tray, for example on a CD-ROM or a removable disk drive.

## Implementation of the Load/Eject Functionality in ASPI_Interface

To add a command, you basically use the same function layout as used for the other commands in ASPI_Interface.pas. The SendASPI32Command() function call needs an SRB structure, so we fill this structure with the correct parameters for our command. Because Load/Eject is an application of the Start/Stop Unit command, the parameters are basically the same as in ASPI_StartStopUnit, with the exception of Byte 4 of the CDB. In addition to the Start bit to determine between a Start and a Stop Unit operation, we need the Eject bit to add the Load/Eject action.

```
SRB^.SRB_HAId:=HA;
SRB^.SRB_Target:=ID;
SRB^.SRB_Lun:=LUN;

SRB^.SRB_BufPointer:=Buffer;
SRB^.SRB_CMD:=SC_EXEC_SCSI_CMD;
SRB^.SRB_Flags:=0;
SRB^.SRB_BufPointer:=nil;        // no buffer:
```

```
SRB^.SRB_Buflen:=0;                    // buffer size 0, for the Start/Stop Unit
                                       // command doesn't transfer data...
SRB^.SRB_SenseLen:=SENSE_LEN;          // default ASPI sense buffer length, 14 bytes
SRB^.SRB_CDBLen:=6;                    // 6-Byte command
                                       // SCSI command block parameters

SRB^.CDBByte[0]:=$1B;                  // Start/Stop Unit $1B
SRB^.CDBByte[1]:=LUN*32;               // LUN shifted 5 bits to the left
                                       // where it belongs ....


if Eject then                          // set SCSI command - start and eject bit
   SRB^.CDBByte[4] := 2
else
   SRB^.CDBByte[4] := 3 ;
```

After filling the SRB structure, SendASPI32Command(SRB) is called and the program polls for the command completion.

```
SendASPI32Command(SRB);
while SRB^.SRB_Status=0 do begin
      sleep(100) ;                     // ASPI command pending  ...
end;
      .
      .
```

Now we check the target status code from the addressed device in SRB_TargStat. This would be the place to implement a better error handler for the command, if needed. This code mainly checks if the command worked or not, but doesn't do more.

```
case SRB^.SRB_TargStat of             // This handler may be used later
                                      // to repeat a command based on
                                      // special conditions


TARGSTAT_GOOD:                        // All done now
  begin
      ASPI_LoadEjectUnit:=True ;
  end;
TARGSTAT_CHKCOND:                     // Check Condition,
  begin                               // e.g. process sense data
      ASPI_LoadEjectUnit:=False ;
  end;
TARGSTAT_BUSY:                        / Device is Busy
  begin
      ASPI_LoadEjectUnit:=False ;
  end;
```

```
      TARGSTAT_RESCONF:                        // Reservation Conflict
        begin
          ASPI_LoadEjectUnit:=False ;
        end;
      else
        begin                                  // there may be some very special cases
          ASPI_LoadEjectUnit:=False ;
        end;
  end ;
```

## Again, the complete function for the Load/Eject call:

```
function ASPI_LoadEjectUnit(HA,ID,LUN:integer; Eject:boolean;
                          var errorcode:integer) : boolean ;
{ Description: Start/Stop Unit with Eject bit set
  Parameters:  HA, ID, LUN of the SCSI device
               Eject bit set true/false
               Errorcode (return value for e.c. - not yet implemented)
               Returns True/False
 }
var Buffer:PSRBBuf;                          // PSRBBuf from Wnaspi32
    SRB:PSRB_ExecSCSICmd;                    // PSRB_ExecSCSICmd from Wnaspi32
begin
  SRB:=New(PSRB_ExecSCSICmd);
  Buffer:=New(PSRBBuf);
  InitSRB(SRB,sizeOf(SRB^));

  SRB^.SRB_HAId:=HA;
  SRB^.SRB_Target:=ID;
  SRB^.SRB_Lun:=LUN;

  SRB^.SRB_BufPointer:=Buffer;
  SRB^.SRB_CMD:=SC_EXEC_SCSI_CMD;
  SRB^.SRB_Flags:=0;
  SRB^.SRB_BufPointer:=nil;                   // no buffer:
  SRB^.SRB_Buflen:=0;                         // buffer size 0, for the Start/Stop Unit
                                              // command doesn't transfer data...
  SRB^.SRB_SenseLen:=SENSE_LEN;              // default ASPI sense buffer length, 14 bytes
  SRB^.SRB_CDBLen:=6;                         / 6-Byte command
                                              // SCSI command block parameters
  SRB^.CDBByte[0]:=$1B;                       // Start/Stop Unit $1B
```

```pascal
      SRB^.CDBByte[1]:=LUN*32;                // LUN shifted 5 bits to the left
                                              // where it belongs ....


      if Eject then                           // set SCSI command - start and eject bit
         SRB^.CDBByte[4] := 2
      else
         SRB^.CDBByte[4] := 3 ;


      SendASPI32Command(SRB);                 // action!
      while SRB^.SRB_Status=0 do begin
           sleep(100) ;                        // ASPI command pending  ...
      end;


      case SRB^.SRB_TargStat of              // This handler may be used later
                                             // to repeat a command based on
                                             // special conditions


         TARGSTAT_GOOD:                      // All done now
         begin
             ASPI_LoadEjectUnit:=True ;
         end;
         TARGSTAT_CHKCOND:                   // Check Condition,
         begin                               // e.g. process sense data
             ASPI_LoadEjectUnit:=False ;
         end;
         TARGSTAT_BUSY:                       // Device is Busy
         begin
             ASPI_LoadEjectUnit:=False ;
         end;
         TARGSTAT_RESCONF:                    // Reservation Conflict
         begin
             ASPI_LoadEjectUnit:=False ;
         end;
      else
         begin                               // there may be some very special cases
             ASPI_LoadEjectUnit:=False ;
         end;
      end ;

                                             // cleanup data structures...
      dispose(SRB);
      dispose(Buffer);
   end ;
```

## Implementation of the Load/Eject Functionality in ASPIApplication

The AspiApplication layer is built from function blocks with simple names like StartStopUnit or LoadEjectUnit that act as call interface for the GUI front end. This layer more or less translates the functional command (Load Tray) in its ASPI/SCSI equivalent by calling the neccessary commands from ASPI_Interface. In our case, this is only the single command Start/Stop Unit, but for a more complex task, this is the place to implement the high-level function.

Error handling from the called function(s) should also be done here, because in multi-command functions, the exact place of the error might need to be checked. Because we have only one command that does the basic checking itself, we have omitted this here.

```
function LoadEjectUnit(Eject:boolean;P:P_ASPI_DevInfo ):boolean;
{ Description: Load or eject medium, depending on Eject bit
  Parameters:  Eject - If set, ejects, if not, loads
               P_ASPI_Devinfo - SCSI device record
  Returns True/False
 }
var
    errorcode : integer ;
begin
    result := ASPI_LoadEjectUnit(P^.HA,P^.ID,P^.LUN,Eject, errorcode) ;
end;
```

## Implementation of the Load/Eject Functionality in the GUI

Calling the new function is the easiest part of all—we need two new buttons in the front end, reasonably labeled **Load** and **Eject**. The ClickEvent of these buttons gets a callback procedure to call our new function LoadEjectUnit with the parameters of the device selected in the DeviceList.

```
procedure EjectButtonClick(Sender: TObject);
procedure LoadButtonClick(Sender: TObject);


implementation


procedure TForm1.LoadButtonClick(Sender: TObject);
var i:integer;
begin
  Screen.Cursor := crHourglass;
  try
```

```
    for i:=0 to ListGUIx1.items.count-1 do
      if ListGUIx1.selected[i]                  // as aGUIve, but 'start' bit
      then                                       // and 'eject' bit true
        LoadEjectUnit(false,DeviceList[i]);
  finally
    Screen.Cursor := crDefault;
  end;
end;


procedure TForm1.EjectButtonClick(Sender: TObject);
var i:integer;
begin
  for i:=0 to ListGUIx1.items.count-1 do
    if ListGUIx1.selected[i]
    then                                         // Stop Unit with 'eject' bit true
      LoadEjectUnit(true,DeviceList[i]);
end;
```

This is it — you just added a new command to your application.

As stated above, there are issues in this example program you wouldn't (and couldn't) accept in a commercial application. But basically, this is a possible way to use the ASPI interface for your own programs.

Have fun in programming, and if you extend the functionality, let us know.

# GLOSSARY

## A

**Adapter**  A card that connects the SCSI bus with the host system's bus.

**Address**  A number that refers to a specific location in memory.

**ANSI**  American National Standards Institute.

**API**(Application Program Interface)  A clearly defined set of software routines and variables that form the interface between related programs.

**ASPI**  (Advanced SCSI Programming Interface)  A software layer that allows SCSI peripheral drivers and applications to send SCSI commands to a SCSI host adapter without needing to know the details about that host adapter.

**Asynchronous SCSI**  A way of sending data over the SCSI bus. The initiator sends a command or data over the bus and then waits until it receives a reply (e.g., an ACKnowledge). All commands are sent asynchronously over the 8-bit part of the SCSI bus. Data may be transferred via either asynchronous or synchronous protocol.

## B

**Backward compatibility**  The ability of newer technology to work with older technology without any modification.

**BIOS**  (Basic Input Output System)  Software stored in ROM or other non-volatile memory in all PCs. The BIOS contains routines that allow the PC to boot from various disk devices and communicate with other vital devices, such as the keyboard and video display.

**Block**  A portion, or sector, of a disk that stores a group of bytes that must all be read or written together. Most current hard disks and operating systems use a block size of 512 bytes. CD-ROM disks have 2048-byte blocks.

**Burst speed**  The maximum speed at which data can be transferred, even if only for a very short time.

**Bus** A set of hardware signals and connections that act together to communicate between SCSI devices. Narrow (8-bit) SCSI provides a 50-pin bus; Wide SCSI uses a 68-pin bus.

**Bus mastering** A method of transferring data across a bus in which the device takes control of the bus from the CPU and performs the data transfer directly to or from memory. Most PCI cards can do this, but some motherboards only allow bus mastering in certain PCI slots.

# C

**Cache** Memory that is used as a high-speed temporary storage place for frequently used data.

**CAM** (Common Access Method) The ANSI standard for SCSI device driver and software layering. It is similar in nature and superior in capabilities to ASPI, but never received as much industry acceptance.

**CDB** (Command Descriptor Block) The bytes that form a SCSI command.

**Chain** A chain is a set of SCSI devices "daisy-chained" together to form a bus.

**Channel** A SCSI channel is a block of hardware that provides an independent SCSI bus. Some SCSI host adapters contain the hardware for two (or more) SCSI buses. Some cards provide separate bus segments that allow isolation of some devices from others and localize signal reflections. A true SCSI channel allows another entire set of SCSI IDs to be connected.

**Cluster** A group of blocks in a filesystem (most commonly FAT16 or 32) that must be used together. The term can also refer to a group of computers that share storage devices and other resources for purposes of maintaining operation even during a hardware failure in one of the systems.

**Cylinder** A collection of tracks all aligned one above the other on multiple disk platters.

# D

**Device driver** A specialized software module that communicates with and transfers data to/from a device or host adapter.

**Differential** (now called high voltage differential [HVD] to distinguish it from LVD)  Uses two wires to drive each signal. Electrically incompatible with single-ended devices! HVD uses much more expensive line driver chips than single-ended interfaces. Differential signaling is more immune to noise because the same noise is picked up on both signal wires and the differential amplifier on the input subtracts the two signals from each other, which causes the noise to be cancelled out.

**Disconnect/reconnect** (also called reselect)  This feature of the SCSI protocol allows a device to temporarily give up control of the SCSI bus. This is typically done when the device is performing an operation that will take some time. For example, it is very important for tape drives, which would otherwise lock out other devices during long operations such as Rewind.

**DLL** (Dynamic Link Library)  A Windows file that contains code that can be shared between applications.

# E

**ECC** (Error Correction Code)  A mathematical algorithm that allows for correcting small amounts of data that were read incorrectly from the disk media.

**EIDE** (Enhanced IDE) The second generation of IDE technology)  Improves the data throughput of IDE hard disks and adds the ability to support ATAPI CD-ROM drives to the same interface.

**ESDI** (Enhanced Small Disk Interface)  An enhanced version of the ST-506 disk interface that provided increased performance for disks only. Has been superseded by SCSI and IDE.

# F

**Fast SCSI**  A synchronous data transfer option, which allows up to a 10 MHz data rate on the bus. Also called Fast-10. Newer variations allow for 20 MHz (also called Ultra) and 40 MHz (Ultra2) rates.

**Filesystem**  A collection of blocks of data and the information that organizes that data so that specific data can be associated with named files. An example of a simple filesystem would be the FAT16 filesystem used by MS-DOS and Windows 95.

Examples of more sophisticated filesystems would be NTFS for Windows NT, ext2fs for Linux, and ISO-9660, used on CD-ROMs.

**Format**  How blocks (sectors) are arranged on the disk medium.

**FPT**  (Forced Perfect Termination)  A sophisticated form of active SCSI terminator that clamps the voltage level of reflected bus signals to minimize the effect of impedance mismatches.

# G

**GB**  (Gigabyte)  Two values commonly represent a gigabyte: One is the binary value of 2 to the thirtieth power or 1,073,741,824 bytes; the other is the decimal value of one billion or 1,000,000,000. Computer engineers generally use the binary meaning; sales and marketing people like the decimal value better (because it makes the disk sound bigger).

# H

**Head**  A very tiny electromagnet used for reading and writing bits on disk media. A disk drive usually has 2 to 20 of these so that data can be read or written to multiple media platters without mechanically needing to move the heads.

**Host adapter**  Also called a host bus adapter or HBA. The interface card that connects your computer's bus to the SCSI bus. Sometimes called a SCSI controller.

# I

**IDE**  (Integrated Drive Electronics)  A hard disk technology that combines the communication, control, and related circuitry on the same physical unit as the disk media. Older ST-506 technology had some of the electronics on the drive mechanism and some on a controller card.

**IEEE 1394**  An interface standard for connecting computer peripherals to a host system that uses a serial protocol (one bit at a time) rather than 8 bits at a time (as does normal SCSI). Apple called their version of this interface Firewire. SCSI-3 provides for sending SCSI commands over IEEE 1394 buses.

**IRQ** (Interrupt Request)  A computer signal used by a device to indicate that it needs the attention of the CPU. IRQs can be shared by PCI devices, but not ISA devices.

# J

**JBOD**  Acronym for Just a Bunch Of Disks. This refers to a group of disk drives that are not organized into a RAID set.

# K

**KB**  Kilobyte. 1024 bytes.

# L

**Logical Unit Number** (LUN)  A LUN is a sub-unit of a target. Most of the time, the LUN is just 0, because most types of target devices don't have sub-units. One example of where you might use LUNs is with multi-disk CD-ROM changers. Many of these units refer to each disk in the changer as a LUN. For example, with the CD-ROM drive set as target ID 4, the first CD disk would be ID 4, LUN 0, the next would be ID 4, LUN 1, and so forth. Another example is an optical disk jukebox where the optical drive might be LUN 0 and the changer might be LUN 1.

Some host adapters ignore LUNs unless the Enable LUNs option is set in the host adapter BIOS or operating system driver configuration. They default to not using LUNs because doing so speeds up the bus scan process and because most targets don't support LUNs anyway.

LUN numbers are generally defined by the manufacturer and can't be changed by the user.

**LVD** (Low Voltage Differential)  A variation on the older high voltage differential signaling used in SCSI-1 and SCSI-2. LVD has the advantage of noise immunity, yet is low in cost because its low voltage levels — and consequently lower power dissipation — allow it to be integrated into single bus-driver chips. It also has the advantage of being able to coexist with single-ended devices on the same bus segment. LVD devices detect what type of bus they're on by looking at the TERMPWR voltage.

# M

**MB** (Megabyte)  1024 kilobytes.

# N

**Nexus**  A complete SCSI address that specifies not only the SCSI ID but bus, LUN, and Queue as well. This is sometimes referred to as an I_T_L_Q nexus.

# P

**P-Cable**  A 68-pin cable used for Wide SCSI.

**Partition**  A logically separate portion of a disk. Partitions are used to allow multiple different filesystems or even operating systems to coexist on a single disk drive. Under Microsoft operating systems, partitions are created and changed by using a utility called FDISK.

**PCI** (Peripheral Component Interconnect bus)  A bus developed by Intel that allows devices to communicate efficiently with the CPU.

# R

**RAID** (Redundant Array of Independent Disks)  A set of disk drives connected in such a way as to allow certain types of access optimization or data security. This can be accomplished either in hardware using a special dual-ported SCSI adapter or completely in software in a special device driver.

A RAID 0 array stripes the data across multiple drives to decrease data latency. A RAID 1 array mirrors the data on multiple drives for increased data integrity. A RAID 5 array uses extra drives in a distributed manner to store parity information that can be used to apply data correction and recover any data in the event of any individual disk failure. This provides high reliability.

# S

**SCA, SCA-2** (Single Connector Attachment)  SCA is a standard for providing a single connector on SCSI devices that contains connections for SCSI signals, SCSI ID selection, drive options, and power. It uses an 80-pin very high density (VHD) connector. SCA devices are aimed primarily at the hot-swap RAID controller market, but adapters can be purchased that allow SCA drives to connect to regular 50-pin or 68-pin SCSI buses. These adapters bring out separate conventional connectors for the various signals and frequently provide an optional terminator. Most SCA drives do not include a terminator on board.

**Segment, bus**  A portion of a SCSI bus isolated by a signal conditioner chip. A bus segment is logically part of a single SCSI bus (e.g., SCSI IDs must be unique) but is electrically separated such that reflections on the segment do not affect other segments. Using bus segments allows longer buses because the signals are cleaned up (edges re-clocked and so on) by the signal conditioner chips. Each segment must have its own termination: one at the signal conditioner chip and one at the far end of the segment. Using a separate bus segment also allows LVD devices to be used on the same SCSI bus as regular single-ended devices.

**Single-ended**  "Normal" SCSI signals. Uses open collector drivers to drive the SCSI bus, meaning that a transistor closes the circuit from the SCSI bus signal to ground to represent an asserted signal. The terminator supplies the current to make the signal go to a high voltage to represent a de-asserted signal.

**SLED** (Single Large Expensive Disk)  The opposite of RAID.

**SSA** (Serial Storage Architecture)  An IBM serial device interface.

**Synchronous SCSI**  Rather than waiting for an ACK, a pair of devices that both support synchronous SCSI can send bytes more efficiently than single-ended devices using the following sequence:

```
send data1 : send data2 : ... : send data3 (max outstanding bytes)
: wait : wait : response1 : reponse2: ...
```

This improves throughput, especially if you use long cables. (The time that a signal spends traveling from one end of the cable to the other end of the cable is not zero.)

# T

**Target**  A device that responds to commands from the initiator.

**Terminator (active)**  In contrast to passive terminators that use TERMPWR, which may not be exactly +5 V, active terminators use a voltage regulator. An active terminator consists of a set of 110-ohm resistors, one from each SCSI signal connected to a 2.85 V regulated voltage source.

**Terminator (passive)**  A group of resistors on the physical ends of a single-ended SCSI bus (and only on these ends) that dampens reflected signals from the ends of the bus. Each terminated signal is connected by a 220-ohm resistor to TERMPWR and by a 330-ohm resistor to ground.

**TERMPWR** (Terminator power)  One of the signals present on all SCSI buses. Supplies current to the terminators at the ends of the SCSI bus. The host adapter is normally responsible for supplying TERMPWR, but other devices may supply it as well.

**Track**  A ring of blocks (sectors) on a disk.

**Twisted pair**  A type of transmission line used for sending electrical signals across a SCSI bus. It is NOT two people who are into kinky stuff. :-)

# U

**UltraSCSI**  Synchronous data transfer option, which allows up to a 20 MHz data rate on the bus. Also called Fast-20.

**Ultra2 SCSI**  Synchronous data transfer option, which allows up to a 40 MHz data rate on the bus. Also called Fast-40. Use of this option also requires the use of LVD bus drivers.

**Ultra160 SCSI**  Synchronous data transfer option, which allows up to an 80 MHz data rate on the bus. Also called Fast-80. The 160 refers to the fact that, because this option also assumes a Wide SCSI bus, you will get a 160 MB/sec maximum transfer rate. Use of this option also requires the use of LVD bus drivers.

# W

**Wide SCSI** Uses a 68-pin P-cable (which contains an extra 8 data bits and an extra parity bit) to send the data 16 bits at a time as opposed to regular narrow SCSI, which only sends data 8 bits at a time (over a 50-pin cable), thus doubling data transfer speed over the SCSI bus.

# X

**X3T10** The former name for the ANSI technical committee responsible for organizing, realizing, and promoting the SCSI standards. The new name is simply T10.

# INDEX

*Italic page numbers indicate an illustration or chart.*

**A**

Abort command, 218, 259, 302
ABORT message, 166
A-cable, 85, 89, 132
  50-pin Centronics-style connectors, 319, 327–*328*
  50-pin high-density connectors, 319, 328, *329*
  50-pin IDC header connectors, 319, 321, 322
  adapter, 96
ACKQ signal, *343*
ACK signal, *137*, 155, 342. *See also* REQ/ACK handshake
active negation, 315
  and FPT, 357
active termination, 45, 47, 355–356
  vs. passive termination, 112
active terminators
  detecting presence of, *116*n
  on differential buses, 46
  features of, 184–185
  measuring the number of, 117
  vs. passive terminators, 112–113, 115, 117
  when to use, 45
Adaptec
  corporate acquisitions, 309–310
  drivers. *See* ASPI drivers
  FTP site with ASPI information, 206
  host adapters, 303–304, 308
adapter cards. *See* host adapters
adapter device drivers (ADDs) for OS/2 2.x, 281
adapters, 40, 42. *See also* connectors
  for 68-pin external SCSI cable connectors, 42
  IBM PS/2, 91
  multi-channel, 371
  P to A transition, 96
  for SCA drives, 91

on single-ended SCSI buses, 182
.add files, 76
add-on cards for the PC. *See* peripheral controllers
addresses
  ASPI HA/ID/LUN (address) triples, 271
  of devices. *See* SCSI IDs
  Logical Block, 160–161
ADDs (adapter device drivers) for OS/2 2.x, 281
AGP bus, 57
Alternative-1 and -2 termination, 184
ANSI (American National Standards Institute), 4
  standards for SCSI, 32, 176
  T10 Technical Committee, 25, 29, 176
Apple Computer
  25-pin SCSI cable connectors, 90
  25-pin Sub-D connectors, 320, 333–*335, 338*, 339
  Firewire. *See* IEEE 1394
  Powerbook 30-pin HDI connectors, 91, 320, 335–*336*
applications
  ASPI demo, 375–387
  using SCSI to develop, 373
ARBITRATION phase, *138, 143*, 145, 149, *343*, 345
  followed by RESELECTION and MESSAGE IN phases, *349*
  followed by SELECTION phase, *349*
ASPI, 69, 172
  demo applications, 375–387
  for DOS, 207–220
  for DOS under Windows 3.x, 220–221
  meaning of, 205
  for NetWare, 292–305
  for OS/2, 279–292
  programming with, 205
  R/W notation for column headings, 207
  SCSI command linking with, 215–216
  for Windows, 221–*242*

for Windows (*continued*)
  for Windows (Win32), 243–*279*
ASPIAPP, 282
AspiApplication.pas, 376, 386
ASPI Command Codes for DOS,
  *210*, 211–220
  0: Host Adapter Inquiry, 211–*212*
  1: Get Device Type, 212–*213*
  2: Execute SCSI I/O Command,
    213–215
  3: Abort I/O Command, 217–218
  4: Reset SCSI Device, 218
  5: Set Host Adapter Parameters, 219
  6: Get Disk Drive Information,
    219–*220*
ASPI Command Codes for NetWare,
  *295*, 296–*303*
  0: Host Adapter Inquiry, 296
  1: Get Device Type, 297
  2: Execute SCSI I/O Command, 297,
    *298*–301
  3: Abort SCSI I/O Command,
    301–302
  4: Reset SCSI Device, 302
  5: Set Host Adapter Parameters,
    303, *303*
ASPI Command Codes for OS/2 2.*x*,
  *283*, 284–292
  0: Host Adapter Inquiry, 284–285
  1: Get Device Type, 285–286
  2: Execute SCSI I/O Command,
    286–290
  3: Abort SCSI I/O Request,
    290, 291
  4: Abort SCSI I/O Request,
    291, 292
  5: Set Host Adapter Parameters, 292
ASPI Command Codes for Windows.
  *See* SendASPICommand
ASPI Command Codes for Windows
  (Win32). *See* SendASPI32Command
ASPI command posting. *See* posting
ASPI drivers, 71–72
  combining, 122
  components of, 205
  for DOS, 207–208. *See also* ASPI
    managers for DOS
  loading in config.sys files,121, 173

for Windows 3.1, 73
for Windows NT, 176
ASPIDRV, 282
ASPI_Entry, 293–294
ASPI functions, calling, 245–247
ASPI HA/ID/LUN (address) triples,
  271
ASPI Host Adapter Number field of
  SRBs, 211
ASPI_Interface.pas, 376, 382–387
ASPI_Load/EjectUnit, 384–387
ASPI managers, 205–206
  support for residual byte length, 252,
    305–308
ASPI managers for DOS
  calling, 209–210
  stack needed by, 207
ASPI managers for NetWare
  handling of more than 16 MB,
    303–305
  scans for new devices, 305
ASPI managers for Windows, 222
ASPI modules, 205, 206, 245
ASPIPostProc, 239
ASPI program for communication
  with SCSI device, 377–381
ASPI Software Developer's Kit (SDK),
  206–207, 282
ASPI_StartStopUnit, 380, 382
ASPI Status Byte field of SRBs, 211
  polling, 238
ASPI-to-CAM translation drivers, 73
asynchronous data transfer, 50–51
  four steps for, 167
  handshaking method, 167–168
  timing diagram of, *350*
asynchronous data transfer rates,
  6, 167
asynchronous SRBs, 249–250, 273–276
ATA (advanced technology attachment), 3
  hard drives, 192
  I/O ports for, *360*
  maximum cable length, 370–371
  vs. SCSI, *10*, 367–373
ATAPI (ATA Packet Interface), 3,
  31, 368
ATN signal, *136*, 156, 342

ATTENTION condition, 344–345
audio data recording, 19
audio/video applications, 30
autoexec.bat file, safeguarding
  your, 77

# B

backplane cases, 101, 324
backups. *See also* RAID systems
  off-site Fibre Channel, 12
  separated geographically, 311–312
B-cable, 132, 133, 337
BIOS on host adapter cards, 60, 78, 111
BIOS (PC)
  calls and functions, 172
  defined, 172
  extending, 79
  option for hardware conflicts, 119
  printing settings in, 77
  troubleshooting, 107
bits
  Direction, 214, 243
  Disconnect Privilege, 147
  Eject, 382
  ID, 130
  Link, 214
  Most and Least Significant, 134
  NACA, 166
  parity, 49
  Post, 214
  S/G (scatter/gather), 308
  Start, 382
block striping, 192–*193*
  with distributed parity, 196, *197*
  with parity, 195–196
  with two distributed parities, 197
block-type drivers (Unix), 176
bootable floppy disks
  creating, 78
  FAT32 filesystems and, 79
bootup problems, troubleshooting,
  110–112. *See also* BIOS (PC)
BSY signal, *136*, 155, 342
bus. *See also* SCSI bus
  architectures, 56–57
  control signals, 135, *143*
  defined, 1

BUS DEVICE RESET
  message, 159, 166
  Windows 95/NT and, 263
BUS FREE phase, *138, 143*, 146, 155,
  *343*, 345
  preceded by MESSAGE IN phase, *351*
bus mastering SCSI controllers, 66
BUS RESET message, 166
bus slots
  defined, 2
  and DMA transfer speeds, 67
  and SCSI, 14
buttons
  Load and Eject, 386–387
  Start and Stop, 379
byte packing, 244

# C

cables. *See also* A-cable; B-cable;
  L-cable; P-cable; Q-cable;
  terminators
  choosing, 84, 85, 183–184, 187
  connecting, 92–93, 182
  diagram of, for SCSI-1, SCSI-2, and
    SCSI-3, *134*
  differential SCSI, 37, *38*, 40, 187
  electrical specs for all, 317–319
  evolution of SCSI, 132–133, *134*
  extending distance of, 37, 60, 86
  external, 40, 88–*89*
  Fast SCSI-2, 6
  flat ribbon, 40, 87–*88*
  HVD SCSI, 187
  icons on, 313, *314*
  IDE, 12
  IEEE 1394, 21, 30
  impedances, 183
  internal, 40, 87–88
  length, importance of, 36, 84
  length vs. ATA cables, 370–371
  lengths to use, 86, *87*
  LVD SCSI, 40
  mixing, 182–183
  narrow, 40, 42
  number of pins, 40
  for printers, 21
  quality, importance of, 84

reference table for, *41*
SCSI-3, 6, 8
SCSI-3 32-bit, 40
single-ended SCSI, 37, *38*
specs, 40
Teflon, 318–319
transceiver specs and lengths of, 180–181
troubleshooting, 118
twisted-pair ribbon, *88*
Ultra2, 27
wide, 40, 42
Y-shaped, 91
caching host adapter cards, 57–59
callbacks. *See* posting
CAM (Common Access Method), 69–70
CAM (Common Access Method) drivers, 72–73
ASPI-to-CAM translation, 73
loading in config.sys files, 121
XPT transport function, 176
CAM (Common Access Method) systems (Unix), 177
camcorders, 310
capacitance, 182
capacity of storage devices, 15
hard drives, 16
CDBs (command descriptor blocks), 160
6-byte, *160*–161
10-byte, *161*–162
12-byte, 162
device driver that loads, 173
nonstandard lengths of, 230
CD burners, 19–20
CD-ROM drives, 19
16-bit Wide SCSI, 181
installing, 78
on non-SCSI interfaces, 3
SCSI IDs, assigning, 100
swapping, between platforms, 11
CD-ROM recorders (CD-R and CD-RW), 19–20
C/D signal, *136*, 155, 156, 342, 344
Centronics-style connectors, 319, *327–328*, 336
channels
number of devices permitted on, 371

character drivers (Unix), 176
CHECK CONDITION status, 165–166
Classic interface. *See* HVD (High Voltage Differential)
CLEAR ACA message, 166
color depth, 21
colored books, 19
command codes for DOS drivers, 173
Command Complete message, 345
command descriptor blocks. *See* CDBs (command descriptor blocks)
COMMAND OUT phase, *139, 143*
COMMAND phase, 151, 152, 160–164, 167, *343–344*, 345, 346
preceded by MESSAGE OUT phase, *350*
commands. *See also* ASPI Command Codes; SRBs (SCSI request blocks)
6-byte, *160*–161
10-byte, *161*–162
12-byte, 162
Abort, 218, 259, 302
for direct-access devices, *163–164*
executing, sequential vs. concurrent, 370
MODE SELECT, 161
the nature of SCSI, 126
REQUEST SENSE, 166
residual byte length of, 252, 305
Start, 377, 379–380
Stop, 377, 379–380
TEST UNIT READY, 345–*346*
command sets
defined, 24
SCSI-3, 31
COMMAND TERMINATED status, 166
communication among SCSI devices, 50–53. *See also* I/O processes
computers
lockups and communication errors, 112–113
SCSI drives for Macintoshes, 11
SCSI drives for PCs, 11
that support SCSI, IDE, ATA, EIDE, and UDMA, 9–11
conductors in external SCSI cables, 85

config.sys file
  examples of, 71, 72, 73, 120, 121
  loading drivers in, 173
  safeguarding, 77
connect, 145–147
connectors, 40–42. *See also* adapters
  25-pin external SCSI cable, 90, 91
  25-pin Sub-D, 320, 333–*335*,
    *338*, 339
  25-pin Sub-D (Future Domain), 320,
    337–339
  30-pin HDI (Apple), 320, 335–*336*
  37-pin Sub-D (Novell and Procomp
    DCB), 320, 340–*341*
  50-pin Centronics-style, 319, 327–*328*
  50-pin external SCSI cable, 90, 91
  50-pin high-density, 319, 328, *329*
  50-pin IDC header, I, 319, 321, 322
  50-pin Sub-D (Sun Microsystems), 320,
    339–*340*
  60-pin high-density Centronics-style,
    336
  68-pin external SCSI cable, 90, 91
  68-pin high-density, 319, 329, *330, 331*
  68-pin high-density Sub-D
    (B-cable), 320, 337
  68-pin internal SCSI cable, 90
  68-pin VHDCI, 320, 332–*333, 334*
  68-pin Wide SCSI P- and Q-cable, 319,
    322, *323, 324*
  80-pin SCA, 42, 91, 101
  80-pin Wide SCSI SCA-2, 319,
    324–*325, 326*
  electrical specs for, 319–341
  external SCSI cable, 88
  high-density, 322
  host adapter cards with multiple, 60
  icons on, 313, *314*
  identifying, 89–91
  internal SCSI cable, 90
  quality, importance of, 84
  shrouded header, 104
  troubleshooting, 104, 119
Contingent Allegiance Condition, 166
Control Byte field of CDBs, 161
controller cards. *See also* host adapters
  defined, 2
  internal and external RAID, 202–203
  for peripherals, 65–68, 126

control signals, data bus, *134*, 135,
  *136–137*
corporate acquisitions by computer
  manufacturers, 309–310
cost of SCSI, IDE, ATA, EIDE, and
  UDMA, *10*, 12, 13–14
CPU load, SCSI vs. ATA, 372
CRC (Cyclic Redundancy Check)
  protection, 26, 28, 50


## D

daisy chain, 91, *92, 93,* 94
data
  copying, among hard drives, 34
  protection. *See* backups; RAID
  protocol for storage of, 312
  reliability problems, 181
data bus
  contents of, *154*
  signals, 134–135
  transferring information across the,
    166–170
data clock signals, 135
DATA IN phase, 153, *350,* 351
DATA OUT phase, *139, 143,* 153, *350,*
  *351*
DATA phase, 167, 343–*344,* 345
data storage. *See* backups
data striping. *See* striping
data transfer. *See also* SCSI bus phase
  sequence
  diagram of, *128*
  high-speed, using DMA, 65–66, 67–68
  large, with ASPI for OS/2 2x, 282
  large, on NetWare networks, 303–305
  large, on Win32 systems, 269–270
  maximum length of, 308
  methods of, 66
data transfer rates. *See also* asynchronous
  data transfer rates; synchronous data
  transfer rates
  defined, 2
  vs. real data rates, 189
  of SCSI-1 devices, 4
  of SCSI-3 devices, 8
  of SCSI, IDE, ATA, EIDE, and UDMA,
    *10*, 12

data transfer rates (*continued*)
of SCSI vs. ATA, 368–*369*
serial vs. parallel, 8
data types for ASPI for Win32, *244*
DAT tapes, 17
DB(0) to DB(7), 342
DB(8) to DB(15), 342
DB(16) to DB(31), *343*
DB(P) and DB (P1), 342
DB(P2) and DB(P3), *343*
DDBs (device descriptor blocks), 174
DDS and DDS-2 tapes, 17
definition file, NetWare, 292–293
development, using SCSI for
applications, 373
Device Bay, 311
device code, 139
device controllers, 2
and SCSI, 3
device descriptor blocks (DDBs), 174
device drivers. *See also* SCSI drivers
block-type and character, 176
conflicts caused by, 111, 363–366
defined, 68, 171
device-specific, 71
for SCSI-3 serial devices, 9
SCSIport, 175, 176
tape class NT, 176
troubleshooting, 119–122
type-specific, 175
virtual (.vxd), 174, 175
device independence, 369–370
DeviceList, 377, 379
device manager drivers (DMDs) for
OS/2 2.*x*, 281
devices. *See also* SCSI devices
defined, 2
external, 11–12
parallel and serial, 4
support for, by SCSI, IDE, ATA,
EIDE, and UDMA, *10*, 11
DEVNODEs, 271–273
differential RS-485 transceivers, 180
differential SCSI bus, 36, 37, 39
cables, *38*, 87
terminators, 46, 48
differential SCSI interfaces, 315,
*316*–317. *See also* HVD (High Voltage
Differential); LVD (low voltage differential)

DIFFSENS, 316
Digital Audio Tape (DAT), 17
digital cameras, 310
Digital Linear Tape (DLT), 18
direct-access (SCSI) devices commands,
*163–164*
Direction bit, 214, 243
direct memory access. *See* DMA
(direct memory access)
Disaster Tolerant Disk Systems, 202
disconnect, 147–148. *See also* discon-
nect/reconnect
Disconnect message, 148
Disconnect Privilege bit, 147
disconnect/reconnect, 51–53
sequence, 151
disk spanning, 193
.dll (dynamic link library) files, 174
DLT (Digital Linear Tape), 18
DMA
for high-speed data transfer, 65–66,
67–68
rates, 57
DMA channels, setting, 67–68
DMA channel usage, *363*
DMA transfer speeds, setting, 67
DMDs (device manager drivers) for
OS/2 2.*x*, 281
Domain Validation feature
(SCSI-3), 28
DOS, ASPI for, 207–220
DOS memory managers and SCSI,
111, 121
DOS Protected Mode Interface
Specification, 220
DOS SCSI drivers, 70–73, 173
troubleshooting, 120–121
double-caching, 59
drives. *See also* CD-ROM drives; hard
drives
letters for, assigned by DOS, *80*
optical disk, 18–20
removable media disk (zip), 16, 17
SCSI command flags for, *264*
tape, 17–18
DT (double-transition) clocking,
26, 28
dual host adapter cards, 60
duplexing, 193–*194*
DVD, Windows 98 support for, 174

DVD-ROM drives, 20
dynamic linking (Windows 95/NT),
    245–247
dynamic link library (dll) files, 174

# E

8mm tapes, 18
ECC (error correction code), 194
EDAP (extended data availability and
    protection), 200–202
EIDE (Enhanced IDE)
    defined, 3
    hard drives, 16
    history of, 368
    vs. SCSI, *10*, 53
EISA boards, I/O ports for, *361*
EISA bus, 56
Eject bit, 382
elevator seeking, 370
Enhanced IDE. *See* EIDE (Enhanced
    IDE)
error checking. *See* parity checking
error detection by SCSI, IDE, ATA,
    EIDE, and UDMA, *10*, 12
error messages
    ASPI for Windows, *242*
    examples of, 105–113, 115
    handling, 103
errors. *See also* RAID; trouble-
    shooting
    ASPI for Win32, 276–*279*
    indicated by CHECK CONDITION,
        165–166
    while loading NLMs, 293
    and speed, 180–181
ESDI, 4,
event notification, 273–274
    with timeouts, 268
ExecSCSICmd Structure Definition,
    *228–230*
expanders, 86
explicit dynamic linking, 245–246
extended contingent allegiance condi-
    tion, 166
extended data availability and
    protection (EDA), 200–202

Extended Host Adapter Inquiry
    command, 305, *306*–308
extended messages, 156
external cables, 40, 88–*89*, 183
    buying, 85
    electrical specs, 318–319
    troubleshooting, 118
external connectors, 90–91. *See also*
    shielded connectors
external devices
    ATA, 371
    data errors using, 318
    SCSI vs. USB, 373
    support for, by SCSI, IDE, ATA, EIDE,
        and UDMA, *10*, 11–12
    terminating, 352–*353*
    typical terminator for, *98*

# F

failures. *See* RAID
false signals, 181
Fast-10 SCSI, 25
Fast-20 SCSI, 7, 25, 27
Fast-40 host adapter cards, 61–62
Fast-40 SCSI, 7
Fast-80 SCSI, 8
Fast SCSI, 25
    cables for, 84
    cable length for, 86
    single-ended interface with, 181
Fast SCSI-2, 5, 6
    cables for, 84
Fast synchronous transfer rates, 169–170
Fast Wide SCSI, 7
FAT filesystems, 79, *80*, 81
FC-AL. *See* Fibre Channel: Arbitrated
    Loop (FC-AL)
female connectors, 89
Fibre Channel, 8, 9, 10, 29, 30
    an alternative to, 30
    Arbitrated Loop (FC-AL), 11, 29, 30
    interface types, 311
    for off-site backups, 12
    over long distances, 24
    storage area networks (SANs) and, 312
Firewire. *See* IEEE 1394
firmware, 139

first-party DMA, 66
fixed disks, 16
flat ribbon cable, 40, 87–*88*
.flt files, 76
FPT (forced perfect termination), 46, 47, 357
FreeASPI32Buffer, *245*, 270–271
FTP sites, Adaptec's, 206
Future Domain 25-pin Sub-D connectors, 320, 337-339

## G

games, using SCSI for, 372
GB (gigabyte), defined, 392
GetASPI32Buffer, *245*, 269-270
GetASPI32SupportInfo, *245*, 247-248
GetASPISupportInfo, 221, 222-223
GetDeviceList, 379
GetHAInfos, 378-379
GetProcAddress, 246
gigabyte (GB), defined, 392
graphics, using SCSI for, 373

## H

HAList, 377
HAListBoxClick, 378–379
handshake, SCSI, 126, 166–170. *See also* REQ/ACK handshake
hard disks. *See* hard drives
hard drive interfaces, 3. *See also* EIDE (Enhanced IDE); IDE (Integrated Drive Electronics); SCSI interface
hard drives. *See also* RAID; SCSI hard drives
  ATA (advanced technology attachment), 192
  choosing, 15, 16
  EIDE (Enhanced IDE), 16
  IDE (Integrated Drive Electronics), 11, 16
  letters for, assigned by DOS, 80
  magneto-optical disk advantages over, 19
  mirrored or duplexed, 193–*194*

mixing SCSI and non-SCSI, 61
  USB (Universal Serial Bus), 31
hardware caching, 58–59
hardware interfaces
  defined, 2
  SCSI impact on, 3
hardware interrupts. *See* IRQs (interrupt requests)
HASTAT_BUS_FREE, *257*
HASTAT_BUS_RESET, *257*
HASTAT_COMMAND_TIMEOUT, *257*
HASTAT_DO_DU, *257*
HASTAT_MESSAGE_REJECT, *257*
HASTAT_OK, *257*
HASTAT_PARITY_ERROR, *257*
HASTAT_PHASE_FREE, *257*
HASTAT_REQUEST_SENSE_FAILED, *257*
HASTAT_SEL_TO, 244
HASTAT_TIMEOUT, *257*
HBAs. *See* host adapters
HDI-30 connectors (Apple), 320, 335–*336*
Hi-9 termination, 42
HIBYTE, 222–*223*
high-density external SCSI cable connectors, 90, 91
high-density IBM 60-pin Centronics-style connectors, 336
high-density Sub-D connectors, 319, 328, *329*
  68-pin B-cable, 320, 337
  for P- and Q- cables, 319, 329, *330, 331*
High Sierra format, 19
Host Adapter Inquiry command, 305, *306*
host adapters, *93*
  Adaptec bus master ISA, 304
  ASPI manager for, 205–206
  BIOS on, 60, 78, 111
  built into the motherboard, 57
  caching by, 57–59
  choosing, 55, 57, 61, 310
  configuring, 8, 62–68
  cost of, 13
  defined, 2
  dual, 60
  EISA, 304

Fast-40, 61–62
fuses, 110
as initiators, 127
installing, 13
IRQs (interrupts), lacking, 64
multiple connectors, using, 60
with other disk controllers, 61
parameters under Win32, *251–252*
PCI, 304
PCMCIA laptop, 44
as SCSI analyzers, 365
setting IDs on, 68, 130
specific drivers for, 71
status reports for, 215
status reports for Win32, 257
terminating, 95–96, *97*
troubleshooting, 105–107, 110, 111
two-channel, 317
host bus adapters. *See* host adapters
host devices, 33
HVD (High Voltage Differential)
cable for, 187
devices, 37, 39
electrical specs, 315–316
icon, *314*
vs. LVD (low voltage differential), 39
maximum length of bus, *87*
terminators, 46, *48*, 53

## I

IBM. *See also* SSA (serial storage architecture)
SCSI adapter cable for PS/2, 91
SCSI connectors, 333, 336
icons, SCSI interface, 313, *314*
ID bit, 130
IDC header connector, 319, 321, 322
IDE (Integrated Drive Electronics). *See also* EIDE (Enhanced IDE)
defined, 3
error reduction technique, 12
hard drives, 11, 16
history of, 368
vs. SCSI, *10*, 53, 367–373
Identify message, 147, 150
and LUNs, 160
IEEE 1394, 8, 30, 310

cables, 30
with USB, 311
I.Link. *See* IEEE 1394
image scanners, 21
impedance, 43
implicit dynamic linking, 247
InfiniBand interface, 31
information transfer control signals, 135, *143*
information transfer phases, 151–155, 343–*344*
command phase and code descriptions, 160–164
control signals, *344*
message phase and code descriptions, 155–159
status phase and code descriptions, 164–166
INITIATE RECOVERY message, 166
initiator devices, 33–34, *36*, 126, 129–130
control signals driven by, *135*
information transfer phases of, *153*
synchronous data transfer, 158–159
Inquiry command, 213, 377
INT 13 extensions, 78
Int 13h, 219, 220
Windows NT and, 263
interface cards. *See* host adapters
interfaces. *See also* ASPI; SCSI interface
defined, 2
intelligent, 3, 125
interlocked, 127
internal cables, 40, 87–*88*
buying, 85
colored stripe on, 92
commonly used, 183
connectors on, 90
electrical specs, 317
troubleshooting, 118
internal connectors. *See* unshielded connectors
internal devices
converting, into external devices, 91
data errors using, 318
terminating, 352–*353*
typical terminator for, *97*
Internet resources
Adaptec's FTP site, 206

Internet resources (*continued*)
  Usenet newsgroups for SCSI, 61, 77, 367, 370
  *See also* Web sites
interrupts. *See* IRQs (interrupt requests)
I/O (input/output) overlapping, 370
I/O ports, 62–63
  usage, *360–361*
I/O processes
  bus operations, 143
  defined, 127, *128*, 129
  disconnect/reconnect effect on, 151, *152*
  DOS handling of, 173
  SCSI device control of, 147
  sending multiple, 150
  Win32 handling of, 248–250
I/O signal, *136*, 155, 156, 342, 344, *344*
IRQs (interrupt requests)
  conflicts, 65
  defined, 393
  the devices that use particular, *361–362*
  freeing for use, 60
  IRQs 2 and 9, 64
  IRQs 10, 11, and 15, 65
  IRQs 14 and 15, 371
  PCI cards and, 62
  and SCSI, 14
  setting, 63–65
  sharing, 65
ISA (industry standard architecture) bus, 56
ISA Plug-and-Play configuration, 362
  I/O ports for, *360*
ISA slots, 2. *See also* PCI slots
isochronous services, 30
I_T_L nexus, 145
  creating, *146*
  establishing, 147
  reestablishing, 140
I_T_L_Q nexus, 145, 150

J

jumpers
  setting SCSI IDs with, 130, *131*
  TP, 98

L

LADDR (layered device driver), 76
laptops
  Apple PowerBook connectors, 91, 320, 335–*336*
  NT drivers for, 175
  SCSI devices and, 44
layered drivers, 69–70, 76
layered programs, 376–377
L-cable, 337
Least Significant Bit (LSB), 134
LEDs on SCSI sniffers, *123*
Link bit, 214
Linux SCSI drivers, 77
Listbox, 379
load/eject ASPI application, 382–387
LoadEjectUnit, 386
LOBYTE, 222
Logical Block Address field of CDBs, 160–161
Logical Unit Number field of CDBs, 160
Logical Unit Numbers (LUNs), 24, 147
logical units, 126
logos, SCSI interface, 313, *314*
Loop Resiliency Circuits (LRC), 29
low-level drivers, 69, 71
low voltage differential. *See* LVD (low voltage differential)
LRC (Loop Resiliency Circuits), 29
LSB (Least Significant Bit), 134
LUNs (Logical Unit Numbers), 35
  specifying, 147
LVD (low voltage differential), 27
  cables for, 40
  devices, 37, 39, 46, 60
  electrical specs, 316–317

Fast-40 (Ultra2) host adapter, 62
icon, *314*
maximum length of bus, *87*
terminators, 46, 53
transceivers, 180–181
LVD/SE SCSI icon, *314*

## M

Macintosh computers, SCSI drives
for, 11
Magneto-Optical (MO) drives, 18–19
male connectors, 89
manufacturers
computer industry, transitory nature
of, 309–310
of SCSI analyzers, 366
MAX_HA_ID, 254
MAX_TARGET_ID, 254
MB/sec (megabytes per second), 2
MCA (micro-channel architecture)
bus, 56
mechanical latency, 147
media trays, program to load or eject,
382–387
megabytes per second (MB/sec), 2
MESSAGE IN phase, *139, 143*, 148, 150,
153, 156, 345
followed by BUS FREE phase, *351*
preceded by ARBITRATION and
RESELECTION phases, *349*
MESSAGE OUT phase, *138*, 146–147,
153, 155, 156, 345
followed by COMMAND
phase, *350*
MESSAGE phase, 155–159, 167,
343–*344*, 345
messages, 156, *157*–158
ABORT, 166
BUS DEVICE RESET, 159, 166
BUS RESET, 166
CLEAR ACA, 166
Disconnect, 148
extended, 156
Identify, 147, 150
INITIATE RECOVERY, 166
Queue Tag, 150
RELEASE RECOVERY, 166
Save Data Pointer, 148

single-byte, 156
terminating a STATUS phase, 164
Microsoft
Diagnostics (mscdex.exe), 86
SCAM (SCSI Configured
"AutoMagically"), 8
support for SCSI, 13
Miniport drivers, 69, 175
mirroring, 193–*194*
MMC-2 (Multimedia Commands), 31
MODE SELECT command, 161
MO (Magneto-Optical) drives, 18–19
Most Significant Bit (MSB), 134
MPD (Miniport drivers), 69, 175
MSB (Most Significant Bit), 134
mscdex.exe, 78
msd.exe, 65
MSDOS. *See* DOS entries
MSG signal, *137*, 155, 156, 342,
344, *344*
multi-channel adapters, 371
multimedia applications, 30
multitasking
activities requiring, 373
with ASPI for Windows, 241
defined, 2
disconnect/reconnect and, 52–53, 144
pre-emptive, 174
by SCSI vs. ATA, 369–370
by SCSI, IDE, ATA, EIDE, and UDMA,
*10*, 12
with Windows 3.*x*, 174
with Windows NT, 175
multithreaded operating systems, 30
Windows NT, 175
music CDs, 19

## N

NACA bit, 166
narrow SCSI, 25. *See also* Wide SCSI
narrow SCSI devices
mixing with Wide SCSI devices,
353–354
setting IDs for, 130
NetWare Loadable Modules (NLMs),
293
networks. *See also* RAID
host adapter cards for, 59

networks (*continued*)
    SCSI on small, advantages of, 371
    storage area, 311–312
newsgroups, 61, 77, 367, 370
nexus. *See also* I_T_L nexus; I_T_L_Q nexus
    forming, with SCSI IDs, *146*
NLMs (NetWare Loadable Modules), 293
noise problems, 181
No Starch Press Web site, 375
notebook computers. *See* laptops
Novell
    connectors, 320, 340–*341*
    NLMS (NetWare Loadable Modules), 21

## O

object file, NetWare, 292, 293
obsolete connectors, 320, 337–341
odd parity checking, *49*
operating systems
    copying data among drives, 34
    multitasking by, 2, 53
    and software caching, 58
    and spatial reuse, 30
    support for device independence and I/O overlapping, 370
    support for SCSI, 11, 13
    that SCSI is recommended for, 373
Operation Code field of CDBs, 160
optical disk drives, 18–20
OS/2. *See also* ASPI: for OS/2
    SCSI drivers, 76
    Warp, 13
os2aspi.dmd, 281, 282
os2dasd.dmd, 281
os2scsi.dmd, 281
oscilloscope, 123–124
    signal, view of, *124*
overlapping I/O, 370

## P

packetized protocol feature (SPI-3), 27, 28
page-locked memory, 243
parallel devices, 4
parallel SCSI-3 interfaces, 27–29, 310, 313
parity bit, 49
parity checking, 48–50
    using, 100–101
parity data bus signal, 135
parity errors, recovery from, 156
partitioning a SCSI hard drive, 79–81
passive termination, 45, 184, 354, *355*
    problems with, 112
passive terminators
    vs. active terminators, 112–113, 115, 117
    on differential bus, 46
    measuring the number of, 116
    problems with, 45
P-cable, 85, 89, 132, 133
    adapter, 96
    shielded connectors, 319, 329, *330*
    unshielded connectors, 319, 322, *323*
    VHDCI connectors, 320, 332, *334*
PC computers, SCSI drives for, 11
PCI boards
    configuration, 362
    I/O ports for, *361*
PCI bus, 57
PCI slots, 8, 13
    defined, 2
PCI-type host adapters, 62, 304
PCMCIA host adapters, 44
performance tuning, 179–189
    with caching host adapter cards, 57–59
    with DMA, 65–68
peripheral controllers, 65, 126, 359–362
peripherals. *See* devices
phases. *See* SCSI bus phases
pin 1 on internal SCSI cable connectors, 92–93

PIO (programmed I/O), 66–67
Plug and Play
  ASPI use of, 271–273
  impact on SCSI, 8
  ISA, *360*, 362
  PCI's advantages, 13
  troubleshooting, 119–120
polling, 64, 238, 275–276, 380–382
port addresses, setting, 62–63
Post bit, 214, 216–217
posting, 216–217, 239, 274–275, 382
  with ASPI for Win32, 243
  for NetWare, 300–301
PostMessage, 241
power supplies, 117
printers, 21
priority on the SCSI bus, 99–100,
  130, *131*
problem-solving. *See* troubleshooting
Procomp connectors, 320, 340–*341*
programmed input/output, 66–67
programming, SCSI for, 373
proprietary SCSI connectors, 333–337
protocol layers, SCSI bus, 137, *138–139*
protocol phases, SCSI bus, *343*
protocols
  defined, 139
  synchronous negotiation, example of,
    158–*159*
  tagged command queuing, *150*
  two sequences of, for a disconnect,
    147–148
PS/2 computers, 336

## Q

QAS (quick arbitrate and selection), 26,
  27
Q-cable, 89, 130, 132, 133
  shielded connectors, 319, 329, *331*
  unshielded connectors, 319,
    322, *324*
  VHDCI connectors, 320, 332–*333*, *334*
QIC (quarter-inch cartridge) tapes, 17
Queue Tag message, 150

## R

RAID
  fault tolerance, 200–202
  implementations of, 202–203
  meaning of, 191
  name games with, 192
RAID Advisory Board (RAB), 199
RAID levels, 191
  level 0, block striping, 188, 192–193
  level 1, mirroring or duplexing,
    193–*194*
  level 2, striping with ECC (error
    correction code), 194
  level 3, byte striping with
    parity, 195
  level 4, block striping with parity drive,
    195–196
  level 5, block striping with distributed
    parity, 196, *197*
  level 6, block striping with two distrib-
    uted parities, 197
  level 10 (0 + 1), mirrored striping
    array, 198, *199*
RAID systems, 35
  RAID 7 proprietary systems,
    192, 198
RBC (Reduced Block Commands), 31
read caching, 56
reconnect, 149–150
  sequence, *151*
red stripe on cables, 87
RELEASE RECOVERY message, 166
removable media hard disk drives, 16, 17
repeaters, 86
REQ/ACK handshake, 155, *156*, 167,
  168, 344
REQQ signal, 343
REQ signal, *137*, 155, 342
REQUEST SENSE command, 166
rescue disks
  creating, 78
  and FAT filesystems, 79
reselect. *See* disconnect/reconnect
RESELECTION phase, *139, 143,* 149,
  *343*, 345

RESELECTION phase (*continued*)
with ARBITRATION and
MESSAGE IN phases, *349*
RESET condition, 344, 345
residual byte length, 252, 305
using, 308
ribbon cable, 87
connecting with round cable, 318
cross-talk rejection by, 183
rotational latency, 16
round cable, 88–*89*
connecting with ribbon cable, 318
cross-section of, *318*
using internally, 183
RS/6000 computers, 336
RST signal, *136*, 342, 345

# S

SANs (storage area networks),
311–312
SASI (Shugart Associates Systems
Interface), 3
Save Data Pointer message sequence,
148
SCA
adapters, 42, 91, 326
backplane cases, 101
LVD drives, 326
SCA-2
connectors, 319, 324–*325*, *326*
SCAM (SCSI Configured
"AutoMagically"), 8
scanners, 21
SCSI-3 command sets for, 31
SCSI vs. USB, 373
SCC and SCC-2, 31
SCSI. *See also* SCSI-1; SCSI-2; SCSI-3
benefits and pitfalls of, 9–14
birth of, 3–4
Common Command Set (CCS), 4–5
Configured "AutoMagically"
(SCAM), 8
features chart, *10*
meaning of, 4
operating systems supporting, 11
pronouncing, 1

resources about. *See* Internet
resources
serial versions of, 7, 29–31, 166
speed of, 12
SCSI-1, 4
cables, 84
connectors, 90, 91
logical unit numbers (LUNs), 147
number of available SCSI IDs, 98
parity checking support, 49, 101
signal grouping, *134*
SCSI-2, 4–7, 25
connectors, 90, 91
logical unit numbers (LUNs), 147
number of available SCSI IDs, 98
signal grouping, *134*
SCSI-3, 7–9
architecture roadmap, *24*
cables, 40, 84, 133
command sets, new, 31
device drivers, 24
and multimedia applications, 30
optimal uses, 24
parallel interfaces, 27–29, 310
parallel interface standards, 26–29
serial interfaces, 29–31, 166
signal grouping, *134*
standards, 23–24, 32
SCSI analyzers, 355–366
SCSI bus. *See also* cables; IEEE 1394;
PCI bus; SCSI bus phases; terminators;
USB
advantages of, 14
vs. ATA/IDE bus, 367–373
characteristics, 127
conditions, 344–345
configurations, 127, *129*
control signals, *136–137*
defined, 91
differential, 57
example of, *36*
example of three devices on, *93*
extending the distance covered by, 37
history of, 367–368
how it works, 35–36
length specs, *41*
maximum lengths, 87
priority of SCSI devices on, 99–100,
130, *131*

QAS improvement to, 28
reflecting signals on, 45
SCSI-1, 4
SCSI-2 maximum data transfer rate, 7
SCSI-3 maximum data transfer rate,
  8, 10
signals, 134–137, 342–*343*
single-ended, 36–38, 39, 44
statistics, *10*
terminating, 94–98
two-segment, 60
SCSI bus phases, 143, 343–346. *See also*
  information transfer phases
distinguishing among, 145
relation to protocol layers, 137,
  *138–139*
SCSI bus phase sequences, 345–*346*
connection, with tagged command
  queuing protocol, *150*
creating I_T_L nexus, 146–147
diagram of, *140,* 140
disconnection, 148, *148*
model, *346*
reconnection, *149*
reconnection, with tagged command
  queuing protocol, *151*
showing save data pointers and disconnect messages, *148*
trace, *141, 142*
with and without disconnection,
  *143, 144*
SCSI bus reset, 268
SCSI bus states. *See* SCSI bus phases
SCSI bus timing, 347–351
SCSI controller cards, 2. *See also* host
  adapters
for peripherals, 65–68
SCSI data pointers, 148
SCSI devices. *See also* initiator devices;
  SCSI drivers; SCSI IDs; SCSI interface;
  target devices
32-bit, 40
absence of all on a system, 109
absence of one on a system, 107–108
ASPI drivers for, 206
ASPI for NetWare scans for
  new, 305
ASPI interface program for communi-
  cating with, 377–381

attaching to the computer, 83–101
attaching to laptop systems, 44
and block addressing, 126
booting from, 60
bootup, order of, 108
with built-in terminators, 94
on a bus, *93*
cases for, 91, 101
characteristics, 127
command sets for, 31
commands for direct-access, *163–164*
communication among, 50–53
communication with computer, 35–39
configuration, 8
conflicts among, 363–366
connecting single-ended, HVD and
  LVD, 39, 60
connection to the bus, 91–94
connectors for, 9
cost of, *10,* 12, 13–14
dead, checking for, 115
drive numbers assigned to, 173
external. *See* external devices
Fast SCSI capability of, 6
host-to-peripheral connection, *127*
HVD (High Voltage Differential), 39
icons on, 313, *314*
installing, 120
intelligence of, 139
internal. *See* internal devices
logical block sizes in, 161
LVD (low voltage differential), 39, 46
maximum number supplying
  TERMPWR, 98
maximum number supported, *10*
mixing narrow and Wide, 68, 96,
  353–354
modular packages for, 311
multi-platform capability of, 9
number of, on a channel, 371
parallel, 4
polling of, 64
with the same SCSI ID, 113–114
SCSI-2, 5
SCSI-3, 7
SCSI-3 serial, 8–9
setting IDs for, 130
setting priorities for, with IDs, 99–100
sharing between two host systems, 68

SCSI devices (*continued*)
  spacing on a single-ended SCSI bus,
    182
  speeds of, 189
  Sun Microsystems' older, 340
  support for different CDB sizes, 162
  technical reference for, 359–362
  terminating, 352–354
  terminating particular, 96–97
  with TP jumpers, 98
  troubleshooting, 119–122
  types of, *10*, 15–21
  types of, under Win32, *254*
  vs. USB devices, 373
  Wide SCSI capabilities of, 7
SCSI drivers, 68–69, 126, 171–178. *See
  also* ASPI drivers
  active negation, 315
  CAM drivers, 72–73
  conflicts caused by, 111
  DOS system, 70–73, 173
  installing, 70, 77–81
  layered, 69–70
  for Linux systems, 77
  loading into upper memory, 71–72,
    72–73
  newest, choosing the, 70
  for OS/2 systems, 76
  translation, 73
  troubleshooting, 119–122
  for UNIX systems, 69–70, 176–178
  for Windows 3.1 systems, 73, 174
  for Windows 95/98 systems, 74–75,
    174–175
  for Windows NT systems, 75–76,
    175–176
  writing, 162
SCSI Harbor, 311
SCSI hard drives, 15–16. *See also* RAID
  booting from, 60–61
  enhancing performance of, 188
  file corruption on, avoiding, 58
  formatting and partitioning, 79–81
  IEEE 1394 and multimedia
    applications, 30
  installing, 78–81
  larger than 8 gigabytes, 78
  letters for, assigned by DOS, 80
  LVD, 46

Mac/PC formatting of, 11
  mirrored or duplexed,
    193–*194*
  vs. other PC drives, 14
  running from sound card's SCSI port,
    111
  SCA, 42, 91
  SCA LVD, 326
  SCSI IDs to assign to, 100
  speeds of, 16
  troubleshooting, 110–112
SCSI host adapter cards. *See* host
  adapters
SCSI IDs, 34
  checking for, 113–114
  and device priorities on the bus,
    130, *131*
  forming a SCSI nexus with, *146*
  number of available, 98
  setting, 68, 99, *100*
  setting priorities for devices with,
    99–100
SCSI interface. *See also* SCSI devices
  compared to ESDL (enhanced small
    device interface), 4
  electrical specs for, 314–317
  Fast SCSI capability of, 6
  functions of, 155
  intelligence of, 125–126
  interlocked nature of, 127
  LVD (low voltage differential), 39
  SCSI-3, 24, 25, 27–31
  serial, 8–9, 29–31
  system-level vs. device-level, 4
  Wide SCSI capability of, 7
SCSI interface cards. *See* host adapters
SCSI'izer, 175
SCSI linking, 215–216
SCSI Parallel Interface (SPI)
  standards, 8, 24, 25, 26, 27
SCSI Phase Disconnection sequence,
  148
SCSI Phase Reconnection sequence,
  *149*-150
SCSI protocol, 126, 137–144
SCSI request blocks. *See* SRBs
  (SCSI request blocks)
SCSI request flags, 211
SCSI requests. *See* commands

SCSI sniffers, 122–123
SCSI standards
  finding documents with, 162
  information transfer phases, 154
  SCSI-1 (X3.131-1986), 4
  SCSI-2 (X3.131-1994), 5
  SCSI-3, 7–8
  SCSI Parallel Interface (SPI), 8
SCSI systems. *See also* RAID
  advantages for home office/small
    business, 371
  vs. ATA systems, *372*
  choosing, 371–373
  configuration, 127, *129*
  daisy-chained, 91, *92, 93*, 94
  data errors with external versus
    internal, 318
  instability, 245
  non-SCSI hard drives with, 61
  optimizing performance on, 52
  performance of, factors that affect,
    179–180
  setting device priorities on, 99–*100*
  sharing devices between, 68
  single-ended, building, 181–183
  terminating, 352–354
  troubleshooting, 103–124
SCSI terminology, 1–3, 25–26
SCSI test equipment, 363–366
SDTR (synchronous data transfer
  request), 158
SE. *See* single-ended SCSI interface
seek time, minimizing, 188
SELECTION phase, *138, 143*, 146–147,
  *343*, 345
  preceded by ARBITRATION PHASE,
    *349*
SEL signal, *136*, 155, 342
SendASPI32Command, *245*, 248–250
  function call example, 382
  reset, where to put, 258
  SC_ABORT_SRB, *249*, 259–260
  SC_EXEC_SCSI_CMD, *249*, 255–259
  SC_GET_DEV_TYPE, *249*, 253-255
  SC_GET_DISK_INFO, *249*, 263-265
  SC_GETSET_TIMEOUTS, *249*, 259,
    260, 266-269, 382
  SC_HA_INQUIRY, 243, *249*,
    250-253

SC_RESCAN_SCSI_BUS, *249*,
  265-266
SC_RESET_DEV, *249*, 261–263
  waiting for completion, 273–276
SendASPICommand, 221
  SC_ABORT_SRB, 233–237
  SC_EXEC_SCSI_CMD, 228–233
  SC_GET_DEV_TYPE, 226–228
  SC_HA_INQUIRY, 224–226
  SC_RESET_DEV, 235–238
SENSE DATA, 165–166
sense data area under Win32, 244
serial devices, 4
  SCSI-3, 8–9
serial interfaces, 8–9, 29–31
serial storage architecture (SSA),
  29, 30
SES (SCSI Enclosure Services), 31
S/G (scatter/gather) bit, 308
shielded connectors, 319–320, 327–*333*.
  *See also* external connectors
ShowSCSI, components of, 375–382
ShowSCSI.pas, 375
shrouded header connectors, 104
Shugart Associates Systems Interface
  (SASI), 3
signal assertion, 314
signal distortion by reflection, 43, 181
single-byte messages, 156
single-ended SCSI bus, 36, 37
  cables, *38*, 181–183
  devices, 39
  maximum length, *87*
  terminators, 44, 53
  TTL transceivers, 180–181
single-ended SCSI interface, 314,
  *314*–315
  for Fast data transfers, 169
  icon for, *314*
SIP (SCSI-3 Interlocked Protocol)
  standard, 27
Small Computer System Interface. *See*
  SCSI
sniffers, 122–123
software caching, 58
Software Developer's Kit (SDK) for
  ASPI, 206–207, 282
software RAID, 203

Sony I.Link. *See* IEEE 1394
Sound Blaster, I/O ports for, *360*
spatial reuse, 29
speed. *See also* data transfer rates
  and errors, 180–181
  of hard drives, SCSI vs. EIDE, 16
  why it isn't everything, 368–*369*
SPI, 8
  naming conventions for, 24, 25,
    26, 27
SPI-2, 26, 27, 28, 320, 324
SPI-3, 24, 26, 27, 28
SPI-4, 26, 27, 28–29
spindle synchronization, 325
SRB_Abort Structure Definition,
  *233–234*
SRB_BusDeviceReset Structure
  Definition, *235–236*
SRB_DIR_SCSI, 243
SRB_GDEVBlock Structure Definition,
  227
SRB_HAInquiry Structure Definition,
  *224–225*
SRBs (SCSI request blocks), 210–211
  associating timeouts with, 259
  command codes, *249*
  effect of bus reset on, 268
  flags, *256*
  flags for SC_GETSET_TIMEOUTS,
    *267*
  structure definitions in Win 16 and
    Win32, 243
  synchronous and asynchronous,
    249–250, 273–276
SSA (Serial Storage Architecture), 8–9,
  29, 30, 310
SS_ABORTED, *232, 242*
  for Win32 systems, 260, *276*
SS_ASPI_IS_BUSY, *232*, 241, *242*
  for Win32 systems, *278*
SS_BUFFER_ALIGN
  for Win32 systems, *277*
SS_BUFFER_TO_BIG, *232*, 241,
  *242*, 243
  for Win32 systems, *278*
SS_COMP, *222, 242*
  for Win32 systems, 255–256, 260, *276*
SS_ERR, *232, 242*
  for Win32 systems, 255–256, *276*

SS_FAILED_INIT, *223, 242*
  for Win32 systems, *278*
SS_ILLEGAL_MODE, *223, 242*
  for Win32 systems, *277*
SS_INSUFFICIENT_RESOURCES
  for Win32 systems, *279*
SS_INVALID_CMD, *242*
  for Win32 systems, *276*
SS_INVALID_HA, *225, 242*
  for Win32 systems, *277*
SS_INVALID_SRB, *225, 242*
  for Win32 systems, *277*
SS_MISMATCHED_COMPONENTS,
  *278*
SS_NO_ADAPTERS, *279*
SS_NO_ASPI, *223, 242*
  for Win32 systems, *277*
SS_NO_DEVICE, *227, 242*
  for Win32 systems, 244, *277*
SS_OLD_MANAGER, *222, 242*
SS_PENDING, *232*, 241, *242*
  and asynchronous SRBs, 273
  for Win32 systems, *276*
ST-506 disk interface, 368
standards
  ANSI, 32, 176
  for CD-ROM disks, 19
  SCSI-1 (X3.131-1986), 4
  SCSI-2 (X3.131-1994), 5
  SCSI-3, 7–8, 23–29, 32
  for SCSI device drivers, 69–70, 176
  SPI (SCSI Parallel Interface),
    8, 24, 25, 26, 27
Start bit, 382
StartStopUnit, 380
STA (SCSI Trade Association), 25
state machine, 139, 343
status byte codes, *165*
status byte format, *164*
STATUS IN phase, *139, 143*
STATUS phase, 151, 152, 164, 167,
  343–*344*, 345
  examples of, 380, 381
status reports
  for host adapters, 215
  for targets, 215
  for Win32 targets, *258*
storage area networks (SANs),
  311–312

storage devices, 15
stripes, 192
striping, 188, 192, *193. See also* block
  striping
  byte-sized, with parity, 195
  with ECC (error correction code), 194
ST (single-transition) clocking, 28
stubs, *41*, 182
Sub-D connectors
  68-pin B-cable, 320, 337
  Apple 25-pin, 320, 333–*335*,
    *338*, 339
  Future Domain 25-pin, 320, 337–339
  Novell and Procomp DCB 37-pin, 320,
    340–*341*
  Sun Microsystems' 50-pin, 320,
    339–*340*
Sun Microsystems' connectors, 320,
  339–*340*
synchronous data transfer, 50, 51, *351*
  handshaking method, 168–170
  messages that negotiate, 156
  protocol example of negotiated,
    158–*159*
synchronous data transfer rates,
  6, 168
synchronous data transfer request
  (SDTR), 158
synchronous offset timing diagram,
  169–170
synchronous SRBs, 249–250, 273–276
system.ini file example, 73

**T**

T10 Technical Committee, 25, 29
  T10/792-M specification, 176
tagged command queuing, 150, 370
  in a connection sequence, *150*
  in a reconnection sequence, *151*
tape drives, 17–18
  SCSI IDs to assign to, 100
target controllers, 126
target devices, 33–34, *36*, 126, 130
  associating with Plug-and-Play events,
    271–273
  control signals driven by, *135*

identifying, 34–35
information transfer phases of, *153*
OS/2 2.*x* and, 281–282
setting timeouts for, 266
status reports for, 215, *258*
synchronous data transfer, 158–159
technical data for all platforms, 313–357
Teflon cables, 318–319
termination, 352–354. *See also* active termination; passive termination
termination ICs (integrated circuits),
  356
terminators, *36. See also* active terminators; passive terminators
  and active negation, 315
  on devices vs. cables, 95
  differential bus, 46, 48, *48*
  FPT, 46, *47*
  functions of, 98
  in "Hi-9 termination" adapters, 42
  on host adapters, 95–96, *97*
  icons on, 313, *314*
  importance of, 86, 134
  measuring, 116–117
  placement of, 94, 185–186
  reasons to use, 43–44
  rules for, 115
TERMPWR
  active terminators and, 356
  decoupling capacitors on, 186–187
  Novell's cable connector and, 341
  placement of, 185–186
  terms to know, 1–3, 25–26
  tools for testing, 122, 124
  troubleshooting, 109, 110, 117–118
  voltage sources, 44, 98
TEST UNIT READY command, 345–*346*
third-party DMA, 66
throughput. *See* data transfer rates
tools
  for benchmarking, 188
  for SCSI driver installation, 70
  for troubleshooting, 105, 122–124. *See
    also* SCSI test equipment
TP jumpers, 98
transceiver specs, 180–181
Transfer Length field of CDBs, 161
transfer rates. *See* data transfer rates

TranslateASPI32Address, *245*, 271–273
translation drivers, 73
transmission line, 43
troubleshooting. *See also* Internet
   resources; performance tuning
   common problems, 105–113
   checking typical issues, 113–122
   initial steps, 103–104
   tools for, 104–105, 122–124. *See also*
      SCSI test equipment
true signal state, 314
TSDs (type-specific drivers), 175
twisted-pair ribbon cable, *88*
type-specific drivers (TSDs), 175

## U

UDF (Universal Data Format), 174
UDMA features vs. SCSI's, 10
Ultra SCSI, 7, 25, 27
   standards for, 27
Ultra2 SCSI, 7–8, 26, 27–28. *See also*
   LVD
   standards for, 27
Ultra3 SCSI, 8, 26, 28
   standards for, 27
Ultra3+ SCSI, 26
Ultra3 (Fast-80 LVD) SCSI, 310
Ultra4 SCSI, 26, 28–29
Ultra160m SCSI, 26
Ultra160 SCSI, 26, 28, 310
Ultra320 SCSI, 26, 29
Ultra Wide SCSI devices, terminating,
   354
Uninterruptable Power Supply (UPS),
   58, 188
Universal Data Format (UDF), 174
UNIX systems, SCSI drivers for, 69–70,
   176–178
unshielded connectors, 319, 321–326
USB (Universal Serial Bus)
   combined with IEEE 1394, 311
   external devices, 373
   hard drives, 31
   scanners, 21
   Windows 98 support for, 174
Usenet newsgroups for SCSI, 61, 77,
   367, 370

## V

vendor-specific connectors, 320,
   333–*337*
very high density connectors. *See* VHD
   connectors
VESA local bus, 56
VHDCI connectors, 320, 332–*333, 334*
VHD connectors, 320, 332–*333, 334*
video
   using IEEE 1394 for, 30, 310
   using SCSI for, 373
virtual machine manager
   (VMM32.VXD), 174
VLB or VL-bus (VESA local bus), 56
voice and digital data delivery, 30
voltage regulators for termination circuits, 112, 356, 357
.vxd (virtual device driver) files,
   174, 175

## W

waiting for completion of
   SendASPI32Command, 273–276
Web sites
   devicebay, 311
   fibrechannel, 311
   nostarch, 375
   scsita, 311
Wide SCSI, 5, 6–7, 25
   68-pin high-density connectors, 91,
      319, 329, *330, 331*
   cables recommended with, 84
   data transfer via, 156
   internal cable connectors for, 90
   maximum devices supported by
      Wide SCSI-2, *10*, 11
   number of available SCSI IDs, 99
   P- and Q-cables for, 319, 322,
      *323, 324*
   SCA-2 connectors for, 319, 324–*325,
      326*
   Wide SCSI-3, 25, 26
Wide SCSI drives
   CD-ROM drives, 181
   mixing with narrow SCSI devices, 68,
      96, 353–354

tape drives, 371

wildcard validity for SC_GETSET_TIME-
OUTS, *269*

Win32, ASPI commands for. *See*
SendASPI32Command

winaspi.dll, 221, 243

Windows 3.1
386 enhanced mode, 174
SCSI drivers for, 63, 69, 120, 174

Windows 3.*x*
ASPI for DOS under, 200–221

Windows 95. *See also* ASPI: for Win32
detecting devices, 266
DEVNODEs, 271–273
handling BUS DEVICE RESET, 263

Windows 95/98
Device Manager, 63
dynamic linking, 245–247
SCSI drivers for, 74–75, 120, 174–175

Windows NT. *See also* ASPI: for Win32
detecting devices, 266
dynamic linking, 245–247
efficient use of SCSI, 175
and FAT filesystems, 79, 81
handling BUS DEVICE RESET, 263
and Int13h, 263
SCSI drivers for, 69, 75–76, 120,
175–176
and TranslateASPI32Address, 271

WM_CREATE message, 239

WM_DEVICE.CHANGE message, 271,
272

wnaspi32.dll, 243, 245

words to know, 1–3, 25–26

WORM (Write Once Read Many) drives,
19

write caching, 56
enabling, 188

# Y

Y-shaped cables, 91

# Z

zip drives, 17

# ABOUT THE CD-ROM

## System Requirements

In order to use this CD-ROM disc, your system must have

- Hardware: A CD-ROM drive (ATAPI or SCSI, any speed)

- Software: Windows 95/98/NT/2000 or Linux (any version with Joliet CD-ROM support, such as Red Hat Linux 5.*x* or newer)

### Recommended Additional Software

A graphical World Wide Web Browser, such as Netscape Communicator 4.*x* or Microsoft Internet Explorer 4.*x* or 5.*x*

### CD-ROM Format

ISO-9660 with Joliet file names (which are longer than the 8.3-character names that MS-DOS FAT allows)

## The CD-ROM includes

- An easy-to-use HTML index that provides hot links to the CD contents and links to other SCSI-related stuff on the Internet

- A searchable copy of the entire text of the book! Find the references to that SCSI buzzword that's been bugging you—in just seconds.

- ASPI example program  Source and binaries to "showscsi" referenced in Appendix E of this book

- ASPI Python  An ASPI function library callable from the Python scripting language

ASPI source code examples:

- ASPI tar utility  Example tape backup utility for MS-DOS and Windows (Uses ASPI interface)
- SCSIDRVR.C Source code for an MS-DOS driver in C

- SCSI utility programs  (Win32 executables) and SCSITool

SCSI utilities courtesy of Western Digital (Win32 executables):

- ASPIMenu  Allows the user to issue SCSI commands

- WDBench  A benchmark utility

- WDScan  Shows you what's on your SCSI bus

- SCSI FAQ  The official comp.periphs.scsi

- SCSI Quick Start Guide  For those in a hurry (SCSI FAQ Lite, if you will)

- SCSI: A Game with Many Rules and No Rule Book  A light-hearted look at hooking up SCSI devices and getting them to work in your system

- Linux SCSI HowTo

- Linux SCSI Programming HowTo

- Some of the most useful links to SCSI information on the Web

## Using the CD-ROM

The CD-ROM included with this book is particularly easy to use. You can use everything directly from the CD, or if you plan to use these utilities a lot, you can copy the whole thing (or any portion) to your hard disk.

### To access the contents directly from your CD-ROM drive

Insert the book's disc into your CD-ROM drive. Your CD-ROM drive appears as a drive letter (D: through Z:). In Windows, it will appear in your "My Computer" folder.

For the easiest access, you should have a graphical Web browser installed on your system.

If you have an Internet connection, you will be able to take advantage of the many *hot links* to SCSI information out on the World Wide Web.

### To install the entire contents onto your hard disk

Make a folder on your hard disk (name it BOS-CD or some other name you like better). Select the entire contents of the CD-ROM and drag it into the folder you made above.

### To access the SCSI programs and information

Using Netscape Communicator (4.*x*): From the "File" Menu, select "Open Page." Click on the "Choose File" button, select your CD-ROM drive, and open the BOS_Cdtour.html file.

Using Internet Explorer (4.*x* or newer): From the "File" Menu, select "Open." Click on the "Browse" button, select your CD-ROM drive, and open the BOS_Cdtour.html file.

If you don't have a Web browser: In Windows, view the files on the CD-ROM directly from Windows Explorer. In Linux, use "ls".

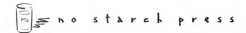
# THE NO B.S. GUIDE TO
# RED HAT LINUX 6

*by* BOB RANKIN

This book is a thorough yet concise guide to installing Red Hat Linux 6 and exploring its capabilities. Author Bob Rankin (*The No B.S. Guide to Linux*, No Starch Press) provides easy-to-follow instructions for installing and running Red Hat 6. Through examples and helpful illustrations, the author guides readers through these topics and more:

- Installation — in ten easy steps!

- How to use and configure GNOME — the new Linux GUI

- How to write Bash or Perl scripts and use the Bash shell

- How to connect to the Internet with SLIP/PPP and how to run the Apache Web server for Linux

- How to access DOS files and run Windows programs under Linux

The CD-ROM contains Red Hat Linux 6 — one of the most popular Linux distributions available. It's easy to install and requires minimal configuration — you'll be up and running in a snap!

BOB RANKIN is a programmer and nationally recognized expert on the Internet. He is a columnist for *Boardwatch Magazine* and a contributor to several computer publications. His books include *Dr. Bob's Painless Guide to the Internet* (1996) and *The No B.S. Guide to Linux* (1997).

1999, 402 pp., w/CD-ROM $34.95 ($54.00 CDN)
ISBN 1-886411-30-1, Item #301

# LINUX PROBLEM SOLVER

*by* BRIAN WARD

- Hands-on, practical guide solves kernel issues

- Helps solve hundreds of problems

A must-have for intermediate to advanced users who already have Linux up and running. Solves technical problems related to printing, networking, back-up, crash recovery, and compiling or upgrading a kernel. Quick and concise in approach, with over 100 problem boxes that help to solve specific problems in addition to those discussed throughout the book.

CD-ROM: Supports the book's contents with configuration files and numerous programs not included in many Linux distributions.

BRIAN WARD is a Unix systems programmer, and is the author of the "Linux Kernel HOWTO", widely circulated on the Internet. A Unix network administrator, he has worked with Linux since 1993. He is currently pursuing a Ph.D. in computer science at the University of Chicago.

350 pp. w/CD-ROM, $34.95 ($54.00CDN)
ISBN 1-886411-35-2, Item #352

# LINUX MUSIC & SOUND

*by* DAVE PHILLIPS

*Linux Music & Sound* offers in-depth instruction on recording, storing, playing, and editing music and sound under Linux. The author, a programmer and performing musician, discusses the basics of sound and digital audio, and covers specific software and hardware issues specific to Linux, including:

- A clear introduction to the fundamental concepts of digital sound

- Linux-specific issues including available toolkits, GUI libraries, and driver support

- Reviews of available software with recommendations

- Recommended components for building a complete system including a digital audio player/recorder, soundfile editor, MIDI recorder/player/editor, and software mixer

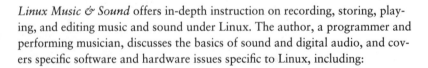

- Coverage of hard disk recording, advanced MIDI support, network audio, and MP3

- A complete bibliography and an extensive list of Internet resources

- A CD-ROM with dozens of software packages

A performing musician for over 30 years, DAVE PHILLIPS became interested in computers as a means for playing, editing, and recording music. He is an expert in MIDI, Csound, and Linux. He currently maintains several educational Web sites on these topics.

300 pp., paperback, $39.95 w/CD-ROM
ISBN 1-886411-34-4

# STEAL THIS COMPUTER BOOK: WHAT THEY WON'T TELL YOU ABOUT THE INTERNET

*by* WALLACE WANG

"*A delightfully irresponsible primer.*" — *Chicago Tribune*

"*If this book had a soundtrack, it'd be Lou Reed's 'Walk on the Wild Side.'*" — *InfoWorld*

"*An unabashed look at the dark side of the Net — the stuff many other books gloss over.*" — *Amazon.com*

*Steal This Computer Book* explores the dark corners of the Internet and reveals little-known techniques that hackers use to subvert authority. Unfortunately, some of these techniques, when used by malicious hackers, can destroy data and compromise the security of corporate and government networks. To keep your computer safe from viruses, and yourself from electronic con games and security crackers, Wallace Wang explains the secrets hackers and scammers use to prey on their victims. Discover:

- How hackers write and spread computer viruses

- How criminals get free service and harass legitimate customers on online services like America Online

- How online con artists trick people out of thousands of dollars

- Where hackers find the tools to crack into computers or steal software

- How to find and use government-quality encryption to protect your data

- How hackers steal passwords from other computers

WALLACE WANG is the author of several computer books, including *Microsoft Office 97 for Windows for Dummies* and *Visual Basic for Dummies*. A regular contributor to *Boardwatch* magazine (the "Internet Underground" columnist), he's also a successful stand-up comedian. He lives in San Diego, California.

340 pp., paperback, $19.95
ISBN 1-886411-21-2

**Phone:**
1 (800) 420-7240 OR
(415) 863-9900
MONDAY THROUGH FRIDAY,
9 A.M. TO 5 P.M. (PST)

**Fax:**
(415) 863-9950
24 HOURS A DAY,
7 DAYS A WEEK

**E-mail:**
SALES@NOSTARCH.COM

**Web:**
HTTP://WWW.NOSTARCH.COM

**Mail:**
NO STARCH PRESS
555 DE HARO STREET, SUITE 250
SAN FRANCISCO, CA 94107
USA

*Distributed to the book trade by Publishers Group West*

# UPDATES

This book was carefully reviewed for technical accuracy, but it's inevitable that some things will change after the book goes to press. Visit the Web site for this book at **http://www.nostarch.com/scsi2_updates.htm** for updates, errata, and other information.

> "Since 1994, No Starch Press has published computer books that make a difference. We hope that this book has made a difference for you."

> — William Pollock, Publisher
> *billp@nostarch.com*

no starch press
555 De Haro Street
Suite 250
San Francisco, CA 94107

**e-mail:** info@nostarch.com
**web:** http://www.nostarch.com
**tel:** 1.800.420.7240
**fax:** 1.415.863.9950

## GIVE US A PIECE OF YOUR MIND

Which book did this card come from?

How could this book be improved?

Did this book meet your expectations?
Why/Why not?

Any suggestions for other computer books?

❏ **PLEASE ADD ME TO YOUR MAILING LIST**

❏ E-MAIL ONLY

NAME: _____

COMPANY _____

ADDRESS: _____

CITY: _____

STATE: _____ ZIP: _____ COUNTRY: _____

PHONE: _____

E-MAIL: _____